QUESTIONS & ANSWERS

About Community Associations

Homeowner Associations

Condominiums

Cooperatives

Topics:

Pets, Pools & Parking

Board Operations

Financial Issues

Legal Issues

JAN HICKENBOTTOM

A Collection of **"Condo Q & A"** Columns
as published in the ***Los Angeles Times***

Second Edition

MILLER PUBLISHING

MILLER PUBLISHING COMPANY

Cover design by Robert Aulicino

All inquiries regarding distribution or quantity discounts should be addressed to:
Condo Consulting Services
PMB 263
4790 Irvine Boulevard, #105
Irvine, CA 92620-1998
ISBN 1-880039-02-8
Printed in the United States of America
First Printing 1991, Revised 2002

DEDICATION

To Chris, Rachel, Jeff, Rob, Megan, Chad and Tyler.

May you experience the joy and fulfillment of striving steadfastly toward your goals and may you appreciate the paths as well as the destinations along the way.

TABLE OF CONTENTS

Chapter 6—Financial Matters 163

Chapter 9—Meetings 283

Chapter 12—Management 343

Chapter 13—Owners' Rights and Buyer's Rights 363

FOREWORD

The term "community association" covers a wide spectrum of common interest developments, including cooperatives, own-your-owns (technically 'community apartment projects'), planned developments ("PUDs"), and condominiums.

As an author preparing the legal documents for these various developments, beginning in the early 1960s, most of my time was spent preparing legal documents for cooperatives. (Interestingly, much of my present time is spent converting cooperatives and own-your-own apartment projects to condominiums.) But the shares of stock or memberships in a cooperative were not then considered interests in real estate, so separate mortgages for each unit were not available. As an interim step, and sometimes instead of a cooperative, a project was developed as an own-your-own where each unit owner owned, along with his co-owners, an undivided interest as tenant in common in the entire development (land plus building) and was given the exclusive right to occupy a particular unit. Since the ownership was an interest in real property (as distinguished from a cooperative share or membership), a lender could, and did, make separate real estate loans for each own-your-own unit.

However, by the end of 1963, laws were enacted in California permitting the creation of statutory condominiums and since 1964 most common interest projects have been developed as condominiums. At first (1964–1967), lenders didn't really understand this new idea of fee title to a cube of airspace. They believed the unit owner should actually own that portion of the ground upon which his unit was situated. So with townhouse-type developments, i.e., no separate unit one above another, planned developments came into vogue. They were called various things: RPDs (Residential Planned Developments), PUDs (Planned Unit Developments) or simply PDs (Planned Developments). Common to each was a recorded subdivision or parcel map showing small separate lots. Each owner was then conveyed a deed to his separate lot, together with the improvements thereon. The lenders were happy.

As more and more condominium projects were developed, the lenders thankfully became, and now are, more sophisticated. Separate ownership of the land beneath the unit was recognized as not necessary because the unit owner owned an undivided interest in the ground as tenant in common with the other condominium owners, plus the unit owner owned fee title to his cube of airspace. Condominiums were accepted and are the norm today.

What all common interest developments have in common is an association of owners which in turn elects a board—-be it a board of directors, board of governors, or board of managers. It is this board that is charged with the responsibility of control and management of the development and enforcement of legal documents that set forth the way the development is to be controlled and managed. Because the legal documents cannot foresee every eventuality, boards are constantly asking questions that cannot be answered by referring only to the project's legal documents.

Enactment of the Davis-Stirling Common Interest Development Act in 1985 (California Civil Code Sections 1350–1376) reorganized the existing laws and set up a uniform set of laws that apply to all common interest developments and reference thereto can answer many questions asked by boards. Additionally, the past 38 years (since 1963) have given rise to many appellate court legal decisions that may answer some questions.

But many questions asked have no direct answer or precedent from either the Civil Code Sections or the appellate court cases, and thus a book like *Questions and Answers About Community Associations* collecting both everyday and sometimes unique questions and answers can indeed be an extremely helpful resource.

Herbert J. Strickstein
Attorney at Law
Los Angeles, California
September, 2001

Herbert J. Strickstein is a 1956 graduate of the University of Southern California Law School. Upon graduation, he spent the next three years in the U. S. Air Force as Deputy Judge Advocate. Thereafter, he entered the private practice of law, specializing in congregate housing types of real estate developments. Active in cooperative housing law prior to 1963 and condominium law since the enactment of the California condominium statutes in 1963, Mr. Strickstein has represented developers and owners in more than 900 residential and commercial condominiums, cooperatives, own-your-owns and planned unit developments, of which more than 300 projects have been the conversion of existing residential apartments, cooperatives, own-your-owns and commercial properties to condominiums.

A past president of the Association of Real Estate Attorneys, Strickstein has lectured throughout the United States on residential and commercial condominiums. He has been chairman of the Continuing Education of the Bar seminar on Condominiums and Planned Developments and in 1990 and 1994 he was a featured panelist at the Continuing Education of the Bar seminar on Planned Developments and Condominiums, He is a member of the State Bar Real Property Section Subsection on Common Interest Developments, former senior member of the Subdivision Advisory Committee of the California Department of Real Estate, a member and past chairman of the Residential Development Subsection of the Real Property Section, Los Angeles County Bar Association and a member of the Real Estate Section of the Beverly Hills Bar Association. Strickstein is currently listed in the 2001-2002 edition of "*The Best Lawyers in America.*"

PREFACE

As you read, you will find that much of the advice in this book is based upon California law because it was originally written for publication in the *Los Angeles Times,* a California newspaper. Readers who live in or own property in other states will want to research the laws in their state and local area. Several states have passed the Uniform Condominium Act or the Uniform Common Interest Ownership Act, which contain laws similar to those cited within the pages of this book.

This book does not attempt to provide legal advice. Regarding their specific questions, readers should consult attorneys, insurance agents or brokers, accountants, engineers, consultants and other professionals who specialize in advising community associations and their members.

ACKNOWLEDGEMENTS

This book would not have been written without the vision of Dick Barnes, the former editor of the real estate section of the *Los Angeles Times*. Dick became the real estate editor in 1989 and immediately began enlivening the section with consumer-oriented columns and articles. People who had glanced through the real estate section in the past suddenly discovered the change in format and found interesting and informative content.

The "Condo Q & A" column was one of many that Dick envisioned. He invited me to write the column because of my experience and professional contacts within the field of community associations. He had seen examples of my writing in a Community Associations Institute newsletter and encouraged me to submit a sample column.

"Condo Q & A" began appearing in the *Times* in June of 1989. We were thrilled with the response and the amount of readership mail that it generated. As more and more readers discovered the column and asked for reprints, compiling a book seemed to be the logical next step. The first book was published in 1991.

Many, many thanks to Dick Barnes for giving me the opportunity to write for the *Times* and to the loyal readers who sent their interesting and thought-provoking questions to me.

I also want to thank those board members who contributed to my knowledge and shaped my future during my first experience as a condominium manager at the Point of France Association in Edina, Minnesota: Howard Lawrence, Albert Cherne, Wendel Burton, Terrance Hanold, George Gackle and Arnold Goldman. I have many fond memories of the experiences I had during my six years at Point of France. What a great opportunity it was for a brand-new manager!

INTRODUCTION

"Community Association" is a relatively new term that means an association of residential property owners. For example, condominiums, homeowner associations, property owners' associations, planned unit developments, residential common interest developments, cooperatives and "own-your-own" community apartment projects are all forms of community associations.

If you live in or work with a community association, I think you will find this book to be a helpful resource. For those who are contemplating purchasing a home, you will find out what to expect from the community association lifestyle.

Whether you have questions about budgeting, voting procedures or parking, you'll find some viable solutions here. If you are a victim of a dictatorial board of directors or the "condo commando," you'll find out about owners' rights.

This book is a collection of material that was originally printed in the *Los Angeles Times* in a column titled "Condo Q & A." The subject matter deals with common issues and concerns of all forms of community associations, not just condominiums, and that is the reason I selected the name *"Questions & Answers About Community Associations"* for the title.

In 1979, I started my career in community association management when I was hired to manage a luxury high-rise condominium in Edina, Minnesota, a suburb of Minneapolis. I quickly found that there was very little resource material to assist and guide the volunteer board members and the managers.

In that first experience as a condominium manager, I was fortunate to have volunteer homeowners serving on the board who were very professional. They were pleased to be my mentors and readily shared their vast management knowledge and experience. We set up the policies and procedures for the association and they fully supported me in carrying out those procedures. They understood that their association should be run in a business-like manner and they understood the liabilities if they failed to perform their duties carefully and judiciously.

After the first six months of my experience as a condominium manager, I felt as though I had taken a crash course in everything from mechanical systems to human psychology. I really needed to be a "Jan-of-all-trades!" I found that a property manager needs to know a lot about many, many subjects in order to manage any property, especially a high-rise building. The association aspects of the job, including board meetings, financial planning and record-keeping, required another set of skills. And the issues of dealing with people, pets, parking and personnel—the list seemed to go on and on. Well, I was hooked. I wanted to be a success in the multi-faceted new career that I had chosen.

Over the next several years, I learned so much about all the specifics of community association management that by the time the real estate editor of the *Los Angeles Times* invited me to write a continuing column for the newspaper, I was pleased to share my experience with the *Times* readers. Writing the column has been a very rewarding experience.

Much of the philosophy contained in this book is just plain common sense. The legal knowledge comes from many courses and continuing education courses provided by the Community Associations Institute and the California Association of Community Managers.

I hope this book will provide guidance that will help associations operate efficiently and foster a happy environment for all who participate in community association living.

CHAPTER 1 THE BASICS

This chapter contains some frequently asked questions and answers on a variety of subjects that are especially helpful for new buyers who have never lived on a community association. Even the old timers may learn something here.

NEIGHBORING ASSOCIATION HAS LOWER ASSESSMENTS

Q *How do we know whether our association's budget is accurate and realistic? A similar association in our area has a much lower budget so their owners pay $50 per month less than we pay.*

A Don't assume that your board is a bunch of spendthrifts. Even though the other association seems similar, there may be many reasons that your association's expenses are greater, such as, type of amenities, size of staff, type of management, amount of landscaping; here's the key item: the amount of reserve funds that are being set aside for repair and replacement of major common area components.

Usually a great deal of time and effort goes into the budgeting process; so don't start criticizing until you have gained some solid information. Talk with your association president, treasurer or management company representative. Don't be surprised if you are asked to serve on the next budget committee!

For more information on this topic, refer to the chapter on Financial Matters.

BUYERS SHOULD STUDY DOCUMENTS BEFORE PURCHASE

Q *I want to purchase a condominium soon. I can afford a one-bedroom unit on my own, but I may purchase with a friend so that we can buy a two-bedroom. What about laundry equipment in the unit and extra storage space? Are these the type of features that will help us when we resell? What other things should we consider?*

A As long as you have a trustworthy friend, go for the unit with as many features and amenities that the two of you can afford. All the things that you mention have a positive effect when it is time to sell. Of course, the most important factor to consider is location.

Don't assume that you can make changes to the unit after you purchase even if your real estate agent assures you that it is possible. For example, if the unit does not have its own laundry equipment, it may be impossible to install. Some older condominiums have drain lines that are inadequate for washers. The venting of a dryer to the outside of the building may be impossible.

Even if the changes seem appropriate, the condominium association has the authority to approve or disapprove alterations to the interior of the unit that might affect other units or the common area. Many condo associations prohibit hard surface flooring and whirlpool tubs because of the noise factor or the risk of water leaks.

Don't fall in love with your dream condo until you have checked out the association's legal documents and financial disclosures. Ask for the declaration of covenants, conditions and restrictions (CC&Rs), the bylaws and the rules and regulations. If you are able to obtain them, read these documents thoroughly before you even sign a purchase agreement. You don't want to buy the place, move in with your St. Bernard and then find out that the association doesn't allow pets.

The annual budget and financial statement will tell you whether the association has reserve funds set aside for roof repairs and other major maintenance expenses. Ask your real estate agent to find out from the seller if the association has had any special assessments recently. These are fees that are charged in addition to the monthly assessment when the association has not budgeted properly or when unforeseen expenses have occurred. If the real estate agent cannot respond, put your questions in writing and request that the information be obtained from the association through the seller.

Request that your agent write up the purchase agreement with a contingency clause that allows you to get out of the transaction if all of the disclosure information is not acceptable to you. These disclosures are among the many disclosures required by California Civil Code, Section 1368, in addition to Civil Code 1102 regarding real estate transfer disclosures, so you are entitled to all of the information.

For more information, refer to the chapter on Owners' and Buyers' Rights.

OWNER WANTS TO KNOW THE MEANING OF CC&RS

Q *As the proud owner of a townhouse in a new homeowners association, I am finding that I have a lot to learn about how my association operates and my obligations as an owner. What are CC&Rs?*

A The term "CC&Rs" stands for the Declaration of Covenants, Conditions and Restrictions. Community associations, such as condominiums, homeowner associations, planned unit developments, residential cooperatives, or "own-your-own" community apartment projects, have unique legal documents that explain the common ownership of the property. These legal documents explain the complex issues and legal responsibilities of the community association and the individual owners or members.

Condominiums and most other forms of community associations have legal documents including a Declaration of the Covenants,

Conditions and Restrictions (CC&Rs), or deed restrictions, that spell out the association's powers and duties and the individual owner's obligations. Among other things, the CC&Rs will state the owners' obligation to pay a pro rata share of the costs of maintenance and operation of the association. Most CC&Rs also include some aesthetic restrictions also, such as restrictions against altering the exterior appearance of the structure without association permission.

In a residential cooperative, owners buy stock in the corporation and receive a proprietary lease or occupancy agreement, which establishes the owner's right to live in the cooperative. The lease or occupancy agreement will state the terms and conditions for occupancy, including the obligation to pay a pro rata share of the costs of maintenance, services, mortgage, taxes and other expenses of the corporation. The documents will also include use restrictions adopted by the board of directors of the cooperative.

The various forms of community associations have varied legal documents. The homeowner association's declaration (CC&Rs) serves the same purpose as the cooperative's occupancy agreement or proprietary lease.

More information can be found in the chapter entitled "Legal Issues."

MOTIVATING OWNERS TO BE ACTIVE IN ASSOCIATION

Q *Most of the owners in our condominium do not want to participate in the operation of the association and we have a tough time finding people who are willing to serve on the board of directors. At a recent annual meeting, we didn't have a quorum present, so the meeting had to be postponed to a later date. What can we do?*

A Let's start by trying to analyze some of the reasons for apathy. First, most people have heavy demands from their work schedules so they are very protective of their personal time.

Second, most people move into a condominium thinking that they don't need to participate in the management or decision-making of the association. In fact, some people don't really understand what they've purchased at all.

Third, as long as the association is running smoothly, most people will not be motivated to participate. It's a fact that if the board starts making unpopular decisions, more people will be inclined to speak up and act.

Fourth, perhaps your current board is stifling interest by discouraging owner input or having "secret" meetings. Secret meetings are against the law and closed meetings are forbidden unless there is a valid reason for an executive session of the board.

If owners feel that the board is ignoring them or operating the association in a disorganized manner, those who might be interested simply give up in frustration or disgust. Sometimes the board members enjoy their power or martyrdom and continually exclaim to all how demanding and unfulfilling it is to serve on the board. Here are some suggestions that may encourage owner involvement:

1. The board should communicate with owners using a brief newsletter to inform owners of board meeting dates, board action, current issues and concerns facing the association. Invite owners to participate. Ask for help.
2. Set up committees such as budget and finance, landscape, building maintenance, social, etc., to give input to the board. Committee members will often become future board members.
3. Several weeks prior to the next annual meeting and board election, schedule a social event, a Neighborhood Watch meeting or a program with interesting speakers, which will draw the owners. During the event, promote the approaching annual meeting, encourage owners to nominate potential board members and urge attendance at the meeting or sending a proxy if attendance isn't possible. Remind them of the added expense and effort that results from failing to get a quorum. Be creative! Offer a door prize!

4. After all that, you may still have to go door-to-door to collect proxies so that the annual meeting can be conducted.

More information can be found in the chapter on "Board Operations."

WISE ASSOCIATION TAKES ACTION AGAINST VIOLATORS

Q *Most of the owners in our 24-unit condominium are elderly, rule-abiding people. Enforcing the rules has not been a problem in the past. However, some new owners have moved in with two grown sons who are disrespectful of our association rules and the rights of other owners. They and their numerous guests take over the pool area for their loud parties, throw their cigarette butts on the carpeted courtyard, and leave litter for other owners to clean up when the party is over. Recently, one of them deliberately stalled the elevator, which caused my wheelchair-bound mother to miss a doctor's appointment.*

I realize that a condominium should not be run like a prison but we need to start enforcing rules. What can our association do?

A All associations need to establish procedures for rule violations and the methods of enforcement. As you have seen, a peaceful environment can be totally disrupted by just one family. It is unfair for the board to allow the misfits to disregard other owners' rights.

The board president should place this matter on the agenda for the next meeting. Meeting minutes will then reflect the action that the board takes. If the board votes to proceed with enforcement by scheduling a hearing with the owners, state law requires that at least 10 days prior notice be given to the owner. The notice should state the type of violation, date that it occurred, and the cost of any damages that resulted. The notice should inform the owners what possible enforcement remedies may be utilized if the owners fail to respond to the notice or fail to attend the hearing.

If the association's legal documents allow the board to levy fines or other penalties, then these enforcement remedies can be implemented after giving the owners the opportunity to respond and defend themselves. The board should carefully follow the procedures for violation notice and hearing that are stated in the association's declaration of covenants, conditions and restrictions (CC&Rs) or bylaws, and California Civil Code Section 1363. Written notification of the board's decision must be sent to the owner within 15 days of the date of the hearing.

Refer the matter to an attorney who specializes in community association law if the owners fail to respond.

OWNER WITHHOLDING ASSESSMENT UNTIL GATE IS FIXED

Q *We have a gated entry to our homeowners association. After several weeks of recurring problems with the malfunctioning automatic gate, the management company decided to leave it open. Even though the gate is still under warranty, the management company has been unable to get the gate repaired.*

In desperation, I have decided not to pay my monthly assessment until the management company has the gate fixed. One of my friends tells me that the association can place a lien on my property. What does this mean?

A It means that you'd better pay your assessment! There might be a number of reasons for the delay in fixing the gate but regardless of the management company's or the board's lack of action, you are obligated to pay your assessment much like your obligation for your mortgage payment. If you don't make your mortgage payments in a timely manner, the mortgage company can file a lien, foreclose on your property and sell it to recover their costs. The association also has the right to file a lien on your property and foreclose (take ownership of your property) if necessary. Owners should never use non-payment of assessments to gain the attention of the management company or the board of directors. It could result in the loss of your home. At the least, it will cause your account to incur further charges that you are obligated to pay.

CAN THE BOARD ALTER OR ELIMINATE AN AMENITY?

Q *Our board thinks that our gas bills for heating the swimming pool are an unnecessary expense. Can they just arbitrarily decide to stop heating the pool? One of our members has threatened to sue the board if they do this.*

A First the board should make sure that they have adequately researched the gas expense records. Then, check the capacity and efficiency of the pool heater. An inadequate size or inefficient heater can greatly increase gas usage. You may need a new heater. Enlist the help of your pool technician to find out how much could be saved by simply lowering the temperature setting or limiting the amount of time or the months of the year that the pool is heated. Look at alternate methods of heating, such as solar heating systems. Analyze the payback of the cost of converting to solar heat.

If the board members feel that they want to discontinue heating the pool water, communication with the owners is necessary. Survey the owners and residents to find out about the number of people who use the pool and the peak periods of use and explain the current costs and the alternate solutions that are being considered. You may find that a majority of the members want the pool heated regardless of the cost. All of these factors should contribute to the board's decision. The board might want to put this matter to a vote of the members.

Bear in mind that the decision may result in some resentment and, in the extreme, even a lawsuit. The board should carefully document the contributing factors to show that they used good business judgment, and, most important, they should communicate openly and honestly with the owners throughout the decision-making process.

You can find more information about the authority of the board in the chapters "The Role of the Board of Directors" and "Board Operations."

IT'S ONE OF THOSE JOBS SOMEONE HAS TO DO

Q *Perhaps you might point out that many board members work very hard as unpaid volunteers on behalf of our neighbors while the majority sit back and do nothing. It can be very time-consuming dealing with the management company and subcontractors, writing newsletters, etc.*

Our board enforces our association's legal documents as fairly as possible, with an eye on our property values. It can be irritating when the only time we hear from some homeowners is when they want to be the exception to the rule. As you have pointed out in your advice column, all homeowners have a legal involvement in their association, and there is a responsibility attached. Could you please comment?

A Bravo! I couldn't have said it better! I have served as the president of the association where I live. Time after time, our board has asked for volunteers to fill vacancies on the board or committees. The percentage of participants is very low.

As a community association manager, I've seen plenty of complainers during my years in this industry. It seems that any decision the board makes will displease someone. I advise putting the complainers on a committee. Give them something constructive to do. You may find that the complainers do not want to participate on the board or committees.

If the board is well organized and efficient, that often results in even greater apathy. As long as the board is doing a good job, board meeting attendance is pretty low. I've heard one manager jokingly say that the only way to get a good attendance at a meeting is to tell the owners that the assessments are going to be increased by 100%!

Well, enough sympathy for the over-worked board members out there. I have a bit of tongue-in-cheek advice. Board members should smile all the time and tell everyone how much fun they are having. That's the only way they'll ever convince someone else to serve so that they can retire from the board.

Now a word to those who chronically complain or never volunteer: If you're too busy to serve your association, the least you can do is attend the annual meeting and participate enough to know who is running for the board. Elect the best people for the job and then support them by abiding by the documents and obeying the rules. If you can't abide by the rules, then you shouldn't be living in a community association.

Treat your neighbor as you'd like to be treated. Some disputes can be resolved neighbor-to-neighbor rather than expecting the board to get involved. When you do have a complaint, be reasonable and speak with someone on the board before it escalates to a confrontation at a board meeting.

The community association lifestyle is here to stay. The responsibility of operating the association rests on the shoulders of a few willing volunteers. My hat is off to all those who continue to serve their associations through turmoil and crisis, with very little appreciation from their neighbors. Keep up the good work!

TEENAGERS ARE CAUSING DAMAGE AND LITTER

Q *I live in a planned unit development that has a large open area that is very appealing to outsiders. Our complex has had a problem with teenagers gathering late at night to smoke marijuana and drink beer. The litter and vandalism is getting worse. A gate and chain link fence have been cut so that they now come and go as they please.*

A locked bathroom near the tennis courts was severely damaged and a light pole was destroyed.

The board of directors has decided to leave the gate unlocked to prevent further damage to the gate and fences.

Obviously, that does not resolve the litter and vandalism issues. The police cannot respond right away and the kids are usually gone by the time that they arrive. A full-time security staff would be too expensive. What can you suggest?

A As you have found, locked gates do not ensure peace and tranquillity. It appears that you and your neighbors are maintaining a nice place for your unwanted guests to "party." There are several reasons that you should be willing to spend some money to get rid of the trespassers. Cleaning up the litter and repairing the damage is costing you money. Vandalism, litter and graffiti will lower the value of your property. The owners who live near this area are probably losing sleep and worrying about what the teenagers will do next.

If you are ready to reclaim your property, I suggest that you call a few security companies and see what it would cost to have random patrols. A security guard driving by or walking through the complex at random intervals would not be as expensive as a full-time guard.

Check with other nearby homeowner associations and shopping centers to get the names of security companies that already provide services in your area. Call your local police, using the non-emergency telephone number, and find out how you can organize a Neighborhood Watch committee.

CONDOS AND TOWNHOUSES: WHAT IS THE DIFFERENCE?

Q *What is the difference between a condo and a townhouse? I've asked many real estate agents and friends who own condos and what a mish-mash of answers I have received! Please let me know the correct definition as we are interested in buying one or the other but not until we know for sure what we are buying.*

A Confusion arises because community associations can have several different architectural designs and legal descriptions. Architectural styles vary from high-rise to low-rise, townhouse to single-family residences. Condominium structures often have public entrances, common hallways and garage areas much like apartment buildings.

A townhouse complex usually has four or five units in one or more buildings. Exterior doors lead directly to each unit with separate garages or carports. This architectural type is sometimes called a planned development and the individual unit owners may also own the land under their units.

Single-family houses on individually-owned lots are sometimes controlled by a homeowners association, another form of planned development. Even though the homes are detached and individually owned, the association will have rules and regulations in addition to other governing documents. The association may have parking rules, for example, and probably has jurisdiction over architectural changes, exterior paint colors and other aesthetics that affect the community.

Community associations are formed for the purpose of maintenance and administration of land and buildings that are owned "in common" by several owners. Membership in the association is mandatory—if you purchase property in the association, you are automatically a member of the association with all the rights and responsibilities outlined in the Declaration of Covenants, Conditions and Restrictions (CC&Rs). Owners pay assessments for the operation and maintenance of the commonly-owned property.

How does legal ownership differ? When you read the legal documents of a "condominium" you will probably discover that the unit owners own a percentage of the land and building structure and common elements (landscaped areas, hallways, recreation rooms, swimming pools) plus the individual owner owns the inner walls and improvements within the condo unit.

This condominium concept has expanded to commercial or office condominiums and even marinas, called "dockominiums."

In a "planned unit development"(PUD), usually called a "homeowners association," the unit owners often own the land on which the individual unit sits, and a proportionate interest in the common elements. Townhouses and single-family residences are often PUDs. Owners in a planned unit development or homeowners association are often responsible for roof maintenance or landscaping around their individual unit. Check the association's CC&Rs for this information.

While we're defining, let's cover the stock cooperative concept. A "cooperative" is a non-profit corporation that owns and pays property taxes on the land and building structure. The owners own shares of stock in the corporation, rather than a percentage of the property. Owners "lease" their units pursuant to a proprietary lease with the corporation, and they pay regular assessments just like the condo or PUD owner. This basic legal difference provides certain advantages for the cooperative. Since the corporation owns all of the property, if the building requires major repairs, the cooperative has the capability of borrowing money secured by a mortgage on the entire building to make the repairs. The downside is that it is often more difficult for a buyer to obtain mortgage financing.

When you purchase in any community association, remember that you are legally bound to abide by the CC&Rs and other legal documents so read them carefully. If you do not understand the governing documents of the association, consult an attorney who specializes in common interest development law.

OWNER IS IRRITATED BY ADVERTISING TERMINOLOGY

Q *We live in a 288-unit townhouse complex in Anaheim. It is very irritating to me that real estate agents list the units as condominiums even though our homes are called townhomes in the original developer's brochures and newspaper advertising.*

Unfortunately, the Articles of Incorporation call us a condominium homeowners association. What can be done to correct this error and rename our association as a townhouse association?

A The term "townhome" or "townhouse" is just a description of the architectural style of your complex. Townhouse complexes usually have several buildings with a small number of units per building. The townhouse units are vertical style, i.e. they are often three-story units with the garage space occupying the ground level, living room and kitchen on the second level and bedrooms on the third level. The units are usually built in a row with shared walls, sometimes called common walls or party walls, between the units. Many townhouse owners like the convenience of having their own garages that connect directly to the living areas of the unit via a private entrance. Most townhouses have a private patio or adjacent lawn area that may or may not belong to the individual owners.

Usually, condominiums are larger buildings that look just like an apartment complex. The traditional condominium complex will have a non-private parking area, a common lobby, hallways and elevators and the individual units are usually like apartments.

Your complex is probably designated as a condominium association in the legal documents because all of the owners share in the ownership of the land. If it were a planned unit development (PUD), each unit owner might own the land under the individual townhouse unit as well as a proportionate share of the common area. Thorough examination of your documents and deed will disclose the land ownership. It is unnecessary for the association to be renamed since the legal documents were probably written to reflect the proper legal ownership of the land and common area.

You obviously feel that a townhouse has more appeal to a prospective buyer, so if your unit is for sale, ask the listing agent to advertise it as a townhouse style condominium.

GETTING "BAD APPLES" TO COOPERATE

Q *Our homeowners association includes a few "bad apples" who do not abide by the declaration of covenants, conditions & restrictions. We have heard of other associations that impose fines against owners who are consistently unresponsive to notices from the association. Can the association levy a fine for CC&R violations? How does the association collect?*

A California Civil Code Section 1366(c) states that the association may collect a late charge from an owner who isn't paying assessments and it sets the amount of the late charge if the association's Declaration of CC&Rs is nonspecific.

If your board wants to fine owners for violations other than nonpayment of assessments, your board of directors should read your CC&Rs to see if the association is given the power to levy fines. If the board has the power to levy fines, follow the procedures as stated in the documents. The *Nahrstedt versus Lakeside Village* legal case established an association's right to enforce the governing documents by levying monetary penalties.

If the power is not stated, the board should seek the advice of legal counsel about adopting an enforcement procedure that will allow them to levy fines. If the board decides to fine owners, they must establish a procedure that will be consistently followed and notify all owners of the new procedure. The board must treat all violators fairly and equally. It is wise to notify the owner of the violation, giving the owner an opportunity to respond within a specified time and informing the owner of the consequences of further violation. Clearly state the nature of the violation and the amount of the fine that will be levied if the violation continues or occurs again.

The owner should be given an opportunity to appear before the board at a hearing in order to establish guilt or innocence and provide due process. The board should give at least a ten-day notice regarding the hearing date and allow the owner to reschedule the date if there is a legitimate reason for postponement. Monetary penalties must be fair and reasonable. After adequate notice and hearing, the owner is entitled to a written response from the association within 15 days following the hearing. If a fine is levied, the board should follow through and make every effort to collect. Fines can be added to the assessment billing. If the owner does not pay the fine, the association may be able to collect in small claims court if adequate records have been kept. The association should show that the owner's due process rights were respected and establish the owner's obligation to pay.

Do not proceed for collection of an unpaid fine by means of a foreclosure. State law forbids foreclosure as a means of collecting monetary penalties other than those resulting from delinquent assessments. Small claims court action is an alternative.

CITY BUILDING DEPARTMENTS KEEP COPIES OF PLANS

Q *The board of directors of our condominium association is investigating the cause of some serious roof problems. If we find that construction defects are involved, our association may decide to file a lawsuit against the builder/developer. We need to have the building plans in order to progress with our investigation.*

The board feels that the builder/developer will not voluntarily cooperate with our research. Does the city have a copy of the plans? Will the city release them to the board of directors since the association now owns the building? We want to do as much as possible ourselves before we call an attorney.

A If you are contemplating the need for construction defect litigation it is imperative that you obtain legal advice. I recommend that all associations establish a working relationship with a good community association attorney.

Leonard Siegel, an attorney with the law firm of Wilner, Klein and Siegel, provides the following advice:

"Sections 19850 and 19851 of the Health and Safety Code now require local building departments to maintain official copies of the plans of buildings, including plans of common interest developments (e.g. condominiums, stock cooperatives, planned unit developments) during the life of the building. Prior to the adoption of amendments to the code in 1989, common interest developments were exempted.

"Other noteworthy provisions of the amendments include:

1. The copy of the plans maintained by the building department may be on microfilm.
2. The plans must be available for inspection at the premises of the building department.
3. The copy may not be duplicated except with the written permission of the professional who signed the original documents and the Board of Directors. The permission by the individual who prepared the plans "shall not be unreasonably withheld." The plans may also be duplicated upon an order of the court.
4. The person requesting permission to duplicate the copy must sign an affidavit stating, among other things, that the plans will be used only for the 'maintenance, operation and use of the building.'
5. The person requesting the plans must also acknowledge that the architect who signed the plans is not responsible for subsequent changes not authorized or approved by the architect.

6. The building department may charge a fee in an amount reasonably necessary to cover the cost of compliance.

"Note: It is not clear whether the requirements of the act apply only to projects developed after the effective date of the amendments or whether they apply to all developments irrespective of the date of construction if the plans are still on file. In many instances, building departments do not maintain records of older buildings. Presumably, the statute will be interpreted to require building departments to maintain plans which it currently has on file which were generated prior to the enactment of these amendments."

NONPROFIT GROUP IS RESOURCE FOR ASSOCIATIONS

Q *What is CAI? How can I get more information about the organization? How can I join?*

A The Community Associations Institute, established in 1973, is a national nonprofit organization dedicated to the successful development and operation of community associations through education and research. The organization includes homeowners, managers, attorneys, real estate professionals, accountants, insurance agents and other professionals, contractors and vendors who work with condominiums, planned unit developments, homeowner associations, cooperatives or other forms of community associations.

Each local chapter provides publications and educational seminars. CAI chapters in California are: Greater Los Angeles chapter, Channel Islands chapter (Thousand Oaks, Ventura, Santa Barbara, Santa Maria and San Luis Obispo areas), Orange County Regional chapter, Inland Empire chapter (Riverside and San Bernardino counties), Coachella Valley chapter (Palm Springs area), San Diego chapter, Bay Area chapter (San Francisco, Oakland, San Jose), California North chapter (offices in Sacramento). Many of the chapters have websites. The national website is www.caionline.org.

CAI has a California Legislative Action Committee (CLAC) that monitors and disseminates information about proposed legislation that would affect community associations. The CLAC website is www.clac.org.

If you do not have access to a computer, consult your local telephone directory and call the chapter in your area for more information or call the national headquarters in Alexandria, Virginia at 703-548-8600.

CAN TERMINATION DATE OF DECLARATION BE EXTENDED?

Q *I live in a planned unit development (PUD). Is it true that after 50 years the PUD can be legally discontinued and then the property would no longer be governed by an association? If this is true, then how would the complex operate and how would the property be maintained?*

A Most common interest developments have some shared property ownership or common area that would require that an association continue to operate.

I have heard of some associations with single-family homes that have decided to disband their association, but each situation must be analyzed as to responsibility for such things as privately owned streets or perimeter lots or landscaped areas that must be maintained. It is usually impossible to dedicate these portions of land to the city or county and terminate the association's maintenance responsibility.

Some associations have declarations of covenants, conditions and restrictions (CC&Rs) that specify a date that the documents expire. The declaration usually states the procedure required to extend the expiration of the association. In most cases, extension requires an affirmative vote of at least 50 percent of the membership.

If your declaration has a termination date with no provision for extension, then California law, Civil Code Section 1357, states that the association members can vote to extend the association's term with a 50 percent affirmative vote or the percentage that the declaration requires for an amendment, whichever is greater.

If the association gets at least a 50 percent affirmative vote but the documents require a higher percentage that is unattainable, the association can petition the superior court using the procedures shown in Civil Code 1356. Consult an attorney whose practice is focused on community associations.

ASSOCIATION SAYS PARKED MOTOR HOME MUST GO

Q *I live in a homeowners association that consists of 150 single-family homes on one- to two-acre lots. Last year, I purchased a motor home and I have been parking it on my property for the last few weeks. The association president called and told me that motor homes are not allowed in the neighborhood. I had no intention of moving the motor home, but before I could get any further information, I received a very official letter. The notice stated that I would be fined if I didn't remove the motor home or attend a hearing to answer the accusation that I am violating the declaration of covenants, conditions and restrictions (CC&Rs).*

I don't have a copy of the CC&Rs but information that was enclosed with the letter says that motor homes, boats and trailers can't be parked or stored on the lots or in the driveways. Why wasn't I informed about this when I purchased my property? Does the association have the right to tell me what I can do? Do they have the right to fine an owner for violation of the CC&Rs?

A The declaration of covenants, conditions and restrictions (CC&Rs) should have been included in the disclosure information that you received prior to the closing of escrow when you purchased your home. You will probably find them filed away with the legal documents that you signed at the close of escrow.

The CC&Rs contain certain restrictions that owners are required to obey. By purchasing the property, you automatically agreed to abide by these restrictions.

The association, through the board of directors, does have the right to enforce the legal documents. You need to read these to find out what obligations you have as an owner and what authority the association has regarding monetary penalties, legal costs or other forms of enforcement.

Remember that the board of directors is a volunteer group elected by the membership (you and your neighbors). Written communication that spells out the alleged violation is a part of your due process rights.

The board president should be able to tell you how to obtain a copy of the CC&Rs. If the association has a property management company, the manager should be able to provide a copy for you at your expense.

I hope that after researching the association's authority you will resolve this problem by removing your motor home. The other owners have the right to expect that everyone will abide by the legal documents. The board has the authority and the obligation to carry out the enforcement process in a fair and business-like manner.

OBTAINING STATE LAWS ON COMMUNITY ASSOCIATIONS

Q *My husband and I live in a 60-unit homeowner association. Your advice has given me the confidence to run for election and now I am serving on the board of directors.*

I know that there are state laws that pertain to community associations but none of the former board members has researched this matter. Could you please tell us where to find out about state laws that govern community associations?

A Get acquainted with your local library. Most libraries have a reference section that contains the California statutes. If this information is not available at your local library, call your county law library and ask if they provide copying service.

Most of the laws governing community associations, whether incorporated or unincorporated, appear in the California Civil Code Sections 1350 through 1376. If your association is incorporated, you will want to consult the California Nonprofit Corporations Code, Sections 7210 through 7238. Statutes of Limitation are covered in the Civil Code, Sections 337 and 338. Disclosure requirements for transfer of ownership of residential property are covered in Sections 1102 through 1107 and Sections 1133 and 1134. Associations that tow cars because of parking violations are subject to the provisions in Vehicle Code Sections 22658 and 22853.

I rely on "*The Condominium Bluebook*" by Branden E. Bickel and D. Andrew Sirkin when I need to find a California law that pertains to community associations. It is a small paperback book, available from Piedmont Press, 1375 Grand Avenue, Suite 200, Piedmont, CA 94610. The e-mail address is piedmontpress@condolawfirm.com. The book is updated each year.

I am glad that you are now motivated to serve your association. Every association needs good volunteers. Good luck with your new board position!

WHEN REAL ESTATE AGENTS ARE ON THE BOARD

Q *In our condominium association, two people on the five-member board of directors are real estate agents. One of the two is a non-resident and rents her condo to tenants. She specializes in sales and rentals in our condominium complex. Would this situation be considered a conflict of interest?*

A The two real estate agents may be responsible, conscientious board members. The fact that they are real estate agents does not mean that there is a conflict of interest.

However, I can think of several examples of board decisions that might bring up concerns regarding conflict of interest. If the board is voting on any issues that might remotely affect sales and rentals, both agents should refrain from voting.

Something must have triggered your concern about this. Do the agents want to keep the annual budget low so that buyers will be attracted by the low monthly assessment? Are the agents lax about rule enforcement against tenants? Are other decisions being made that lead you to believe that the agents are interested in their own income from resales and rentals rather than the well-being of the association?

Have either one of the agents asked the board to endorse them as the exclusive listing agent or rental agent for the association? Owners have the right to use any real estate agent they choose and the association should not be allowing the agents to present the appearance that owners must use their services.

Board members have the obligation to ask themselves, "What is best for the whole association?" and then put their own selfish interests aside when making decisions. Of course, some people can do this better than others.

If any board member is acting for their own financial gain or self-interest, the other board members should question the actions and decisions of that board member and try to avoid the appearance of a conflict of interest. The board can pass a resolution that requires disclosure of interest by all of the board members. Homeowners have the right to review board meeting minutes to ascertain if conflict of interest appears to be clouding any board policies or decisions.

BOARD VIOLATES BYLAWS BY APPOINTING EXTRA MEMBER

Q *We live in a homeowners association that consists of 102 lots with single-family homes. Our association's five-member board of directors decided to increase the size of the board. They appointed a sixth board member without changing the bylaws and without a vote of the general membership.*

When questioned, the board members said that they needed the expertise of an architect to advise the architectural control committee and they wanted him the have the "status" of board member. Is this legal?

A Boards should not make decisions like this without consulting legal counsel. Every association should select an attorney that they can rely on when legal questions arise. If the attorney has the association's legal documents on file, a quick answer may keep the cost down. Legal consultation is usually well worth the expense and should be a budgeted item for every association.

I am not an attorney, but in my opinion your board's appointment of an additional member is questionable. The association's declaration or bylaws will usually specify the number of people who serve as the board of directors. If these documents state a specific number of directors, then the only legal way to add another director would be to go through the amendment process to change the wording of the governing documents. The amendment procedure and the amount of votes required will be stated. If the board wants to expand their number, I would suggest changing to a seven-member board. An even number of directors can result in deadlocks when tie votes occur.

Now I can hear some of you out there saying, "What harm does it cause if the board just increases the number of board members? Why go through the expense and hassle of amending the documents?"

My response is that the board is elected to uphold and enforce the legal documents. The board members should operate the association accordingly. The owners have a right to expect nothing less. If the board members choose to ignore the mechanics of the way the board is supposed to be constituted, I wonder what other portion of the documents they will decide to ignore in the future.

If the architect is a member of the architectural committee, he or she should be protected by the association's directors' and officers' liability insurance. The board should check their insurance coverage to ensure that committee members as well as board members have the protection of the association's insurance.

OWNER QUESTIONS SPECIAL FEES AND PENALTIES

Q *I have questions about some of the rules and regulations of our 30-unit condominium complex. We charge a non-resident owner fee of $50 per month for owners who rent out their units. Our move-in and move-out fee is $50 for owners and $120 when a renter moves in or out. The cost of the common area key that opens both exterior and interior common area doors is $50. The penalty for late payment of assessments is double the amount owed. We pay board members an honorarium of $20 per month.*

Are these procedures and fees legal? Are they fair?

A Many of the fees that you have described are either illegal or discriminatory and, therefore, probably unenforceable.

Charging a higher assessment or additional fee from non-resident owners is probably illegal unless the legal documents specifically grant the association the authority to do so. The fee for renters' move-ins and move-outs is considerably higher than the fee for owners and, therefore, is discriminatory. What move-in service is the association providing to the renter that specifically makes the renter's move-in more expensive?

California Civil Code, Section 1366.1 states, "An association shall not impose or collect an assessment, penalty, or fee that exceeds the amount necessary for the purpose or purposes for which it is levied." The $50 fee for the common area key may be proper if it is an expensive type that is impossible to duplicate. Again, I would refer you to the law stated above. Many associations charge a high fee for common area keys to discourage owners from having several keys made.

Some people feel that if one has a lot of keys, one will tend to be more careless with them or distribute them to friends.

Your association's penalty for owners who pay late is way out of line. The lawful penalty for late payment of assessments is 10% or $10, whichever is greater. Charging a higher amount is contrary to the California Civil Code. If your association's governing documents specify a lesser amount, then the association must charge the lesser amount.

The "honorarium" of $20 per month for board members is unwise. It also may be in violation of the governing documents of your association. The California Civil Code Section 1365.7 provides protection from personal liability to *volunteer* board members of non-profit corporations. Paying the board members deprives them of the protection that the law affords since they are no longer volunteers.

I urge you to consult an attorney who is well versed in community association law in order to get a legal opinion on all of your association's fees and procedures. Operating with your current procedures is unwise and could result in lawsuits.

CHAPTER 2 THE ROLE OF THE BOARD OF DIRECTORS

WHAT IS THE BOARD SUPPOSED TO DO?

The members of a community association meet at least once a year to elect the directors who are charged with the responsibility of running the association and carrying out the duties of the association. The directors then elect their officers according to the procedures in the association's bylaws. The Board of Directors is ultimately responsible for the entire operation of the association. Though certain duties or tasks may be delegated to committees, manager or service providers, the responsibility to see that the association is run properly rests on the shoulders of the elected board members.

The goals of the board should be to preserve, maintain and enhance the association's property in such a way that each owner's investment is protected. The association must be operated as a business, even though it is, legally, a non-profit entity. Prudent business management practices should always prevail. The board must operate the association in the best interests of the entire membership. Board decisions must be reasonable, fair and consistent. If the board members are unsure about any decision, they should rely on professional advice.

Many states have specific legal requirements regarding the operation of community associations. In California, whether the association is incorporated or unincorporated, it must comply with the Davis-Stirling Common Interest Development Act (California Civil Code Sections 1350–1376), which deals with budgets and annual reports, financial disclosures, maintenance responsibilities, insurance disclosures and many other legal requirements.

Specific powers and authority are granted to the board in the governing documents of the association. The governing documents include:

The Articles of Incorporation and Condominium Plan, if applicable

Declaration of Covenants, Conditions and Restrictions (CC&Rs)

Bylaws

Rules and Regulations

In most governing documents you will find a list of board responsibilities, such as:

Physical maintenance of the property

Financial planning, budget preparation

Assessment collection, financial record keeping, annual audit or review

Enforcement of the governing documents

Legal action, as needed

Supervision of employees, agents, and contractors

Procuring proper amounts of insurance coverage and fidelity bonds

Compliance with meeting notice requirements, board meeting procedures, annual meeting procedures

Compliance with local, state and federal statutes.

Unless the governing documents state otherwise, board members are not paid and are not entitled to any special privileges or benefits beyond those available to all owners. Board members should be exemplary in their compliance with the CC&Rs, bylaws and rules of the association.

It is the board's responsibility to comply with and enforce the association's legal documents in a fair and consistent manner. The meeting minutes, financial statements and all records of the association should be made available to all board members. Board meeting minutes (or a summary of the minutes, or draft of the unapproved minutes) are to be made available to any owner within 30 days after a board meeting. With few exceptions, owners are entitled access to most association records and they have photocopying rights if they pay for the costs (production of the information, copying and postage, as necessary). Refer to the chapter on Owners' Rights.

Board members should not engage in any self-dealing. I recommend that all work done for the association should be done by outside entities, individuals employed by the association or independent contractors. If a board member, or a board member's firm provides services to the association, or if a board member has any financial interest or remuneration from a firm doing business with the association, that board member should disclose the conflict of interest and exclude himself or herself from the board deliberations and voting process regarding contractual agreements and payments. If the association does pay a board member for services, sealed competitive bids should be obtained and the bidding process should be documented in order to protect the board and the individual board member from any possible appearance of conflict of interest.

Serving on the Board can be a thankless job. Those who enter into association service for the power, glory or attention are often quickly disillusioned. It is an inescapable fact that other owners within the association hold board members to a high standard. Board members should expect some criticism and be able to accept it without undue distress.

It is self-defeating for board members to spend a great deal of time and effort doing everything for the association. The board should attempt to minimize the time required for board meetings, committee meetings and other association business. Board members should not be treated as unpaid servants during their tenure. This is not only unfair; burnout and resentments soon begin to cause repercussions within the association. Board members' complaints about the amount of time and effort that they spend on association business will undoubtedly discourage others from wanting to serve on the board.

CONDUCTING EFFICIENT MEETINGS

One board meeting per month is sufficient for most associations, unless the board is putting together the budget or is faced with a special project or legal issue that requires more meeting time. All homeowners have the right to know when and where meetings take place so that they can attend. Executive sessions of the board are private meetings held for a specific purpose and homeowners are not entitled to attend unless the agenda topic pertains to that individual homeowner.

Meetings should be conducted in an organized manner, according to some form of parliamentary procedure so that the time spent will be productive, efficient and rewarding. Special board meetings should be called only when absolutely necessary. Proper annual planning and delegation of duties will help to eliminate the need for special meetings.

Each month, the board president or manager should prepare a detailed agenda listing any matters that require discussion or action at the board meeting. Sometimes, management will perform this task without much input from the president. All board members have the right to have an item placed on the agenda.

The agenda should state the date, time and place of the meeting. Attached to the agenda should be the financial report, actual bank statements (reconciled), written committee reports, correspondence and any supporting data that will be needed so that the board can make informed decisions at the meeting. The agenda packet should be distributed a few days prior to the meeting so that the board members have adequate time to read the material. Any board member's questions about the material should be clarified and answered prior to the meeting, if possible.

The board must allow time for owners' questions or concerns. Usually, I find it works best to hold this "open forum" before the meeting is called to order. The board should have a procedure that limits the speaking time so that owners are not allowed to ramble on and on or take over the meeting. It is the president's job to keep the meeting focused and running in a business-like manner. Everyone should be treated with respect.

If an owner's question, complaint or concern requires research, discussion or action, the president may appoint someone to follow up, put the matter on next month's agenda or refer the matter to the appropriate committee. The Board should not be pressured into taking action immediately if the matter is a new issue. If there is some pressing topic (health and safety issue) that needs immediate attention, the matter can be added to the agenda and handled during the meeting.

FISCAL RESPONSIBILITIES AND COLLECTING ASSESSMENTS

The board is responsible for determining the funding that is needed for the operating expenses and reserve funds. Then an annual budget is produced and distributed to the owners.

In California, Civil Code 1365.5 spells out the specific responsibilities for overseeing the bank records and accounting reports of the association. The decision to use reserve funds must always be documented in the board meeting minutes. Checks for expenditures from the reserve account must be signed by two officers of the association and must be approved by the board, with documentation in the minutes. The board is responsible for engaging a certified public accountant to prepare the year-end financial reports and tax returns.

One of the board's important duties is the collection of assessments. The association must have money to operate. It is the board's duty to collect the assessments in a fair and consistent manner. The board must adopt a "Delinquency Procedure" that conforms to the governing documents and state law, distribute it to the owners every year with the operating budget and then enforce it. Successful enforcement is dependent upon accurate record keeping and diligent follow-up. If a volunteer treasurer is unable or unwilling to go after delinquent accounts, the board must hire an accounting service or management company to perform this service.

It is unwise to allow any delinquency to go beyond three months without filing a lien on the separate interest (unit or lot). There are collection services that specialize in the collection of community association assessments. Attorneys also provide collection services. Any and all reasonable collection costs can be billed to the delinquent owner.

The "good neighbor" approach (allowing a delinquency to build up) is no kindness to the delinquent owner. The board has a duty to comply with the collection responsibilities in the CC&Rs. It is a disservice to all of the other owners who are paying on time and who will have to shoulder extra assessments in the future if some owners are allowed to remain in delinquent status.

OWNERS' RIGHTS

California Civil Code Section 1363.05 explains exactly what constitutes a board meeting, who can attend and the owners' right to be heard at a meeting. Corporations Code Sections 8310 through 8320 state that written minutes, records and accounting reports must be kept and that members have a right to review the books and records of the association. Even committees must have written records of their meetings. The meeting minutes can be less formal than board meeting minutes, but they should include the date, time and place of the meeting, who attended and the decisions made at the meetings.

Owners have the right to be informed about the association and its business affairs. They have the right to attend board meetings and membership meetings and communicate with the board. Owners have the right to attend an annual meeting and vote in the annual election as required in the governing documents. Owners may petition the board to call a special meeting of the owners by following the procedures contained in the governing documents (usually found in the bylaws). Owners are entitled to the list of names and addresses of other owners if the list is being used for association-related purposes (California Corporations Code Section 8330).

An owner is not entitled to attend executive sessions of the board of directors. According to California law, the board may hold executive sessions when the following matters are being considered: personnel matters, litigation, third-party contracts and owner discipline. An owner is not entitled to have access to the minutes of executive sessions of the board.

If an owner is accused of a violation of the governing documents, the owner has a right to be heard and to defend his or her position or opinion prior to the board levying any penalty. Proper written notification of a hearing, citing the alleged violation and the possible penalty, must be provided to the owner. The owner should be told that he or she is being given the opportunity to be heard and the possible ramifications if the owner fails to respond or fails to attend the hearing.

If an owner's voting rights are in jeopardy (according to the association's authority granted in the governing documents) the owner should receive notice and be given the opportunity for a hearing prior to any board action to remove the owner's voting rights. Even if the governing documents state that the board has the right to remove voting rights (i.e. for delinquent assessments), most attorneys recommend that the board send proper written notice and conduct a hearing prior to taking this action.

According to California Civil Code Section 1365, the association must distribute a comprehensive disclosure packet with the annual budget information. Another distribution of documents must be sent with the annual financial report, which is either a "review" or "audit" of the financial records after the close of the fiscal year. The review or audit must be performed by an independent certified public accountant who has no personal interest or investment in the association. There are specific guidelines used by the American Institute of

Certified Public Accountants that pertain to homeowner associations, condominiums and stock cooperatives. The reserve fund disclosures are an integral part of the CPA's report.

California law specifies that the amount of funds received from a compensatory damage award or settlement of a construction defect claim, and the expenditure of those funds, must be reported to the owners at the end of the fiscal year as *separate line items* under the cash reserves.

Civil Code Section 1375.1 states that the disclosure of the status of claims for defect or design shall include those defects that the association reasonably believes will be corrected or replaced and a good faith estimate of when the association believes that the defects will be corrected.

Questions and answers about owners' rights appear in a subsequent chapter.

CHAPTER 3—WHO IS RESPONSIBLE?

ASSOCIATION FAILS TO REPAIR ROOF LEAKS

Q *During heavy rains several months ago, my condominium unit was damaged because of roof leaks. Water came into my unit in three or four places. My insurance company paid for the cleanup and repairs but the condominium association's board refuses to make any repairs to the roof. The board says that the roof drains were clogged and that is the reason that the leaks occurred.*

I have contacted roofing companies and their workmen have told me that the roof does need repairs. Even after a strong letter from my attorney, the board still refuses to address the problem. I can't sell my unit without disclosing the roof problems.

The condominium complex has many deferred maintenance projects that need to be done. The board recently increased the monthly assessments and a special assessment of $500 per unit was approved. However, I'm told that none of this money will be used to repair the roof. My unit is the only one that leaks. It appears that since none of the board members has this problem, they do not care about making the repairs. Isn't the board supposed to represent all of the owners?

A Yes, the board has an obligation to maintain the roof so that your unit is not damaged again. If the board believes that clogged drains were the cause of the original leaks, water testing could have been done to ensure that the roof did not require repairs. Water testing could be done now to alleviate your concern.

It appears that your insurance company paid for repairs prior to ascertaining that the leak was repaired. The insurance company knows that it is wise to take care of water damage quickly so that mold and mildew does not become a problem.

You do not have the authority to get bids and have work done on the common area. You followed the right course by having your attorney put the association on notice that you will hold the association responsible for future leaks.

Perhaps the next step would be to request evidence that water testing has been done and that a maintenance program has been put in place so that roof drains will be kept clear in the future. Follow your attorney's advice and document your concerns by writing to the board.

WHO IS RESPONSIBLE FOR REPLACING THE FENCES?

Q *The fences in our homeowners association are not being maintained. The painting contractor informed the association when the fences were painted the last time that the fences would need to be repaired before he would paint again.*

The board of directors admits that the fence is common area but they say that the association's maintenance requirements are limited to painting. The board states that owners are responsible for replacing or repairing the fences between neighboring lots. As he warned previously, the painter has refused to paint the fences because they have deteriorated so badly.

Does California condominium law clarify the responsibility for common area maintenance?

A According to California Civil Code Section 1364, if the association's declaration states that the fences are common area, rather than "exclusive use common area," the association is responsible for repairing, replacing or maintaining the fences. The board has the responsibility to adopt a budget that adequately serves the needs of the association. Poor financial planning or inadequate reserve funds are not valid excuses for failing to maintain the common areas. The board can approve a special assessment equal to five percent of the annual budget in order to pay for common area expenses.

CLEAR-CUT RESPONSIBILITY FOR WINDOWS

Q *I am on the board of directors of our 18-unit condominium association. One of the units has just been sold and the new owner has requested that the association replace some cracked windows in his unit. In 25 years of operation, we have never had to deal with this issue. Is the association responsible for the windows? What about the window screens?*

A First, look at the association's legal documents. The declaration and the condominium plan should define ownership and differentiate between common area maintenance and unit owners' responsibilities. It may also refer to "exclusive use common areas" such as balconies or garage spaces that, for practical purposes, are a part of the unit because they are used exclusively by the individual unit owner.

If the association's documents do not specify the association's maintenance responsibilities and the owners' maintenance responsibilities, then the California Civil Code, Section 1364, states that exclusive use common areas are the responsibility of the individual unit owner. *Unless stated otherwise in the association's documents*, the windows and screens are defined in Section 1351 as "exclusive use common areas." If the association's documents are unclear, consult an attorney who specializes in community association law. Consulting an attorney is wise when you consider the cost of maintaining the windows and screens for the entire life of the project. Some associations are willing to pay for maintenance of balconies, awnings and other "exclusive use common areas" for the sake of uniformity and quality control.

TREE ROOTS CAUSE HAZARDOUS SIDEWALK CONDITION

Q *I live in a planned development consisting of attached townhouse-type units. I have informed the association that tree roots have elevated a section of sidewalk in front of my unit. The uneven concrete is a hazard especially at night because the lighting is not adequate. My family and guests are more at risk than anyone else. Since the raised concrete is a part of the common area, am I allowed to correct the problem if the association fails to take care of it?*

A In general, the association has the exclusive authority and obligation to repair, maintain, modify or improve the common area. Therefore, you would not have the right to take care of the repair yourself. I recommend that you report the problem in writing to the board members. You could remind them of the association's increased liability when a common area hazard is knowingly allowed to exist. If your association is professionally managed, send a copy of your letter to the property manager.

The board has an obligation to see that the problem is corrected. If they continue to drag their feet after receiving your written notice, I would suggest that you report the problem to the association's insurance agent.

COMMON AREA HAS INFESTATION OF TERMITES

Q *Our association's declaration does not have any guidelines regarding the responsibility to treat a termite infestation. We have 36 units in our complex. Six units on the top floor are infested and localized treatment during the past two years has not eradicated the termites. The infestation is in the common area and obviously is spreading from one unit to the next.*

It seems that the board of directors should be responsible for acting on behalf of the association to protect the building's structural integrity. Does this issue require a majority vote of the owners?

A In California, the Civil Code defines the responsibility for termite abatement if the association's declaration ignores the issue. Condominium associations, community apartment projects ("own-your-own" apartments) and cooperatives have different responsibilities than planned unit developments (PUDs). You must refer to your declaration to see what form of association you have or check the explanations of the different types of common interest developments as defined in Civil Code Section 1351.

The responsibility for termite abatement appears in the Civil Code beginning with Section 1364(b), as follows:

1. In a community apartment project, condominium project or stock cooperative, as defined in Section 1351, unless otherwise provided in the declaration, the association is responsible for the repair and maintenance of the common area occasioned by the presence of wood destroying pests or organisms.
2. In a planned development, as defined in Section 1351, unless a different maintenance scheme is provided in the declaration, each owner of a separate interest [unit] is responsible for the repair and maintenance of that separate interest as may be occasioned by the presence of wood destroying pests or organisms. Upon approval of the majority of all members of the association, the responsibility for such repair and maintenance may be delegated to the association, which shall be entitled to recover the cost thereof as a special assessment.
3. The costs of temporary relocation during the repair and maintenance of the areas within the responsibility of the association shall be borne by the owner of the separate interest affected."

In subsequent paragraphs, the Civil Code also provides that the association has the authority to require that occupants vacate the building for termite treatment and it specifically states the association's responsibility for giving sufficient and proper notice to occupants. An occupant is described as an owner, resident, guest, invitee, tenant, lessee, sublessee or other person in possession of the unit.

The notice to temporarily vacate must be given not less than 15 days nor more than 30 days prior to the treatment date. The notice must state the reason for the requirement to vacate the unit, the date and time that treatment will be started and the date and time for termination of the treatment.

Notice to the occupants must be given as follows: 1) personal delivery or first class mail delivery of a copy of the notice to the occupants at the unit address and 2) mail delivery of the notice must go the unit owner if different than the occupants.

OWNER WANTS ASSOCIATION TO COMPLETE REPAIR JOB

Q *How can I get my condominium association to complete repairs to the common area plumbing that involves repairs in my condo unit?*

New pipes were installed, which required tearing out some of the wall in my unit. The plumbers damaged some plumbing fixtures and did a poor job of replacing and painting the drywall. Repeat visits to correct the defects have proven that the damage cannot be fixed without major rework and expense.

The association and I are at an impasse regarding the extent of the repairs and the responsibility for payment. What can I do to get them to correct the problems and is the association responsible for the cost of the repairs?

A This is one of those situations where a bit of communication and some written assurances before the work started would have been helpful. You should have been told whether or not the association would be responsible for all of the finish work to restore your wall to its original state.

If the facts are correct, as you have stated them in your letter, the association is probably liable for the repairs. Fixtures that were damaged by the plumbers during the course of the work should be covered by the plumber's liability insurance. The association should have protected your interests by making sure that the company has adequate liability insurance.

Sometimes it is impossible to restore a wall to its original condition if there are wall coverings or improvements that cannot be matched. You will have to be understanding and work out a compromise if that is the case.

Write a letter to the board citing dates of the original work and repair work and requesting that they place this issue on the agenda for the next board meeting. This will give you an opportunity to speak with the board and discuss possible solutions. Ask the board how you can assist them in resolving the matter. If the board is uncooperative, one of your options would be to have the work done yourself and then try to collect in small claims court. Before doing so, inform the board in writing, including your estimate of the cost of repairs and your intent to collect from the association, so that you have full documentation for your court case.

If the repair cost is less than $5,000, you should attempt mediation or arbitration before filing legal action.

SUPERVISING CONTRACTOR IS BOARD RESPONSIBILITY

Q *The janitorial company that provides cleaning services to our condominium is doing a poor job. The corridors are vacuumed only once a week and there is dust on the light fixtures. An old newspaper has been lying in the garage for about ten days. I am furious about the condition of our building but the board of directors refuses to fire these janitors. What can I do?*

A Don't be too critical of the janitorial firm until you have learned all of the facts. Does a contract specify the type of cleaning that is to be done and the frequency of the cleaning? If you think that more frequent cleaning is needed, let the board know how you feel and find out if other owners agree with you. Communicate with the board rather than speaking directly to the cleaning crew about your dissatisfaction.

You could volunteer to submit suggested cleaning schedules to the board for their review. If the board approves, the cleaning duties could be increased or expanded.

The board of directors may be economizing on the cleaning costs or contracting for services based upon the wishes of a majority of the owners. It is not easy to please everyone. Some may want more services while others want to minimize costs.

Try to think of the entire complex as your home. If you see litter or debris, why not just pick it up? You could wait for the cleaning crew to find it, but they may not do a thorough inspection of the complex each day. Depending upon their schedule, that newspaper could lay in the garage for another ten days. Garages usually do not get the same amount of attention as the entrance, lobby, elevators and corridors.

DOES BOARD HAVE THE AUTHORITY TO REMOVE TREES?

Q *The landscape committee recommended that several trees be removed from the grounds of our condominium association. Some of the owners feel that is a radical approach. Half of the owners, only those surrounding the courtyard where the trees are located, were asked for their input.*

Is it legal to remove these trees without asking all of the owners for their opinion?

A The landscape committee reports to the board. Apparently, the committee and the board have good reasons for removing the trees. Trees are an asset because of their beauty, shade and oxygen-producing qualities. Perhaps the trees are diseased or overgrown and thinning them out will be advantageous. The board should rely on the opinions of an arborist before taking drastic measures.

It is commendable that the board is communicating with the owners and seeking their opinions, however the board has ultimate authority to decide how the association's assets will be maintained.

You have a right to let the board know how you feel about this issue, but the board has the authority to make the final decision.

OWNER OBJECTS TO REMOVAL OF SHADE TREE

Q *When I moved into my condominium two years ago, I was elected to the board of directors and this year I am president. Serving on the board has been an interesting experience, but not always pleasant.*

We have a difficult problem as a result of the removal of a tree. The board approved the pruning of several large trees that had been neglected for over five years. Many of the trees had grown over the roofline so that leaves and debris were collecting on the roof and clogging the rain gutters.

Three of the five board members were present when we negotiated with the tree trimmer. We agreed that one large tree, which was growing between two other very large trees, should be removed. After the tree was cut down, the homeowner whose unit was directly under the tree has threatened to sue the association. The owner wants remuneration for the loss of the tree's shade and the additional electricity expense for air conditioning.

The board members felt that we were acting in good faith by protecting the roof and properly maintaining the trees. Now we are faced with the possibility of a lawsuit. What can we do?

A The board can show that their action was taken to protect the association from roof damage, falling tree limbs and overgrowth of the trees. The board has the authority to make decisions about the manner in which the association will maintain the property. The opinions of the owners should be respected but sometimes trees have to be pruned or removed even though the individual owners don't like the results. Most judges in a court of law will not question the decisions of a board that studied the alternatives, relied on professional advice and acted in good faith.

Obtain a statement from the arborist or tree trimmer regarding the reasons that the tree had to be removed. Send a copy to the unit owner and invite the owner to a board hearing. I don't believe that the association has any responsibility for the owner's electricity. It would be difficult to determine a dollar amount since temperatures and the need for air conditioning vary so much each year.

HOW CAN OWNER OBTAIN COOPERATION OF NEIGHBORS?

Q *The condominium complex where I live consists of 10 buildings with 12 units in each building. The garage and laundry room are on the first floor of my unit, the kitchen and living room are on the second floor and the bedrooms are on the top level.*

My unit is infested with black wingless bugs that range from very tiny to 5/8 inch in length. They do not appear to be termites or roaches. How can we get rid of these pests without the cooperation of the other unit owners in our building? Getting the other owners to contribute financially will not be easy.

What do you suggest?

A Overcome any reticence about disclosing your unwanted guests and talk to your neighbors about the problem before you call the exterminating companies. The neighbors may want to rid their units of the critters also. If you are able to coordinate with your neighbors, the exterminating companies will probably drop the per-unit cost according to the total number of units that are treated.

Capture some of those critters and then call some exterminators to find out the identity of the pests and obtain bids. The exterminators will be able to determine what type of eradication method is necessary.

Wood-destroying pests or organisms are the responsibility of the association if your association is a condominium, community apartment project (commonly called an "own your own" apartment complex) or a stock cooperative. In a planned development, as defined in Civil Code Section 1351(k), the individual owners are responsible for termites unless the declaration of the association states otherwise. A planned development may be responsible if a majority of the members have voted to make the association responsible for treatment and repairs.

For localized treatment in your own unit, boric acid powder is effective against most household pests. You can buy boric acid at any hardware store. Be careful to follow the instructions on the container label and use it only as directed.

RESTRICTED COMMON AREA IS OWNER'S RESPONSIBILITY

Q *The board of directors of our homeowner association recently engaged the landscape contractor to plant and maintain the area behind several homes. These areas are designated as "restricted common area/homeowner maintained" in the declaration of covenants, conditions and restrictions (CC&Rs). The board felt that they were acting properly because weeds had become a fire hazard in the unmaintained areas.*

I notified the board in writing that they did not have the authority to change the maintenance responsibility that is stated in the CC&Rs. I feel that a more appropriate action would be fining the owners who have failed to maintain their restricted common area and calling the fire department to enforce weed abatement.

The manager told me that the board might advocate a CC&R amendment and conduct a homeowner vote. The board is displeased that I questioned their actions and it appears this may escalate to a legal battle. What can you suggest?

A The CC&Rs may have a provision that allows the association to bill the owners for the cost of maintaining the areas that the owners failed to maintain. Perhaps that is the board's intent. Make sure that you are fully informed about the entire matter before you criticize the board's action.

The board has an obligation to uphold the CC&Rs. In my opinion, they should have notified the owners who were in violation of the maintenance requirements of the CC&Rs, conducted hearings to encourage the owners' cooperation, and levied monetary penalties against those owners who failed to correct the problem. If the CC&Rs allow the association to pay for correcting the problem and then bill the owners, that would be an alternate course of action.

Relying on the fire department to enforce weed abatement is a good example of using outside sources and governmental services to assist the association. Your suggestion is a good one.

It is not appropriate for the board to use association funds to pay for expenses that are beyond the scope of the association's responsibility as stated in the governing documents. They should have obtained legal advice. If they treat you as the enemy because you disagree with their decision, they are just compounding their error. The board members should not take offense when other owners disagree with their actions. Boards sometimes make improper decisions. They should be willing to revisit a decision and change it.

It is ridiculous if this disagreement escalates to legal action. The board needs legal advice to learn about the scope of their authority and alternative enforcement methods. It is appropriate and prudent to use funds to get the professional advice of an attorney.

If the board fails to correct their alleged bad decision, you can request mediation to air your concerns, listen to their viewpoint and try to resolve the matter.

UPSTAIRS FLOOR FAN CAUSES DISTURBANCE

Q *We live in a two-story condominium where an owner on the second floor uses fans that are placed on the floor of his unit. The hum and vibration bothers the unit owner on the first floor. After many complaints, the upstairs owner raised the fans off the floor but the downstairs owner still complains that he is losing sleep from the disturbance. The fan owner refuses to discuss the problem.*

Is this a dispute that the association should be trying to solve? Some owners feel that the two owners should resolve this between themselves. However, the first floor owner is the board president so he has directed the management company to hire an attorney and many letters have been written to no avail.

Our declaration states that either the association or any individual owner can take steps to enforce the restrictions against "unreasonable noises, which interfere with the enjoyment of other residents." If this results in litigation, will the association have to pay all of the costs? A counter suit has been threatened so the legal expenses could be substantial.

How do we determine whether this is a private problem between the two owners or an association problem?

A The lawsuit threats are flying and that just escalates the animosity. In my opinion, this is a problem that should be mediated between the two owners. According to California Civil Code, some form of alternative dispute resolution should be attempted prior to filing a lawsuit in this type of situation.

If no one else is affected by the noise, the board members should vote to determine whether the association will accept the responsibility to cure the problem. In a neighbor versus neighbor dispute like this, it is helpful if a neutral person from the association can convince the two parties to talk about the problem.

It appears that it is too late to settle this in a congenial manner unless someone can convince the two parties to be reasonable. Perhaps if the second story neighbor is given the opportunity to visit the downstairs neighbor and hear the sound of his fans, he will agree that they are too noisy. The first floor neighbor has a right to peace and quiet, especially at night.

Hiring a mediator or arbitrator is the next step. The board members should decide whether the association will be involved in the mediation as one of the parties or whether this should be a neighbor-to-neighbor arrangement.

The board president exceeded his or her authority if attorney fees are accumulating without the approval of the rest of the board members. In my opinion, the board president who is personally involved in the dispute should not even vote on whether the board should engage the attorney. The president probably overstepped his authority when he instructed the manager to consult the attorney.

OWNER WITHHOLDS MONEY BECAUSE OF DIRTY WINDOWS

Q *I am having a dispute with the board of directors and the management company of my condominium complex. The stucco walls had to be pressure-washed prior to painting the exterior of the building. My clean windows were left streaked and dirty.*

I phoned the management company and asked to have my windows washed but the management company refused. I then wrote a letter stating that if the windows were not cleaned within one month, I would hire someone to wash the windows and deduct the cleaning cost from my monthly assessment payment. The management company again refused to pay, so I deducted the $30 cleaning cost from my subsequent assessment payment.

Now I am being charged a late fee for the unpaid $30. They caused the problem and I feel they should acknowledge their responsibility to clean my windows.

How should I proceed?

A Sorry, but I can't be sympathetic to your complaint or the way you have chosen to deal with it. The association is probably not responsible for cleaning your windows even though the dirty windows resulted from the association's maintenance of the building exterior. Window cleaning is usually the unit owner's responsibility. A possible exception might be in high-rise buildings where the windows must be professionally washed from the outside of the building.

After the pressure washing was completed and you were left with dirty windows, perhaps it would have been reasonable for you to ask the board of directors if all of the windows in the complex could be washed at the association's expense. It is not reasonable for you to expect the association to pay for yours and not pay for other owners' window cleaning. That could result in a lot of angry neighbors who would complain that you received special treatment.

In any case, a unit owner does not have the right to arbitrarily deduct any amount from the monthly assessment. By doing so, you have just caused more expense. You must pay the $30 and the late fees. If you don't pay, the association has the right to file a lien in order to collect. Then you will have to pay the additional costs of the lien filing and lien release when you finally decide to give up your battle.

By the way, your disagreement does not involve the property manager or the management company. The manager is just carrying out the instructions or procedures that the board of directors has approved. The manager could not have used association funds to pay for the cleaning unless the board approved it.

WHO IS LIABLE FOR DAMAGE FROM WATER LEAK?

Q *The condo above our unit had a water leak. Our whole bathroom ceiling fell down and the walls and wallpaper also had to be repaired. The association had a plumber come in to repair the leak and then billed the owner of the unit above us.*

We repaired the ceiling, walls and wallpaper and when we tried to collect from the association, we were told that the association was not at fault. Who is responsible for our damages, the association or the owner above us? How can we collect?

A If the leak had resulted from common plumbing within the walls, I would say that the association would be responsible for repairing the ceiling and walls and you would be responsible for replacing the paint, wallpaper or other surface decorating. Your board should rely upon legal advice regarding the association's governing documents and the precedent that has been established in prior incidents of this type. However, it appears that the leak occurred in piping within the upstairs owner's unit since the association billed the other owner for the plumbing work and declined to pay for your repairs.

In most cases, the association would be responsible for ensuring that the ceiling was replaced, because that is probably common area. The owner's responsibility is usually the paint or wall covering or other improvements that are applied to the ceiling.

It's too late now, but this is what you should have done when the leak occurred. After mopping up the water and doing everything you could to protect your unit from further damage, your next step should have been to contact your manager or board president to find out who was responsible for the damage. If the association was not responsible then you should have filed a claim with your own homeowners' insurance company because some CC&Rs have clauses that protect the upstairs owner from liability in this type of situation. Some insurance companies might not process a subrogation claim against the owner where the leak occurred. Perhaps it might be difficult to collect unless negligence can be proven.

Read your CC&Rs and talk to your own insurance agent to determine if anything further can be done to recover the cost of your repairs. Be sure that your insurance policy protects you against this type of damage that may occur in the future.

WHO IS LIABLE FOR TREE PLANTED IN COMMON AREA?

Q *I live in a planned unit development of 19 townhomes. Each unit has a private patio and beyond the patio there is a small area of land that is common area owned by the association.*

Over the years, the owners have "done their own thing" with this small area adjacent to their patios. The association now has a problem with a tree that was planted on the common area 15 years ago by one of the owners.

Now the tree is overgrown and is leaning to one side, making it a possible hazard. Neither the owner who planted the tree nor the association want the tree removed, but trimming is necessary. The owner who planted the tree is willing to pay for the cost of trimming it. Since it has been on common property all these years, who is responsible for trimming and maintenance of the tree? If the tree falls, would the association be liable for any damage that might occur?

A Your questions give me an opportunity to point out that associations should not allow owners to plant flowers, trees or add other enhancements to the common area. The association has the responsibility to maintain common area; therefore the association, through the board of directors, should control what is planted or placed in the common area of the association.

I am neither an insurance claims adjuster nor an attorney, but I will give you my common sense response to your questions. The tree has been there for many years. The association's sprinkler system has probably watered it, the association's gardener has mowed around it, and raked the leaves under it. I would say that the association is responsible for trimming it, too. Since the tree is on common property that is under association control, any damage caused by falling limbs would probably be the association's liability.

Boards should bear in mind that when an owner wants to plant a tree, or present the association with a statue or a birdbath, they should consider all the consequences before allowing this kind of improvement to the common area. If the board expects an individual owner to be responsible for the maintenance of an improvement, then a document should be signed that fully states the owner's and successive owner's responsibility.

WHO SHOULD PAY TO CORRECT CONSTRUCTION DEFECTS?

Q *I live in a condominium complex of nearly 300 units. Several of the units have water intrusion due to faulty construction. After three years of delay, the board is finally negotiating with the developer.*

The developer only wants to pay for half of the cost of the corrective work. In addition, he is demanding that the association indemnify him and sign away any future claims. What are the consequences?

The association does not have enough money in the reserve funds to split the cost with the developer. Does the board have the right to approve a special assessment without a vote of the owners?

A If the water intrusion problems are the result of poor design or construction defects, the developer is obligated to pay for all of the corrective work that is needed. The developer may not have the funds to do all of the work but a competent construction defect attorney will seek out the insurance companies that insured the developer during the original construction.

I hope that the association board is being advised by legal counsel who is very knowledgeable about the statute of limitations and procedures for proceeding with litigation that are outlined in the state law. California laws specify the steps that must be taken when an association is considering legal action because of construction defects.

Prior to settling with the developer, the board should be advised regarding their liability if latent defects become known after the settlement. All alternatives should be addressed and fully discussed with legal counsel in executive session with the board.

If the board decides that they are going to use reserve funds for work that the developer has an obligation to complete, they should have adequate documentation to show why they chose their course of action. They also must have a plan to replenish the reserve funds.

The board has the authority to approve a special assessment that is no more than five percent of the total budgeted expenses for the fiscal year. A larger special assessment requires a vote of the members at a meeting that more than fifty percent of the members attend. Approval of the special assessment requires the affirmative vote of a majority of those members in attendance.

ARE OWNERS LIABLE FOR TENANT'S AND GUEST'S ACTIONS?

Q *Our association's declaration states that the owners are legally liable for the actions of their tenants and guests. How can one person be liable for another's actions? Is this provision in the legal documents enforceable?*

A Yes, you are responsible to the association for any actions such as rule violations or damage to the common property that is caused by any person that you invite into the complex. This would include even workmen who might cause some kind of common area damage or create a problem for any of the other owners.

This provision is enforceable. It is a good reason for you to have liability insurance and to require that any companies doing work for you be licensed and have liability coverage, vehicle liability and workers' compensation coverage. For instance, the association has the right to hold you responsible if your plumber backs his truck into the common area wall and damages it.

DAMAGE RESULTS FROM TILE INSTALLED ON BALCONY FLOOR

Q *I bought my condominium unit about a year ago in spite of the seller's disclosure that there was a stain on the ceiling from an unknown leak. The real estate agent assured me that it was the condominium association's responsibility to fix the leak and repair the ceiling.*

Due to recent heavy rains, my ceiling now has more damage and the board of directors is not addressing the problem. The property manager says that the leak is the result of tile that was installed on the balcony of the unit directly above mine.

I have tried to contact my upstairs neighbor to see if we could amicably resolve the problem. She refuses to discuss it with me.

The board president said that the tile was installed without the approval of the board or the architectural control committee.

Where do I go for help?

A The board of directors has the authority to require that your neighbor cooperate with the efforts to find the source of the water leak. This is especially true if architectural control provisions in the association's legal documents have been ignored. If the neighbor refuses to cooperate, the board of directors has the right to demand correction of the problem. The board may have to pay for the legal assistance and the experts who can define the problem and recommend a solution. Then, if the neighbor's tile installation is found to be the source of the problem, the board can demand that the owner pay for any legal costs and other expenses that the association incurred in order to enforce the association's legal documents. In addition, the owner can be compelled to take care of and pay for the necessary repairs.

The board has an obligation to assist you in resolving this matter. If the board fails to take action, you have the right to enforce the legal documents as stated above and then attempt to pass on your costs to your uncooperative neighbor.

A letter explaining the association's authority and your rights could be sent to the neighbor. If she continues to be uncooperative, the next step should be obtaining legal advice. Perhaps a letter from the association's attorney will get her attention.

WHO SHOULD MAINTAIN DECKS, BALCONIES AND FRONT DOORS?

Q *Our townhome association has received conflicting advice regarding the responsibility to maintain the deck surfaces in the complex. Our former manager insisted that California laws specify that "exclusive use" decks, balconies and front doors are the maintenance responsibility of the individual owners. Our current manager is not aware of any law that would supersede the declaration of covenants, conditions and restrictions (CC&Rs). He insists that the CC&Rs should be our guide to determine the maintenance responsibility. Who is right?*

A Both of the Civil Code sections that apply to this situation refer to the provisions in the association's declaration, so first you should find out what the declaration says. Section 1351 of the

California Civil Code defines "exclusive use common area" as a portion of the common area designated by the declaration for the exclusive use of one or more, but not all, of the individual owners.

If your association's declaration (CC&Rs) does not define "exclusive use common area" then you can rely on the following portion of Section 1351 for clarification: "Unless the declaration otherwise provides, any shutters, awnings, window boxes, doorsteps, stoops, porches, balconies, patios, exterior doors, door frames and hardware incident thereto, screens and windows or other fixtures designed to serve a single separate interest [unit], but located outside the boundaries of the separate interest, are exclusive use common areas allocated exclusively to that separate interest."

In Section 1364 of the Civil Code, you will find the explanation of the responsibility for maintenance. Again, the law refers to the declaration (CC&Rs): "Unless otherwise provided in the declaration of a common interest development, the association is responsible for repairing, replacing or maintaining the common areas, other than exclusive use common areas, and the owner of each separate interest is responsible for maintaining that separate interest and any exclusive use common area appurtenant to the separate interest." Many associations have run into conflicts over the meaning of the words "repair, replace, and maintain." In my view, the words have separate and distinct meanings.

Though some property managers are very knowledgeable about legal matters pertaining to your association, I recommend that your board of directors consult an attorney whose practice is primarily focused on community association law. After thorough review of your declaration, the attorney will be able to advise the association about the legal responsibility for the maintenance of the deck surfaces in your complex.

The association should get a legal opinion and then the board of directors can adopt a resolution regarding exclusive use common area repair, replacement and maintenance. The board of directors should distribute the information to all of the owners so that these responsibilities become standard operating procedure.

IS ASSOCIATION RESPONSIBLE FOR RAIN GUTTERS?

Q *We live in an eight-unit condominium association. During recent rains, we had water damage that included soaked carpet, damaged interior drywall and interior wood shutters. We have been told that the repairs are not covered under the condominium association's insurance and our homeowner's insurance company has denied the claim.*

The damage resulted from clogged rain gutters and lack of rain gutters in some areas. The association's legal documents state that the association is responsible for all exterior maintenance. Who is responsible for the internal repairs when damage results from poor exterior maintenance?

A An attorney would want to review all of the association's governing documents before giving you a definite answer. If the damage is significant, you should obtain legal advice.

Relying upon the information that you have provided, I would expect the association to pay for the repairs. Since the damage resulted from lack of maintenance of the rain gutters or lack of proper drainage of the roof and driveway, the association should be responsible.

You have a right to file a claim with the association's insurance carrier. If the association's insurance company accepts the claim, the association should pay the deductible. If the insurance company denies the claim, you may want to file an action in small claims court. The association may be held liable for all of the repairs if you can successfully argue your case in small claims court. In California, small claims action has a $5,000 limit.

WHO IS RESPONSIBLE FOR BROKEN WINDOW?

Q *A bottle was thrown through the front window of a second-story condominium unit. Is the broken window an association expense or must the owner pay for it? Since the window is a part of the exterior of the building, who is responsible?*

A Sometimes the answer to this question can be found in the association's governing documents. The "condominium plan" is a document that often explains the actual ownership of the common areas and the units and the accompanying responsibility. Sometimes the Declaration of Covenants, Conditions and Restrictions (CC&Rs) states whether the owner of the separate interest (condominium unit) or the association is responsible for window repair and replacement. Many condominium documents state that the unit owner simply owns the cube of airspace or, in some cases, the paint or wall covering or other improvements on the interior of the unit's walls. The structure is owned by the association.

This is a legal question and an insurance question that requires the expertise of an attorney and the association's insurance agent. Vandalism like this may be covered under the association's insurance policy. However, many policies exclude windows. In addition, the amount of the deductible may preclude filing a claim.

Every year, the association is supposed to disclose the names of the insurance companies, the amount of coverage and the amount of the deductible. To help clarify the line between owner responsibility and association responsibility, the association's insurance agent should send a letter to the association informing the owners of the types of losses that the association's insurance policy covers and those that the owners' policies should cover. The owners should be informed about the amount of the deductible so that they can adjust the coverage on their own policies accordingly.

The association needs to seek professional advice. This issue could easily come up again. If the association assumes the responsibility for the repair, a precedent may be set for more repairs and maintenance in the future.

COMMON AREA LANDSCAPING IS ASSOCIATION'S RESPONSIBILITY

Q *Several homeowners are paying the association's gardeners to have them plant shrubs and flowers in the common area near their residences. The board does not want to upset any of the homeowners so they are allowing the plants to remain in the common area.*

Maintenance of the common area is an association responsibility. Don't I have the right to expect that the board will treat each person fairly and not allow individuals to alter the common area?

A In my opinion, it is a mistake to allow individual owners to plant their own shrubs and flowers in the common areas of the complex. The owners simply do not have the right to put their own plants in the common area. The entire common area belongs to every owner. By adding their own plants, these owners are saying, "I'm claiming this portion of the common area and I'm going to plant it the way I want it." This is an example of disrespect for one's neighbors and disrespect or ignorance of the association's documents.

There are other reasons that I am against individuals adding their own plants. Any board that is faced with owners who want to add their own flowers, shrubs or trees should consider these issues:

The association will lose control of the general landscape plan. The landscape plan should take into consideration many issues: the cost of the plants, the amount of water, the amount of maintenance and the type of care that is needed. All of these things affect the association's landscaping costs. When the association's board decides on the types of plants that will be used, then everyone should support the plan because the board has the authority to make those kinds of decisions.

When individuals add their own plants, neighbors might complain about the choice of plants or the colors or the size. After the shrubs and plants are installed, who is going to maintain them? Who is going to decide when they need to be fertilized, cultivated, trimmed and who will pay for the extra care these plants will require? Will the owner hold the association responsible if the plants die and expect that the association will replace them?

Owners do not have the right to upgrade the common area around their individual homes. The common area belongs to everyone in the association.

PLUMBING RULE CONFLICTS WITH THE DECLARATION

Q *My condominium association has a rule that states, "All plumbing problems within the walls and ceilings, i.e. waste lines, drains, and p-traps are the responsibility of the unit/units connected to said lines."*

The association's declaration specifically states that pipes and utilities that are not within the unit, including sewer lines, are part of the common area.

Recently, one of my neighbors had a blocked drain in the kitchen sink. She called a plumber who cleared the drain and then sent bills for one-fourth of the cost to each of the owners of the other three units in her part of the building. The association also sent a letter threatening to impose a fine on any owner who fails to pay his/her share to the owner who called the plumber.

Can the association impose a fine for this purpose?

A The board of directors should consult the association's attorney to determine whether the rule is enforceable. The association's board is threatening to impose a fine, but they may not have the legal right to do so. They cannot enforce a rule that is in conflict with the association's declaration. The declaration is the association's "constitution" and it is the controlling governing document in this situation. The declaration may state that the board has the authority to adopt rules and regulations; however, the board does not have the authority to adopt a rule that is in conflict with the declaration.

There is standard procedure for handling clogged drains in condominiums. At the time that a clogged drain is reported to a board member or manager, the association's billing procedure should be explained to the unit owner. If the blockage occurs in a sink p-trap, garbage disposal, tub, shower or toilet in a unit, it is usually due to something that the owner or occupant of the unit put into the drain. The unit owner is typically billed for clearing the drain. If the blockage occurs in the main line or if the plumber's snake has to be extended into the drain line that serves more than one unit or an entire stack of units, the association typically pays for the plumbing work.

It is most efficient for the manager or board member to call a plumber who is familiar with the building. The plumber will be able to advise the association whether the blockage was in the individual unit or the common area drain line. To ensure that the association's plumber gets paid, the association will usually pay the bill even if the unit owner is at fault. Then the cost of the plumbing repair is added to the owner's assessment billing.

The association board should obtain legal advice and adopt a procedure for clogged drains that complies with the declaration. Then the owners should be informed how this situation will be handled in the future.

WHO IS RESPONSIBLE FOR LEAK FROM SLIDING GLASS DOOR?

Q *I own a condominium unit on the third floor of a three-story building. I have a rain leak from a window and I'm not sure who is responsible for the repair. The window is the stationary section that is part of the sliding balcony door. It is leaking water from the bottom of the door into the living room of the unit.*

Is the condominium association responsible for repairing and paying for the cost of the repair? Are there situations where the owner might be held responsible and other situations where the association would be responsible?

A First, let's determine if this is a door or a window. From your description, it seems that the leak is occurring at the bottom of the stationary side of a sliding glass door. The stationary door and the sliding door are mounted in the same doorframe, so I would consider this to be a door leak, not a window leak. In some associations, windows are treated differently from doors.

Your association's declaration of covenants, conditions and restrictions (CC&Rs) may state whether the association or the unit owner is responsible for repair or replacement of doors. If so, your association should rely upon the CC&Rs.

If owner or association responsibility is not stated in the CC&Rs, then two sections of the California Civil Code will provide clarification of responsibilities. Civil Code 1351(i) states the "exclusive use common area" means "a portion of the common areas designated by the declaration for the exclusive use of one or more, but fewer than all, of the owners of the separate interests [units] and which is or will be appurtenant to the separate interest or interests." The code continues:

1. Unless the declaration otherwise provides, any shutters, awnings, window boxes, doorsteps, stoops, porches, balconies,

patios, exterior doors, door frames, and hardware incident thereto, screens and windows or other fixtures designed to serve a single separate interest, but located outside the boundaries of the separate interest, are exclusive use common areas allocated exclusively to that separate interest.

2. Notwithstanding [in spite of] the provisions of the declaration, internal and external telephone wiring designed to serve a single separate interest, but located outside the boundaries of the separate interest, are exclusive use common areas allocated exclusively to that separate interest.

To find out who is responsible for repair, replacement or maintenance, refer to Civil Code Section 1364, which states:

(a) Unless otherwise provided in the declaration of a common interest development, the association is responsible for repairing, replacing or maintaining the common areas, other than exclusive use common area, and the owner of each separate interest [unit] is responsible for maintaining that separate interest and any exclusive use common area appurtenant to the separate interest.

Therefore, depending upon the wording of an association's CC&Rs, sometimes the owner will be responsible for a particular repair while another association's documents might make the association responsible for the repair.

If you need clarification of the association's governing documents or the civil codes that pertain to associations, then you should rely on the advice of an attorney whose law practice is focused on the representation of community associations (common interest developments). After thorough review of your documents, including the condominium plan, if one exists, the attorney will be able to provide an opinion letter that definitively states the repair and maintenance responsibilities of the association and the owners. This information will help to prevent disputes about legal responsibilities.

INSURANCE WON'T PAY FOR DAMAGE FROM ROOF LEAK

Q *During some recent rainstorms, a roof leak damaged the ceiling and carpet in my townhouse. The homeowner association is responsible for the roof. The association's insurance company refuses to reimburse individual owners for interior damage resulting from roof leaks. I do not have insurance coverage on my individual unit that would pay for interior damage.*

It was my understanding that the association has financial responsibility for damage that results from a deficiency in the common property. Therefore, I expect the association to pay for the damage to my unit.

Can the association refuse to pay for the damage?

A The answer probably lies within your association's declaration of covenants, conditions and restrictions (CC&Rs). There may be an exculpatory, or nonliability, clause that lets the association off the hook even if negligence is a factor in the deficiency in the common roof. The association's insurance may not be responsible for paying for your claim if this type of exculpatory clause appears in the legal documents.

The insurance company could also deny your claim if the association has had a history of roof leaks in the past. Insurance companies soon get wise to associations that defer their roof maintenance and then expect the insurance coverage to pay for interior damage. A past history of roof leaks can result in cancellation of the association's policy.

In my opinion, it is wise for each unit owner to obtain insurance coverage for the interior of the unit and its contents. This will only assist you in case of future losses, of course. When obtaining this coverage, you should also consider loss assessment coverage, which will reimburse you in the event that your association must levy a special assessment due to an insurance loss. This type of coverage is very helpful if your association is affected by a fire, earthquake or flooding, for example.

Consult an attorney who specializes in community association law. After reviewing your association's legal documents and insurance policy, he or she will be able to advise you about your rights and the association's obligations.

AFTER ROOF WAS REPLACED, LEAK DAMAGED CEILING

Q *We live in a townhouse complex. The homeowner association is responsible for all common areas including the roof. After the association replaced the roof, we had a leak that damaged our ceiling. The contractor was unable to fix the leak right away, so our unit has extensive ceiling and wall damage. We asked the association to repair the damage that resulted from the common area roof being improperly replaced.*

The association denied our claim stating that any interior repairs were the unit owner's responsibility. How can the association escape responsibility?

A Without having an attorney review your association's legal documents and insurance policies, this is a tough call. The liability of the roofing contractor needs to be examined. It may be possible to file an insurance claim with the association's insurance carrier. Several legal issues are involved, so you may want to contact an attorney to ascertain your rights and alternatives. Even when there is no legal basis for denying responsibility for a claim, some association boards try to "stonewall" homeowners.

If your declaration of covenants, conditions and restrictions (CC&Rs) states that the association owns the walls and ceilings, then the association is probably liable for the repairs to the drywall inside your unit. However, some declarations state that the association is not responsible for interior damage, other than common area, regardless of the cause. Most condominium associations are responsible for the drywall and ceiling repairs and the owner would be responsible for the paint or wall coverings.

The association should have required that the contractor provide evidence of liability insurance. If the association was negligent by not requiring liability insurance or if they did not require the contractor to make repairs in a timely manner, there may be liability on their part. You could file a claim against the board's errors and omissions insurance, sometimes called director's and officer's liability insurance.

Since the association was the party that entered into the contract with the roofing contractor, I believe that the association would be the only party that could present a claim to the contractor's liability insurance carrier. You should document everything in writing with photographs and delay doing any of the repairs yourself, if possible.

Another option is filing a claim with your insurance carrier for your interior damage and then your insurance company may be able to subrogate the claim. Subrogation occurs when your insurer pays your claim but then the insurer goes after the contractor's insurance or the association's insurance if there is legal basis for doing so.

Small claims court may be the way to go if the damage will cost less than $5,000 to repair. After you have fully documented your claim, repair the damage, keeping receipts for all work. Then file a claim in small claims court against the association. You can seek the advice of an attorney regarding your small claims case but you cannot be represented by an attorney in small claims court.

CHAPTER 4 LEGAL MATTERS

SUGGESTIONS FOR SELECTING ATTORNEY

Q *Our association does not have an attorney. One of our board members is insisting that we need to have legal advice on an architectural matter. One of the owners is an attorney, but he has declined to provide legal advice to the association because he specializes in another area of legal practice. How should we select an attorney? Will we have to pay a monthly retainer fee?*

A Seek a law firm that has several community association clients and ask for the names of some of the firm's clients so that you can obtain references from board members of those association clients. If your association is professionally managed, the manager or management company personnel can provide the names of several attorneys. Attorney referral services for California are listed on the Internet at www.calsb.gov or www.calbar.gov.

Some associations have more than one attorney. For instance, an association might have a law firm that is handling construction defect litigation while another provides advice regarding interpretation of the governing documents, rule enforcement and assessment delinquencies. If your association employs a manager or other on-site personnel, the association needs an attorney who can provide advice about labor laws. Vendor contracts are another area that requires legal advice from time to time.

Interview several different attorneys. If you like a specific attorney, find out whether he or she will handle all of your work or delegate some or all of the day-to-day work to associates within the firm.

In the interviews, discuss the following: 1) the attorney's specific areas of knowledge and length of experience, 2) his or her litigation experience, 3) the attorney's experience with associations having similar architectural controls, 4) some of your current problems or concerns, 5) the hourly rate and billing procedures, 6) references and 7) find out about the attorney's voluntary affiliation with nonprofit groups such as Community Associations Institute and the California Association of Community Managers.

Do not expect free legal advice during the interviews. A good attorney will not offer glib answers to legal questions without having the opportunity to review your association's governing documents.

After the interviews, verify the attorney's membership or affiliation with the bar association and the organizations named previously. Check the references that the attorney provided. Ask the references if the attorney returns phone calls within a reasonable length of time. Ask about the types of problems that the attorney has worked on for the client.

Do not select an attorney based upon the cheapest hourly rate. Fees vary based upon retainer fees, clerical fees and other considerations. Some attorneys offer a choice of an annual or monthly retainer or hourly billing. One person from the board should be the contact person in order to monitor the billing statements. The individual has a duty to keep the other board members informed and he or she must be trusted to represent the entire board in its dealings with the attorney.

When the board is ready to select an attorney, rely on all of the information gathered from the interviews, the verification of professional license, references from managers and the attorney's association clients.

ASSOCIATION'S AGE RESTRICTIONS MAY NOT BE ENFORCEABLE

Q *I own a condominium in an association that has age restrictions. The board has not enforced these restrictions for a number of years. The governing documents (CC&Rs) state that "Each unit shall be occupied by at least one person not less than fifty (50) years of age and no person under eighteen (18) years of age shall permanently reside in any unit." A 36-year-old renter has been a resident here for about six years. Another resident who is under fifty has resided here for a number of years. She recently purchased another unit and moved into it. Since the CC&Rs have been violated regarding age restrictions for a number of years, can we enforce the restrictions now? In the future, can a property owner be restricted from selling to someone less than fifty years of age? These are questions that have divided our board of directors and angered a number of owners. One attorney that I contacted said, "If the board has knowledge of a violation of the CC&Rs, and does not respond in writing to the offender before another board meeting occurs, that represents the board's approval." Can you provide some insight?*

A Senior housing is usually restricted to persons who are 55 or over, though a younger person may be a "qualified resident" as defined by laws governing discrimination in housing. Your attorney is not very well informed or you would have obtained more definitive answers to your questions. The attorney should be aware of California's Unruh Civil Rights Act (Civil Code Sections 51 through 53) and the federal laws pertaining to age discrimination. The federal Fair Housing Amendments Act of 1988 prohibits denying residence on the basis of age. With some exceptions, unless your condominium complex provides specific design, services or amenities for the physical and social needs of senior citizens, it may not qualify as senior housing. Therefore, your association may be in violation of state or federal law and subject to harsh penalties if your association attempts to enforce your outdated legal documents.

The specific requirements to qualify as senior housing are numerous and complex. I suggest that you consult with an attorney who is familiar with the federal and state laws regarding age restrictions and senior housing requirements if you wish to explore the possibility of enforcing your age restrictions.

In general, when a violation occurs, the board does not have to take immediate action; however, it is preferable to act as soon as possible.

IS BOARD LIABLE FOR ACCIDENT IF CHILDREN DISOBEY RULES?

Q *I live in a planned unit development in which several units share a common driveway. Some of the children ride their bikes in the driveways even though the association's rules prohibit it. As a member of the board of directors, could I be held personally liable for the injury or death of a child in this circumstance where the child was violating a rule?*

A Since I am not an attorney, I urge you to seek the advice of your association's legal counsel regarding the association's ability to enforce the rule and California Civil Code Sections 1365.7 and 1365.9, which specifically address board members' liability and the liability of the individual owners.

The law states that a volunteer director "shall not be personally liable in excess of the coverage of insurance" to "any person who suffers injury, including, but not limited to, bodily injury, emotional distress, or wrongful death, or property damage or loss as a result of the tortious act or omission of the volunteer officer or volunteer director if all of the following criteria are met:

1. The act or omission was performed within the scope of the officer's or director's association duties.

2. The act or omission was performed in good faith.
3. The act or omission was not willful, wanton, or grossly negligent.
4. The association maintained and had in effect, at the time the act or omission occurred and at the time a claim is made, one or more policies of insurance, which shall include coverage for
(A) general liability of the association and
(B) individual liability officers and directors of the association for negligent acts or omissions in that capacity; provided that both types of coverage are in the following minimum amount:
   a) At least five hundred thousand dollars ($500,000) if the common interest development consists of 100 or fewer separate interests [units], or
   b) at least one million dollars ($1,000,000) if the common interest development consists of more than 100 separate interests."

There are further stipulations within the law that clarify who is and isn't protected under the law based upon their volunteer status and whether the officer or director lives in the complex or owns more than two units.

Civil Code Section 1365.9 protects the association's individual owners from liability if the association maintains general liability insurance policies that provide at least $2,000,000 of coverage if the association has fewer than 100 units, or $3,000,000 of coverage if the association has more than 100 units.

OWNER WANTS TO CONSULT WITH ASSOCIATION'S ATTORNEY

Q *I contacted the office manager of our condominium and asked for the name and phone number of the association's attorney. I was told that if I call the attorney, I must pay for the attorney's time* *even though the condominium association was the subject of my inquiry. There is nothing in our rules regarding this matter.*

It would seem that through the monthly assessment, each owner is contributing to any legal costs and would be entitled, within reason, to inquire regarding the legality and accuracy of procedures and information promulgated by the board. To what extent can an individual owner seek legal clarification from the association's attorney?

A When you see the gardener working on the property, would you ask him to install a flower garden for all to admire and then expect the association to pay for it? What if your neighbor wanted a hedge around the pool? And another owner might order more fertilizer or weed control for the common areas. As you can see, controls need to be exercised so the board of directors has the responsibility to authorize expenditures of this type.

The attorney provides legal advice to the association and the board is elected to run the business affairs of the association. Your dollars help to pay for legal services, but the board decides how those dollars are spent. If individuals call the attorney for advice on association matters, the bills could mount up without the board or management being aware of the situation. Also, the board may have already asked for a legal opinion on the same subject.

If you have concerns about the legality of a board action then you should briefly explain this to the attorney's secretary, state that your association is a client and ask what the fee would be for consultation. Perhaps your question could be answered very briefly and there would be no charge at all. On the other hand, the attorney may refuse to speak to you because you are not a board member. In that case, you will have to consult with your own attorney.

NEIGHBORING CHILDREN USE POOL WITHOUT PERMISSION

Q *We live in a five-unit association in North Hollywood. We occasionally have neighborhood youngsters (not children of our residents) who let themselves in and use our pool. They range from ages 10 to 16 years. Needless to say, we are concerned about our liability in the event that one of these uninvited children gets injured or drowns.*

The two pool gates automatically close and lock; however, it is quite easy to reach over the top of the gates and turn the inside knob in order to gain access.

Would it be legal to install self-locking latches on these gates that would require a key to exit from the pool area and to enter the pool area?

I called the Los Angeles city attorney's office and they could not provide an answer.

A I am aware of other associations that have the kind of locks that you describe. In my opinion, you need to control access more effectively by modifying the gate or the locking mechanism. Many associations have gates that require a key to enter and exit.

Check with your local code enforcement officers to find out what health and safety codes or ordinances might apply to this situation. The codes vary from city to city so I do not want to give an answer that would apply only in one municipality.

Discuss your concerns with your association's insurance agent and attorney. If you are aware that these children are using the pool without permission, you must be honest with your experts and ask for advice on obtaining insurance coverage that will protect you from liability. The attorney may be aware of appellate cases, which limit the association's liability if the guests are uninvited.

You may want to call the police the next time you catch the children in the pool without permission, since these children are trespassing on private property.

For more questions and answers about pools see the chapter, "Parking, Pools & Pets."

UNLICENSED BOARD MEMBER IS DOING ELECTRICAL WORK

Q *One of the board members in our homeowners association takes care of minor repairs and painting in our complex. Everyone seems to appreciate his work because of the money he is saving the association.*

I recently learned that he has been doing some electrical work in addition to his handyman duties. He is not a licensed electrician. I have talked to the rest of the board members but no one is concerned about the risks and liabilities involved.

If someone is injured because of faulty work, isn't the association liable? Would the association's insurance policy cover the association for an injury or damage claim if the board knowingly hires an unlicensed person?

A In my opinion, the association should play it safe. The board should hire licensed contractors who have sufficient workers' compensation and liability insurance coverage. Most cities require that permits be issued for electrical work. If the proper permits are not obtained and unlicensed workers are employed, the association is taking a risk that could result in a large property damage or personal injury claim against the association due to fires or electrical shocks.

Your board members should discuss these concerns with the association's attorney and insurance agent. Are there exclusions in the insurance policy that would allow the insurance company to deny a claim? If the insurance company does not cover a loss, can the association afford to pay the damage claims?

Board members who focus only on saving the association's money sometimes lose sight of the risks. They should remember that they have a responsibility to make sound business decisions that protect the association from liability.

The unlicensed board member may not be aware of his personal risk when he performs these good deeds for the homeowners association. An unlicensed person whose work results in personal injury or damages can be taken to court for additional damages of triple the amount of the loss, up to a maximum of $10,000.

CEILING AND PAINT ARE DAMAGED FROM ROOF LEAK

Q *My condominium unit is on the top floor of the building. The roof is common area. For the past two years, the roof leaks every time it rains. The ceiling and paint in our unit have been damaged and discolored with mold. I have begged the board of directors to repair the problem before the next rainy season begins. I am afraid the next rain will cause the ceiling to collapse.*

The association's handyman has made four attempts to fix the leak, but the problem still exists. The board will not call a licensed roofer. Do I have the right to repair the roof myself?

A As an individual owner, you do not have the authority to engage a roofing contractor or repair the leak yourself. You should resort to self-help only after your written requests and deadlines are ignored by the board. The damaged ceiling may be harboring molds and mildew that could be injurious to your health.

You can file a claim with your insurance company or file a claim under the association's coverage. Since this is a two-year-old problem that the board has not resolved, the association's directors and officer's liability insurance may protect you if all else fails.

Write to the board of directors giving them a 30-day response deadline. Your letter should state the number of times that the roof repairs have failed to correct the leak. Enclose interior photographs with your letter and keep copies of pictures and correspondence for your own records.

The board has a duty to hire someone who can determine the cause of the problem and complete the repair in a reasonable amount of time.

The board's failure to take appropriate action has caused damage to your unit. Their cheap solution has created a costlier problem because they can probably be held responsible for the interior repair in your unit. Because of the probability of mold growth, an expert such as a certified industrial hygienist, should investigate the damaged area of the ceiling as soon as possible. When the roof repair has been completed and water-tested, mold remediation can occur and the ceiling can be replaced.

If the board ignores your written demand, perhaps a letter from your attorney will spur them to action. Follow your attorney's advice regarding alternative methods of resolving the problem.

Civil Code Section 1354 states that your claim against the association, if less than $5,000, should be submitted to mediation or arbitration prior to filing legal action.

SECURITY OFFICERS ACCUSED OF BIAS AGAINST OWNER

Q *Our condominium association has a security staff that is discriminating against certain owners. Some of the security people speak openly of "selective enforcement." I have numerous witnesses to the fact that I am their "selected party." Can citations and fines by our security personnel be appealed to the state courts?*

Do we give up our rights when we buy a condo?

A Your association's enforcement proceedings are completely separate from the state court system. However, you have due process rights.

The association must provide an appeal process before a fine is collected. You have the right to a hearing before the board of directors. If you are being denied due process, then I urge you to discuss your options with an attorney. I am adamant in my support of the board if you have disobeyed a fair and reasonable rule. Rule enforcement is often a difficult and thankless job. On the other hand, if the rules established by the board are unfair or if they are being enforced unfairly, then you should take action to change things. Ask to have the matter placed on the agenda of the next board meeting. You have a right to be heard. If the board does not allow you to speak, then put your request in written form and try again. When you are given the opportunity to speak, be reasonable and courteous and have your thoughts well-organized so that your comments are brief. You have the right to bring your attorney if you feel that it is necessary.

BOARD REFUSES TO HIRE EXTERMINATOR

Q *What can be done about a condominium association that refuses to do anything regarding a termite problem?*

Our condominium unit was examined by a pest control company over a year ago and it was determined that we had termites. Every time we contact the board of directors, they refuse to do anything about it. I might want to sell my condo, but I know it will never pass inspection. I have considered withholding my monthly assessment, or contacting an attorney. What do you suggest?

A First, don't withhold your assessment payment. I'm sure you've heard that two wrongs don't make a right. The association has the authority to file a lien on your property to collect unpaid assessments and you will end up paying the expenses for the collection process.

Unless the CC&Rs state otherwise, the association is obligated to take care of this problem. I would refer the board of directors to Section 1364(b) of the Civil Code: "In a community apartment project, condominium project, or stock cooperative...unless otherwise provided in the declaration, the association is responsible for repair and maintenance of the common areas occasioned by the presence of wood-destroying pests or organisms." I would assume that the termites are within the common walls of the building. Perhaps you can simply show the board of directors the California Civil Code and request their cooperation. Otherwise, you may have to pay for an attorney to enlighten your board.

COMMON AREAS CAN'T BE SOLD TO OTHERS

Q *The developer of our association has taken portions of the "common area" and sold them to individual owners as "exclusive easements." These "exclusive easements" include surplus garage spaces, closets and storage spaces, which have electrical service provided by the association. Shouldn't the funds derived from these sales be deposited in the association's account? Does the developer have the right to sell these areas?*

A In general, the developer does not have the right to grant "exclusive easements" to individual owners when the association pays the electricity and the spaces are designated in the documents as common area. However, there may be wording in your association's declaration (CC&Rs) that gives the developer the authority to grant these easements. Some association documents give the developer the power to do almost anything. You need to consult with an attorney that specializes in common interest development law.

BUILDER ADVISED TO HALT DEVELOPMENT

Q *I am building 14 houses that share a private road and some common area that is landscaped. Some of the houses share common walls. How do I go about setting up an owners' association that will be responsible for repair and maintenance of the common areas and the private road.*

A Hold everything! If your development is being built in California, the Department of Real Estate is the governmental agency that controls developments of this type. Before you proceed any further, check with the Department of Real Estate to find out what the requirements are and how to draft the necessary documents for filing with the state. You are involved in a project that requires a great deal of legal groundwork and document preparation both with the state and the local municipality if the property lies within a city's boundaries.

AGENT STATED HOME WAS NOT IN AN ASSOCIATION

Q *Our real estate agent told us that our new home was not in an association. We believed him because this is a development of single-family homes and there are no amenities or highly visible common elements. At the time of the closing we received a copy of the CC&Rs and bylaws but we did not understand the significance of these documents. We were shocked to find out that we had to pay assessments for private streets, street lighting and some landscaping around the perimeter of the property. We have recently read the CC&Rs and find several restrictions that we do not like. What can we do about this agent?*

A The real estate agent has a legal obligation to know the pertinent facts about any property that he or she is selling. Full disclosure is the seller's and the agent's responsibility. The fact that the association exists is definitely a pertinent fact that you should have been informed about before you even signed an offer to buy the property.

Consult the Department of Real Estate and the local Board of Realtors and then you can decide whether to file a complaint with one of these agencies and/or consult with a real estate attorney for further legal advice.

ASSOCIATIONS CAN USE SMALL CLAIMS COURT

Q *Our association has spent a lot of money on attorney's fees in attempting to collect past due assessments. Wouldn't it be cheaper to file a claim in small claims court?*

A California Civil Code, Section 1366, states that the association may charge to the delinquent owner any reasonable costs incurred in collecting delinquent assessments, including reasonable attorney's fees. If your attorney has not advised you of this, you need to find an attorney who is knowledgeable in the field of community association law.

Small claims action is an option, but someone must represent the association in court. If you have a management company they may provide this service for a fee. If a volunteer from your association is knowledgeable and willing to represent the association in court, the volunteer is entitled to reimbursement of his or her expenses while appearing in court on behalf of the association.

There are several companies that specialize in the collection of delinquent assessments, lien filings, small claims action, and foreclosures. Here again, reasonable expenses can be collected from the delinquent owner.

BOARD WON'T REPAIR FLOOR LEAK

Q *My ground floor unit is built on a concrete slab. Moisture seeps through the foundation and my kitchen floor is ruined; the linoleum is discolored and the seams are curled up. There is so much dampness that mold accumulates around the metal base of the patio doors.*

For four years I have spoken to and written to the board members about this. A contractor suggested that a waterproofing material be applied and a trench along the exterior should be dug out and filled with gravel. Instead of following the contractor's advice, the association had a cheaper waterproofing material applied on part of the outside wall. The repairs were not effective and moisture continues to seep into my unit.

I was promised that my floor would be replaced but when I asked for a written statement that the association would take care of it, I was put off.

How do I get the association to stop the leaking and repair my linoleum?

A Your sad letter just makes me want to jump in and act as your ombudsman! You have been unduly patient with an association that has been very unresponsive. The situation that you describe is unhealthy. Write to the board and demand that they tell you how they are going to deal with this problem. Give them a reasonable deadline, possibly 30 days, for responding to you. Request that a claim be filed with the association's insurance company as either a general liability claim or a directors' and officers' liability claim because of their failure to take appropriate action. Since this is an on-going problem, it is not too late to find out what the insurance company will do for you.

After the waterproofing work is successfully completed, the insurance company may pay for new linoleum. The association must follow through on this for you. They may be obligated to pay for the flooring if the insurance company denies the claim.

If the association fails to act within a reasonable amount of time, call the building and safety division of your city to see whether your moisture problem is a health and safety code violation. The board would then have to correct it if the association is cited by the city.

You may have to contact an attorney or Legal Aid or a mediation service to force the board to take action. An alternative plan would be to pay for the work yourself and try to collect from the association through small claims court or civil court action.

IS ASSOCIATION LIABLE FOR INJURY TO HANDYMAN?

Q *Our association employs a handyman who is probably an illegal immigrant without a green card. He is paid $9.00 per hour in cash at the end of each week. He sometimes pays his friend a small amount out of his own salary when the friend helps him with small jobs.*

If the handyman or his helper is injured while working for the association, could the association be required to pay the medical bills? The board president says that the worker is an independent contractor and, therefore, the association is not responsible. I cannot convince the other board members that we have any liability. What can you tell us?

A The cheap labor that you are using could end up with a high price tag. Your association is violating a number of laws in addition to immigration law. First, it is doubtful that the worker would qualify as an independent contractor. Therefore, the association is responsible for payroll taxes, workers' compensation insurance, compliance with OSHA regulations and other employer requirements. If a complaint is filed, the association could be charged with heavy penalties for ignoring these laws.

Board members who ignore the law are not serving the best interests of the association and its owners. Though I am not in favor of board recall in most situations, I recommend board recall in this case if the board refuses to obey the law. The owners should petition for a recall vote as soon as possible. It will take some effort on your part to get the support of the other owners and make the board recall successful.

PARALEGAL PROVIDES POOR ADVICE

Q *Our homeowners association was recently contacted by a paralegal from a neighborhood legal and bookkeeping service. We were told that the association's declaration of covenants, conditions and restrictions (CC&Rs) must be updated every year. He also stated that the association must have an audit done every year.*

The cost of the legal work seems very reasonable, but we are wondering whether the advice regarding updating the CC&Rs is correct. What do you advise?

A Stay away from the cheap paralegal who is giving you bad advice. I recommend that the association obtain the services of an attorney who specializes in community association law and stays informed about all of the laws and new legislation that govern common interest real estate developments and nonprofit mutual benefit associations.

Associations do not have to update their CC&Rs every year. Amendments to the CC&Rs should be done only when necessary because amending the CC&Rs usually requires the approval of either two-thirds or three-fourths of the voting membership. Amendments must be recorded with the county recorder upon certification of the prescribed number of affirmative votes from the full membership.

All condominiums, homeowners associations, planned developments, cooperatives and "own your own" community apartment projects must distribute a financial report each year. Associations with annual income greater than $75,000 must have a financial review prepared by a state-licensed accountant. A full-scale audit is not required annually unless the association's legal documents specifically state that an audit is mandatory. Incorporated associations with annual income between $10,000 and $75,000 must prepare a financial report and make it available to the association members according to Corporations Code Sections 8321 and 8322.

Please refer your questions to an attorney who can review your association's legal documents and advise you. Obviously, this particular neighborhood paralegal and bookkeeping service is not a reliable resource.

LAWS ABOUT COMMUNITY ASSOCIATIONS ARE ACCESSIBLE

Q *Our condominium board has learned through your column that there are many laws that govern community associations. Thank you for educating our board and all of the owners in our association.*

We have heard about the Davis-Stirling Act and I believe this is the law that you usually cite in your column as the California Civil Code. Is the California Civil Code included in the Davis-Stirling Act? How can I obtain a copy of the California statutes that govern condominiums?

A The Davis-Stirling Act was passed in 1985 and took effect January 1, 1986. It consolidated certain existing provisions in the Business and Professional Code and the Civil Code so that most of the laws having to do with common interest developments, or community associations, now appear in Sections 1350 through 1376 of the Civil Code. Nearly every year there are changes to this statute so you need to stay informed about new legislation. The law firms that have many association clients often send out newsletters to inform their clients of new legislation and appellate court cases that have some bearing on association operations.

There are provisions in the Corporations Code and the Nonprofit Corporations Code that can be referenced when researching voting procedures, board powers and responsibilities and members' rights. Most public libraries have a law reference section where you can read these laws and make copies for your use.

TEN PERCENT PENALTY CAN BE CHARGED FOR LATE PAYMENTS

Q *Our condominium association is collecting a special assessment from all the owners to pay for major repairs. Does the association have the right to request payment of a special assessment before the repair work is even started? Can the association add a ten percent late charge if the special assessment is not paid?*

A When major repairs are necessary, the association may need to accumulate a major portion of the money before the work is started. Construction companies often require deposits to pay for materials, permits and other "up front" costs. Some companies require proof that the association can afford to do the work before they will enter into a contract.

Unless your association's legal documents specify a smaller percentage or amount for late charges, California law states that unpaid regular and special assessments are subject to a late charge of either ten percent of the assessment amount or $10.00, whichever is greater.

CAN BOARD APPROVE THE SETTLEMENT OF A LAWSUIT?

Q *Our homeowner association filed a lawsuit against the developer. The association's attorney settled the suit on less than acceptable terms. What authority does the board of directors have in this matter? Can the board authorize the settlement without a vote of the owners? Since all the owners are paying the legal expenses, shouldn't all owners participate in the decision-making on this important issue?*

A Several attorneys have advised me that in most instances the board does have the authority to settle a suit filed on behalf of the association. The board is elected annually by the general membership of the association. The duly elected board has the responsibility of managing the affairs of the association, often making decisions that affect millions of dollars of association assets. Their authority is usually very broad with certain specific limitations found in the association's legal documents.

Read your declaration of covenants, conditions and restrictions (CC&Rs) to find out about the board's specific powers and duties. I have often seen CC&Rs that specifically authorized the board to take legal action on behalf of the association members. On the other hand, I have also read legal documents that require a vote of the membership before legal action is taken.

If you feel that the board's action is not in the best interests of the association, contact an attorney who specializes in community association law.

OWNER QUESTIONS LEGALITY OF ASSOCIATION OPERATION

Q *I live in an 11-unit townhouse complex. Since I purchased my unit in 1995 there has never been a board meeting or annual meeting of owners. One of the owners is the president of the association but we do not know of any other board members.*

There are many problems that are being ignored. We have never received any kind of financial report or any other information about the operation of the association. Some of the owners are not paying their monthly assessments. I am told that one owner owes assessments for about three years.

We have some repair work that is needed, but the president said that he would have to increase the association assessments since there are no reserve funds to cover any additional expenses. Is it legal to increase the assessments without a vote of the owners? Has the board president been breaking the law? Can he be held liable for making the repairs or charged with mismanagement?

A It appears that your association has been operating without an elected board of directors for some time. The one active board member has made a serious mistake by not fulfilling his fiduciary duty to conduct the association according to the legal documents.

Even small associations like yours must operate in compliance with the law and provide certain reports and financial statements to the owners. A dictator is operating your association. It may be a benevolent dictatorship but the results are simply not acceptable.

The owners have a right to elect a board of directors to handle the management of the association. The president may say that there weren't any other owners who were willing to serve on the board but that is not a valid excuse. Annual meetings must be conducted in compliance with the legal documents of the association. Then if there were no owners willing to serve on the board, the rest of the owners would have been informed of the situation and they might have been able to find willing volunteers at that point.

Assessments must be collected from all owners based upon an annual budget. It is illegal for the board president to increase the assessments without the vote of a duly elected board of directors. With proper board vote, the assessments can be increased up to twenty percent above the previous year's assessments.

The board has a duty to collect delinquent assessments. If all of the owners had been paying their fair share, it is possible that there would be enough funds to take care of the required maintenance and repair. It is time for you and the rest of the owners to take action to protect your rights and your investment.

There are many things wrong with the scenario that you describe. The board president can be held responsible for the apparent mismanagement that has occurred. You and the rest of the owners may want to band together and seek the advice of an attorney who specializes in community association law. I would advise you to have an audit done to determine where the funds were spent and to uncover the extent of the delinquencies on the part of the non-paying owners.

It is possible that the self-appointed president is a good person who was unaware of all of the legal requirements and responsibilities of operating the association, but the legal documents cannot be ignored.

CAN PARALEGAL UPDATE THE LEGAL DOCUMENTS?

Q *I live in a small homeowner association. Some of the owners would like to update the association's declaration and bylaws; however, there is no money in the budget for this purpose. Can we keep the cost down by hiring a paralegal?*

A The board should adopt a budget that adequately covers legal expenses for the association. There are proper procedures that must be followed when the documents are being changed or you may find that the revised documents are unenforceable.

Revision of the legal documents should only be done by an attorney who specializes in community association law. A community association manager or consultant might be able to assist you with the preliminary stages of the project but the attorney should review all of the documents and rewrite the sections that are being revised. As stated earlier in this chapter, the laws pertaining to community associations are changed in some fashion nearly every year.

The attorney will advise you about the approval procedure for amended or revised documents and he or she can handle the recordation with the county.

ASSOCIATION BOARD DOES NOT COMPLY WITH THE LAW

Q *Our condominium association has 200 units with pools, tennis courts and other amenities. Our annual budget is about $1,000,000 and we have about $1,000,000 in our reserve funds for future repair and replacement of major components of the complex.*

In a recent board election, the campaign was a nasty one. Negative stories about the previous board appeared on the front page of a local newspaper. Owners of multiple units were taken to lunch by the proxy gatherers and lawsuits were threatened against the opposition.

The new controlling majority, three of the five board members, was elected through a well-organized proxy collection effort. They include an attorney, a wealthy real estate investor and another person who always votes with the attorney and the investor.

After the election, the new board fired the management company that had performed well for five years. The new management company appears to do whatever the majority of the board wants, even though the action is in violation of the association's legal documents or state law.

Your advice has warned us against many of the actions that the board has taken. For example, reserve funds are being withdrawn with only one board member's signature and without any board discussion. In the last four months, our reserve funds have been depleted by $100,000 even though no reserve expenditures have been discussed or approved at a board meeting.

Our association's declaration of covenants, conditions and restrictions (CC&Rs) requires accrual accounting methods for our financial records. The new management company switched to cash accounting methods and changed the chart of accounts. We are now six months into the contract year and the management company has not been able to produce a single financial report in time for review at the monthly board meeting. They blame the prior management company's lack of proper records.

Without any board discussion, the law firm that was handling our foreclosure procedures for delinquent assessments has been dismissed. The association now uses a non-judicial procedure for foreclosures.

Please answer the following questions: Does the association's board have an obligation to comply with the legal documents? Does a manager with the Professional Community Association Manager designation have an obligation to comply with the law? When professional "wheeler-dealers" take control of the board, what can an owner do? What protection is available other than expensive legal action?

A The board of directors has almost all of the power and authority in a community association. That is why the election of directors is so important. The owners should be very careful to elect people who are known to be fair, honest, competent and loyal to the common good.

Once elected, the board has an obligation to comply with state and federal laws and enforce the governing documents of the association. Accurate financial records must be supplied to the board so that they can review actual expenditures and income and compare the association's current financial status with the budget. State law requires that the board review accounting records and bank statements at least every three months. For an association of 200 units, this should be done at each monthly board meeting.

Accrual accounting provides a more complete picture of the association's finances since it shows accounts payable as soon as the obligation is incurred and income is accounted for as soon as it is billed. Cash accounting, on the other hand, does not take into account any unpaid bills that may be accumulating without the board's knowledge. In my opinion, modified accrual accounting is better, especially for a large association such as yours. That is probably why your association's CC&Rs require the accrual method. However, some management companies do not provide accrual accounting. These companies say that, as long as the annual review or audit is performed using accrual accounting methods, they are in compliance with the state law.

Board meeting minutes must be kept of any and all important board decisions, especially firing attorneys, changing assessment collection procedures and approving reserve expenditures. If these decisions are being made in between board meetings, California Corporations Code, Section 7211(b), gives specific procedures: "Any action required or permitted to be taken by the board may be taken without a meeting, if all members of the board shall individually or collectively consent in writing to such action. Such written consent or consents shall be filed with the minutes of the proceedings of the board."

In other words, all board members must not only participate in the decision, they must all agree in writing to any action that is taken outside of a meeting.

Regarding your manager's failure to provide timely financial reports, this is a serious problem. The change in management companies should not delay the printing of financial reports. The reports do not have to balance with the prior management company's records. The new management company starts with the current status of the assessment billings, accounts payable and the current bank balances to prepare their reports. After a management change, a licensed accountant who is experienced in community association accounting should conduct an audit. Perhaps the audit will clear up any discrepancies in the accounting records.

Your manager's Professional Community Association Manager (PCAM) designation means that he or she has a professional level of community association management education and experience and that the person has agreed to abide by a professional code of ethics established by the Community Associations Institute. In my opinion, the manager is causing or allowing the association to be in breach of the law and he or she is in breach of the PCAM professional ethics if financial reports are not being provided on time and reserve funds are being used without proper signatures and without documentation in the board meeting minutes.

The PCAM Code of Professional Ethics requires that the manager accept only those contracts that he or she can perform with professional competence. A complete copy of the ethics code can be obtained from your local chapter of the Community Associations Institute. A written complaint about the performance of a PCAM can be sent to the president of the organization, at the national C.A.I. office, 225 Reinekers Lane, Suite 300, Alexandria, VA 22314.

California Civil Code, Section 1365.5(b), states that the withdrawal of reserve funds requires two signatures, either two board members should sign or it is permissible to have an officer who is not a member of the board and a board member as the signers. The manager should be aware of this law and, in my opinion, he or she should inform the board in writing if reserve funds are not being handled properly. In your letter, you have accused some of your board members of being wheeler-dealers, but you and the other owners have elected them and you are the only ones who can remove them from power. There is no state agency that oversees the operation of community associations after the original developer has completed the project and turned it over to the owners.

You may want to talk with an attorney who specializes in community association law. If the election was unfair, or if you can prove that deception or proxy fraud was involved, you can petition the superior court to review the voting records and possibly the election will be set aside. Your petition must be filed within nine months of the election.

California Corporations Code Sections 7527 and 7616 cover the means of challenging an election.

If a majority of the owners are now displeased with the board, the owners can petition the board for a recall election. I do not recommend board recall because bickering and resentment last a long time after the battle is either won or lost. Even if a board recall is successful, it is almost always detrimental to the association in the long run. You can decide if the board's illegal action is serious enough to attempt to unseat them.

Another option is to start working discreetly to elect new board members at the next annual meeting who will comply with the law and uphold the legal documents of the association. If you cannot find others who are willing to challenge the ones who are currently in power, the association could be in serious trouble.

OWNER'S CONCRETE SLAB HAS CRACK—WHO PAYS FOR REPAIR?

Q *A section of the concrete slab of our condominium has settled, resulting in a wide crack across our kitchen floor. The floor on one side of the crack is about one-half inch lower than the rest of the floor.*

The declaration of covenants, conditions and restrictions (CC&Rs) does not specify who is responsible for repair of the slab. Does this relieve the association from the responsibility for the cost of the repair?

A Several legal issues are involved. If your association is less than ten years old, and this problem is a latent construction defect that was just discovered recently, the builder-developer might be responsible for the repairs.

The second legal issue involves maintenance responsibility based upon ownership of the structure of the building. If your unit is a typical condominium unit, the association owns and is responsible for repairs to the common areas, which would include anything below the carpet or floor covering. Refer to your association's legal documents, including the CC&Rs and a document called the condominium plan that explains the legal boundaries of the individual condominium units. You should also read your property deed for specific information about your ownership.

In general, individual owners are not required to make structural repairs to the common area that is owned by the association. If the slab is designated as common area and, therefore, is owned by the association, you would not be required to pay for the cost of repairs. The repairs would be the responsibility of the association. The board of directors would be responsible for approving the methods and cost of the repairs. The cost would be paid with the association's funds. On the other hand, if your association is a planned unit development (PUD) and you own the ground that the unit sits on and the structure of the building between the common walls of the adjoining units on each side, then you would be responsible for repairing the slab.

If you and your association are unable to come to an agreement on the responsibilities because of ambiguous legal documents, the board should consult the association's attorney, preferably one who specializes in community association law. If the board fails to deal with your problem, you have the right to contact an attorney to act on your behalf. With proper legal advice, this can and should be resolved without conflict.

ASSOCIATION WANTS TO KEEP LEGAL COSTS UNDER CONTROL

Q *Our board of directors for our homeowners association sincerely appreciates the worthwhile advice we obtain from your column. You often recommend that community associations refer their problems to an attorney.*

One of our board members feels that we have the right to make decisions without checking everything with an attorney. He is very concerned about the cost of legal services, while the rest of us are concerned about the liability of dealing with many of the issues facing the association.

Can you give us some tips for keeping our legal expenses under control?

A Ask questions about the attorney's billing rates and billing procedures. You have a right to know the hourly rates of the attorneys, paralegals and other staff members who may be doing work for the association. You should receive a detailed billing statement on a monthly basis to know how much is being charged to the association's account.

If someone in the association has already researched a problem and compiled information that would be useful to the attorney, this will probably reduce your cost. Good record keeping is always a time saver.

If you want the attorney to write an opinion letter, ask what the estimated cost will be and request that the attorney notify you when your account has reached a specified dollar amount.

Only one person from the board of directors should be communicating with the attorney. If everyone on the board calls the attorney with their individual concerns, the bills can add up very fast. Individual homeowners should not expect to have direct communication with the association's attorney for the same reason. The association engages the attorney; so individual owners cannot use the association attorney as their own legal counsel.

It is advisable to establish a working relationship with an attorney of record who will have your legal documents in the file ready to provide timely advice when it is needed. It will save dollars for the association if the chosen attorney focuses his or her practice in community association law. Less research time is needed if the attorney is already familiar with the statutes and the case law that has evolved from appellate court decisions.

The attorney should be asked to review contracts involving large expenditures, especially a management contract, for example. The money spent is well worth the peace of mind and the reduction in potential liability.

NEW BOARD MEMBER IS DELINQUENT IN PAYING ASSESSMENTS

Q *Our association recently held its annual meeting and new board members were elected. One of the new board members is delinquent in the payment of his monthly assessment. Some people believe that he ran for the board of directors so that he could have his delinquency forgiven when he became a board member. There is a rumor that he intends to sell his unit or make arrangements with the mortgage lender to release him from his financial obligations.*

What can be done if the rest of the board members go along with his scheme?

A The association's governing documents may state that only members "in good standing" can be elected to serve on the board. In that case, the election could be challenged if less than nine months have elapsed since the meeting.

The board of directors is not entitled to special privileges. The board members must pay their monthly assessments just like all of the rest of the owners, unless the governing documents state otherwise. All of the board members have a fiduciary duty to oversee the finances of the association in a prudent manner and enforce the collection procedures fairly and consistently. Failure to collect from one owner means that all the rest of the owners will eventually pick up the tab. This affects every owner.

You have the right to request a review the financial records if you believe that the board is failing to collect the delinquent assessments. Send a letter to the board requesting permission to have access to the records. The board should respond to your request within ten days. If the board fails to disclose information to you, that may be an indication that they are not actively pursuing the delinquency. The board may think that they should protect the delinquent owner's privacy but they also must consider the other owners' right to know whether delinquent accounts are being collected.

Board members can be held responsible if they fail to carry out their fiduciary duties. If you feel that the board members are willfully neglecting their responsibilities or if you want to challenge the election, consult an attorney who specializes in community association law.

SOME OWNERS HAVE EXTENDED PATIOS ONTO COMMON AREA

Q *Several owners in our homeowner association have extended their concrete patios and wood fencing beyond their own lots. The board members have approved these changes and, in fact, some of the board members have extended their lots onto the common area also.*

I believe that the board's action has given unfair advantage to certain owners. Complaints to the board have been ignored. What should we do?

A Some of the board members thought it was such a good idea, they wanted a part of the action. The straight truth is that the board of directors does not have the authority to allow certain individual owners to claim any portion of the common area that legally belongs to everyone.

The owners all pay the property taxes for the common area because the taxes are assessed to each of the owners according to their percentage of ownership. Now you are paying taxes on common area property that you cannot use and enjoy.

This complicated situation has many other issues relating to the board's conflict of interest, enhanced or decreased property values for the individual owners, maintenance responsibility and resale disclosure.

These are issues that should be discussed with an attorney if you want to take action to protect your rights. Consult an attorney who specializes in common interest developments and community association law.

BOARD REFUSES TO OBTAIN LEGAL ADVICE

Q *I was recently elected to serve on the board of directors of our 16-unit condominium association. Our board of directors has made some questionable decisions in the past. I feel that the board should seek legal advice now and then.*

The board president often says that we are protected by our insurance policy if anyone questions our procedures. She does not want to pay for legal advice. Perhaps she wants to run things her way whether it is legal or not. What can I do if I disagree with some decision that a majority of the board members approved?

A At a board meeting, you can make a motion to refer the matter to an attorney. If the motion fails because no one seconds it, you have the right to request that your motion be noted in the board meeting minutes. The board secretary should comply with your request.

Any time that the board is voting, you have the right to have your vote noted in the minutes. It should not be necessary to do this for every board vote. However, if you think that a particular vote may have some legal significance at some time in the future, I recommend that you exercise this right. It may protect you from liability if the board's decision proves to be illegal.

Community associations should always have liability insurance and, in addition, a specific policy that covers director's and officer's liability. However, board members should not assume that they will always be protected by this insurance when a legal question arises. The insurance policy will have several exclusions that the board needs to keep in mind when faced with difficult decisions.

Board members probably do not have expertise in all of the issues facing the association. They should be wise enough to seek professional advice when it is needed.

STOCK COOPERATIVE MUST GIVE OWNERS A FINANCIAL REPORT

Q *I live in a stock cooperative. I have requested a financial statement or some type of accounting records to show the monthly expenditures. The board of directors says that a cooperative is not like a condominium association and they do not have to give out information regarding how the money is being spent.*

In January, my monthly assessment was increased by a large amount but there was no explanation of why the additional money is needed.

Do I have a right to get an itemized accounting of the monthly expenses? Am I entitled to an annual statement of the financial status of the cooperative? How can I communicate with the board so that they will respond to my questions and concerns?

A It sounds like your board of directors just needs some education about the California laws that govern community associations. A community association is a nonprofit corporation or unincorporated association that was created for the purpose of managing a common interest development. And what is a common interest development, you ask? The law defines a common interest development as a community apartment (or "own your own") project, a condominium project, a planned development or a stock cooperative. This means that even though you are a shareholder in a cooperative, you are entitled to the same financial information that a condominium, planned development or community apartment owner would receive.

The California Civil Code states that an association must provide an annual budget that itemizes expenses and discloses detailed information about the reserve funds needed for future repair and replacement of the common elements of the building or complex.

If the association board did not distribute the budget at least 45 days, but not more than 60 days, prior to the beginning of the fiscal year, then they do not have the authority to increase your assessments. The owners would have had to vote to approve the increase.

In addition, at the end of the fiscal year, an independent licensed accountant must prepare an annual financial review if the association's annual income exceeds $75,000. This information is supposed to be distributed to the owners within 120 days after the close of the fiscal year. Any incorporated association must distribute an annual financial report if income exceeds $10,000.

If the board of directors is not giving you this information, you should refer them to the California Civil Code, Title 6, Sections 1350 through 1376, also known as the Davis-Stirling Common Interest Development Act. These statutes were adopted in the mid-80s and have been amended many times. Community association boards need to have familiarity with the current laws. It appears that your board has simply not kept up with the times.

You can visit your local library's law reference section to do your own research. Perhaps you should make some photocopies for your board of directors. If they ignore your attempts to educate them, you may want to consult an attorney who specializes in community association law.

More information can be found in the chapter entitled "Financial Matters."

ASSOCIATION DOES NOT COMPLY WITH GOVERNING DOCUMENTS

Q *Several months ago my partner and I purchased a unit in an upscale condominium association as an investment. At that time, we did not know about the association's lack of compliance with the governing documents. Now that we are aware of some problems, we would like your advice about the way that the association is being operated.*

Here are some of our concerns:

1. A special assessment was voted upon at the annual meeting without prior notice to the owners that a vote would be taken.

2. The board of directors has been setting an unrealistic budget each year, deliberately keeping the monthly assessments at a low amount, and then passing a special assessment each year to replenish reserve funds that are used for operating expenses.

3. The declaration states that the fiscal year must coincide with the calendar year but the board has established July 31 as the fiscal year-end.

4. The board has not mailed out the annual budget or the year-end audit.

Perhaps we would not have purchased the unit if we had known about the association's failure to abide by the declaration and bylaws. Now that we are owners we would like to protect our investment by urging the board to improve their procedures. We would appreciate your comments on the board's current practices. One board member says that they can run the association the way that the owners want. Does the board have the authority to disregard the association's governing documents?

A You've cited a number of serious problems. The board cannot disregard California laws or the governing documents. The board has a fiduciary duty to protect every owner's investment by upholding and enforcing the association's governing documents.

Every owner should be concerned about operating the association in a haphazard manner, which exposes the board members and the association to liability and may put the association in jeopardy of a lawsuit.

The board could be in a real pickle if you decide to sell your unit. Certain documents must be provided to an owner who is selling a unit. The owner has the right to submit a written request to the association asking for the most recent financial statement which was prepared and distributed in compliance with California Civil Code Section 1365. State law requires that this information be provided within ten days. The purchaser could hold the association responsible for any damages and, in addition, the association could be charged a penalty of $500 if the information is not provided within the ten-day period. If a lawsuit is filed, the prevailing party may be entitled to recover attorney's fees.

For the protection of all of us who own property in a community association, most states have laws that require that the community association board conduct the association's affairs in a business-like manner.

In some of the examples that you cited, the board is not only disregarding the association's legal documents, but also the state law. As stated earlier in this chapter, the state law requires specific financial reports be provided to the owners.

Instead of being openly critical of the board, offer your help to get the association on the right track. The board may resent your discovery of their shortcomings but if they see that you want to be helpful instead of combative, they will probably accept and appreciate your help.

CAN CITY CODES ON OCCUPANCY LIMITS BE ENFORCED?

Q *One of the houses in our homeowner association has about 12 occupants. The association's declaration of covenants, conditions and restrictions (CC&Rs) does not have any limitation on the number of occupants. Can the association enforce city codes regarding occupancy limits if there are no restrictions in the CC&Rs?*

A If this is an ordinance or code in the city where you live, the association does not have to get involved. Any resident has the right to inquire about the city's occupancy limitations and file a complaint with the city's code enforcement division if a violation exists. If an infraction is outside of the association's scope of authority, then it is better that an individual take on the responsibility of filing a complaint.

If a city or county code violation is also a violation of the CC&Rs or association rules, such as parking violations or animal control issues, the board of directors should ask for city or county enforcement in addition to enforcing the association's legal documents. Working closely with local government will strengthen the association's control.

NEW BOARD OBJECTS TO LEGAL EXPENSES OF PRIOR BOARD

Q *Without discussion with the rest of the owners, the board of directors of our small condominium association decided to consult with an attorney about possible legal problems. They paid the attorney a $2,000 retainer fee even though the association didn't have the funds available. Two of the board members paid several months of their assessments in advance so that enough money could be accumulated to cover the $2,000.*

Six months later, a new board was elected and decided the attorney's advice was unnecessary. They attempted to get a refund of the $2,000 but the attorney said that the retainer fee was entirely used and, after some delays, provided dates and times spent working with the former board, including the initial meeting with them to explain his services. The board apparently consulted the attorney whenever they wanted. Many of the owners feel that we were cheated by the attorney or the board members or both. What do you think?

A The board has the authority to consult professionals regarding the operation of the association's business affairs. In general, legal issues often are a challenge for both inexperienced and experienced board members. You should not expect your board members to be legal experts. I think that they were being prudent to consult with legal counsel. Two of them were so convinced that this advice was needed that they prepaid their assessments. Though owners don't have the authority to earmark their assessment money for a specific purpose, the board members' action is an indication of the seriousness of the matter. Perhaps you are concerned about the cost but preventive legal advice can be much cheaper than hiring an attorney after the board has made a poor decision or set a bad precedent. Advice that keeps you out of trouble or avoids a costly lawsuit is good advice and protects the association from mistakes before they happen. A retainer fee is not always necessary, however. Some attorneys will charge an hourly rate based upon the exact number of hours of service.

Remember, the board members have ultimate responsibility and are granted most of the decision-making power in the association. They did not have to inform all of the owners before spending the money for legal advice. However, if they had communicated with the owners about it, they might have eliminated this controversy.

Your letter doesn't state any specific reasons that the board hired the attorney. You imply that the board did not keep accurate records about the reasons that they referred problems to the attorney and the content of the advice that was received. This information would be helpful to future boards and would keep them from subsequently seeking advice about the same matters.

It is easy to find fault with the former board's decisions if you are unaware of the problems that they faced. Perhaps they were protecting someone's privacy by not disclosing the reasons for the consultation.

My advice is to give the former board the benefit of the doubt and get off their back. Don't contribute to an "us against them" campaign when you disagree with board decisions. If you have the opportunity to serve on the board you will find that it isn't always easy to make prudent decisions without some professional guidance. Board members who think they know all the answers are often the ones who make the biggest mistakes.

Boards should plan ahead during the budgeting process and set aside enough funds for legal, accounting and management advice so that funds are available when the need arises.

CAN OWNERS BE SUED FOR INJURIES IN COMMON AREA?

Q Our 184-unit association is concerned about an appellate court decision that gives persons who are injured on the association's property the right to sue the individual owners to cover medical and therapeutic expenses. Our association has $2,000,000 of liability insurance coverage. The board of directors has advised the owners to add "loss assessment coverage" to their individual homeowner's insurance policies. However, my insurance company does not offer this type of coverage and I'm not sure that it would protect an owner from this type of injury claim.

Should our association purchase more liability insurance? What is the purpose of the loss assessment coverage on an individual's policy? What can we individual owners do to protect ourselves?

A First, consult your insurance experts to discuss both the association's coverage and your individual policy. Most associations are now purchasing an umbrella liability policy in the range of 3 to 5 million dollar limits. An umbrella liability policy is relatively inexpensive. It is additional coverage beyond the regular liability policy that would cover a catastrophic claim.

In the case of a catastrophic loss, the association members might need to contribute to a special assessment to cover the expenses. Loss assessment coverage on your individual policy probably would pay for this type of assessment. Since every claim is different and every policy seems to have exclusions, I cannot assure you that loss assessment coverage is guaranteed to cover any assessment that might be levied against you.

California Civil Code Section 1365.9 says that an injured person cannot sue individual owners if the association carries at least $2 million of liability coverage if the association has 100 units or less. Since your association has more than 100 units, it would be required to have $3 million of liability coverage.

The association must inform the owners of the type of insurance that the association carries and the policy limits. Then the individual owners can consult their own agents to discuss the association's policy limits, investigate loss assessment coverage and determine whether it is worth the cost.

CAN PLANNED UNIT DEVELOPMENT DISBAND ASSOCIATION?

Q *I live in a planned unit development (PUD). Is it true that after 50 years the PUD can be legally discontinued and then an association would no longer govern the property? If this is true, then how would the complex operate and how would the property be maintained?*

A Most common interest developments have some shared property ownership or common area that would require that the association continue to operate.

I have heard of some associations with single-family homes that have decided to disband their association, but each situation must be analyzed as to responsibility for such things as privately owned streets or perimeter lots or landscaped areas that must be maintained. It is usually impossible to dedicate these portions of land to the city or county and terminate the association's maintenance responsibility.

Some associations have declarations of covenants, conditions and restrictions (CC&Rs) that specify a date that the document expires. The declaration usually states the procedure required to extend the expiration of the association. In most cases, extension requires an affirmative vote of at least 50 percent of the membership. If your declaration has a termination date with no provision for extension, then California law, Civil Code Section 1357, states that the association members can vote to extend the association's term with a 50 percent affirmative vote or the percentage that the declaration requires for an amendment, whichever is greater.

OWNERS CAN GET NAMES AND ADDRESSES OF OTHER OWNERS

Q *Must the board of directors of our homeowners association furnish a complete name and address list of all homeowners to an individual owner if the owner requests these records?*

A In California, owners are entitled to the name and address list of members as long as the request is association-related. The owner requesting this information should put his or her request in writing and state the reason for the request. The reason can be stated as, "I am requesting the name and address list so that I can contact other owners regarding association matters." The association must respond within 10 days or state the reason why they cannot provide the list. The board can offer another means of communication; for example, the board can offer to have the management company mail the communication for the requesting owner and they can charge a reasonable fee for the service and the postage.

The owners are entitled to have access to the records of the association. This has been established in a number of legal cases around the nation as cited in *The Law of Condominium Operations* by Attorney Gary A. Poliakoff. Having the right of access to records also includes the right to make notes or request photocopies at a reasonable cost. Florida's Condominium Act explicitly gives association members that right and several other states have similar laws.

Association boards should adopt procedures for allowing this type of access and should instruct their managing agents accordingly, if the association has a management company that keeps the records.

It is unwise for associations and management companies to make this process a difficult one for the owner who wants information.

BOARD HIRED COLLECTION SERVICE FOR UNPAID ASSESSMENTS

Q *The board of directors of my condominium association recently voted to hire a collection service to collect unpaid assessments from the owners who are not paying their share. Does the board have the authority to hire this service without a vote of the owners?*

A In the association's declaration, the board is usually given broad powers and duties to operate and maintain the association, including the duty to collect assessments from all of the owners. These assessments pay for the common expenses of the association and therefore, if owners fail to pay, the association's fiscal stability is jeopardized.

Selecting a collection service or lien service company to perform the task of collecting delinquent assessments is a very effective way of fairly and consistently enforcing the association's collection policy.

In most cases, the association does not have to pay for this service because the association is entitled to pass along to the delinquent owner any reasonable costs of the collection procedures, including attorney's fees, lien filing fees and other reasonable costs. In my opinion, unless your association's legal documents require a vote of the owners for approval of contracted services, your board does have the right to obtain the assistance of a collection agency or lien service.

ASSESSMENT INCREASE NOT DISCLOSED TO NEW OWNER

Q *I recently purchased a townhouse. Fifteen days after the close of escrow, I received notice of a homeowner meeting. The notice of meeting was dated one day prior to my closing date and it referred to an imminent assessment increase. The board approved a 20 percent increase in the monthly assessment. Then I learned of water intrusion problems and costly testing that is being conducted. Neither of these matters was disclosed to me prior to my purchase. I informed the management company that I was very disturbed about the lack of disclosure.*

What recourse do I have?

A It is especially important to seek the advice of an attorney prior to purchasing a home in a community association. Any sales transaction is accompanied by several disclosure documents. Of course, there are more documents connected with the transfer of property situated in an association than the number of disclosure forms required in the sale of a home that is not in an association.

If the assessment increase and water intrusion matters were known to the seller, the seller had the duty to disclose them and the real estate agent had the duty to inform the seller about full disclosure of any anticipated increase in assessments, construction problems and many other matters.

Your agent should have protected you by ensuring that you received from the seller, or seller's agent, a form called the Real Estate Transfer Disclosure Statement that includes information completed by the seller and the seller's agent. Additional disclosure information required in Civil Code 1368 is supposed to be provided by the seller "as soon as practicable before transfer of title" so that the buyer has an opportunity to reject the offer if any of the disclosure information is unacceptable. The lender usually reviews this specific disclosure information prior to deciding whether to fund the mortgage. If the disclosure was sent to your lender and not provided to you, that is another mistake on the part of the agent or the escrow company.

Information required in Civil Code Section 1358 includes, along with many other disclosures, "Any change in the association's current regular and special assessments and fees which have been approved by the association's board of directors, but have not become due and payable as of the date disclosure is provided." This information should not be held back and presented to the buyer at the escrow closing when there isn't adequate time to review all of the documents and forms.

From your information about the specific dates of the transfer of ownership and the notice of meeting about the impending assessment increase, it appears that you should have been informed about it.

Seek the advice of a real estate attorney who can review all of the documents and advise you of any recourse and deadlines. Until you obtain legal advice, continue to pay your assessments in full or the association could file a lien on your unit and complicate your legal issues even more.

DOES STATE LAW REQUIRE A RESERVE STUDY?

Q *The board of directors of our homeowner association voted to have a reserve study prepared several months ago, but our accountant said we didn't need one because we have only 16 units in our building. Does state law require the reserve study? Are small associations like ours required to have reserve studies?*

A Yes, state law requires that all associations, incorporated or unincorporated, have a reserve study prepared every three years. Your small number of units does not exempt your association from the requirements of California Civil Code 1365.5 (e). If your accountant is not aware of this law, he or she is probably not experienced enough to provide accounting services to your association.

In a small association, the owners are especially vulnerable if there is no reserve fund. The first step is the preparation of a reserve study. The board of directors should review the reserve study each year, consider the items that were repaired or replaced during the fiscal year, determine what items need repair or replacement during the next fiscal year and use that information in preparing the reserve budget.

More information can be found in the chapter on "Financial Matters."

BOARD FAILS TO MAKE REPAIRS AND ENFORCE RULES

Q *The board of directors of my condominium association is not enforcing the governing documents, including the articles of incorporation, the declaration of covenants, conditions and restrictions and the rules and regulations. I have made written requests for repair and maintenance of common area amenities and enforcement of pet restrictions. The board still refuses to take action on both of these issues, though it seems obvious to me that they are obligated to take action.*

Since there is no governmental agency that can require the board to act, can I sue the board? Are my legal costs recoverable?

A You have the right to sue the board, but filing a lawsuit should be the last resort. Normally, individual owners have the right to enforce the pet restrictions if the board fails to take action, so you can also sue the owner of the pet. The judge may award reasonable legal costs if you take the case to court and win.

Obtain legal advice regarding the strength of your case and how to comply with California Civil Code Section 1354. This law requires that you attempt mediation or arbitration prior to filing a legal action. Both you and the association will save time, effort and money if you submit your dispute to mediation or arbitration.

The board should also seek legal advice if they choose not to uphold the governing documents.

ASSOCIATION MUST PROVIDE ESCROW DOCUMENTS

Q *Our association believes that a real estate agent committed fraud in a recent sale of a unit. He orally promised a new owner, prior to the close of escrow, that her dog complied with the association's weight restrictions for dogs. He knew that the dog weighed twice the allowable weight. At the same time, he orally assured the board of directors that the new owner did not even own a dog.*

The agent did not give the new owner a copy of the governing documents until after she moved into the unit. The board will grant her an exemption for her pet because she was an innocent victim, but we don't want to deal with this agent again.

Can the association refuse to process the documents required for escrow if a particular real estate agent is involved with the sale?

A The association is required by law to respond to escrow document requests from the seller of a unit. You cannot discriminate against a seller just because this agent is involved in the sale. However, the board has no obligation to accommodate the new buyer by making an exception for her and her dog. Both the buyer and the association could file a lawsuit against the agent, the broker and possibly the escrow company for misleading the buyer and failing to provide the governing documents in a timely manner. The agent, broker and escrow company are supposed to have written documentation that the buyer received the governing documents prior to the close of escrow. In fact, the governing documents and other disclosures are supposed to be provided to a buyer "as soon as practicable before transfer of title."

Though you cannot refuse to deal with this agent in the future, there are more effective ways of letting the agent know that you will not tolerate his sales tactics in the future. You can report him to his broker, the local Board of Realtors or the local office of the California Department of Real Estate. Real estate agents are not required to be a member of the Board of Realtors, a trade association, but the agent must be licensed by the Department of Real Estate.

More pet problems can be found in the "Parking, Pools and Pets" chapter.

ASSESSMENTS WERE DELINQUENT AT CLOSE OF ESCROW

Q *Our association consists of 95 single-family homes. The escrow companies seem to be unaware that our association exists because they do not communicate with the management company or request legal documents from the association prior to the closings.*

Sellers should be notifying their real estate agents, but some homes have been sold without the buyer being told about the homeowner association. Recently, an owner who owed the association several months of assessments was able to sell his home and the association did not receive the delinquent assessments after the closing.

How can the association protect itself?

A You can still file a small claims action against the seller to recover the unpaid assessments. If the sale was a typical real estate transaction, I am surprised that the title company and the escrow company both failed to communicate with the association.

To protect the association and notify the real estate industry that an association exists, the association can record a Notice of Assessment statement at the county recorder's office of the county in which your association is located. This will identify your association as having assessment collection authority and inform any escrow agent where to send escrow forms to your management company. Self-managed associations can record the name of their treasurer. The statement must be amended when this information changes.

California Civil Code 1363.6 is the state law that provides for this recordation. Contact your association's attorney if the management company needs legal advice regarding recording this important document. The county will charge a recordation fee that is based on the recorder's per-page recording fee.

ASSOCIATION WANTS NEW BUYER TO PAY DELINQUENCY

Q *I just bought a condo and I am already having problems because the former owner was delinquent. The homeowner association is threatening me with a lien if I do not pay the monthly assessments and late fees that the former owner did not pay.*

The association says that the escrow company failed to collect the unpaid assessments from the seller. The association had released the lien because they thought that the escrow company would collect the delinquent assessments and fees from the seller. What can I do?

A You are not obligated to pay the delinquent assessments. If the escrow company was notified of the delinquent assessments, the escrow company should have collected the money from the seller, regardless of a lien having been released.

You should obtain legal advice immediately. There may be some facts that are not contained in your letter. This is a serious matter that you must not ignore because the association has lien rights and the association can foreclose on the unit.

OWNERS WANT TO GET OUT OF THE ASSOCIATION

Q *We live in a group of twenty-two homes, the final phase of a homeowners association of 267 homes. A different builder constructed our phase. Our homes were completed and brought into the association two years ago. All 22 homes are on a cul-de-sac. We would like to separate ourselves from the rest of the association. What is the procedure for breaking away?*

A Your phase of 22 homes is an integral part of the association. You don't have the right to "opt out" after two years. You purchased a home in a community association and you are obligated by the legal documents to remain a part of the association. The legal fees would be very expensive to even attempt to change the legal structure.

All of the other 245 homes would be affected by any change in the total number of homes, so they would have to approve the separation of your 22 homes.

If you read your legal documents and your annual budget, you will probably see that all 267 homes share the responsibility for maintaining all of the association's common areas. The budget in many large associations includes the common expense of maintaining streets and street lighting, as well as swimming pools, green belts and other community assets and amenities.

I am curious about the reason that you want out of your association. Your brief letter does not state the reason for your disenchantment. If you don't like the association or its rules, then your best option is to sell and move to a neighborhood that is not a part of a community association. The cost of selling and moving will surely be less than the cost of your battle for independence.

BOARD FAILS TO COMPLY WITH ASSOCIATION'S RULES

Q *What agency oversees homeowner associations and condominiums? Will the agency enforce the CC&Rs and bylaws? My neighbor and I would like to file a complaint about our board of directors for failure to comply with the association's legal requirements.*

A There is no local or state agency that oversees the community association after the association is past the involvement of the original developer. The developer of a new common interest development must go through a lengthy approval procedure with the California Department of Real Estate. During the marketing phase of the project the Department of Real Estate will follow up on complaints about non-compliance with the legal documents of the association.

After the association is transferred to the control of the homeowners, there is no further supervision by any public agency. The owners who are elected to serve on the volunteer board of directors are sometimes qualified and sometimes woefully inept. Homeowners should actively participate in the association and carefully elect board members who are knowledgeable, fair and committed to the common good of the association members.

The board of directors has a fiduciary duty to operate the association in compliance with the governing documents. Peer pressure from the owners will often cause a board to be more diligent and responsible. If this is not effective in your association, you can elect new directors when the next election occurs.

If the board is misappropriating the association's money or is engaged in other criminal activity, you may want to hire an attorney who specializes in the representation of community associations. Perhaps with the attorney's guidance you can gather enough evidence so that you can report the board of directors to the police or file a civil suit. The attorney can also assist you in preparing for the next election so that new directors will be able to take control.

CHAPTER 5 BOARD OPERATIONS

INFORMATION FOR NEW BOARD MEMBER

Q *Our homeowner association has had numerous conflicts and lawsuits in the past. Now it is almost impossible to get anyone to serve on the board because they are afraid of being sued. I was recently appointed to the board of directors but I really don't know what my responsibilities are. What can board members do to limit our liability? What resources can you recommend?*

A First, you should make sure that the association has directors' and officers' liability insurance, adequate property insurance, fidelity bond coverage and workers' compensation coverage. Make sure that you comply with all the insurance requirements in your declaration of covenants, conditions and restrictions (CC&Rs). The directors' and officers' liability insurance will not protect you if you fail to adequately insure the association.

Second, read all the legal documents of the association, and the board meeting minutes, contracts, financial statements and management reports for the past year.

Third, educate yourself by attending seminars given by the Community Associations Institute. Check your local phone directory or call directory assistance for the chapter near you. CAI has many publications that would be helpful. A basic resource is a booklet titled "Community Association Leadership: A Guide for Volunteers." Topics covered include the role of the officers, effective meetings, committee operations and fiduciary responsibility. More information about CAI can be found in the first chapter.

BOARD REFUSES TO APPROVE TENTING FOR TERMITES

Q *Spot treatment has not successfully eradicated termites from our condominium. Several people in my association do not want tenting to occur because of the expense and inconvenience of temporary relocation. We have elderly residents who say that they are simply unable to relocate with their pets and large house plants. The board refuses to approve tenting. What recourse do I have?*

A Based upon a Supreme Court decision, you may not have any recourse if your board has thoroughly researched the alternatives and decided to take another course of action.

Community associations throughout the state should take note of the California Supreme Court 's decision in the *Lamden v. La Jolla Shores Clubdominium Homeowners Association* case in 1999.

This case reinforces the standard that boards of directors should be able to show good reasons for their decisions. Boards must act within the scope of the association's governing documents and California law. The board must exercise their legal authority and responsibilities by acting in good faith, consulting professional advisors as appropriate, weighing the facts carefully and making decisions in the best interests of the entire association membership. This standard, commonly known as the "business judgment rule," protects volunteer board members from liability as defined in Corporations Code Section 7231.5.

The *Lamden v. La Jolla Shores* case was filed because Ms. Gertrude Lamden, a condo owner, disagreed with the board of directors of the La Jolla Shores Clubdominium Association. The board decided to treat termite infestation with localized treatment rather than having the exterminating company fumigate the entire structure. Ms. Lamden sued the association seeking to obtain a court order to require the tenting and fumigation of the entire building where her unit is located.

The trial court found that the association board had acted properly and required Ms. Lamden to pay several thousand dollars of the association's legal fees. However, Ms. Lamden filed an appeal and the appellate court's decision favored Ms. Lamden. This was a precedent setting case, which might have placed board decisions in future lawsuits under the scrutiny of judges who might then overturn board decisions based upon criteria other than the "business judgment" language in the Corporations Code.

The association appealed to the California Supreme Court. The La Jolla Shores board of directors showed that there were several factors that caused them to decide to spot-treat the termite infestations rather than using fumigation. They had considered the cost of total fumigation, inconvenience to residents and the risk to residents' health. The association board felt that even fumigation might not obliterate the termites since the wooded, coastal area is fraught with the wood-destroying pests. In addition, the board had approved a two-year exterior renovation project that would include the removal and replacement of any termite-damaged wood.

The Supreme Court decided in favor of the association, upheld the standards of the "business judgment rule" and created a "deferential standard" meaning that courts will defer to a board's decisions when those decisions are within the scope of authority granted in the association's governing documents and the decisions are reached in a business-like manner. The court's findings stated that boards of directors are better equipped "to make the detailed and peculiar economic decisions necessary in the maintenance of homeowners associations." The court's decision will probably reduce the likelihood of future litigation over association boards' decisions.

Daniel C. Shapiro is an attorney with the law firm of Wolf, Rifkin and Shapiro and Past Chair of the California Legislative Action Committee of Community Associations Institute. Shapiro states, "While the Lamden case is a landmark decision affecting boards of directors of California homeowners associations, it is important to note that the Lamden decision does not remove the long established duty to guard against unreasonable risks to residents' personal safety. Stricter standards are still applicable to such situations."

BYLAWS CONTROL BOARD MEMBER TERM LIMITS

Q *The resort condominium association where I live was formed in 1976. I believe that the bylaws need updating because they have led to an unduly close relationship to the manager/developer of the complex. The current president has served for over four years.*

Are there any laws that control the length of time that a president or a board member can serve?

A The California Nonprofit Corporations Code states that the term of office for directors shall be as stated in the association's articles or bylaws, but shall not be any longer than four years. In other words, when a board member's term is expiring, he or she may run for office and be elected for another term. By limiting the term of office to the number of years stated in the bylaws or a maximum of four years, the law requires that a director be re-elected by the membership in order to serve beyond the initial term of office.

For example, if an association has two-year terms of office for directors, a director could be elected for several consecutive terms if the number of terms is not limited in the bylaws. Some associations have bylaws that limit the number of terms that a director may serve but this is not typical of most of the bylaws that I have read.

In general, it is not in the best interests of the association to have the same people serving for several years. Four years is not too long if the current board is doing a good job. On the other hand, four years would be much too long if the board members are not fulfilling their duties appropriately.

Your concern about the president's close ties to the developer may warrant further investigation. Board members have a duty to make decisions based upon the needs of the whole association membership.

Since you live in a resort area, many of the owners probably have another home as their primary residence. It may be difficult to find other people who are willing to serve on the board, so it will probably take some work on your part.

ASSOCIATION BOARD SHOULD COMPLY WITH BYLAWS

Q *We have a small association and only three people are supposed to serve on the board according to the bylaws. We would like to appoint two more people to the board because one of the board members is often out of town. The board president says that we have to operate according to the bylaws. How can we get around this provision in the bylaws?*

A It is not proper to "get around" your legal documents. The board president is correct. If you would like to appoint committee chairs to advise the board, that is acceptable; however, these extra people should not be voting members of the board. If you want to change the bylaws to provide for more board members, refer to the bylaws to see how they can be amended.

COMPLEX DETERIORATING UNDER VETERAN LEADER

Q *I live in a 40-unit condominium in Palm Springs that has had the same president/manager for 14 years. The owners have never received a financial statement or an audit report. Our assessments are $200 per month.*

The condition of our property continues to deteriorate and the owners have no input even when services are being cut. One of the swimming pools has been shut down and appears to be permanently closed. Three men on the board of directors are non-resident owners who have their units listed for sale. They seem to allow the president to do anything he chooses. I, like most of my neighbors, cannot afford to move. We are elderly folk who feel that we are being ripped off. What can we do?

A Every member has the right to speak at a board meeting within reasonable time limits. Speak to the board at the next meeting and request attention to the specific maintenance items that are being neglected. If the board is not scheduling regular meetings, then send a letter to all the board members stating your concerns and requesting a response by a reasonable date.

You are entitled to review the minutes of prior board meetings so that you can find out what is happening in your association. The board must keep minutes and make copies available to an owner at the owner's reasonable expense.

California Civil Code Section 1365 stipulates that all the association members are entitled to receive a copy of an annual financial report. The report must be prepared by a state-licensed accountant for any year in which the gross income to the association is greater than $75,000. A copy of the report, either a review or audit, must be distributed 120 days after the end of the fiscal year, *unless* the governing documents provide more restrictive requirements. For instance, some associations' governing documents require that the report be distributed within 90 days.

If your association is incorporated, California Corporations Code Section 8321 requires that an annual financial report be made available to association members if the association's gross revenues exceed $10,000.

Your association's annual assessment income is $96,000 so ask for your copy of the most recent annual review. If you do not receive it, put your request in writing and continue to pursue the matter until you get some action.

It seems that your board members have lost sight of their fiduciary responsibility to run the association properly. If this board is unresponsive, you and other concerned owners will need to find members who are willing to serve on the board and perform their duties as board members responsibly. Work to get these new people elected. This may not be easy, but the amount of money that you have invested in your home is definitely worth the time and effort.

Board members have an obligation to run the association in a manner that is in the best interests of all of the members. If malfeasance or misappropriation of funds is discovered, then perhaps you will need to pool your resources and hire an attorney to represent you and the other owners.

For more information about owners' rights, refer to Chapter Thirteen.

SMALL ASSOCIATION NEEDS LEADERSHIP

Q *I live in an eight-unit association. I am one of the three owners who serve on the board of directors. There are several maintenance items that are not being cared for properly. The sidewalk is lifting because of some tree roots and we have wrought iron gates that are so rusted that they now need to be welded.*

The current president just resigned. He is moving out of the area and has his unit listed for sale. The other board member is not concerned about termite abatement and other association responsibilities.

I am trying to be a good board member but I can't get the other board members to do anything. Should I resign?

A The sidewalk problem is an insurance risk that should be corrected immediately before someone is injured. First, you should get the other board member to assist you in getting the sidewalk repaired. Then you can deal with replacing the person who has resigned.

Your association bylaws will explain how to replace a board member. Usually, the remaining board members have the authority to appoint a person who will finish out the term of the retiring person. Some bylaws require an election to replace a board member. Then the board elects their officers. You sound like you would make a good president.

Perhaps you can find someone to serve who understands the fiduciary responsibility of caring for the building as you do. I don't think you should resign unless there is a lack of support and cooperation from the other owners.

In a small association, all of the owners should be willing to serve on the board when needed. That is the best way for the owners to protect their investment. The owners should support the board in their fiduciary responsibility to adopt a budget that is sufficient to maintain the property and also set aside reserve funds for the future repair and replacement of the common areas.

HOW SHOULD BOARD HANDLE A RESIGNATION?

Q *As a homeowner, I am curious about the way our association board has handled a board resignation. If one of the board members in our association resigns, can he rescind his resignation at the following meeting and continue to serve on the board? Would an election be required to fill the vacancy?*

A You should be able to find answers about the procedures for resignations and vacancies on the board by reading your association bylaws.

Sometimes in the midst of a heated discussion, a board member will say that he or she is resigning but after calming down, the board member reconsiders and decides not to submit a written resignation. If there is no written resignation, the board is not required to take any action.

In most associations, the board has the authority to appoint someone to fill a vacancy on the board. If a board member is recalled (voted out) by a vote of the owners, then the owners would have the right to vote on a replacement.

It is possible that the board member submitted a resignation, reconsidered his resignation and the board then appointed him to finish out the term. If so, this should be reflected in the minutes of the meeting.

CAN JOINT OWNERS BOTH SERVE ON THE BOARD?

Q *Our association's declaration states that the board of directors shall consist of five people. Can two people who are owners of the same unit serve on the board at the same time? One of the two does not vote, but that reduces the voting members to only four. Can you give us your opinion?*

A In my opinion, it is unfair to have an individual unit or lot represented by more than one person on the board. However, unless the declaration or the bylaws state that only one person from a unit may serve on the board, it is probably legal for both to serve.

The scenario that you describe fails to provide the voting power required in the governing documents. The board is supposed to have five voting members so that an uneven number will prevent tie votes and stalemates.

BOARD SHOULD RELY ON ADVICE OF EXPERTS

Q *Our association has spent over $30,000 in the last two years on roof repairs. We still have leaks and we are having difficulty getting any response from the roofing contractor since recent rains have damaged some interiors.*

Some of the board members have obtained bids for a new roof but we aren't sure that a completely new roof is necessary. The bids vary greatly in price and scope of the work. We don't know where to go for help.

A Many roofing contractors do not provide any warranty if they aren't replacing a large portion, or all, of the roof.

This is a big decision for your association. A new roof is usually a very large expenditure. No one expects the board members to be roofing experts. They should rely on the advice of professionals, thereby reducing their liability.

I recommend that you contact some independent roofing consultants and then select one who will examine your existing roof and write detailed specifications for the necessary work. Then you can obtain competitive bids from several roofing contractors based upon the written specifications that the consultant provides.

An independent consultant is an objective third-party who provides professional guidance but does not actually perform the roofing work. The independent consultant sometimes supervises the work of the roofing contractor after the contract has been negotiated and signed. The consultant saves the board members' time and energy and sometimes prevents the association from making a disastrous and costly mistake. By using a paid expert to verify the contractor's licenses, warranties, insurance coverage and references and write the specifications, the board members reduce their liability if problems do arise.

PUSH CONDO BOARD FOR ACTION ON FENCE REPAIR

Q *I live in a condominium with over 150 units. I am one of the few owners who attend board meetings. The board procrastinates with everything that needs to be done. We have several wood fences that need repair because of a windstorm over a year ago, but the board keeps telling the management company to get another bid.*

One board member is holding out for concrete block walls even though there isn't enough money in the reserves for this. The property manager tells me to put my complaint in writing by sending a letter to the board. I have written several letters but there is never any response, not even a phone call. Most of the owners are not informed or do not care. What can be done to make the board respond?

A You have a choice based upon your level of frustration and the amount of time you are willing to give to the association. How bad are the fences and how drastic should your response be? What would you do if you were in the board's shoes? Think about these factors before you take further action. It is easier to sit in judgment of the board rather than serving on the board of directors. The board is probably just as frustrated with this situation as you are and they obviously have differing opinions. However, they do have a duty to take action on this matter.

A helpful approach would be to volunteer to serve on a committee to obtain bids based on uniform specifications and make a recommendation to the board for the fence repair. The aggressive approach would be to write to the board again, requesting a written response by a reasonable date. If no action to repair the fence is taken and the board does not respond to your letter, you might contact an attorney who could write a letter reminding the board of their responsibility to maintain the property.

BOARD MEMBER HAS A FIDUCIARY DUTY

Q *I am the manager of a condominium association. It is becoming very difficult to deal with one of the association board members who makes demands that are unreasonable and unfair. He appears to be serving on the board for his own selfish reasons. When he needs something done in his unit, he expects the maintenance man to be his handyman.*

Recently, an electrician was doing some work for the association and this board member wanted an outlet repaired in his unit. He wanted the electrician to add it to the association's bill. The electrician refused to do the work. The board member wanted me to convince the electrician but I declined. Now he is mad at me. I am ready to resign even though I really like my job and most of the owners are very pleasant. What can I do?

A You work for all the owners and have an obligation to act in the best interests of the association as a whole. You and the employees that you supervise should not do special favors for any of the board members or owners.

Most association managers are faced with this kind of problem from time to time. Now you have let this person know that you will not cooperate in obtaining services for him so he is angry with you. If it happens again, remind him of your obligation to all the owners. Don't give in to his demands.

Before resigning from a job that you like, I suggest that you inform the other board members. The board should reinforce your position and prevent this man from pressuring you.

SHOULD PLAYGROUND EQUIPMENT BE REPLACED?

Q *Our homeowner association's five-member board is considering the replacement of expensive playground equipment that was vandalized by some of the older children in the complex.*

Our association cannot afford to purchase unnecessary items. Our financial condition is not good because we have a number of unit owners who are not paying their assessments on time.

We have two owners who want the playground equipment replaced because they are providing child care services. Two children have had minor injuries in the past so we are concerned about the association's liability.

Two of the board members have their units on the market to sell so they want new equipment to make their units more desirable to potential buyers. The other board members do not feel that we are obligated to replace the equipment, especially since it may be destroyed again.

Perhaps the decision should be put to a vote of the owners because of all of the complicating issues.

Three board members do not want to replace the equipment but the other two board members constantly bring up this matter. Are we wrong if we don't vote to replace the equipment? Should all of the owners vote on it?

A It sounds like you have already taken a board vote but the three that were in the majority are still feeling the pressure from the other two.

Your dilemma could be resolved by discussing the following questions with the association's attorney and insurance risk analyst: What is fair for everyone? Should the day-care providers expect the association to replace the equipment even if it is a hardship for the association to pay the cost? Do the day-care providers have adequate liability insurance and have the parents of the children signed an agreement freeing the association from liability? Is the playground an important amenity for all of the owners? Does it enhance the value of the property? Does it increase the association's liability or insurance costs? Is it fair to all of the owners to vote and let a simple majority decide the fate of an amenity? Would a special assessment be needed or does the association have reserve funds to pay for the replacement? Are these reserve funds needed for other immediate priorities? Is the association taking appropriate steps to collect the delinquent funds? Could the association recover the cost of the equipment from the owners whose children were responsible for destroying it? Does the association have insurance to cover vandalism? What is the best solution that is fair and reasonable? Is the solution good for the whole association?

If the association does not have the funds to replace the equipment, the board should provide all of the pertinent details to the owners and invite their input at a board meeting. In my opinion, the equipment should probably be replaced unless the board determines that it would be highly imprudent to do so after weighing all of the issues. Do not put this issue out for a vote of the owners without referring this matter to the association's attorney. After the decision is made by either a board vote or written vote of the owners, the board members should agreeably abide by the decision of the majority and refrain from reviving the controversy at subsequent meetings.

CALIFORNIA LAW DEFINES MEETING REQUIREMENTS

Q *The board of directors of my association recently took a phone vote to take care of some business. Shouldn't they have met in person?*

A You haven't provided enough information for me to give you a definite answer. However, if this was considered a "teleconference meeting," California Civil Code Section 1363.05 states that members of the association are supposed to be informed of the meeting, allowed to attend and speak to the board at any board meeting unless the meeting is in executive session. The law allows an emergency board meeting to be called if some unforeseen occurrence requires immediate board attention and/or action.

California Corporations Code Section 7211(a)(6) states: "Members of the board may participate in a meeting through use of conference telephone, electronic video screen communication, or other communications equipment . . . if all of the following apply:

1. Each member participating in the meeting can communicate with all of the other members concurrently.
2. Each member is provided the means of participating in all matters before the board, including, without limitation, the capacity to propose, or to interpose an objection to, a specific action to be taken by the corporation.

3. The corporation adopts and implements some means of verifying both of the following:
   a) A person participating in the meeting is a director or other person entitled to participate in the board meeting.
   b) All actions of, or votes by, the board are taken or cast only by the directors and not by persons who are not directors."

In addition, Section 7211(b) of the Corporations Code states: "An action required or permitted to be taken by the board may be taken without a meeting, if all members of the board shall individually or collectively consent in writing to that action. The written consent or consents shall be filed with the minutes of the proceedings. The action by written consent shall have the same force and effect as a unanimous vote of the directors."

SMALL COMPLEX MEANS MANY BOARD DUTIES

Q *I am considering buying a condominium and have wondered about the merits of a small association of three to six units versus a large association. I would like to have your opinion.*

A If you decide to purchase in a small association, be prepared to volunteer your time as a working board member. What do I mean by a "working" board member? In a large association, serving on the board may involve merely coming to a board meeting once a month to vote on policies and procedures while a management company is responsible for the financial operation, maintenance and day-to-day affairs of the association.

In a small self-managed association, each owner should be willing to participate in the work of the association including the accounting, maintenance, record keeping, insurance, and other operations of the board. Read the legal documents that state the powers and duties of the board and make sure that you are willing to participate in some way. In many very small associations, one overworked individual often does all the work, from replacing light bulbs in the hallways to overseeing contractors, and continues to do it simply because none of the other owners will volunteer.

Serving as a board member in any size association is a big responsibility because of the legal requirements, financial decisions, insurance obligations, rule enforcement and record keeping. In a large association, there is the likelihood of having more volunteers who are willing to serve or the association may have professional management; whereas in a small one, it is very difficult to find volunteers and they quickly tire of the job because of the greater burden of hands-on participation without professional management.

RECALL OF ENTIRE BOARD IS NOT BEST SOLUTION

Q *Our association had a tyrannical board until some of the owners came up with the answer—board recall. We recalled our entire board, despite their objections and despite their using our association attorneys at the association's expense to try to keep their jobs!*

We now have a board that is much more responsive simply because they know that malfeasance, favoritism and ignoring board responsibilities will no longer be tolerated. Please comment.

A I always recommend working with the board and supporting them if possible. Sometimes board recall is the only solution. However, I must add a few words of caution. One should not enter a recall endeavor without considering all of the consequences. Recall is unpredictable. Sometimes, it is unsuccessful. Whether the recall election unseats the board or not, it always causes dissension and leaves resentments that linger. Neighbors end up not speaking to one another and personal vendettas sometimes continue long after the matter is resolved.

A new board that takes office as the result of a recall election often has a difficult time because of the lack of continuity and the criticism from former board members who are still trying to defend their honor.

Board recalls are unpredictable especially if the association bylaws allow cumulative voting. I know of an association whose members were dissatisfied with the board's decisions so some of the dissenting owners organized the recall effort and a recall election was scheduled. At the special election meeting, the board defended themselves with eloquent speeches and impassioned pleas and when the votes were counted, all of the board members were reelected, as the dissenting owners stood by "with egg on their faces."

These warnings should not discourage those who really have valid reasons for wanting to get rid of errant board members. When a board blatantly disobeys CC&Rs, engages in illegal acts or makes decisions that endanger the association, then they should be replaced. This can often be done at a regular annual election, however, which takes less effort and causes less resentment. Board recall should only be attempted if you have the advice of an attorney so that every detail of the procedure is followed. If proper procedures aren't followed, the recall election can be challenged.

WAS SCREEN DOOR PURCHASE QUESTIONABLE?

Q *I live in a 16-unit condominium. The president called a meeting of the owners, the first one in two years. He reported that debts incurred during his tenure caused the need for an increase in the assessments.*

At the meeting, someone suggested installing screen doors on the front and back doors of the units. A month later, the president gave a bill for the screen doors to each owner and said that we should pay the bill within two weeks. There were no competitive bids shown. We owners have to install the door ourselves.

Was this done in the right manner, or do I smell something fishy here?

A Perhaps you could talk to the other board members to see if they participated in the decision to increase assessments and if they approved the purchase of the new screen doors.

Decision-making is often rather loose in a small association, but regular board meetings must occur and written minutes must be made available to all of the owners who request them. The president should be able to give you some further documentation to show why the increase is necessary. How do expenses compare with the budget? Has a new budget been prepared based on the increased assessment or is the president just telling everyone how much he or she has to pay? How long has it been since the last increase? Are all the owners paying their assessment or is the shortfall caused by delinquencies that the board should be collecting? These are some of the questions I would ask.

In my opinion, the screen door matter was not handled properly. You have a right to question the president's methods. Bear in mind that this could escalate to a confrontation resulting in long-lasting resentment. Before you take further action, you may want to talk to your neighbors to see if they are concerned about this, too.

Perhaps after careful consideration and conversations with your neighbors, you will decide to discuss the president's actions with him and the other board members.

If your sense of "something fishy" results in the ultimate decision that a change in board members is needed, find out when the next annual meeting is scheduled and start looking for good candidates for the board. Here is another important question for you to ponder: Are you willing to serve on the board?

BOARD MEMBERS MAY BE LIABLE FOR DICTATOR'S ACTIONS

Q *I own property in a homeowner association in a ski resort area in Northern California where most of the owners have other homes for their primary residence. Even though I am on the board, a lot of decisions are being made by one of the board members (a full-time resident) who is taking action on her own, without prior board approval.*

At each quarterly board meeting, we learn about more unauthorized decisions. Her decisions sometimes affect the level of comfort and enjoyment of our owners, such as the cancellation of contracts or services. Since a large number of owners are only here for short intervals, they are either unaware that this board member is acting alone or they feel powerless to stop her. Other board members either support her actions or do not wish to confront her since it hasn't helped in the past. By the way, she even controls the content of the minutes since she is the secretary. What can I do?

A A community association is supposed to be a democracy. In a democracy, people have the right to opt for non-participation.

In the situation you describe, the democratic process is slipping because of this lack of participation and your association is on the fast train to dictatorship—and it isn't even the president who is the dictator!

First, every association should have director's and officer's liability insurance. Many CC&Rs require it.

Second, you need to determine how much support you will have when you challenge "the dictator." If you do not have support from other board members and homeowners, you may want to resign in order to protect yourself from liability. Remember that all board members may be liable for the mistakes of one board member, especially if those mistakes are challenged by an irate owner who sues the association. If you decide that you want to continue to be on the board, you may want to try to get the support of some other owners to elect someone else to "unseat the dictator" at the next election.

As a last resort, you may want to recall this board member. Consult your CC&Rs for the explanation of the procedures for board member recall. If your association is incorporated, the California non-profit corporation code, Section 7222, also stipulates methods of removal.

Finally, it is extremely important that you insist that the board meeting minutes reflect your disagreement with any action that has been taken without proper authority. In addition, you may want to consult an attorney to find out other ways to limit your liability.

SUGGESTIONS FOR DEALING WITH INACTIVE BOARD

Q *Our association board of directors appears to be totally inactive. Since I bought my unit three years ago, there has only been one homeowners association meeting, mainly for the purpose of electing a new board. The board does not have regular meeting times. Every time I have questioned the board president about this matter, I was told that since very few people have attended in the past, the board did not see any need for holding more regular meetings. My letters to the board regarding the lack of maintenance in the building have generally gone unanswered. Meanwhile, the building is deteriorating and many of the owners and tenants are frustrated with the board's inaction. What can we do?*

A Your association bylaws will explain the meeting requirements. There is a possibility that your board is holding meetings without publicizing them. California Civil Code Section 1363.05 requires that owners be given four days notice prior to board meetings. Send the board a written request for copies of the minutes of the board meetings of the past year. You are entitled to read the minutes or obtain copies. (However, the minutes of executive sessions involving legal issues, contract negotiations or personnel matters are usually kept confidential.)

You also have a right to be informed about future board meeting dates so that you can attend the meetings. If your association consists of a small number of units, regular monthly meetings may not be necessary, but your comment about deterioration indicates that the board members may be ignoring their fiduciary responsibility of meeting at least on a quarterly basis as required in Civil Code Section 1365.5.

It sounds like you would be interested in serving on your board. If you want to protect your happy home, you may have to do just that!

It is always best to try to work with your board rather than starting a movement to throw them all out of office. A board recall leads to the deadly "us-against-them syndrome" which can be a very negative and divisive factor in an association. In general, boards should communicate more and homeowners should be more involved in a constructive way.

ASSOCIATION MEMBERS ARE VICTIMS OF CORRUPT BOARD

Q *I feel that the owners in our association are the victims of a dictatorship that exists in our association. The board's lack of maintenance has reduced the value of our townhouses and many people have lost their homes due to assessment lien foreclosures simply because of poor bookkeeping procedures on the part of the management company. There is collusion among the non-resident Realtor board members, foreclosure attorneys and the management company.*

The board president has threatened the lives of owners who have indicated an interest in running against any of the incumbents. Many of our owners have tried writing to congressmen, city officials, the local board of realtors and the attorney general. Nothing has been done. The cost of litigation is beyond our means. What can we do?

A You cite several broad examples that show that you have a general distrust of the board as well as the association attorneys. You have a right to file a complaint with the state Attorney General.

If you fail to get a response, then you will have to rely on your own devices. I suggest you consult an attorney who can represent you and any other owners who are dissatisfied with the board's operation of the association.

Most of the government agencies do not have enforcement capabilities against the guilty parties unless you submit written complaints with specific evidence to back up your claims or file a legal action through an attorney.

If civil codes are being violated, then you and the other honest owners will have to consider whether you can pool your resources for legal assistance. Criminal acts should be reported to the police. In general, the police do not investigate claims of impropriety unless you can provide evidence of wrongdoing.

OWNER HAS COMPLAINTS ABOUT ASSOCIATION BOARD

Q *My homeowners association has not had an annual meeting to elect a board of directors for over two years. Aren't associations required to have annual meetings?*

The president has been giving preferential treatment to certain people. The board has paid for projects that benefit them personally. I feel that the president should be removed from office.

The intercom system, which had not been operating for quite some time, was recently repaired. The electrician installed the wiring in the hallway so that it is visible rather than being inside the wall. The transformer is plugged into an outlet right next to my door at eye level. After I notified the board president that the installation was unacceptable, the electrician came back and placed a piece of wood over the wiring. Now it looks worse than before and the transformer inside my unit is still exposed.

I think it is time for me to contact an attorney. What else can you suggest?

A First, the association should be having annual meetings to elect board members. You can verify the association's meeting requirements by reading your bylaws.

It will be very difficult to remove the board president if you are the only person who is dissatisfied. I urge you to find out when the next annual meeting is going to occur. Talk with some of your neighbors about their opinions of the current board members and their willingness to serve on the board. You will then be able to decide whether to work toward electing new people.

Repairs should be done properly to protect the association from liability. If you feel that the installation of the wiring is unsafe or improper, you have the right to call a city building inspector to have the installation checked.

CAN NON-RESIDENT OWNERS SERVE ON THE BOARD?

Q *I have served on the board of my 20-unit condominium for several years. Two of the board members are non-resident owners. They both have their units leased to tenants. These two board members only come to the building once a month for the board meeting. They are not around to help when problems arise. Is it legal to have non-resident owners serving on the board of directors?*

A The governing documents of your association contain the answer to your question. You should review the declaration of covenants, conditions and restrictions (CC&Rs) and the bylaws. In most cases, the documents give all owners the right to serve on the board whether they are residents or non-residents.

I understand your complaint that these non-residents are not around to share in some of the day-to-day workload. The board should hire someone to manage the association. You probably get stuck with letting in a repairman who needs access to the building or you are the person who has to respond to the other owners' questions or complaints if there is a burnt-out light bulb or a water leak. There are going to be times when you just want some help with these tasks and those other board members are not around. Perhaps you get a bit resentful that you are the one with all these burdens. Wouldn't it be nice if you received a "thank you" now and then?

Many associations have a difficult time finding any volunteers, either resident or non-resident, to serve on the board. All volunteer board members deserve a pat on the back for giving their time and talents to the association. In some associations, non-resident owners contribute a great deal to the successful operation of the complex.

A non-resident board member who is willing to share in the decision-making process is just as interested in protecting his or her investment as you are. All board members should make decisions based upon what is best for the whole association. Unless the governing documents forbid it, the non-resident owners have a right to serve on the board.

BOARD MEMBER'S CONFLICT OF INTEREST

Q *I am the property manager for a large homeowner association. One of the board members is related to a contractor who has done some large projects for the association. The contractor keeps on submitting bids for a great deal of work and in some cases these bids are being accepted without getting competitive bids from other contractors.*

The board is responsible for these decisions, but I feel that there is a conflict of interest. What is my obligation to disclose information to the rest of the board members? Is the board member the only one that is responsible for the disclosure? Should the rest of the board members require that the relative of the contractor refrain from discussing and voting on any pending projects?

A In my opinion, the property manager has an obligation to disclose the possibility or the appearance of a conflict of interest to the rest of the board members. You could contact the board member and ask him or her to disclose the relationship with the contractor. By giving the board member the opportunity to tell the others, you will avoid the appearance of being the tattler.

If the board member fails to do so, you should bring it up at the next board meeting or write a short memo to the board members so there is a permanent record in the files. In order to protect the board member from future criticism, the information about a potential conflict of interest should be noted in the minutes and the minutes should reflect that the board member refrained from voting on any bid from this particular contractor.

Conflict of interest can be a very negative influence on the association's board of directors. All board members have an obligation to make decisions based on the best interests of the association as a whole. However, some board members who are concerned about harmony may go ahead and approve the bid that would directly or indirectly benefit the non-voting member with the conflict of interest.

The property manager and the board members should make sure that competitive bids are documented in the minutes to show that the board is properly researching and comparing bids prior to voting on contracts.

BOARD VACANCY PROCEDURES FOUND IN THE BYLAWS

Q *Our condominium association has no provision for filling vacancies on the board of directors. The declaration of covenants, conditions and restrictions (CC&Rs) does not address this matter.*

At an annual meeting, the membership passed a resolution giving the board of directors the authority to appoint an interim director to fill a vacancy only until the subsequent annual meeting. Then the appointed person must be confirmed by a majority vote of the homeowners. Is this legal and binding? If not, what should the procedure be?

A If you only looked in the CC&Rs, you may have missed the boat. You should also read the bylaws. Most bylaws give the board of directors the authority to fill vacancies, except when the vacancy occurs because of a recall vote of the owners. In my opinion, the resolution passed by the homeowners is legal as long as it does not conflict with the governing documents. The governing documents include the Articles of Incorporation, the CC&Rs, the bylaws and the rules and regulations.

The resolution passed by the membership can be changed at future membership meetings with a majority vote. If the association wants the resolution to be more binding, then a vote to amend the bylaws is necessary. The procedure for amendments can usually be found by reading these legal documents.

Your association board should seek the advice of an attorney who specializes in community association law. In California, the Corporations Code Section 7224 governs the authority of the board to fill vacancies.

SHOULD ASSOCIATION HAVE KEYS TO RESIDENTS' UNITS?

Q *Our condominium association has several elderly residents. Some of these residents are deaf. An emergency could be life threatening for any of these people. Our board is also concerned about residents who might become ill and need assistance.*

Is it reasonable for the association to require that owners have a key to their unit kept in a locked key box in the office?

A You are to be commended for caring about your neighbors' welfare, but bear in mind that having the keys on file in the office brings certain liabilities on the association. If a burglary occurs in one of the units, the owner may accuse a staff person or try to hold the association responsible because the key could have been obtained in the office. If an owner dies, will relatives complain that the association was negligent for not entering the unit to check on the owner? These examples of possible insurance liabilities should be discussed with the association's insurance agent and attorney.

It is certainly reasonable to request that owners have their keys on file in the office if the association wants to accept the accompanying liabilities. I don't think that you can demand that an owner provide a key unless there is provision in your association legal documents that requires it.

Perhaps if the association board provides a safe place for unit owners' keys and establishes the proper security procedures to control the use of the keys, then the owners will cooperate.

It is very beneficial to have a "buddy system" in the building or to have resident captains on each floor who will see that each unit is checked in an emergency.

If an emergency arises and you don't have a key to gain access to a particular unit, you should rely on the judgment of the police or paramedics regarding forced entry.

BOARD WAIVES LATE PENALTIES FOR BOARD MEMBER

Q *I live in a planned unit development consisting of almost 50 townhomes. I have reason to believe that one of the board members is not paying her monthly assessment. In the past, the board has waived any late penalties when she was delinquent.*

Last month, my assessment payment was late and the board treasurer notified me that I would have to pay a $10 late charge. I believe that I am being treated unfairly. I have lived here for ten years and I have never been late with my payment until last month. I would gladly pay the penalty, but I think the board has a duty to be fair to all owners.

I would like your comments, please.

A The board of directors should treat everyone in a fair and consistent manner. When they grant favors or make exceptions to their enforcement policies, they are vulnerable to criticism.

Board members have an obligation to uphold the governing documents and the policies and procedures of the association. They are not entitled to privileges beyond those granted to other owners.

The association's written delinquency procedures should be distributed to all of the owners so that everyone is aware of the penalties.

Since you concede that you were late with your payment, I would suggest that you pay the penalty. However, you have a right to expect the board to require that all other owners will abide by the same rules. Perhaps you will want to write to the board to let them know that you expect that, in the future, all delinquent owners will be penalized equally. You have a right to attend a board meeting to request that the late penalty be waived for this one exception based upon your good payment record in the past.

CAN BOARD APPOINT A DIRECTOR WHO WASN'T NOMINATED?

Q *One of the board members of our condominium association resigned just two months after we held the annual meeting to elect the board of directors. The board has not scheduled another election.*

There are rumors that the board has appointed someone who wasn't even nominated at the annual meeting. Shouldn't the association members be allowed to vote on the person who will replace the board member who resigned? If the board has the authority to appoint a new director, shouldn't they appoint the person from among the losing nominees who had the highest number of votes?

A The answer to both of your questions is probably "no." The board is usually responsible for filling any board vacancies that occur between annual meetings.

You can find out about your association's procedure for dealing with vacancies by reading your bylaws. Sometimes the declaration of covenants, conditions and restrictions (CC&Rs) will contain this information but it is usually in the bylaws.

Most associations have legal documents that give the remaining board members the authority to appoint a new director when a vacancy occurs. The remaining board members do not have an obligation to appoint someone who was nominated at the annual meeting. The board should use their best judgment to select a person who will serve the association in the best interests of all of the members.

WHAT IF NO ONE WANTS TO SERVE ON THE BOARD?

Q *Our ten-unit condominium complex is about ten years old. I have served on the board and given a lot of my time to the association in the past but I am unable to continue as a board member.*

Our annual election is coming up soon and no one has offered to serve. Some people feel that they do not have the skills or the time to be a board member.

One member who frequently files lawsuits against the association also intimidates several of the owners. No one wants to serve with the threat of lawsuits from this unreasonable owner. The person who is currently handling our assessment billing has asked the board to find someone else to do the job.

What happens when the owners are unwilling to serve on the board? If no one else will volunteer, do the current board members have an obligation to continue to act on behalf of the association?

A Many associations have bylaws that state that a board member serves until his or her term expires or until a new board member is elected or appointed. There is no way to attempt to keep someone from resigning from a board position. Lack of owner participation can occur for several reasons: a board member who does such a good job that no one else wants to try to fill his or her shoes, an erosion of respect for the board and the association because of mismanagement, or a board member who continually complains about serving on the board so that no one else wants to take the job.

It seems that few individuals have that volunteer spirit that compels them to serve for the common good. There are many charities, churches and other places where the altruistic person can give his or her time. Often the board's enforcement role will deter volunteers. Most people do not like to confront their neighbors about rule violations.

So what can we say to convince people to serve their association? Most people who serve on community association boards say that they do so to protect their investment. It is obvious that a dysfunctional association will cause everyone's investment to deteriorate, so that is a good way to convince someone to participate.

Of course, unreasonable owners and lawsuits tend to reduce the number of people who are willing to volunteer. An owner who thrives on conflict can be a nightmare for any board. You would probably like to hang a sign around the difficult owner's neck that reads, "This person should not live in a condominium" and then kick him out the door. However, that is not possible.

This continuing feud needs to be resolved so that the association can function effectively. The board needs to listen to the owner's complaints and see if he has valid reasons for challenging the board's actions. Perhaps mediation can effectively bring out and resolve the underlying causes of the owner's dissatisfaction.

In order to find nominees for the election, the board of directors should write a letter to all of the owners to let everyone know that the association is looking for volunteers to serve on the board. Some people will not volunteer even if they have the skills and the time. The board must put out an urgent appeal and recruit people by knocking on doors and talking face to face with the other owners.

During this search for volunteers, the board will get an earful of excuses and complaints about what's wrong with the association and the reasons why people don't want to volunteer. But in the process, the owners will have a chance to express their feelings about the association and they may decide to give some of their time if they find that their opinions and their skills are needed and valued.

If this search for board members is unsuccessful, then it is time to call a meeting of the owners, prior to the election, to discuss the consequences of a dysfunctional association. Talk about ways to reduce the board members' duties such as hiring a management company or an accounting firm to handle the financial and administrative functions. Contracting for these services will increase the association's expenses so that is another consideration for the owners to discuss. If owners don't want to volunteer, then they should be willing to pay for the services. In my opinion, that is a fair way of sharing the burden; moreover, reducing the board's duties may convince other owners to participate.

Even small associations need to hire professionals if volunteers are not available. Paying the bills and collecting assessments cannot be ignored. Insurance policies must be renewed, the property must be maintained and rules must be enforced. The board can delegate these duties but the board retains the overall responsibility of operating the association.

If the board fails to function, the owners can file a court petition to have a court-appointed receiver manage the association until an election is held or until the court finds that the association can function properly again. This can be very expensive because the receiver will charge for his or her time and may not make decisions that are fiscally prudent.

If I were you, I would stay on the board and urge the other board members to continue serving until the election. Meanwhile, work on getting other owners to volunteer.

LANDSCAPE COMMITTEE CHAIR CANCELS ORDER

Q *Our homeowner association has a landscape committee that oversees the maintenance of the grounds. The chairman of this committee has taken more and more control so that she is now giving instructions to the landscape crew and ordering new plants and work to be done. The board recently approved an expenditure that she did not recommend so she cancelled the order.*

How should the board deal with this situation?

A In this situation, the board president or other board member should meet with the landscape committee chairman to discuss her powers and responsibilities. Be aware that if she is hurt by an insensitive attitude, the association may lose its volunteer. On the other hand, if the board allows this person to continue to override their decisions, they are setting themselves up for lack of control or more conflicts in the future.

The committee should have some written objectives regarding the purpose of the committee and the committee's role in relationship to the board of directors. The board members and committee members should understand the following: Committees assist and often make recommendations to the board but final decisions rest with the elected directors.

In general, the board appoints committees and they serve for a specific purpose. It is reasonable to appoint committee members for a specific term. Then if they are inactive or uncooperative, they should not be reinstated when their term expires.

Written objectives can usually prevent the kind of problem that you are experiencing. The committee members will then know what is expected of them and power struggles are less likely to occur.

BUSYBODY BOARD MEMBER DISTURBS OWNERS

Q *My wife and I live in a condominium. We are very fond of many of our neighbors and we love our unit with its view of the city skyline. However, we are so disturbed by the actions of one of the board members that we are about ready to move out. This person has served on the board for years and no one wants to challenge him.*

During the past year he has become more and more of a pest. He "polices" the building, questioning owners about their guests, checking unit doors to see if owners have left them unlocked and leaving notes on people's doors chiding them for petty things, many of which are not even rule violations.

We would like to see him removed from the board if possible but we don't want to start a recall. He has served several two-year terms. Is there a limit of the number of years that a board member may be elected to serve the association?

A If there were any limits on the number of terms or number of years that one can serve on your board of directors, this restriction would probably appear in your association's bylaws.

Have you spoken to the other board members about your dissatisfaction? Every board needs to have people who are not afraid to enforce rules but this guy sounds like he is definitely overstepping his authority. The other board members need to speak up and take control of this situation. If this board member has no hobbies or other interests, it may be very difficult to change his ways. In fact, he may continue with his policing if he is obsessed with the enforcement role.

I think your first step should be to talk with the other board members to find out if other owners are complaining and to discuss a few ways to deal with the situation. Perhaps you will want to submit your name for nomination at the next election. It will be impossible to replace this person if no one else wants to run for the board.

SELF-APPOINTED PRESIDENT REFUSES TO PREPARE BUDGET

Q *I live in a 16-unit homeowner association that is unincorporated. One of the owners has designated himself as president and whenever an unusual expense comes along, he just sends an extra bill along with the monthly assessment bill.*

I have learned from reading your newspaper column that the association is supposed to have a budget. The president says, "It's too much fuss and bother." Since ours is a small unincorporated association, he believes that a budget is not required. Is he right?

A No, the president is not correct. Every community association in California, whether it is incorporated or unincorporated, large or small, must prepare an annual budget and distribute it to the owners between 45 and 60 days prior to the beginning of the fiscal year. Community association is the term for any of the following forms of common interest residential developments: condominium, planned unit development, residential cooperative, homeowner association, community apartment or "own-your-own" apartment project.

According to California Civil Code Section 1366, the association cannot increase the assessment unless the pro forma budget has been properly prepared and distributed. Your letter indicates that the board president is, in effect, levying a special assessment every time he feels the need to do so. The owners are entitled to better financial planning and controls from a board of directors.

If the board members don't have the time to run the association in a business like manner, then the association members should be willing to hire a management company or consultant to do the budget preparation and other financial work so that the association is operating in compliance with the law.

BOARD MEMBER HAS THE RIGHT TO SEE BANK RECORDS

Q *I was recently elected to the board of directors of my condominium association. I am concerned that our manager does not have a fidelity bond. I asked to see the bank records for the operating account and the savings account but the other board members will not release the records.*

My lawyer says that I will have to spend several thousand dollars of my own money to file an injunction in order to force them to disclose the records that I am legally entitled to see.

What alternative course of action would you recommend? Does the law requiring arbitration apply to this type of dispute?

A Didn't your attorney suggest simply writing a letter? Have letters been ineffective in the past? Sometimes corresponding with the rest of the board is very effective.

Since you are a board member, you are entitled to see the bank account records. However, if you are the type of person who would use this information to find fault with the board's fiscal policies or the manager's purchasing and payment methods, this may be the reason that the other board members are holding you off. When you review the records, try to be objective. There is a difference between a watchful board member who is fulfilling a fiduciary duty to protect the association's finances and one who is nitpicking about every bill that is paid.

There are several steps that you can take prior to filing legal action: mediation or arbitration would be an effective way of getting your point across without the expense of filing an injunction. I am not an attorney, but in my opinion, your attorney should have discussed these less expensive alternatives with you. Filing an injunction should be your last resort.

First, you can write a letter to all of the other board members requesting access to the financial records that you want to review. As a board member, you should have access to any and all records of the association. There is one precedent-setting legal case that prevents a board member from seeing the ballots of an election so that the privacy of the voters is protected; however, in most circumstances, a board member should have access to association records.

In your letter to the board, there are certain laws that you can cite which may educate the board.

According to California Corporations Code Section 8334: "Every director shall have the absolute right at any reasonable time to inspect and copy all books, records and documents of every kind and to inspect the physical properties of the corporation of which such person is a director."

In addition, the California Civil Code, Section 1365.5, states that the board of directors of a community association must do all of the following:

1. Review a current reconciliation of the association's operating and reserve accounts on at least a quarterly basis and review the most recent statements prepared by the financial institutions where the association's operating and reserve funds are kept.
2. On at least a quarterly basis, review the current year's actual reserve revenues and expenses compared to the current year's reserve budget and review an income and expense statement for the association's operating and reserve accounts.

If the association's governing documents impose more stringent accounting duties on the board of directors, then your board must perform their duties according to the governing documents.

After you or your attorney write a letter to the board citing all of these reasons why you should have access to the records, the board members will surely grant your request. If they ignore your letter, then the next step is an attempt to mediate or arbitrate the dispute prior to seeking a court injunction. You do not have to be represented by an attorney in a mediation or arbitration.

BOARD MEMBERS WANT TO HAVE STAGGERED TERMS

Q *Our homeowner association board has decided that it would be beneficial if the director's terms expired at different times in order to provide continuity. We currently have a five-member board.*

One person has suggested that we elect three board members each year and that terms be two years. Each year only three people would be leaving the board instead of having the possibility of a complete turnover in board members. Should we change our bylaws so that we can have six board members who serve two-year staggered terms? How should we make the change?

A I am not an attorney so I always recommend that the association consult legal counsel before changing the legal documents. Most governing documents specify an uneven number of board members so that there will always be a majority deciding every action of the board.

Talk to your attorney about amending the bylaws to provide for two-year staggered terms. Then at the next annual meeting, the three directors getting the highest number of votes will serve two years and the other two will serve one-year terms. At each succeeding annual election the membership will be voting on only two or three directors depending upon the number of directors whose terms are expiring.

WHO ELECTS THE BOARD PRESIDENT?

Q *I want to start a vigorous campaign so that I can be elected president of my homeowners association. I am not interested in holding any office other than president. Our board needs a change in leadership and I believe that my being president is the only way that change will happen.*

One of the people who is currently serving on the board of directors told me that a person must first be elected as a director. Please explain the election process.

A At the annual meeting, the members elect the individuals who will serve as the board of directors. The officers of the board are not elected by the membership as a whole. The board of directors elects their own officers at the first board meeting following the annual membership meeting.

Usually, a detailed explanation of the election process can be found in your association's bylaws. If you are planning on running for the board of directors you will want to thoroughly read all of the legal documents. The board is responsible for abiding by and enforcing these documents.

BOARD MEMBERS ARE BEING PAID FOR SERVICES

Q *I own a community association management company in the Los Angeles area. In the past few months I have been invited to present management proposals to five associations.*

These five associations have been self-managed without any professional management advice. Each of these associations has been paying one or more of their board members for their association services. The payments are not for reimbursement of expenses but rather a form of salary for serving in a "volunteer" position.

Some of the associations waive the monthly assessments for their board members and some have devised clever ways to avoid accounting for the missing revenue. It is possible that the other owners do not know that the board members are being paid. One of the associations pays its board members by issuing checks out of the operating funds.

I have explained to them that volunteer directors have some protection from liability because of their volunteer status and paying themselves jeopardizes that protection. In every case, they stated that paying the board members was the way that they kept the board positions filled. They claimed to be unaware that this procedure is probably in violation of their governing documents.

One of the associations asked their attorney about paying the board members and the attorney advised them that it was okay.

I would appreciate your comments.

A The ideal "textbook" association is structured so that the volunteer board of directors is the decision-making body. The board has the authority to delegate all administrative, accounting, property maintenance and other association responsibilities to contractors, vendors and professionals. The board has the duty to adopt a realistic budget and assessment schedule to operate the association. That is the fair way for the owners to share the actual cost of running the association.

Almost every association is set up this way, but some boards of directors like to save money by doing the work themselves or they think that is what they are supposed to do. I have never seen an association declaration that says that the condominium board members have to vacuum the halls. Board members should not feel obligated to be the unpaid accountant, attorney, janitor or handyman for the rest of the owners.

I advise board members not to perform services for the association that should be paid services. It is unfair for the other owners to expect board members to perform association services. Eventually no one wants to serve on the board because of the time commitment and the work that is involved.

When board members take on responsibilities like cleaning the pool, mowing the common area lawn or performing other services, they sometimes decide they should be paid for their work or receive some secret benefit. At that point, the director should resign from the board. Payment or any other form of remuneration to board members is not consistent with most associations' governing documents unless the payment is reimbursement for actual expenses.

The association is a nonprofit organization and the members (owners) are entitled to know if board members are being paid. The annual financial report, if prepared according to generally accepted accounting practices, should disclose any conflict of interest or financial dealings with volunteer directors according to Corporations Code Section 8322.

Some associations have requirements in their legal documents that any member who performs paid services must have the approval of the membership. In other words, both disclosure and member approval are required.

I don't agree with the attorney who opined that paying board members is acceptable. There are many legal, accounting, insurance and tax considerations. As you point out in your letter, liability is an important issue that should be discussed with the association attorney and insurance agent. The directors' and officers' liability insurance coverage could be affected if board members are paid, especially if the board members are aware that payment is prohibited in the association's legal documents.

Board members have a duty to comply with the association's documents. They are not entitled to special privileges or benefits. In my opinion, associations should not hire any owners or residents to perform paid services. When disagreements or negotiations arise, the association is better off dealing with a third party.

MUST BOARD DISTRIBUTE MINUTES OF MEETING?

Q *Civil Code Section 1363.05 states that board meeting minutes are supposed to be available to the owners within 30 days of the meeting. Some associations do not distribute minutes at all or they wait until the board meeting minutes are accepted at a subsequent meeting before making them available. Please comment on the association's obligation to comply with the law. Does the law require that they be distributed?*

A The board has a duty to comply with the Civil Code and other laws pertaining to community associations. The law states that "The minutes, minutes proposed for adoption that are marked to indicate draft status, or a summary of the minutes, of any meeting of the board of directors of any association, other than an executive session, shall be available within 30 days of the meeting. The minutes, proposed minutes or summary minutes shall be distributed to any member of the association upon request and upon reimbursement of the association's cost in making that distribution."

In other words, the board is supposed to have some form of the minutes ready for distribution within 30 days of a meeting. The law does not say that the minutes have to be distributed to every owner. Accessibility or distribution must be provided to those owners who request the minutes. The association has a right to collect payment for copying, postage and other related costs before the minutes are sent out.

Each year, the association is supposed to distribute an explanation of where and how an owner can obtain copies of minutes. The association board should establish a policy on distribution of the minutes. Many owners do not care about reviewing the minutes. Therefore, associations could be wasting labor, paper and postage to send them to everyone.

ASSOCIATION FAILS TO PROVIDE DISCLOSURE DOCUMENTS

Q *My daughter is purchasing a townhouse in an association that does not have professional management. She reads your column and knows that she is entitled to see financial reports, the reserve study and other documents.*

The volunteer board member who serves as treasurer was rather curt with her and said, "We've never had anyone else ask for this information. I don't know where to find all of this." My daughter is persisting. I just wanted you to know that there are probably lots of associations that don't know about the law and couldn't care less, especially if it inconveniences them to comply with the legal requirements.

A It is the seller and the seller's agent who should be obtaining the documents from the association. As your daughter has learned, if she relies on others she may not get what she needs.

I believe that some associations that seem indifferent really know what is expected, they just don't want to be bothered or they simply want to run things their way.

There are escrow officers who think that no one reads the association's governing documents anyway, so they wait until the closing and dump all of the documents on the buyer at the last minute. That's not the way it is supposed to be. The seller is supposed to supply the governing documents and other pertinent information noted in Civil Code 1368 "as soon as practicable before transfer of title."

I have owned properties in community associations for over 15 years and served as a board president. I would never purchase property in an association without getting all of the disclosure information within the contingency period and well in advance of the close of escrow. Even the most informed buyer who obtains all of the transfer disclosure documents still can be surprised by dictatorship, board indifference or other association problems. At least, your daughter is forewarned about the level of service that she can expect from this particular board.

TWO BOARD MEMBERS APPROVED ASSESSMENT INCREASE

Q *Our association board recently passed an assessment increase. I am curious about the board's ability to approve the increase since only a board president and an "interim" vice president were serving on the board at the time of the increase. The interim vice president soon resigned after the assessment increase was announced.*

A It appears that the board may have been a few cards short of a full deck, but they played the game anyway. Your association's legal documents, perhaps the declaration (CC&Rs) or, more likely, the bylaws, will tell you the number of members that constitutes a board of directors.

For instance, if your bylaws say that your association has a three-member board, then it would be possible for two board members to approve an action. If your association is supposed to have a five-member board, two board members would not have the authority to act. The board needs a majority (quorum) to conduct a meeting and take action.

BOARD MEMBER IS HIRED BY ASSOCIATION TO PAINT TRIM

Q *Our association has 161 new garage doors that have been installed recently. The board meeting minutes state that one of the board members is a painter and the board unanimously voted to hire him to paint all of the trim around the garage doors at the hourly rate of $20 per hour plus the cost of materials. It is not clear whether brushes, ladders and other equipment will be purchased at association expense. There is no estimate of the total cost and no restriction of time. The board member who was hired as a painter is a real estate agent according to information that was distributed with election materials.*

A $20 per hour handyman was hired to repair damaged stucco around the garage doors. It seems that he could have been hired to do the painting also.

Isn't there a conflict of interest when a board member is hired to do work for the association? Who is responsible if he is injured while performing work for the association?

A Yes, there is a conflict of interest when a board member is hired to do work for the association. The board member should not have participated in the vote to hire himself. The board should have a written agreement with him and someone should be verifying his hours worked. The board member should take steps to ensure that his honesty is unquestionable.

The association should have a workers' compensation policy that covers the handyman and any other paid workers. Volunteer board members should be covered as well as board members who are hired to do work for the association. The insurance agent can answer any questions about the risk of coverage being in jeopardy if a board member works for the association.

In my opinion, it is not appropriate to hire homeowners, especially board members, to do work for the association. Board members who want to work for the association should resign from the board. I have seen many examples and heard many tales of woe regarding the pitfalls of hiring association members.

HOW CAN WE NETWORK WITH OTHER ASSOCIATIONS?

Q *How can our association board of directors network with other boards and discuss common problems and compare enforcement and assessment collection techniques? We'd like to learn from others' mistakes and share our successes.*

A Call the local chapter of the Community Associations Institute (CAI). This is a national nonprofit organization with more than 50 chapters around the country. There are several chapters in California. Seminars, publications, legislative updates and other resources are available to CAI members and non-members who want to learn how to run their associations more effectively. If you cannot find a listing in your local phone directory, call the national office at

(703) 548-8600. If you have a computer with access to the Internet, the organization's website is www.caionline.org.

DOES BOARD PRESIDENT HAVE THE RIGHT TO VOTE?

Q *Our community association manager told our board of directors that the board president should only vote on motions when the vote results in a tie. I have read our bylaws and find no basis for this procedure.*

Now, one of our directors has resigned so instead of having five board members, we only have four. It doesn't seem right that a motion could be approved with only two board members' votes if one of our board members is absent or abstains from voting. Doesn't the board president have the right to vote in such instances?

A Your question is a common one. The board's method of voting is basic procedure. They should rely on the advice of the association's attorney whenever the association's documents are unclear.

Though I am not an attorney, I attend many law seminars and rely on the advice of the instructor attorneys who specialize in community association law. The board president is elected by the membership and has as much right as any other director to have his or her vote recorded on every motion. With a five-member board, you need three board members for a quorum. In order for a motion to pass, a majority of the board members in attendance at the meeting must vote for the motion. Therefore, if only three board members attend a meeting, approval of motions would only require the affirmative vote of two board members.

Since board members are not allowed to give their proxy to other board members, it is very important that board members make every effort to attend board meetings and exercise their right to vote.

In order to avoid tie votes, the vacancy on the board should be filled as soon as possible. Consult the bylaws to find the procedure for filling board vacancies. In most associations, the remaining four board members can vote to appoint a new board member.

OWNER WANTS A LIST OF OTHER OWNERS

Q *I live in a condominium in a resort area. Very few owners are year-round residents. Some of the board members have served for 15 years or more. They do not give advance notice of meetings.*

I have decided that I will run for the board in the next election. However, with the high percentage of non-resident owners, the board receives a great number of proxies. I have asked to have a roster of owners distributed, but the board will not allow it. How do I have a chance of being elected? Can I demand a list of the owners?

A The board does not have the authority to keep you from contacting the other owners. You have the right to obtain a list of the names and addresses of the other owners as long as you are not using the list for improper reasons such as soliciting clients for your business or selling the names to mass marketing advertisers.

To obtain a list of the members and their mailing addresses, write to the board of directors. You must tell them the reason that you are requesting the list. For example, you can state, "I would like the names and addresses of the owners of Happy Acres Association for the purpose of contacting my fellow owners regarding the annual election."

According to California Corporations Code, Section 8330, the board has only ten days to respond to your request. It would be very unwise for them to deny your request. They can allow you to photocopy the information at your expense or they can offer an alternative method of allowing you to exercise your right to contact the other owners. The alternative must be a written response from the board.

I recommend that boards establish a written procedure for distribution of the mailing list so that when a request is received, the association is prepared to deal with it in a timely manner. Some associations will mail out notices to the other owners for an individual if the individual agrees to pay for the cost of the photocopying and postage. Some associations will provide the mailing labels at the owner's cost.

CAN MEMBERS CALL MEETING TO ELECT NEW DIRECTORS?

Q *Our homeowner association is supposed to have a five-member board. Two of the directors resigned several months ago. The board members have not scheduled an election to fill the two vacancies. Can the members call a meeting and elect two new directors?*

A The association's bylaws will state how board vacancies are to be filled. In most cases, the remaining board members have the authority to appoint new directors when vacancies occur. The board should appoint new directors as soon as possible if qualified people are willing to serve. Perhaps the board has tried unsuccessfully to fill the vacancies.

The members do not have the authority to schedule an election even if the board does not appoint new directors. The members can petition for a special meeting.

The bylaws will state the method of petitioning the board for a special meeting or election. The board then has the obligation to act within the time period specified in the bylaws.

CHAPTER 6 FINANCIAL MATTERS

ASSESSMENTS MUST BE COLLECTED FROM ALL OWNERS

Q *I live in a 16-unit townhouse complex. One of the association board members has not paid her assessments in several months. Two of the board members are her friends and the rest don't seem to know what should be done. Don't we need a procedure for collecting unpaid assessments?*

A The obligation of all owners to pay assessments is usually stated in the Declaration of the Covenants, Conditions and Restrictions (CC&Rs). The board has a fiduciary responsibility to uphold and enforce the CC&Rs and to establish a delinquency procedure.

The association's budget should accurately reflect its expenses without any padding to compensate for those who do not pay. Therefore, the board must diligently collect assessments or the association will have a negative cash flow and will be unable to pay its operating expenses.

California Civil Code Section 1365 states that the association must disclose its practices in enforcing lien rights against its members or other legal remedies for default in assessment payment. After the board has adopted a delinquency policy, they must provide proper notice to all of the owners prior to putting it into effect. When budget information is distributed to all of the owners each year, your delinquency procedures should also be included.

TREASURER DELAYS PRESENTING BUDGET FOR APPROVAL

Q *I have served on the board of directors of our homeowners association for three years. We are an association of 124 lots with single-family homes. We have private streets and street lighting, swimming pools, spas and several acres of landscaping that must be maintained.*

The board treasurer takes sole responsibility for preparing the annual budget. He procrastinates and always waits until December to present the budget to the board for approval. Our fiscal year begins on January 1.

What is the legal requirement for distribution of the budget to the owners? What other fiscal deadlines or disclosures about reserve funds are required of the board?

A Even if the treasurer handles the preparation of the budget, all board members have a responsibility to see that the budget is a realistic one and that its distribution complies with the law.

In California, as in several other states, the legal requirements are very specific. The annual budget must be sent to all owners not more than 60 days nor less than 45 days prior to the beginning of the association's fiscal year. These requirements apply to all forms of community associations whether they are incorporated or unincorporated.

The budget must include estimates of the association's operating and reserve expenditures, plus the following reserve funding information:

1. Identification of the major components belonging to the association that will require future repair and replacement,
2. The estimated replacement cost of these components and the estimated remaining useful life of each one,
3. The current estimate of the amount of cash reserves necessary to repair, replace, restore or maintain the major components,
4. The percentage of total funds needed that are currently accumulated for reserve expenditures,

5. A statement regarding the likelihood of a special assessment being levied during the fiscal year, and
6. An explanation of the procedures used to calculate the reserve needs of the association.

The budget information could also include the association's delinquency policy since the written procedure for collecting unpaid assessments is supposed to be sent to owners some time within the 60-day period prior to the beginning of the fiscal year.

Another important deadline comes 75 days after the close of the fiscal year, which is the date for filing the association's tax returns. If your fiscal year ends on December 31, your tax returns must be filed by March 15. If your association's total income for the year is $75,000 or more, an annual financial report must be sent to all owners within 120 days after the fiscal year-end. If the association's declaration is more restrictive, the board must comply with the declaration. In addition, California Corporations Code Section 8321 requires that each member receive specific financial reports within 120 days after the close of the fiscal year if the association's annual gross receipts are $10,000 or more.

If your association charges penalties for violation of the legal documents, all owners are entitled to receive a schedule of the amount of the monetary penalties or fees that the association charges.

Your board treasurer should be reminded that even volunteers have deadlines that are important. The rest of the board should assist him in meeting those deadlines because you may all be held responsible if the board's failure to comply with the law results in legal problems. If the board intends to increase the assessments, they will need a vote of the owners to approve the increase if they fail to meet the legal deadlines.

COLLECTING SPECIAL ASSESSMENT BEFORE REPAIRS ARE MADE

Q *Our condominium association is collecting a special assessment from all the owners to pay for major repairs. Does the association have the right to request payment of a special assessment before the repair work is even started? Can the association add a ten percent late charge if the special assessment is not paid?*

A When major repairs are necessary, the association may need to accumulate a major portion of the money before the work is started. Construction companies often require deposits to pay for materials and permits. They usually want progress payments when each phase of the project is completed. Some companies require proof that the association can afford to do the work before they will enter into a contract.

Unless your association's declaration specifies a smaller percentage or amount for late charges, California law states that unpaid regular and special assessments are subject to a late charge of either ten percent of the assessment amount or $10, whichever is greater.

POOR MAINTENANCE BRINGS EXTRA EXPENSES LATER

Q *My homeowner association doesn't perform repairs when they are needed. The board doesn't want to raise the assessments and consequently we don't have sufficient staff to maintain the building and grounds properly. Those of us who want the property maintained have no influence. There is no way to make the repairs ourselves. What can we do?*

A You can remind the board that they have an obligation to maintain the property in a manner that protects the owners' investment and provides a safe and habitable environment. The board of directors isn't doing you any favors by keeping the assessments low.

The annual budget should allocate funds for adequate maintenance of the property. The budget must include a reserve analysis that estimates the current replacement cost, the remaining useful life and the methods of funding the future repair or replacement of the major components of the common areas. The downward spiral created by poor maintenance is sometimes very difficult to overcome. Some of the consequences might be extra expense caused by the lack of preventive care, special assessments due to inadequate financial planning, decrease in marketability of the units, and vandalism and other damage due to a lack of pride in the property.

You and the other owners who are concerned about this matter should offer your help to the board. Volunteer to serve on the budget committee and work with them to help them learn about their fiduciary responsibilities. If the board is unresponsive, then you may want to work to replace them in the next election.

OWNERS SHARE COSTS AS STATED IN THE DOCUMENTS

Q *Our association has less than twenty units. Some of the units need to have the roofs replaced. We need to know how to allocate special assessments based upon square footage of the units that need repair.*

A All of the owners share in the cost even though all units are not going to be repaired. The association's method of allocating special assessments can be found in the declaration of covenants, conditions and restrictions (CC&Rs). If the declaration states that assessments are apportioned according to square footage, then the apportionment pertains to all of the units in the association. Some owners do not understand this concept of shared costs.

The following scenario is an example of the lack of understanding that exists in some associations. A condominium owner purchased a unit on the ground floor of a three-story building. When the roof needed to be repaired, he complained that he should not have to share the cost because the leaking roof did not affect his unit. The association board approved a special assessment and billed all of the owners appropriately for their share of the cost of the roof repair work. No one could convince the stubborn owner that he was obligated to pay the special assessment for the roof. After three months, the association filed a lien against the unit because of the unpaid special assessment. The owner was adamant. He came to every board meeting to protest the unfairness of the assessment. After several months he finally hired an attorney who reviewed the association's CC&Rs and explained that he would have to pay the special assessment plus the association's collection costs. By the time he understood the meaning of the CC&Rs, he owed several hundred dollars of late fees and attorney fees in addition to the special assessment.

This illustrates the importance of communicating with all of the owners regarding the purpose of the special assessment and how the allocation of the assessment is dictated in the association's governing documents. The association's attorney should be consulted. If the special assessment is less than five percent of the annual budget, the board has the power to approve the special assessment without a vote of the owners.

Notification of the special assessment must be sent to all owners at least 30 days, but no more than 60 days, prior to the date that the special assessment is due.

CAN BOARD USE RESERVE FUNDS FOR EMERGENCY REPAIR?

Q *The board of directors of our condominium association has determined that the association is responsible for some repairs that will cost approximately $10,000. This is an unforeseen expense for an item that is not included in our reserve study.*

Since our association has only 14 units, it will be impossible to accumulate this amount of money immediately so that these emergency repairs can be done. I understand that the owners are entitled to 30 days notice prior to the due date of a special assessment. The repairs must begin right away in order to prevent further damage and more costly repairs in the future.

Does the board have the authority to use $10,000 from the reserve funds even though the reserves are designated for other expenses? What steps must be taken to replenish the reserve funds?

A The use of reserve funds is covered in Section 1365.5 of the California Civil Code. The board does have the authority to transfer money from the reserves for this unexpected emergency repair if they follow the proper procedures.

First, the board must document the reasons for the use of the reserve funds and the amount of the reserve funds that will be used. Then the board must decide how to replace the reserve funds and how soon they will do so. The reasons for the use of the funds and the method of replacing the reserve funds and the amount of time that will be needed to replace the funds must be noted in writing in the board meeting minutes. This is the first step in the disclosure of information to the owners.

The money should be replaced within one year. If the board finds that they have a good reason to delay the restoration of the funds beyond the one-year time limit, they must document this information and the reasons for their decision in the board meeting minutes.

The board may decide to approve a special assessment that will replenish the funds over a period of time. However, if the special assessment exceeds 5 percent of the budgeted annual expenses, the board would not have the authority to approve it. The owners would be entitled to vote at a special meeting called for the purpose of voting on the special assessment. The special meeting can only occur if a quorum is present. Then, a majority of those owners present would have to vote in favor of the special assessment. If a special assessment is not approved, the board can increase the annual budget as much as 20 percent for the next fiscal year to replenish the reserves.

If the special assessment is due to a true emergency as defined in Civil Code Section 1366, the board would have the authority to approve the special assessment regardless of the amount. The emergency situations specifically defined in the law are:

An extraordinary expense required by an order of the court.

An extraordinary expense necessary to repair or maintain the common area where a threat to personal safety is discovered.

An extraordinary expense necessary to repair or maintain the common area that could not have been reasonably foreseen when the board was preparing the annual budget.

Prior to the approval of the special emergency assessment, the board must pass a resolution containing the written findings as to the necessity of the special assessment and why the expense was unforeseen.

CAN BOARD USE FUNDS FOR SOCIAL EVENTS?

Q *I live in a 250-lot development of homes. The developer turned over control of the association to the homeowners about a year ago at our first annual meeting. The five board members unanimously voted to have a social gathering during the holidays. The party will be held in the association's recreation facility and will be paid for with association funds.*

Our budget doesn't have money set aside for this purpose. I asked the treasurer why the association was spending money on a party that not every homeowner would be interested in attending. She said that the party is to build goodwill and encourage people to get acquainted so that the owners will be interested in serving on the board in the future. Our next annual meeting will be in January but I think it's just an excuse for the board members and their friends to get the association to pay for their holiday party.

Should the association's funds be spent for social events?

A The board has the authority to spend association money according to the governing documents of the association. The budget is a financial road map but it is not meant to keep the board from spending funds for something that is beneficial to the association. In general, the board can spend money on a party if it is for "building community." All of the owners should be invited, of course. You think that not every homeowner will want to attend. That is probably correct, however, owners should want to be involved with their association.

I think that this is an appropriate use of association funds if the amount spent is within reason. In fact, I often suggest social gatherings as a means of dealing with owner apathy or in preparation for an annual meeting. Owners are more apt to attend a meeting or run for a board seat if they know other people in the association. In a large association like yours, some people probably don't even know their next-door neighbors.

New associations need to generate some interest and make the owners aware that the destiny of their association lies in the hands of the volunteers who give their time to serve on the board or on committees.

COMPARING COST OF IN-HOUSE LABOR VERSUS CONTRACT

Q *I live in a condominium association that is comprised of over 200 units. The landscaping features of our complex are labor-intensive because of water features. Until recently the association employed our own on-site employees who took care of the day-to-day maintenance and repairs. The board of directors decided to outsource the maintenance by using contractors instead of employees.*

I would like to perform a comprehensive cost analysis by comparing in-house labor to the independent contractors. I know there are intangible benefits and some liabilities regarding in-house labor. Surely other associations must wrestle with similar decisions. Are there any resources that could shed some light on this topic?

A One publication that might be helpful is a booklet called "Grounds Maintenance for the Community Association" by Bette Weseman. It is published by the Community Associations Institute and can be obtained by calling one of the local chapters of the organization or accessing the CAI website at www.CAIonline.com. The booklet provides the advantages and disadvantages to having your own employees; however, it doesn't address the cost analysis directly. The following lists of advantages and disadvantages point out some of the cost factors that should be considered. The actual figures must come from your association's accounting records.

Bear in mind that it is inappropriate for you to obtain information about employee salaries and other cost factors if you are not on the board. Most associations protect the privacy of their employee records and contracts.

The booklet lists these advantages when contractors are used for grounds care:

1. Workers perform productively since contract provisions must be carried out.
2. Contractors' specialized expertise increases quality and efficiency of work performed.
3. Association is not required to invest in equipment, maintain it or keep track of the equipment.
4. Contracted workers require less supervision time from association.
5. Costs are fixed if the contract includes weed control, fertilization and other incidental expense.

6. Contractor is responsible for insurance liability and personnel record-keeping.
7. Work force is stable if the contractors perform well and treat their employees well.

The disadvantages are:

1. Association loses some control over how well and when jobs will be done.
2. Association may have higher costs.
3. Maintenance personnel may turn over more frequently if work is unsatisfactory and contractor is changed.
4. Personnel are less likely to be available to respond to emergencies unless specified in their contract.

If you are not a board member, you should not be interfering with or contesting the board's decision. The association board may have decided that the employees did not have the knowledge or skills to maintain streams or ponds, trim trees and take care of other landscaping needs. Lawn care is more complex than just mowing. Problems with supervision or discovering employee dishonesty will often lead a board toward relying upon contract labor, though this information should be kept confidential to protect the association from liability. Even if the tangible costs are higher for contractors, the board may have determined that hiring contractors was more beneficial to the association in the long run. You should abide by their decision.

BOARD SPENT HALF OF RESERVE ON RENOVATION

Q *In the past six months, our board of directors has spent 50 percent of our reserves in addition to about $50,000 that was in the checking account. The board approved a major renovation of the lobby and hallways and paid for it over a period of several months to avoid having to get approval of the homeowners to spend the money.*

The redecorating has changed our "old English inn" decor to cheap-looking contemporary. What recourse do I have?

A The board has the right to use reserve funds for the repair, replacement or improvement of the property. Your reserve study should disclose when major expenditures are anticipated. When a large portion of the reserves is being depleted, the board must have a plan for replenishing those reserve funds. Prior to the work being done, the board had an obligation to show that the association could afford to do the remodeling without jeopardizing the overall financial stability. If there are no other major repairs, such as roofing, which will be needed in the near future, then the board may have acted properly.

I sense that you are more upset with the choice of decor than with the large expenditures. I have never heard of a major improvement that 100 percent of the owners supported. As an individual homeowner you have the right to be heard, but if the majority of the owners like the improvements, what can you do? Now that the work is completed, it seems unreasonable to expect that the association would spend even more funds to change it.

When you purchase in an association, you are automatically giving a tremendous amount of control to your board of directors. Most owners are glad to sit back and let the board make these major decisions for them. It is either boon or blessing depending on your viewpoint. This is why some owners decide that the condominium lifestyle is not their preference.

CAN BOARD USE RESERVE FUNDS TO PAY FOR LAWSUIT?

Q *Does our homeowner association's board of directors have the authority to use reserve funds to pay attorney fees for a lawsuit against the builder/developer?*

A Yes, but the board must follow the same procedure of documentation and disclosure in the board meeting minutes as stated in the previous answer. The association must notify all of the owners when the decision is made to use reserve funds or to temporarily use reserve funds for litigation.

The board must notify the owners at its earliest convenience by mailing a copy of the minutes or by including the information in the next regularly published newsletter that is mailed to all owners.

The notification must include information about the availability of an accounting of the litigation expenses that are transferred from the reserves. The board must make accounting records regarding the litigation available for inspection at least on a quarterly basis at the association's office. If the association's legal documents require a higher level of accounting disclosures, then the association must comply with those requirements.

Prior to filing legal action against the builder for construction defects, there are other legal requirements and disclosures that must be made. These requirements are primarily contained in Civil Code Section 1375 and 1375.1. The association board should rely on the advice of legal counsel to ensure that all legal requirements are met.

ANNUAL BUDGET WAS SENT AFTER THE DEADLINE

Q *Our homeowner association's fiscal year begins on January 1. The board of directors did not mail the budget for next year until November 17, stating that Section 1365 of the California Civil Code permits mailing this information as late as 45 days prior to January 1, superseding the CC&Rs which state that it should be mailed 60 days before the beginning of the new year.*

Some owners feel that the budget information was not mailed in compliance with the law, so the owners must approve the $10 increase in monthly assessments before it can be collected. Is this correct?

Can the association spend money without a properly approved budget, or must invoices wait until the owners approve a budget? Can the association follow the current budget until next year's budget is approved?

A California Civil Code Section 1365 starts out with the phrase "Unless the declaration imposes more stringent standards...." Perhaps your attorney advises otherwise, but I believe the budget and other financial information should have been sent to the owners before the 60-day deadline as required by your CC&Rs.

I firmly believe in abiding by the CC&Rs and the Civil Code, but the board members thought that they were doing the right thing. In this situation, an argument over the missed deadline and the cost of time and money for some owners to contest the validity or legality of the budget is just counter-productive.

Remember, the board of directors is a group of volunteers who are serving because they were elected to represent all of the owners. They cannot be experts in every aspect of the operation of the physical property and the association's business. Sometimes they will make mistakes. When that happens, the other owners should be reasonable. It isn't prudent for "concerned owners" to go to extremes and work against the board. After all, you should all be playing on the same team, working for the good of the association.

Whether the budget is proper or not, the bills keep coming in and they must be paid on time or the association's credit will suffer. The dissidents can't make everything stop until this is resolved. If the association is forced to go back to last year's budget, there may be a shortfall that would require a special assessment. One way or the other, the owners have to pay the costs of operating the association.

Will it benefit the association to force the board to put the new budget to a vote of the owners? In my opinion, it isn't necessary, but that may be the only way to restore harmony. Since a $10 increase seems reasonable, wouldn't most of the owners vote for it? While the board is wrestling with this brouhaha, what other problems are they ignoring or putting on hold?

My suggestion to the board would be to decide quickly whether they are going to stick to their guns and keep the new budget or organize a vote of the owners to approve it. Once the question has been decided, how about putting the owners who are questioning the legality of the budget on the finance committee for next year with the goal of distributing the budget information properly?

Association living would be so much more satisfying if people would have patience with one another. Bickering not only wastes a lot of time, it is very detrimental to the association because it creates an atmosphere that discourages owners from serving on the board.

CAN BOARD INCREASE THE BUDGET AND ASSESSMENTS IN MID-YEAR?

Q *In January, the beginning of our condominium association's fiscal year, the board of directors increased this year's budget by about five percent. The person who was the treasurer at that time influenced the rest of the board members and kept them from adopting a realistic budget.*

I was recently elected to the board of directors of our condominium association. Most of the other board members feel that our monthly assessments need to be increased. We have had our reserve study updated and we should be allocating more funds to the reserve funds for future repair and replacements.

I understand that the association's budget can be increased as much as twenty percent above the previous year's amount. Since the increase this year was only five percent, can the board now revise our budget and increase it by an additional ten percent for the remainder of the fiscal year?

A The budget that took effect on January 1 should have been distributed to all of the owners between 45 and 60 days prior to the beginning of the fiscal year. If this was done properly, then the board of directors has the authority to increase the budget up to twenty percent above last year's budget in accordance with the California Civil Code.

Since the board only increased the budget by five percent, your plan to increase the budget by an additional ten percent would be within the legal limits. Some owners may question the board's authority to approve a mid-year budget increase; however, the board can send out a revised budget explaining the reserve study update and providing the actual numbers that justify the additional funds.

California Civil Code Section 1366 requires that the owners be given at least a thirty-day notice, but not more than 60 days' notice, prior to an increase or special assessment going into effect, so give adequate notice with a full explanation and attach a revised budget showing which line items in the budget need to be increased.

Prior to approving the second increase, inform the owners that the board is considering another increase because of the recent reserve study. Invite the owners' attendance at the next board meeting and get their feedback and answer their questions prior to approving the new budget. This is a good way to build consensus if you feel that some owners will be angry about another increase. Remind the owners that the board has a duty to adopt a budget that will fulfill the present and future needs of the association.

ACCOUNTANT IS ALWAYS LATE PREPARING FINANCIAL REPORT

Q *Our association board is aware that our community association must distribute an annual financial report to the owners within 120 days after the close of the fiscal year. Our homeowners association has not complied with this legal requirement.*

Since our annual income exceeds $75,000, an accountant is preparing the report. This is the second year that the accountant has not completed the work on time. As a board member, I am concerned about this. The manager says that she has done everything she can to get the accountant to complete the report.

I am frustrated with both the manager and the accountant. What can we do?

A The board should write to the accountant stating that your association must comply with California Civil Code, Section 1365(b). Request that the accountant send a letter stating the reasons for the delay and the estimated date of completion. Then you will be able to distribute the accountant's letter to your owners to show that you have made an effort to comply with the law.

If the accountant is also responsible for preparing the association's federal and state tax returns, you should check on the status of those also. Penalties will be owed if the returns are late and an extension has not been filed.

In the future, I recommend that you contract with a licensed accountant who understands the association's legal requirements and agrees to complete the work in a timely manner.

HOW TO MAKE SURE RESERVE FUND IS ADEQUATE

Q *The governing documents (CC&Rs) of our association state that we must set aside funds every month for a reserve account, but a specific amount is not given. How do we know if our reserve funds are adequate? What happens if we have an emergency and the reserve funds are not sufficient to cover the expense?*

A Your questions bring up some common concerns for most homeowners and board members. It's good that your governing documents don't state a specific amount for your reserve funds since inflation and changing needs of the association have an effect on the total reserve amount required as time rolls along.

Let's look to our state laws for guidance. California Civil Code Section 1365, states that the annual budget information must include: (1) an estimate of the current replacement costs, (2) the estimated remaining useful life, and (3) the methods used to defray the cost of future repair, replacement, or additions to, the major components which the association is obligated to maintain. In order to determine if the reserve fund is adequate, the board must identify all the major components of the common elements (e.g. roofing, swimming pool, common area furnishings). Then all the factors listed above must be established. The association board should contract with a company that provides reserve studies or reserve analysis reports. The cost and the end product will vary considerably from one company to another.

If an emergency arises and reserve funds do not cover the cost of repairs or replacement, your board will have to approve a special assessment or obtain a loan from a lending institution. (Unfortunately, not all lending institutions are interested in lending money to community associations.) Each homeowner's assessments will then be increased temporarily.

Special assessments can be either lump-sum payments or paid over a period of months depending on how the board determines to collect the special assessment. Consult your association documents to see what restrictions apply to special assessments. In addition, California Civil Code Section 1366(b) does not limit the amount of special assessments for specific emergency expenditures, so be aware that a new roof, for example, might require a very large special assessment.

The reserve study is an important part of the budgeting process. Proper budgeting and reserve planning will protect you from special assessments, which are always unwelcome surprises!

OWNER QUESTIONS WORTH OF RESERVE STUDY

Q *Our association has more than 400 units with parks and swimming pools. The board spent thousands of dollars on a reserve study to determine the cost of long-term maintenance and replacement. They announced that the law requires that the association provide this information to the owners.*

I just received the annual audit report and I am frustrated that the very expensive reserve study is simply a one-page report that I believe was a waste of our money. Why does the law require this ridiculous expenditure of the association's money?

A A reserve study is not a waste of the association's money. It is an important document that discloses the association's maintenance responsibilities and current fiscal condition to the owners and potential buyers. In California, state law requires a reserve study every three years. It is a complete list of all of the components and amenities that the association must maintain. The study identifies the estimated remaining useful life of the components, an estimate of the cost of repair, replacement, restoration or maintenance of each component, and the total amount of funds that should be accumulated for the future repair or replacement.

The reserve study then becomes a long-term financial plan. A portion of the assessment funds should be placed in a separate reserve account to be used for future maintenance, repair or replacement of the association's common area. Annually, the reserve study and the analysis of the expenditures from the reserves can be used as a tool to formulate the budget for the next year. As soon as a maintenance item, such as replastering the pool, is expensed from the reserves, the reserve funds should be built up again incrementally for the next expenditure.

Since your association is a large one with several amenities, the one-page report that was included in your annual audit was probably just a summary of the actual reserve study. The law states that distributing a summary of the reserve study to the owners is acceptable. If you read the report, you will probably find information about who to contact so that you can obtain a copy of the full report and analysis. The photocopying costs are the responsibility of the requesting owner.

HIRE COLLECTION SERVICE FOR UNPAID ASSESSMENTS

Q *As a board member for our association, I have been assigned the task of collecting delinquent assessments. An investment company owns one of the units. The delinquent assessments for this unit total over $3500. We have so many expenses that our association really needs this money. How can we collect right away?*

A This is a common problem that occurs when the board does not establish or enforce procedures for collection. Many small associations fail to set up effective delinquency procedures and then when a delinquency occurs, the board is unsure how to collect. I urge you to lay the proper legal groundwork before you go any further.

Consult the California Civil Code, Section 1365(d). If your association's CC&Rs do not spell out delinquency procedures, the first thing you must do is establish a delinquency procedure and notify your owners by distributing the new policy to all owners. Then enforce it fairly and consistently.

I also recommend that you contact an assessment collection service for assistance with this process. Under normal circumstances, all collection costs, including reasonable attorney fees, are chargeable to the delinquent owner.

Most management companies and collection companies recommend that a lien be filed as soon as an account is more than sixty to ninety days past due. By using the services of a professional collection service, chances are that the association will recover all of the delinquent fees including collection costs. In the case of corporate ownership, there are methods of collection that do not require you to locate the individual owners.

Small claims action is another way of collecting but you must file a claim before the delinquency gets beyond the $5,000 maximum limit for small claims cases.

WAYS TO PROTECT AGAINST EMBEZZLERS

Q *A neighboring condominium association has recently been informed that an employee of their management company embezzled some of the association's funds. What can we do to ensure that our association will not have the same problem?*

A Whether you are managed by a management company or not, the board is obligated to review the association's reconciled bank statements for the operating and reserve accounts on at least a quarterly basis. Make sure that your bank accounts for your reserve funds require two board signatures for the transfer of funds. Some management companies are not aware of these legal requirements. If you have a management company, you must not assume that your finances are being maintained properly. It is the board's fiduciary responsibility to ensure that funds are protected.

In addition, every association should have a fidelity bond for protection against loss of funds through malfeasance or embezzlement. The fidelity bond should cover all board members as well as the management company staff. Many management companies will tell you that they have their own fidelity bond coverage, but their coverage does not protect your association's funds unless your association is specifically named on their fidelity bond coverage. The management company's fidelity bond usually only protects the management company's funds, so be sure to investigate thoroughly and consult your association's insurance agent.

UNDER-FUNDED RESERVE COULD BRING PROBLEMS

Q *We live in a 17-unit condominium complex that is self-managed. When a reserve study was done two years ago, it was recommended that $75 out of each unit's monthly assessment be deposited to the reserve fund. The annual budget, based on this recommendation, was rejected by the homeowners. The approved budget allocates only $37 of each unit's monthly assessment to the reserve fund. This means that our reserve account continues to be grossly under-funded, according to the original reserve study.*

Homeowners who plan to move within three to five years are against building up the reserves, assuming that keeping the assessments low will enable them to sell more easily. Those of us who plan to live here a longer time are faced with the probability of large special assessments when major repairs are needed. We would appreciate your comments.

A Usually, it is the board's responsibility to set the annual budget. Evidently, the board recommended more than a 20 percent increase, which required an affirmative vote of the owners.

If the board is concerned about the under-funded reserves, I recommend that the board increase the assessments each year at the rate of 20 percent, which is the maximum allowable under California law without the vote of the owners. (The law recognizes some exceptions, such as unforeseen emergency expenditures that necessitate an increase greater than 20 percent.) A special assessment of five percent of the annual budget is legal if it becomes necessary.

It is important that the board members understand their responsibility for prudent financial planning. Board members are obligated to adopt a realistic budget.

With the current disclosure laws, copies of the reserve study must be distributed to all owners and the association cannot hide the fact that the reserves are under-funded. More and more buyers are becoming aware of the importance of adequate reserve funds. I recommend that buyers review the annual budget, reserve study and the annual financial report prior to signing a purchase agreement.

NO FORMULA FOR AMOUNT OF RESERVE FUND

Q *We have 27 units in our condominium. Each unit pays assessments of $100 per month. How much reserve should we have on hand?*

A Unfortunately, there is no way to pluck a number out of the air. Years ago, some experts said that the reserves should equal ten percent of the annual operating budget. That advice is no longer appropriate.

State law now dictates that the association must distribute to the owners specific financial information which includes a list of major components of the property, an estimate of the current replacement cost and the remaining useful life of each of the components, and the method of funding that the association is using to pay for the future repair or replacement. All community associations must abide by this law whether they are large or small, incorporated or unincorporated. Read the question in this chapter entitled "How To Make Sure That Reserve Fund Is Adequate."

LAW PERMITS BOARD TO INCREASE ASSESSMENTS

Q *I would like more information about a community association board's authority to raise assessments up to 20 percent per year. I live in a condominium that passed an amendment to the declaration allowing increases only with the approval of 60 percent of the members except for emergency situations. Does the law displace all previous provisions in the association's documents? How can a board of directors stay informed about changes in the law?*

A Yes, Section 1366 of the California Civil Code specifically states that regardless of more restrictive limitations in an association's documents, the board may increase regular assessments up to 20 percent of the previous year's assessment. The board may also impose a special assessment that does not exceed five percent of the budgeted expenses.

Higher increases are legal if more than 50 percent of the owners attend a meeting at which a majority of those present approve the increase. Proper notice must be given and the meeting must be conducted according to Section 7510 and Section 7613 of the Corporations Code. Your board can research the law by going to the county law library. Some local public libraries also have excellent legal reference books available. Since the law is changing frequently, make sure that you have current information.

The board has the authority to approve an assessment increase greater than 20 percent if the increase is directly related to an emergency situation, such as: 1) an extraordinary expense required by a court order, 2) an extraordinary repair or maintenance expense where a threat to personal safety is discovered, or 3) an extraordinary expense necessary to repair or maintain association property that was unforeseen at the time of preparation of the annual budget. The board must pass a resolution containing written evidence of the need for the repair and reasons why the expense was unforeseen. The resolution must be distributed to all the members with the notice of the assessment increase.

The California Civil Code, Section 1366.1 prohibits the association from collecting an assessment, penalty or fee that exceeds the amount necessary for the purpose for which it is collected.

The Community Associations Institute provides seminars and newsletters to keep boards of directors, managers and other professionals informed about changes in the laws governing community associations. The attorney members of CAI often send out newsletters informing other members of changes in the legal requirements for associations.

SHOULD OWNER ASSESSMENT BE BASED ON UNIT'S SIZE?

Q *It is my understanding that many condominiums have a monthly assessment that is the same amount for all owners regardless of the square footage of the unit or percentage of the common area. However, our association's documents set the monthly assessments and special assessments based on the size of the unit. The low-paying owners outnumber the owners who pay the larger assessments, so it is unlikely that a vote would result in any change. Are you aware of any action taken to rectify this situation?*

A The California Department of Real Estate usually requires that assessments for each unit be prorated based upon the square footage if the square footage varies by more than 10 or 15 percent.

I am aware of many associations that have debated and are debating this issue. Unequal assessments and unequal voting percentages are often a nuisance for the budget preparer, the bookkeeper, the accountant and the election judge at the annual meeting, so in my opinion equal assessments are sensible. However, the issue of fairness is always brought into the discussion.

Many people assume that the owner of a penthouse unit should pay more for the monthly assessment because the owner paid a higher purchase price, but what effect does the penthouse view, which probably influenced the purchase price, have on the maintenance cost to the association? Is it unfair to automatically assume that the owners of the larger units will have higher water and electrical usage?

Here's my advice: You knew or should have known what the assessment differential was when you purchased your unit. If you were willing to live with it then, perhaps you can live with it now. It is probably unrealistic to try to change it if you don't have the support of a majority of the owners. You will simply make enemies if you try. If you are upset by the way the assessment variance is handled, you should consider selling your unit and moving.

BOARD HAS POWER TO APPROVE SPECIAL ASSESSMENTS

Q *The board of directors of our condominium complex has approved a $350 special assessment. They did not call a special meeting to discuss it with all the owners. We have been told that we must pay the special assessment on time or we will have to pay late charges. Shouldn't the owners be allowed to vote on a special assessment?*

A The board has the authority to adopt the annual budget and approve special assessments. If the special assessment is more than 5 percent of the annual assessment, then the board should allow the owners to vote on the issue.

California law allows special assessments of more than five percent for emergencies only. If the special assessment is necessary due to an emergency that is a threat to health and safety of owners, then the board must act immediately. A vote of the owners would not be required. The board does have an obligation to communicate with the owners regarding the reasons for the special assessment.

An association board usually approves a special assessment only if it is absolutely necessary. No one likes a special assessment, especially the board members who are often subjected to criticism regarding financial matters. Board members sometimes postpone budget increases or vote against special assessments because they are afraid of criticism from their neighbors though they have a responsibility to act in the best interests of the association, even when their decisions are unpopular. Owners should support the board and value their experience unless there is a reason to suspect that they are poor decision makers.

Special assessments are subject to late fees just like regular assessments if they remain unpaid after the due date.

SMALL ASSOCIATIONS NOT EXEMPT FROM RESERVES LAW

Q *I own a condominium in a 36-unit complex. Our association is unincorporated. The board of directors contends that the California statute regarding reserves for the repair and replacement of common property does not apply to our association because we are not incorporated.*

Are we exempt from establishing and maintaining a reserve fund? How do we comply with this law if we are required to do so?

A California Civil Code, Section 1351, defines an association as a "nonprofit corporation or unincorporated association created for the purpose of managing a common interest development." Your association is not exempt from the California statutes governing community associations. Even small associations must comply with this law and disclose the status of reserve funds to the owners. Prospective buyers are entitled to this information.

Civil Code Section 1365 states that the association must provide an operating budget. The annual budget must include related financial information that shows the current cash reserves that are set aside, a list of the major components that the association is responsible for maintaining, the current replacement cost, the estimated remaining useful life of the components, and the methods of funding that will defray the future repair or replacement. The association must also disclose the procedures used to calculate the reserve funds.

Many association boards are finding that they do not have the time or the skills to prepare an adequate reserve analysis for their association so they hire a reserve study professional in order to comply with the law.

TREASURER HAS RIGHT TO GET BANK STATEMENTS

Q *I am the treasurer of my homeowner association. The management company controls the bank accounts for both the operating funds and the reserve funds. They write the checks and sign them and then provide a monthly financial statement showing income and expenses. I have asked to see copies of the bank statements but the manager says that the financial statement prepared by the management company has all the information that I need. Should I demand copies of the bank statement?*

A Yes. You are relying too heavily on the honesty and integrity of the management company. As a board member and the treasurer of the association, you and the rest of the directors have a responsibility to see that the funds are properly handled.

Here in California and in several other states, two board officers or directors must sign any checks or withdrawals from reserve accounts. Board members should never remove funds from the reserve account unless approved by formal board action that is noted in the meeting minutes.

The association should carry fidelity bond insurance on the individuals who have access to the funds. If possible, obtain a fidelity bond that also covers the manager.

Request copies of all statements from your bank or savings institution. California law requires that the board of directors review the "account statements prepared by the financial institution where the association has its operating and reserve accounts."

STATE LAW SUPERSEDES BUDGET LIMIT IN CC&RS

Q *The California Civil Code, Section 1366, limits the regular assessment increase to twenty percent "notwithstanding more restrictive limitations placed on the board by the governing documents."*

Our association's CC&Rs limit the annual assessment increase imposed by the board to ten percent. Since the CC&Rs are a contract among the homeowners, I question if Section 1366 can nullify that contract.

A You are not the only person who is confused by the wording of this law. The confusion arises because of a misunderstanding of the meaning of the word "notwithstanding." Notwithstanding is a legal term that means "in spite of" or "regardless of." One of my dictionaries uses the following example: "He bought it notwithstanding the high price."

I have attended many legal seminars where this section of the law was thoroughly explained by nationally recognized experts in the field of community association law. Even though I am not an attorney, I am certain that I can stand by my advice, which is: According to California law, the board has the right to impose a 20 percent increase over the prior year's regular assessment. The law takes precedence over more restrictive controls in your association's legal documents.

STATE LAW SUPERCEDES ASSOCIATION AMENDMENT

Q *In 1983 our homeowner association passed an amendment to the declaration that states that a special assessment greater than $100 per unit per calendar year must be approved by at least 51 percent of the total membership.*

The board recently approved a special assessment of $155 per unit without a vote of the membership. The purpose that the money will be used for is not an emergency. The association has $100,000 in the reserve fund. Can the association legally approve this special assessment?

A The California Civil Code supercedes the amendment that you describe. However, the code states that if the special assessment is greater than five percent of the current annual assessment, then the membership must vote on the matter. Emergency special assessments are exempt from a vote of the owners as explained in previous answers in this chapter.

The association has $100,000 in the reserve fund but you haven't told me whether a reserve study has been done. Perhaps $100,000 is far below the amount needed for maintenance and repair. Obviously the board of directors feels that the current reserve fund is inadequate so they approved a special assessment.

I doubt if the board would have voted for it without thorough discussion and study. Board members do not like passing special assessments because they know that they may be criticized for improper budgeting in previous years.

From the information that you have given me, I would say that the board deserves your support for increasing the reserves before an emergency arises. If a reserve study has not been distributed to all the owners, then you have the right to question the board's action. California law requires homeowner associations to prepare a reserve study that identifies the major common area components and the cost of future repair and replacement.

BOARD USES RESERVE FUND FOR OPERATING EXPENSES

Q *The previous board of directors in my homeowner association was frugal and maintained a reserve fund for future repair of streets, tennis courts and gates. Our present board has apparently spent all of our operating funds for the year and now must dip into the reserves to pay for the remainder of the year. Our assessment fees for next year will probably be increased.*

I thought that the purpose of the reserve study was to determine the amount of money needed for the future and that none of the money should be used until the full amount has been accumulated. What does state law say about spending reserve funds?

A The law states that a reserve study must be done to determine the amount of funds that will be needed for future repair and replacement of association property. The association does not have to wait until the tennis court reserve is fully funded before using the money to resurface the court, for instance. Each year, as money from the reserves is used, the reserve budget for the following year must be revised to allocate more money as needed.

If the board is using reserve funds to make up the shortfall in the operating funds for this year, the budget for next fiscal year should be increased to adequately pay for operating expenses and to cover the replenishment of any reserve funds that are used during the current fiscal year.

In other words, if the association is now using reserve funds to pay the gardener for landscape maintenance, the operating budget for next year will have to be increased to reflect the true cost of the landscape maintenance. Then the reserve budget will have to be increased to replace the funds that were used for the operating expenses this year.

Reserve funds can be used for emergencies at the discretion of the board, but in this case it might have been more prudent to have a special assessment rather than use the reserve funds. Using the reserve fund for ongoing operating expenses is a poor way of managing the association's money.

SHOULD ALL OWNERS GET FINANCIAL STATEMENTS?

Q *I live in a 34-unit condominium that is managed by the volunteer board members. I went to a board meeting this week, the first one that the board has held in five months. At this meeting, the treasurer was absent and she did not provide a financial statement.*

Though no financial report was given, there was some discussion that an increase in assessments may be necessary. Should all homeowners be receiving financial statements on a regular basis? Should I be concerned about the infrequent meetings and lack of participation by the treasurer?

A Check the association's bylaws to find out how often the board is supposed to meet. According to California law, Civil Code Section 1365.5, the board should be reviewing, at least on a quarterly basis, the financial records and reconciled statements from the financial institution where the association's operating funds and reserve funds are deposited.

Normally, only the board members would receive the monthly or quarterly financial statements, however copies should be provided to other owners if requested. The requesting owner is obligated to pay copying and postage costs, if applicable. All owners should get an annual financial report that is distributed at association expense.

If the treasurer is a volunteer, it may be difficult to require that she prepare a financial report each month. However, I believe that even volunteers should have some guidelines from the board on what their responsibilities are. Of course, the board's procedures should comply with the state law.

CLARIFYING THE LAW ON LATE CHARGES

Q *I own a condominium unit, which is rented out to a tenant. The condominium association's monthly newsletter recently stated that the California Civil Code permits a late charge of ten percent plus interest.*

I am unfamiliar with this information and would like to know exactly what the law says. Can the association assess a late charge of $14.00 to save computation time rather than computing the ten percent late charge?

A Here is the wording of Civil Code Section 1366(e): Regular and special assessments levied pursuant to the governing documents are delinquent 15 days after they become due. If an assessment is delinquent, the association may recover all of the following:

1. Reasonable costs incurred in collecting the delinquent assessment, including reasonable attorney's fees.
2. A late charge not exceeding ten percent of the delinquent assessment or ten dollars ($10), whichever is greater, unless the

declaration [CC&Rs] specifies a late charge in a smaller amount, in which case any late charge imposed shall not exceed the amount specified in the declaration.

3. Interest on all sums imposed in accordance with this section, including the delinquent assessment, reasonable costs of collection, and late charges, at an annual percentage rate not to exceed 12 percent interest, commencing 30 days after the assessment becomes due.

Civil Code Section 1366(f) states "Associations are hereby exempted from interest-rate limitations imposed by Article XV of the California Constitution, subject to the limitations of this section."

It appears that your association's late charge of $14.00 is a combination of the flat ten dollar fee plus a four dollar collection fee. The association may levy the late charge in this manner without computing the percentage unless the declaration specifically states otherwise.

Refer to your association's declaration to see if the specified late charge is a smaller amount. Civil Code Section 1366(c)(2) is one example of a statute that does not supercede the association's legal documents.

The association's delinquency procedures are supposed to be distributed to the members annually.

OWNER ASSESSED FOR LAKE HE DOESN'T USE

Q *Many members of our homeowner association must pay a $162 annual fee to a lake association. The requirement is part of the property deed. The lake is not contiguous to the property and most of the owners do not even use the lake. Is it legal for a developer to require homeowners in a condominium association to belong to a recreational facility that is not contiguous to the property?*

A Yes, it is legal. If this is a deed restriction that runs with the property, I don't see that there is any way that you can stop paying the fee to the lake association. You could refer this matter to an attorney who can review all of your legal documents and give you a legal opinion.

You bought the property under those terms and you probably will have to live with it. Even though you do not live on the lake or use it for recreational purposes, it is an amenity that enhances the value of your property. When you sell, you may find that buyers are very interested in the nearby lake and recreational facility.

OWNER REFUSES TO PAY BECAUSE REPAIRS NOT MADE

Q *I serve on the board of directors for a new condominium development that has just recently been turned over to the homeowners by the developer. One of our owners is seriously delinquent in paying his monthly assessments. The delinquent owner refuses to pay his assessment because the developer has not completed some repair work inside his condominium unit. What can we do?*

A First, your board must enforce the established delinquency procedures that should have been adopted as soon as the association was formed. Always enforce these procedures fairly and consistently with all owners who are delinquent.

Perhaps a friendly visit between the delinquent owner and the board president or treasurer will clear up the problem. It should be easy to reason with the owner, especially now that the association is no longer under the developer's control. You can explain to him that the assessment fee pays for common area expenses or common utilities. For example, the domestic water is probably a common expense. Ask him if he thinks that his neighbors should have to continue to pay his share of the water bill. Another example would be the lighting in the common corridors. These are services that he is using every day and not paying for it.

The owner has an obligation to pay the assessment regardless of the condition of his own unit. His "beef" is with the developer and the association has no control over when the developer will complete the repair work. In my opinion, the board should not assume any responsibility to assist the owner in getting the work done.

BOARD HAS AUTHORITY TO USE COLLECTION SERVICE

Q *The board of directors of my condominium association recently voted to hire a collection service to collect unpaid assessments from the owners who are not paying their share. Does the board have the authority to hire a collection service without a vote of the owners?*

A Yes, the board has the authority to do this. In the association's declaration, the board is usually given broad powers and duties to operate and maintain the association, including the duty to collect assessments from all of the owners. These assessments pay for the common expenses of the association and therefore, if owners fail to pay, the association's fiscal stability is jeopardized.

Selecting a collection service or lien service company to perform the task of collecting delinquent assessments is a very effective way of fairly and consistently enforcing the association's collection policy.

In most cases, the association does not have to pay for this service because the association is entitled to pass along to the delinquent owner any reasonable costs of the collection procedures, including attorney's fees, lien filing fees and other reasonable costs.

In my opinion, unless your association's legal documents require a vote of the owners for approval of contracted services, which would be very rare, your board does have the right to obtain the assistance of a collection agency or lien service.

STATE MANUAL CAN HELP IN ESTABLISHING BUDGET

Q *As the treasurer of my homeowners association, I am responsible for budget preparation. We would like to cut our expenses, particularly landscape maintenance and electrical costs, but we want to adopt a budget that is realistic.*

What resources are available to help us determine whether our current expenses are reasonable?

Our association might hire a management company or a bookkeeping service to do the monthly assessment billings and other accounting work. How much should we put in the budget for these management services?

A The California Department of Real Estate (DRE) publishes a manual that is especially useful to developers in estimating the operating costs of a new development. The data for the most recent revision was compiled early in 2000. Some portions of the manual's instructions, data and worksheets may not apply to your association.

The manual provides formulas for estimating landscape costs and electrical costs. By using this data and your financial history from previous months and years, you should be able to formulate a realistic estimate of your operating costs and reserve funding.

The cost of financial services depends upon the scope of services performed. The DRE manual estimates that an association can contract for assessment billing, collection, payment of bills, collection of delinquent accounts and preparation of a financial statement for $11 per unit per month or $750 per month, whichever is greater. To ascertain the actual cost, you will have to obtain bids from companies that perform this type of service.

You can obtain a copy of the DRE Operating Cost Manual for Homeowners Associations by sending a check for $10.83. Make your check payable to California Department of Real Estate. Mail your request to: Book Orders, Dept. of Real Estate, P. O. Box 187006, Sacramento, CA 95818-7006.

PAY YOUR ASSESSMENT EVEN IF BILL IS NOT RECEIVED

Q *I am having an ongoing argument with the management company that sends out the billing statements to the owners for our homeowners association's monthly assessment. I did not get a bill for the month May so I didn't send in a payment. When the June bill arrived, it showed that a late charge has been added to my account.*

I don't think that the management company or the association can add a late charge if they didn't send me a bill. What can I do?

A Pay the bill, including the late charge. The payment of your assessment is mandatory. You should consider the association fee to be much like a mortgage payment or your property tax assessment. The billing statement is just a reminder. The bill could be lost in the mail or maybe it wasn't even mailed to you through some error or oversight, but that doesn't relieve you of your responsibility to pay.

LACK OF RESERVE FUNDS IS CAUSE FOR CONCERN

Q *My husband and I are very concerned about the lack of financial planning in our condominium complex. Even though I am serving on the board, I am unable to convince the other directors that we need to start accumulating reserve funds to pay for some of the major expenses that we know will be needed soon. A majority of the board members seem to think that special assessments can pay for any need or emergency that arises. Can you help us?*

A I frequently get questions about reserve requirements. I'm sure that this is a controversial issue in many associations.

The board has a fiduciary duty to adopt a budget that serves the best interests of all of the owners. In my opinion, that means setting aside money for major repairs that will be needed in the future. Special assessments cause too much of a hardship on the owners.

A proper reserve study identifies all of the major components that will require future repair or replacement, the estimated cost of the repairs and the anticipated lifespan of the components. At the present time, the state law does not require that money be set aside for this purpose, but full disclosure must be made as to the methods of funding, or lack thereof.

Some owners say that they don't want to pay for a roof that may not be needed until after they have sold their unit. What would happen if all of the owners decided to sell their units before the major expenditures are required? If your reserve analysis indicates that your 50-unit condominium complex will need a new roof within five years, is everyone just going to sell out in four years so that they can escape before it is special assessment time?

Potential buyers and mortgage lenders are getting very wary of associations that do not have adequate reserves. An owner who is unable to sell his or her unit because of this factor may decide to take legal action against the board of directors.

Since you are a member of the board of directors, make sure that your views are clearly noted in the association's meeting minutes when any votes are taken on this subject. You should make every effort to protect yourself from liability.

BOARD SHOULD PURSUE LATE ASSESSMENTS

Q *I live in a five-unit townhouse complex. Each unit pays a monthly assessment of $150. We try to keep our assessment collection on a personal, friendly basis. One of our owners is often two to four months late in paying his assessment. Many reminders and phone messages have been unsuccessful in getting full payment. The rest of us are feeling very frustrated with the time and effort that it takes to collect from him. What action can we take?*

A With a small association, it is especially important for the owners to pay their assessments on time. When one owner fails to pay, the association has to delay paying bills or defer maintenance until the money is received. This can have a detrimental effect on everyone's investment.

California Civil Code Section 1366, allows community associations to charge a late fee if an assessment is more than 15 days late. The monthly assessment is due on the first day of the month and delinquent if unpaid on the fifteenth day of the month. Unless the association's legal documents specify a smaller amount, you can charge the delinquent owner a late charge of ten percent of the unpaid amount or ten dollars, whichever is greater. You are also entitled to collect a reasonable fee for extra bookkeeping or extra notices that are sent.

Many other states have adopted the Uniform Condominium Act or the Uniform Common Interest Ownership Act with similar provisions for collecting assessments.

Read your association's declaration of covenants, conditions and restrictions (CC&Rs) to find the enforcement procedures that you can use to collect delinquent assessments. If the late charge specified in the declaration is less than the state law allows, then you must charge the lesser fee unless you can justify additional collection costs. The association can charge interest at the rate of 12 percent per annum if the monthly assessment is still unpaid thirty days past the due date.

The association can file a lien for the unpaid assessments and charge the cost of lien filing and other legal expenses to the delinquent owner. If the owner ignores the lien, the association can foreclose and take the unit.

The board should review the association's legal documents and vote on the methods they are going to use to collect unpaid assessments. If the association's board of directors adopts a new delinquency procedure, all of the owners must be informed. The association is obligated to distribute the written delinquency procedures annually to the owners during the 60-day period prior to the beginning of the fiscal year. Consult a property management company, a lien service or attorneys that specialize in community association matters if you need professional guidance. Always enforce your delinquency procedures fairly and consistently with all of the owners. When the delinquent owner is informed that your association will enforce its procedures and charge him for any additional costs, he may decide to pay on time in the future.

TEN PITFALLS IN THE BUDGETING PROCESS

Q *The board members for our condominium association are working on the annual budget. Since our fiscal year ends on December 31, I understand that we have a narrow window of time during November when we must deliver a copy of the new budget to all of the members of the association. Can you give us any last minute advice that we can use to debate with our treasurer who always wants to cut corners and adopt a "bare bones" budget?*

A Your question is often asked by board members and other concerned owners. You are correct about the requirement for distribution of the new budget. It must be distributed to the owners 45 to 60 days prior to the beginning of the fiscal year.

I am glad to provide some suggestions for your discussion with the treasurer. I have very little patience with treasurers who keep such a tight fist on the association's money that the whole complex suffers from deferred maintenance and inadequate reserve funding. Being frugal is fine but treasurers and, indeed, all of the board members have a responsibility to adopt a realistic budget and to act in the best interests of the whole association.

I recently found an article from the Community Associations Institute's newsmagazine titled "Ten Budgeting Mistakes Made by Community Associations." It was written several years ago but the advice in it is timeless. The authors, Arthur W. Hiban and James T. Derry, certified property manager and certified public accountant, respectively, give the following advice:

The annual budget is the most comprehensive planning tool available to the condominium or homeowners association. If properly approached and carefully conceived, the budget will become the basis for successful management of the property.

The budget must be approached with the goal of providing for efficient operations and for funding adequate reserves to meet long-term requirements.

When an association loses sight of this goal, the result is usually an inadequate budget, improper management and a community burdened by seemingly insurmountable problems.

Your association cannot afford to ignore the aging process. Each year, maintenance costs become more expensive. More money must be spent on preventive maintenance in order to preserve the life expectancy of your mechanical systems and other major components. An example of an expense that some associations scrimp on is landscaping costs. They budget for mowing, fertilization and weed control when more comprehensive services are needed as the landscaping matures.

Proper tree care and trimming is expensive but necessary, because mature trees are an asset that should not be ignored. The association should plan for replacement of shrubs and trees that may be affected by drought or inclement weather.

Don't underestimate maintenance costs. Anticipate that you will have emergencies and plan your budget accordingly. A leaking roof must be repaired. A broken water line must be replaced.

Your property insurance will not pay for these emergencies because they are maintenance expenses. Insurance may pay for the damages that result from an emergency but the insurance carrier will soon refuse to pay for claims if your facility isn't properly maintained. A high number of claims will affect your insurance costs in the long run.

It is a mistake to low-ball your budget and then expect to find contractors who will meet your price. Don't assume that you should always accept the lowest bid for repair projects. The board must make prudent business decisions based upon complete specifications including warranties, compliance with deadlines, and many other considerations in addition to the quality of the materials and the cost of the labor.

The board needs to determine the type and quality of the services that the owners expect. How often are the corridors going to be vacuumed? Do the garages need cleaning by an outside contractor on a periodic basis? How many times per week does the swimming pool require service? Would the owners like to hire a management company that will provide 24-hour emergency service?

Hiban and Derry encourage the association to define the level of service or maintenance standards. They state:

Too many communities ask: What can we afford? What is the lowest price we can get for services? How can we reduce the condominium fee?

They ignore the standards before preparing the budget. The results can be disastrous. If you prepare a budget without first considering standards, then the standards, goals and specifications will be determined by the budget and not the other way around.

Maintenance should be done *before* it is apparent that maintenance is needed! Waiting to paint until the surface needs extensive preparation is being "pennywise and pound foolish." Painting extends the life of the wood or stucco and seals out termites and other wood-destroying organisms. The association should schedule repainting before the surface is at risk. You may plan to have the paint last for seven years, but be prepared to revise your maintenance plan when it is apparent that painting is needed earlier. You may try to ignore the shabbiness, but a potential buyer will notice it.

I strongly believe that associations should plan their budgets so that they can afford to rely on the advice of experts when the need arises. The association should rely on professionals to assist in their decision-making on complex matters or legal issues because doing so reduces the board's liability.

For example, the association may want to hire an independent insurance appraiser to establish the insurable value of the property. *The director's and officer's liability insurance will not protect the board members if they have made an error that causes the association to be under-insured when a loss occurs.* The association may need to hire an independent roofing consultant to determine the scope of the work, write specifications, and supervise the contractor's progress when major roofing work is required.

Here is a common problem that I see all too frequently. Too many associations spend an incredible amount of money on a "Band-Aid" approach to roof repairs because they don't want to face the decisions involved in a total reroofing project. Board members are not expected to be roofing experts. If you aren't an expert, be prepared to hire someone who is.

I encourage associations to set aside funds for hiring a licensed accountant to prepare the year-end financial reports and tax returns. Don't rely on the services of a volunteer board member, even if he or she is a licensed accountant. The board should eliminate the appearance of a conflict of interest. The association should have the funds available so that an attorney can be consulted when legal issues or questions arise. Legal issues will, most assuredly, arise. Be prepared by having an attorney selected who is familiar with new legislation and the laws that govern community associations, ever-changing case law and your own association's legal documents.

A serious pitfall for budget preparers is basing the budget on political considerations. Hiban and Derry cite the following examples:

The developer wants to make sure that the monthly assessments are low enough to sell the units quickly; the board president wants to be able to "sell" the budget to the community; the managing agent wants to prepare a budget that makes him look good so he can keep the contract; and the treasurer was elected to the board on a platform of holding down the condominium fees.

Basing the budget on these "political" reasons will sometimes result in financial crisis.

When I hear a board member say proudly, "We haven't increased the assessments in five years!" I tend to wonder about deferred maintenance, shortsighted decision-making and under-funded reserves for future repair and replacement.

Perhaps the budget was grossly overestimated five years ago but this is unlikely. Long-term planning is essential if the association is going to be financially secure. No one likes special assessments to pay for major projects. If the annual budget is not adequate, the association may pay a greater price later on because of the lack of preventive maintenance.

Finally, in my opinion, preparation of the budget is a yearlong project, a continuing evaluation of the service levels that are desired by the general membership, and an analysis of the adequacy of the reserve funds that are being accumulated for the future. Boards that adopt bare-bones, unrealistic budgets will find themselves pinching pennies in order to stay within the budget and future boards will have to resolve their mistakes. Budgeting controversies and special assessments may lead to criticism of the board and unwillingness on the part of others to run for the board in the future. All of these factors have an affect on the overall value of the condominium complex.

Board members should be aware that their first and most important responsibility is to preserve and protect the investment that each of the owners made when they purchased their unit. Boards not only have the authority, but also the fiduciary responsibility, to approve a budget that is both adequate and realistic.

An association that is properly funded and well maintained means proud owners, ease of finding mortgage lenders for refinancing or for potential buyers, general community respect and retention of property values. These are important considerations for all board members to keep in mind when they are making their final decisions about the bottom line of the annual budget.

SHOULD WE POST NAMES OF "DEADBEAT" OWNERS?

Q *One of the board members in our homeowners association said that we should post the names of "deadbeat" owners in the common area of the property. Is this an effective way of collecting from owners who are continually late in paying their monthly assessment to the association?*

A No, I definitely do not recommend posting the names of late payers in the common area or printing this information in the association's newsletter. This kind of peer pressure may be effective in collecting late dues at your country club or social organization, but community associations have means of collecting delinquent assessments that are more effective than using public embarrassment.

It is unwise for the association to attempt to collect delinquent assessments in this manner. Occasionally, accounting errors occur. It would be very upsetting for the owner and the association might be held liable if the information that was publicized turned out to be incorrect.

RESERVE BUDGET IS LOWER THAN STUDY RECOMMENDED

Q *The board of my association engaged a qualified consultant to provide a reserve study but now they have decided not to follow the recommendations in the study.*

The board has extended the expected remaining life of some of the reserve components while keeping the replacement cost constant. As a result, the board's reserve budget is significantly lower than the recommendations of the consultant.

Does state law require that the board adopt a budget that follows the reserve study recommendations?

A The law requires that the board provide disclosure to the owners. A reserve study must be prepared and the study or a summary of it must be distributed to the owners. The board does not have to follow the consultant's recommendations. If the board has documentation to show their reasons for not heeding the advice found in the reserve study, that information should be shared with all of the owners also.

The board may have good reasons for varying from the reserve study. The study may provide an estimate of roofing costs, for instance. However, if the board has written estimates from reputable contractors that are lower than the roofing estimates in the reserve study, that would be a valid reason for reducing the amount of reserves in the budget. The law requires that a general statement of the method of calculation be disclosed in the reserve study that is distributed to the owners.

MOST OF RESERVES TO BE SPENT ON TERMITE CONTROL

Q *Our condominium has sixteen units and the complex is 15 years old. The board of directors is a three-member board. We have approximately $32,000 in the reserve fund and our reserve study was done about four years ago.*

Our board president plans to update the reserve study using software that we recently purchased. The original analysis did not include any funding for termite control. The president plans to add this and other items to the new reserve study. He then wants to spend all of the *reserve funds on these items. Localized treatment of termites during the last seven years has been unsuccessful and tenting the whole complex will cost $22,000.*

The board president insists that it is legal to spend all of our reserves as long as the money is spent on items included in the reserve study. He does not think the money has to be replaced even though these expenses were unforeseen four years ago when the reserve study was done.

I disagree with his opinions. What advice can you provide?

A When funds are used from the reserves, a plan should be set in motion that will replenish those funds. If your board is contemplating using a major portion of the accumulated fund, you must determine what other needs are likely to arise in the next few years. How will the association pay for other reserve expenses that arise in the near future before the reserve fund can be built back to the level that is needed?

A reserve study analyzes the future repair and replacement needs of the association for 20 years or more. A reserve study should include a complete list of all components for which the association has maintenance responsibility. Even in a relatively small complex, the component list can be quite extensive. In your association, these components might include roofing, heating/cooling equipment, elevators, lobby and hallway redecoration, lighting, security gates or garage doors, painting, swimming pool and/or spa, and other common area items.

The association should have funds available for these large expenditures. Otherwise, maintenance is deferred and the entire complex is in danger of slow deterioration. The downward spiral is sometimes hard to detect until only levying hefty special assessments can reverse the situation. A special assessment is an extra fee levied in addition to the regular monthly assessment. A special assessment is necessary when the association does not want to use reserve funds or when the reserve funds are not adequate to cover the expenditure.

Boards tend to dislike levying special assessments because they don't want to make unpopular decisions. However, if reserve funds are inadequate, the only way to build them up is to increase the assessment that each owner is paying to the association.

If your board allows the reserve funds to be substantially depleted, this could have a negative impact on the value of your units. Buyers, real estate agents and mortgage lenders look favorably on associations that have adequate funding in their reserves. If special assessments are levied to fund major expenditures, unit owners may not be able to afford to pay the extra fees and delinquencies, and foreclosures will occur.

Every association, large or small, needs a board that can provide sound financial planning or find the outside sources to do so. If the other board members do not agree with your president's views on spending the reserve funds, they have a duty to explore other ideas. Obtain competitive bids on the termite work. Survey the owners to find out if they would prefer paying a special assessment rather than depleting the reserve funds. It is basically a "pay me now or pay me later" type of situation because the reserve funds used for the termite work must be replaced.

DEFERRED MAINTENANCE LEADS TO SPECIAL ASSESSMENT

Q *I recently bought a unit in a seven-unit condominium association. After moving in, I realized we have deferred maintenance. Our monthly assessments barely cover the expenses. The treasurer does not believe in having a reserve fund because the interest earned is taxable. The other two board members seem to agree with him. Any unexpected expense, such as roof repair, will require a special assessment.*

I am concerned about the poor maintenance. How can I protect my investment? What are my rights?

A You had the right to know about the lack of reserve funds prior to purchasing the unit. The law does not require that the association have reserve funds. However, the association must have a reserve study and the information in the reserve study must be disclosed to potential buyers as well as the owners.

Now that you are an owner, you have the right to attempt to change the board's philosophy. Unless you and the other owners can convince the board to adopt a budget that provides money for reserve funds, you will probably continue to have deferred maintenance. The board has a fiduciary duty to adopt a budget that is adequate to cover the monthly expenses including routine preventive maintenance. In addition, it is good business judgment to have some money in the reserve fund for repair or replacement of major components.

If you have no reserves, the association will have problems accumulating money quickly when an emergency occurs. How many of the owners would be able to immediately pay their share if a new roof is needed? If a large special assessment is levied, how many owners will bail out by selling their unit rather than paying the special assessment when it is needed? How will the association collect from an owner who refuses to pay? These are all questions that should be discussed by the owners.

The "pay as you go" method protects everyone's investment. When funds are not available, deferred maintenance is the inevitable result. When repairs are postponed, you will often pay more in the long run. Most boards will resist approving a special assessment until it is unavoidable. By that time, the downward spiral of deferred maintenance will have taken its toll. The recovery is often difficult and more expensive.

DUE TO MANY FORECLOSURES, ASSESSMENTS MAY BE RAISED

Q *I own a unit in a 30-unit condominium association. The bank has foreclosed on eight units in the complex. The manager has sent a letter to all owners stating that he needs to raise the amount of the monthly assessments because he is unable to collect assessments from the units that went to foreclosure.*

Can the manager raise the assessments without the approval of the board members? Some of the owners want to change management. We need your advice.

A In times of crisis, it is important to prioritize the issues that face the association. Your concern should be focused on collecting the assessments. Your association may have lost quite a bit of money prior to the foreclosures. As soon as the lender forecloses on a unit, the lending institution then owes the monthly assessments from the date that the foreclosure took place. Now the manager should be sending assessment billing statements to the lender. A title company can verify ownership after the foreclosure. Sometimes it takes diligence and a lot of telephone calls to find out the name of a responsible individual at the lending institution who will process the payments.

Using California Civil Code Section 1366 as a guide, the association board should adopt lien procedures that can be used against delinquent owners. Collection of delinquent accounts should be among the duties performed by the management company. Liens can be filed against any delinquent owner, including lending institutions. Delinquencies will increase if the board does not have an aggressive procedure in place.

The association's board of directors should be checking on the manager's collection efforts and discussing their collection problems with the manager. The board may have to consider changing management companies if the company's staff is unable to follow the association's collection procedures effectively. That is a board decision, so you should discuss your management concerns with the board.

With the high number of foreclosures, it is obvious that your manager's letter to the owners was meant to inform everyone of the serious financial situation. Now it is the board's responsibility to analyze cash flow and determine if an increase in the assessments is needed.

BOARD REFUSES TO PROVIDE DELINQUENCY REPORT

Q *We own two condo units. One of them is in California and the other is in another state. The bookkeeper for the out-of-state association sends a quarterly financial report that includes the assessment payments from all of the owners.*

We would like our association in California to provide the same information but the board of directors refuses to provide it. Is there some basis for the board's withholding delinquency information?

A Most boards wisely refrain from giving out information about delinquencies because they wish to protect the privacy of the delinquent owners. Associations that post delinquency information or print delinquency reports run the risk of publicizing incorrect or outdated information.

In this situation, the board must weigh the individual owner's right to privacy balanced against the other owners' right to have access to records of the association. In some associations, the more protective the board is with the records, the more suspicious the owners become. Most attorneys urge associations to keep their assessment collection records confidential, though there are situations when the owners should be aware of delinquencies.

Many association documents require that owners who are running for the board of directors be members "in good standing." When association elections occur, I think it is proper for board candidates to voluntarily reveal the status of their assessment accounts in order to show that they are in compliance with the requirement to be in good standing.

I have heard of associations in which the board members were delinquent and they were not enforcing delinquency procedures against their fellow board members. This is a clear breach of duty. Board members can be held liable if they protect delinquent board members and practice inconsistent collection procedures.

ARE MOVING FEES LEGAL?

Q *Someone moved out of our condominium complex and they left a mess in the trash area. In my opinion, the board overreacted to this one incident when they adopted a new policy. Our association now charges $100 for move-ins and move-outs. If the unit is rented to a tenant, the owner of the unit is billed for each move. In addition, the owner is billed for any damage that occurs during the move.*

I view this policy as a penalty to the non-resident owners who have tenants moving into and out of their units. Damage that has occurred in the past has not been repaired. Why should the association charge for the damages if the repairs are not going to be done? Are move-in and move-out fees legal?

A The association may charge a reasonable moving fee. The fee should relate to the association's actual cost of services performed for the move. California Civil Code Section 1366.1 states: "An association shall not impose or collect an assessment or fee that exceeds the amount necessary to defray the costs for which it is levied."

Typical association costs might be for staff services such as: 1) changing the name of the new resident on the directory, mailbox, and the association's resident roster; 2) putting protective pads and floor mats in the elevators; 3) keying off the elevator for the exclusive use of the movers; 4) escorting utility workers who turn gas, electric, telephone or cable service off and on; 5) disposal of boxes and packing materials; or 6) monitoring the common area for security and safety purposes during the move. Your association may have other services that go beyond those listed. You have a right to know what services are provided.

The association has the authority, usually granted in the CC&Rs, to charge an owner for the cost of repairing damage that the owner or his/her family member, guest or tenant causes. However, I would expect repairs to be completed, if possible. Sometimes, damage cannot be immediately repaired. If carpet is permanently stained and no matching carpet is available, replacement may be the only way of correcting the problem. That is the type of damage that may have to wait for redecorating of the common area.

There are some ways that you can protect yourself from damage charges. You could require that your tenants use a licensed, insured moving company that will be liable for any damage to your unit or the common area. The terms of the lease should allow you to use the tenant's damage deposit for either damage to the unit or the common area.

It would be discriminatory if the association charges only non-resident owners for tenant moves, but your letter does not state that only tenant moves are charged.

I recommend that you ask the board or manager about the services that the association provides so that you will understand the charges. All owners should protect their investment by attempting to eliminate any damage to the common areas and reporting to the board or management those who do cause damage.

INADEQUATE RESERVES LEAD TO SPECIAL ASSESSMENTS

Q *We live in a 35-unit condominium association located on a lake. The Declaration of Covenants, Conditions and Restrictions (CC&Rs) includes the following: 1) the monthly assessments should include a contribution to a maintenance reserve fund. 2) If there is a surplus at the end of the year, it should be equally divided and returned to each unit owner. 3) Monthly assessments and special assessments are proportional to the size of each unit based upon the number of bedrooms. We have one, two and three- bedroom units in our complex.*

Until about five years ago very little money was allocated to the reserves. Because surplus funds were supposed to be returned to the owners at the end of the year, the boards apparently believed that they did not have to put money into the reserves.

As repair or replacement of roofs, swimming pool, irrigation systems and other common area components became necessary, $1,000 to $2,000 special assessments were levied equally to each owner. At some point in past years, the proportional assessment directive in the CC&Rs was dropped because everyone pays the same amount for their monthly assessments and special assessments.

Now we are faced with a major problem. We are told that we need to replace the boat dock and it will cost over $5,500 per unit owner. There are no reserve funds.

Is it fair to expect owners who bought in the last few years to contribute as much as the ones who have been living here for several years and failing to buildup the reserve fund? Can the board of directors levy special assessments according to the number of years that an owner has owned his or her unit?

A No, the board must follow the CC&Rs. That may be a new philosophy for your association, but the board must get the association back on track. Now everyone will suffer the consequences of the lack of financial planning during the previous years.

First, if the CC&Rs were not amended by a supermajority vote of the membership, as stipulated in your CC&Rs, then your monthly assessments and special assessments should be proportioned on the one, two and three-bedroom basis. Boards cannot arbitrarily decide to change the way the assessments are levied.

Second, all owners share in the cost of special assessments just as stated in the CC&Rs. There is usually no provision in the CC&Rs to protect new owners from their obligation to pay special assessments. That is the reason that buyers should carefully review the association's financial disclosures and find out about the amount of the reserve funds before they purchase. According to California law, detailed information about the reserves is available to purchasers prior to closing the sale. If recent buyers looked at the reserve disclosure information, they should not be surprised that special assessments are necessary.

Apparently, your association has determined whether the dock can be repaired rather than replaced. If repairing it is not an option, then the board must decide how to fund the new dock. Since the special assessment is probably more than five percent of your annual budget, approval of the owners will be required.

SHOULD RESERVE FUNDS BE IN A SEPARATE ACCOUNT?

Q *Until recently, our small association was self-managed by the board of directors. The board treasurer handled the bank account. Assessment income was deposited into the bank account each month.*

When the account accumulated enough excess income over a period of time, the treasurer purchased certificates of deposit from the bank. We have about $20,000 and four certificates of deposit. We have not been putting a designated amount into the reserve funds each month.

We now have a manager who prepared an annual budget for the next fiscal year. We will be setting aside $800 each month, which will be for reserve funds. The manager says that we need to set up a new bank account just for the reserve funds. Do we have to have a separate bank account for reserves? Are special procedures necessary for using the reserves when they are needed?

A Your manager is providing correct advice. The operating account should be used to deposit your monthly assessment payments and checks are drawn on that account to pay for contract services, maintenance, insurance, utilities and other association expenses.

Each month a check for $800 should be written from the operating account and deposited into the reserve account. California law requires separation of the operating cash from the reserve funds. The Internal Revenue Service regulations also require separation of the two funds.

When reserve funds need to be used, the expenditure should be approved at a board meeting and the reason for the expenditure should be noted in the meeting minutes. The board motion should clearly state who or what company is being paid and the amount of the expenditure. This formal board action authorizes the manager to generate the payment.

The board may delegate check-signing authority to the manager only for the operating account. Two members of the board of directors or two officers must sign checks or withdrawals from the reserve account.

BOARD PRESIDENT IS HIRED FOR REMODELING

Q *The Board of Directors of our condominium association has hired the board president to remodel the lobby. The project includes replacing the lobby mailboxes, new floor tile, paint and wallpaper. The board did obtain three bids and the president's bid was the lowest so he was selected for the work.*

Then the president immediately said that the painting of the hallways would cost $14,000 instead of $7,000 because his original bid was based on one coat of paint and one coat was not going to be acceptable. I believe there is conflict of interest here but the board president is intimidating and it looks like everyone is going to just let him clean out our funds.

Now he wants to put new carpet in the hallways and the fire stairways. The building is twenty years old and the fire escapes have never been carpeted.

We need your advice.

A I hope you are not the only person who thinks it is time to hit the brakes on this project! I realize there are at least two sides to every association issue, but this sounds suspicious to me.

It is very likely that your concerns are already making you the unpopular "trouble maker" but you just may be the only person who has the fortitude to ask the right questions. I would have lots of questions if I were you.

During my many years in the condominium management business, I have seen far too many remodeling projects like yours and that is why I believe it is almost always a mistake to contract with a board member. Perhaps the board president isn't even a contractor. Your letter doesn't state whether he has the business background or qualifications to handle this type of project.

It is clear to me that your association's problems started even before the bidding process. First, the board should have looked at their reserve funds and decided how much they were going to renovate and approximately how much money they were willing to spend.

The next step is getting some professional advice on the scope of the work, costs, specifications, contract terms, qualifications of the bidders and several other matters. Advice from your accountant, reserve study professional and attorney should have been sought right from the beginning.

If your president is such an expert, why weren't thorough specifications written that included all of the work that the association board authorized?

The fact that the painting cost doubled should have been a huge red flag for the rest of the board members. They then had the responsibility to go back to the original bidders to bid the project based upon the revised specifications (two coats of paint). The quality of the paint and lots of other factors are important too. If the paint is watered down, that explains why the walls need two coats and then that doubles the association's labor costs.

It appears that the board president is not handling any of this in a professional manner. There are several reliable paint manufacturers that will send out knowledgeable people to write the specifications for you so that bids will then be easy to compare.

If the board president is presenting himself as an expert, then he shouldn't mind answering questions and fully disclosing to the rest of the board members what an honest, qualified, experienced guy he is.

Again, the board needs to rely on professional advice! They should have interviewed several general contractors and decorators. Remember, if you are having these kinds of problems just with the painting, there is still a lot more at stake. Carpet in the fire escapes? Someone should check with the fire marshal before this is even considered.

The entire board can be held liable if this project goes awry, especially if they fail to make the board president participate in fair and competitive bidding. The job description for board members does not say, "be a friend to the president," does it? The board's role is to protect the association and that often means that they cannot just "rubber stamp" everything that the president wants to do. The board should approve each step of the project and thorough documentation should be written in the board meeting minutes.

If any of the board members vote against the president regarding the manner that the project is being handled, they have the right to have their dissenting vote written in the minutes.

WHO SHOULD MAKE INVESTMENT DECISIONS?

Q *Our association's reserve funds total about $200,000. Our board treasurer is doing a good job of investing our money in certificates of deposit and treasury notes.*

Who is responsible for making decisions about investing our money? Should the board treasurer have this responsibility, or the management company, or should we delegate this task to an outside money manager?

A The board of directors has the duty to protect the association's funds. Though the board can delegate the authority to a financial advisor or banker or the management company, the board is ultimately responsible for the decisions regarding investments.

The board should abide by any requirements in the association's legal documents. Many associations have specific guidelines that require placing the funds in relatively risk-free, government-secured investments.

All board members have a fiduciary responsibility to know how and where the association's money is being invested or spent.

Even though you feel that your board treasurer is making good decisions, the funds should never be under one person's control. California law requires two board signatures for withdrawal of reserve funds. Any reserve expenditure or withdrawal of reserve funds should be with the approval of the board of directors noted in the board meeting minutes.

CAN ASSOCIATION CHARGE FOR USE OF POOL?

Q *I live in a 25-unit condominium building that is about 20 years old. The board is considering an increase in the monthly assessment to cover the cost of painting and repairs.*

Our monthly assessment is now $175 per month. I feel that higher assessments could scare off potential buyers. I would like to raise money some other way.

Perhaps we could charge a $3.00 fee for guests who use the pool. We could also charge a yearly maintenance assessment based on the number of occupants per unit. For example, two people would pay $200 and a couple with child would pay $300. Could these methods be used to raise the money for the needed repairs?

A Could it be that you are a single person who never invites guests to use the pool? Sorry, but your creative financing ideas will not fly. Your first suggestion would create work for someone because the pool guest fee would have to be collected from the owners. I doubt that you are going to want to set up a ticket booth at the entrance to the pool. The association does not have a way of billing the guests and the honor system probably would not be very effective. Owners will not be pleased if they have to start paying for their guests when the pool has been a free amenity in the past.

In addition, the pool guest fees would create more work for the tax accountant because the fees would be taxable income. The small amount of revenue is not worth it. The arguments against the fee would far outweigh the arguments in favor of it.

Regarding the yearly maintenance assessment based upon occupancy, I assume that you are suggesting that this would be an extra charge in addition to the monthly assessment. I am certain that the association's declaration does not authorize an extra charge based on occupancy.

The cost of operating the building is shared on the basis of the percentage of ownership (square footage) or is shared equally among the

25 unit owners. Some associations have a more complicated equation that is a combination of the two cost-sharing methods. Each owners' share should be clearly explained in the governing documents of your association and it probably also is included in the deed to your property. Any other method of computing the owners' financial obligation is illegal.

Perhaps you think that you could get the owners to vote to change the declaration. In my opinion, this type of amendment would require 100 percent approval of the owners, and possibly the lenders, since it is an issue that deals with percentage of ownership and each owner's financial obligations.

BOARD INCREASED MONTHLY ASSESSMENT BY 18 PERCENT

Q *Our condominium association's board of directors increased the monthly assessment amount by 18 percent when the fiscal year began on the first of January. We were notified in advance that this increase was going into effect so we tried to stop it.*

My husband and I argued against it because the legal documents of our association state that the owners must approve any assessment increase that is five percent more than the previous year's amount.

The management company representative says that there is a state law that gives the board of directors the authority to increase the assessment amount by as much as twenty percent without the consent of the owners.

We purchased our unit with the understanding that the association is governed by the declaration, bylaws and other legal documents. Is it true that a state law makes our documents invalid?

A Your association manager is correct. California Civil Code, Section 1366, specifically states that it overrides more restrictive limitations that appear in the association's governing documents. However, there are certain requirements imposed on the board.

First, the board must distribute the annual budget between 45 and 60 days prior to the beginning of the fiscal year. If the board fails to distribute the budget to the association members in the proper manner, then they do not have the authority to increase the budget beyond the limits stated in the association's documents. With a properly distributed budget, the board may increase the annual budget by twenty percent and, in addition, may impose a special assessment of five percent or less.

A special assessment of an emergency nature may be approved without limits if expenditures are required by a court order or some type of threat to the safety and health of the owners or others exists.

I can understand your concern when you learned that state law has superseded restrictions on budget increases in your association's legal documents. In my opinion, each owner should note in the margin of the pages in their documents a reference to the state law so that future buyers obtain correct information.

Many other states have laws that are similar to California's, especially those that have adopted the Uniform Condominium Act or the Uniform Common Interest Ownership Act.

BOARD WON'T ACCEPT PARTIAL PAYMENT

Q *The Board of Directors of our homeowner association proposed a special assessment of $2,400 to fund certain substantial and long-delayed maintenance projects. The proposal was voted on by the membership and was approved by a slim majority of 52 percent.*

The payments are to be made in four installments of $600 each. My husband and I were unable to pay the full amount of the first installment so we paid $200 instead, and requested an extension that would allow us to pay the special assessment over a two-year period. Our check was cashed and credited to our account, but a $10 late fee was levied.

The board of directors, through the association's attorney, has informed all the homeowners that liens will be placed on the property of any delinquent owners. Foreclosure proceedings will be instigated if the full $600 is not paid on each established due date. They also informed us that no partial payments will be accepted, even though our $200 check was accepted and cashed.

With the regular monthly assessment of $170, we are unable to pay the additional money. All appeals to the board have been ignored. Do we have any recourse to save us from foreclosure? We would appreciate any advice you can give us.

A It is unfortunate that your association's financial condition required such a large special assessment. It may not be easy to accept; however, you have been living in an association that was obviously under-funded in the past. If you and the rest of the owners had been paying an adequate amount in previous years, this special assessment would not have been necessary.

You and the other members of the association voted to elect board members in the past who did not adopt a realistic budget. Deferred maintenance resulted and now all of you are burdened with a lump sum "wake-up call." A special assessment is the proverbial rude awakening, never the best way to fund your association's maintenance needs. Another negative aspect is that it sends a warning to real estate agents and potential buyers that the association is under-funded and that more special assessments may be required in the future.

I often hear board members bragging, "Our board of directors hasn't increased our monthly assessments in four years," or similar examples of holding down the budget of their associations. I ask, "How have you been able to cut your expenses? What are you neglecting to maintain?" Time marches on and, in general, associations need to increase their maintenance expenditures as the complexes become older and require more preventive maintenance and repairs.

Sometimes board members need to be strongly reminded that they have a responsibility to adopt a budget that will adequately fund realistic operating expenses and reserve funds. That is one of the primary ways to protect every owner's investment and preserve the association's real property and collective assets.

It appears that the association's board of directors has followed proper procedure by obtaining a majority vote of the owners. You cannot contest the collection of the special assessment on the grounds that it was not properly levied. The association's delinquency procedures are legal and these procedures were properly disclosed and distributed to all owners as required by state law.

The association needs the money and you must pay it. The board of directors must take a strong stance on collecting it. How can the association pay its bills if a number of the owners defers payment? The association or its management company accepted your partial payment but they did not waive the late fee. This, too, is proper procedure and I would advise the association's board that they are correct in doing so. Accepting the partial payment does not remove the association's right to levy a late fee, lien the property and eventually foreclose.

My advice is to continue to pay as much as you can while trying to arrange a short-term personal loan or an equity loan from a financial institution. If that is impossible, perhaps a relative can assist you with a loan.

By making partial payments until you can get some additional funds, you will show the association that you are trying to comply. Communicate with the board in writing and tell them how you are trying to resolve the problem. This written communication is very important. It will possibly keep the board of directors from starting foreclosure procedures if they see that you are making an effort to pay.

CHAPTER 7 GOVERNING DOCUMENTS

TWENTY-YEAR-OLD CC&RS PROBABLY NEED UPDATING

Q *I live in a condo development (149 units) in the city of Oceanside, California. Twenty years have gone by and we haven't revised our CC&Rs. They reflect what the developers wanted. Since they are out of the picture, shouldn't our association make a complete revision?*

A committee has been formed to review the CC&Rs and bylaws and make recommendations for revisions. What advice can you provide?

A After twenty years, your documents probably warrant a review and may need revision. If minimal changes are needed, I would urge you not to start over but to simply amend the portions that are outdated.

Consult the California Civil Code, Section 1355 and 1356, which governs amending association documents. There is specific authority granted in Civil Code Section 1355.5 that allows the association to delete references to the developer in the governing documents. As you will read about later, these changes are supposed to be voted on by the membership.

Seek the guidance of your association attorney before you begin and rely upon the attorney for the actual wording of the amendments and the approval process. If member approval, notification and recordation are not done properly, the amendments will likely be invalid.

OWNER HAS CONCERNS ABOUT AMENDING THE DECLARATION

Q *Our condominium management company urged the association to have our declaration of covenants, conditions and restrictions (CC&Rs) updated to be in compliance with the Davis-Stirling Common Interest Development Act. The association members voted not to have the document rewritten.*

Doesn't the Davis-Stirling Act supersede the CC&Rs? If that is the case, I don't understand the need to update our declaration. If we need to update the CC&Rs each time a law is changed, this could be a costly process.

Should we have our declaration updated?

A There are good reasons to have your CC&Rs updated but it is important that the update is handled correctly and that the owners understand all of the reasons and ramifications if certain changes are made.

The state law does not supersede the CC&Rs in every situation. For instance, if the CC&Rs include late charges for unpaid assessments that are less than the Davis-Stirling Act allows, the act clearly states that the association must charge the amount specified in the declaration.

There is a clause in Civil Code 1364 regarding "common area" and "exclusive use common area." This section of the code states that the association's responsibility to maintain, repair and replace these areas is controlled by the CC&Rs if the CC&Rs differ from the responsibilities spelled out in Civil Code Section 1351 and 1364.

For some associations, the incentive to change the CC&Rs would be to eliminate association responsibilities that are in the current document. For instance, repair of balconies, window boxes, garage doors or other exterior components or fixtures may be designated in your current CC&Rs as association responsibility. In older associations, the owners may have been relying on this and paying into reserve funds for several years.

By removing the specific wording in the CC&Rs that makes the association responsible for these components, some associations are moving this financial burden to the individual homeowners. The owners need to weigh carefully the financial impact of this change. In addition, architectural harmony and uniform maintenance standards may be affected if owners are responsible rather than the association.

In some associations, boards have been negligent in budgeting and reserve planning. They have failed to accumulate adequate reserves to fulfill the association's responsibilities. Switching the financial burden to the individual homeowners is a questionable method to keep from having to levy special assessments in order to maintain, repair and replace components that are association responsibility.

In some cases the owners are told that they are required to update their association CC&Rs when, in fact, they may be better off with the current wording. For instance, here is a scenario that is happening with great frequency. Let's say that the owners have contributed to the reserve funds for several years and part of the money was designated as balcony repair and replacement because the balconies are the responsibility of the association. Obviously, the board has an obligation to adopt an adequate budget to take care of this responsibility but they have failed to increase the assessments for many years.

After several years of deferred or minimal maintenance, the balconies are falling apart. Now the association is in a financial crisis, so the board says that they aren't going to maintain the balconies any longer because the state law says that balconies are "exclusive use common areas" that are the responsibility of the individual owners. They cleverly fail to inform the owners that the association's declaration is the controlling document, not the state law in this instance. In this scenario, the board is purposely misinforming the owners in order to cover up prior negligence of maintenance responsibilities and lack of adequate financial planning.

I received a letter from a townhome owner who said that his association's governing documents state the association is responsible for roofs and exterior walls. However, the association had sent out a letter stating, "The California Supreme Court has ruled that responsibility for exterior walls is ambiguous and associations may not be held responsible." The person who wrote that letter for the association is being extremely creative in his or her interpretation of case law.

If the *Lamden v. La Jolla Shores* case is the one being cited as the precedent, that particular case involved the board's authority to determine the type of termite abatement that was being implemented. The court's decision did not remove the association's responsibility to maintain, repair or replace common area when that responsibility is stated in the governing documents.

In summary, if there is specific language in your CC&Rs regarding the association's responsibility for maintenance, repair and replacement of specific components of the property, neither state statutes nor current case law supersedes that requirement.

There are legitimate reasons for updating the CC&Rs and all of the governing documents. Effective January 1, 2000 associations are required to remove any language that may be discriminatory. Even though the discriminatory language is unenforceable, the association must remove the discriminatory clauses in all of the governing documents including the articles of incorporation, the declaration, bylaws and rules. The association should consult a legal firm that focuses its practice on the representation of community associations.

If a complete revision or restatement of the documents is proposed, owners should carefully review what is being changed and for what reasons. The attorneys who are rewriting documents to bring them into compliance with state law are aware that the Davis-Stirling Act is changed in some way nearly every year so provisions for future changes in the law should be included.

NEIGHBOR POSSIBLY LIABLE FOR DAMAGE

Q *On two occasions pipes have burst in our condominium causing flooding in my unit on the first floor. It was necessary to gain access to the unit above mine to fix the pipes. Both times the owner refused access for three days, which delayed the work and caused further damage. What recourse does the association have when this type of emergency occurs?*

A Your association's governing documents should clearly state that in an emergency the association or its agent (manager) is granted "right of entry" in order to perform the necessary repairs. An amendment to your documents may be necessary. Then an uncooperative owner could be held liable for any further damage resulting from the delay. I am aware that some condominiums require that a master key or keys for all units be kept in a safe place in the management office for emergency access in case of fire or other life-threatening emergency.

Regarding recourse against the uncooperative owner in the two cases that you cite, contact your attorney or the board of directors may want to contact the association's attorney.

CAN BOARD ADOPT RULES AND ENFORCE WITH PENALTIES?

Q *Our association has board-established rules, many of which are arbitrary and selectively enforced. Are there any court decisions that give authority to the association or its board of directors when that authority does not appear in the governing documents? Can the board levy fines or monetary penalties to enforce the documents if that authority is not granted in the declaration or bylaws?*

A The board should be fair and consistent with its enforcement policies and those policies must be distributed to all owners. Most associations have CC&Rs or bylaws that give the board of directors the authority to adopt reasonable rules and enforcement procedures.

Civil Code Section 1363 (g) states: "If an association adopts or has adopted a policy imposing any monetary penalty, including any fee, on any association member for violation of the governing documents or rules of the association, including any monetary penalties relating to the activities of a guest or invitee of a member, the board of directors shall adopt and distribute to each member, by personal delivery or first-class mail, a schedule of the monetary penalties that may be assessed for those violations, which shall be in accordance with authorization for member discipline contained in the governing documents." Redistribution of the schedule of penalties must occur only when the board's policies of enforcement are changed.

The *Nahrstedt v. Lakeside Village* case upheld the board's authority to levy reasonable fines for the purpose of enforcing the governing documents. If you feel that your association's board is not abiding by the law or is enforcing rules inconsistently, seek the advice of an attorney.

LIMITED PARTNERSHIP HAS CONTROL OF BOARD

Q *After eight years, the developer of our complex still owns 51 of the 65 units. Three board members are from the developer's limited partnership so that he controls all board action. How can the other fourteen owners amend the CC&Rs to provide for one vote per member rather than one vote per unit?*

A The 14 individual owners comprise only 22% of the total membership. Under the circumstances you will be unable to amend the CC&Rs. It would not be legal to restrict the owner of 78% of the units to only one vote. It looks like you are stuck in an association that will continue to be controlled by the limited partnership that owns the majority of the units. If the board is not acting in the best interest of the entire association, then you may have to initiate legal action in order to make your voice heard. Legal action should be a last resort. You may decide that selling your unit is the preferable solution.

ASSOCIATION BOARD MUST DELETE ANTI-CHILDREN CLAUSES

Q *I am president of our association. I recently received a noise complaint, which cited a two-year-old child as the source of the noise. The complaint also cited a clause in our declaration of covenants, conditions and restrictions (CC&Rs) that prohibits children under the age of 18 from being residents.*

Our CC&Rs were written in 1980. Are we allowed to prohibit children?

A No, your CC&Rs are outdated and unenforceable because there are federal fair housing laws and state laws that prohibit age discrimination. These laws supersede your CC&Rs. Age restrictions can be enforced only in senior housing developments.

The federal laws are very specific so consult a community association attorney regarding deleting the offending language from your governing documents. The penalties for age discrimination can be considerably high.

California Civil Code Section 1352.5 states that the board of directors must remove any discriminatory language (against persons of a particular race, color, religion, gender, familial status, marital status, disability, national origin or ancestry), without a vote of the owners.

If the association is informed of discriminatory language and fails to act within 30 days to delete the language, any person may file an action for injunctive relief and the court may award attorney fees to the prevailing party.

All associations are supposed to attach a cover sheet to any governing documents that are distributed to anyone, including new buyers. The cover sheet must state the following in 14-point boldface type:

"If this document contains any restriction based on race, color, religion, sex, familial status, marital status, disability, national origin, or ancestry, that restriction violates state and federal fair housing laws and is void and may be removed pursuant to Section 12956.1 of the Government Code. Lawful restrictions under state and federal law on the age of occupants in senior housing or housing for older persons shall not be construed as restrictions based on familial status."

BOARD MEMBER MAKES CC&R CHANGES

Q *We currently have an attorney on our association board who is revising our CC&Rs. When I asked why this was being done, he stated that he is updating them according to the recent changes in the state law.*

I believe that our documents (written in 1973) may need updating, but I would also like to know what the changes are and verify that they are legal and proper. The attorney who is making the changes says that the owners will not be voting on this matter since the law mandates that these changes can be made without a vote of the membership. What advice can you give us?

A The only type of change that doesn't require notification of the owners is the removal of discriminatory language. Refer to the previous question and answer regarding age restrictions.

Some other types of new legislation supersede the association documents, in which case, changing your documents would not be mandatory. It is preferable to have the legal documents agree with the law, but that means that each time there is new legislation, the association will be amending the documents if proper wording is not used.

On the other hand, certain phrases such as "unless the association's declaration otherwise provides" appear in several sections of the law. This means that the law does not supersede the association's documents.

Certain wording in your association's CC&Rs regarding the declarant (developer) can be deleted by board action, but the specific changes must be submitted to all of the owners and the matter must be considered at an open meeting of the owners as required in Civil Code Section 1355.5.

The procedure for amending, other than discriminatory or declarant language, is explained in your CC&Rs. If the amendment procedure is not explained, then you should refer to California Civil Code, Sections 1355(b) and 1355.5, where it is spelled out in detail. If the proper procedure is not followed, the amendment is not valid and would not be accepted for recordation by the county.

If your board wants to have the CC&Rs revised, I recommend that you engage another attorney who specializes in community association law to provide further legal advice after your attorney/board member makes his recommendations on changes in the wording.

BOARD NOT ENFORCING LANDSCAPE STANDARDS

Q *In our townhouse complex, each unit has a private landscaped area that has no enclosure so the area is visible to the public. Our association documents state that all landscaping, including private property, must be maintained in "first class condition." Some owners have neglected these areas or have failed to plant proper landscape. The board will only allow the association gardeners to weed them. I have asked the board repeatedly to enforce the documents and establish some sort of minimum landscaping requirements. The board refuses to act. What is the board's responsibility and how should they enforce the documents?*

A The board is obligated to enforce the documents. If a majority of the owners are happy with the current level of maintenance by their neighbors, then the documents should be changed to comply with the wishes of the owners and remove the "first class condition" clause. When the documents stipulate "first class condition" then the board should enforce adequate maintenance.

If the board is allowing the association gardeners to perform work on the private property of the negligent owners, then it is unfair to those owners who are caring for their property responsibly. In fact, it is probably illegal to use association funds to maintain these private areas. It is unfortunate that the board is allowing certain owners to ignore their obligations. Poor maintenance is contagious and in the long run, property values will suffer. Even if the board is motivated to change things, it will be difficult to do so if they have ignored the problem for a lengthy period of time.

The board members may not know how to get themselves out of this problem. Because you are very interested in this, perhaps you could draft some proposed minimum standards and present them to the board, or volunteer to start a landscape committee and enlist other owners. It may be the incentive that the board needs to take action. Good luck!

OWNER WANTS PERMISSION FOR CHRISTMAS LIGHTS

Q *We live in a 29-unit condominium complex. Our association documents state that nothing is to be attached to the common area or the exterior of the homes. Could the board make a temporary exception and allow Christmas lights to be attached to the building with some simple guidelines to be followed by the homeowners?*

A Yes, it is usually within the board's power to make exceptions for good reason. The board members may not want to deal with this matter because of the time it would take to draft a proposed policy. Therefore, I suggest that you speak with the board and volunteer to write up a draft of a new temporary holiday lighting policy that the board can then consider for adoption. You might want to include the type of lighting that is acceptable and the post-holiday date that the lighting must be removed from the home. Your governing documents probably already contain language that makes the owner responsible for any damage that may occur as a result of his or her decorations.

Bear in mind that any form of religious observance offends some people, while others say that this type of lighting has no religious connotation. This issue has resulted in controversy in several associations and municipalities.

BUYER SHOULD EXAMINE ALL GOVERNING DOCUMENTS

Q *We are thinking about selling our house and purchasing a condominium. We would like to see the legal documents including the rules and regulations before we buy but our real estate agent says that we will receive them at the close of escrow. Is there any way that we can review these documents prior to purchasing?*

A Yes, you should not be shy about demanding to see the declaration of covenants, conditions and restrictions (CC&Rs), the bylaws, rules and regulations including architectural guidelines, board meeting minutes, financial statements, annual budget and reserve study. Your real estate agent's response was definitely incorrect. The escrow closing is not the proper time to receive this important information. In California, the escrow officer usually obtains all of the required disclosure documents from the seller or the association's management company. When disclosure documents are requested, the response must occur within ten days.

If you sign a purchase agreement prior to receiving the documents that you request, the contract should include a contingency clause that gives you ten days after receiving the documents to review the information. You have the right to cancel the contract if the legal documents and related disclosure information do not meet with your approval.

BOARD SHOULD HIRE LAWYER TO UPDATE DOCUMENTS

Q *Our condominium association's documents need to be updated. We do not want to pay attorney's fees. Where can we purchase a model set of CC&Rs that correlates with the current laws? Would we be able to obtain another association's documents that we could adapt for our association?*

A Don't attempt to take the cheap solution. I am not aware of any "boiler plate" documents that you could copy and I certainly would not recommend that approach. The amendment process is one that requires the expertise and guidance of an attorney who is knowledgeable about community association law. You can read in previous answers in this chapter about federal and state laws that supersede the CC&Rs.

Associations that wish to amend their documents should first determine that it would be possible to get the approval of the required percentage of owners. After the board has determined the changes that are necessary, then consult with your attorney who will prepare the wording of the proposed changes and assist with the notification of members for the vote. If the amendment is approved, it must be recorded with the county recorder and then distributed to all of the owners.

I do not understand why association boards are unwilling to consult with attorneys when the need arises. The board is not expected to know all the answers. They should be willing to pay for expert help, which will often prevent costly problems arising at a later date. By relying on professionals, the board is reducing its liability.

If you are concerned about the cost, discuss this during the initial consultation and see if the attorney will do the work for a flat fee or at least give you a "not-to-exceed" estimate of the total cost. Request a monthly billing statement so that you can keep track of the cost as the work progresses.

RULES AND REGULATIONS SHOULD BE REASONABLE

Q *Our condominium complex has just been painted white and the board has issued a new set of rules and regulations, one of which specifies that all patio furniture must be white. However, this rule applies only to half the members whose private patios are visible from the street. Owners whose patios face the back (which includes all members of the board) have no color restriction for their patio furniture. How frivolous can a board be when making new rules?*

A Your board probably thinks that this new rule is perfectly fine, but in your opinion their action is frivolous.

Rules should always serve the common good and benefit the association. Here is what I recommend to boards members who are contemplating adopting rules. The following questions should be considered:

1. Is the proposed rule legal?
2. Does the board have the authority to adopt rules?
3. Is the proposed rule needed?
4. Is it reasonable and fair?
5. Is it enforceable?

If all these questions can be answered affirmatively, then after deciding on the clear and concise wording of the rule, the board should notify the owners of the proposed rule change. Then owners should be given an opportunity to give feedback to the board before the rule is adopted. The board should seek this input in order to remove opposition and build consensus. Many associations hold a hearing before adopting any new rule or policy.

If the board votes to adopt the rule, abide by the legal documents' specifications for the notification of owners and residents. Be sure to provide ample notice and clearly state when the rule takes effect.

Did your board make prudent decisions when adopting the "white patio furniture rule"? Did the owners have an opportunity to give their opinion about this rule? If not, the board may have a tough time enforcing it. If you cannot abide by this rule, request an open hearing where you and the rest of the unhappy owners can talk with the board about it. You may find that they are willing to consider changing the new rule.

A more detailed answer about changing or amending rules can be found in subsequent pages of this chapter.

UNIT OWNER WANTS TO COMBINE TWO UNITS

Q *A unit owner in our condominium is considering purchasing the adjacent unit and expanding to make his unit larger. Our association's legal documents state that there are a certain number of units in the condominium. Is changing the number of owners subject to the consent of all the owners?*

If the two units were combined into one, would the owner have to pay assessments for one unit or two?

A Before the association addresses the issues that you have raised, I recommend that the board require the owner to hire an architect and a structural engineer to determine whether fire barriers and load-bearing walls will be affected. The owner who wants to combine the units should pay the cost of these consultants.

The percentage of ownership and the assessment amount are legal issues that should be referred to the association's attorney. I am aware of several condominiums where an owner has combined units. In most instances, the owner simply owns two units, pays assessments for two units and votes accordingly. Changing the percentage of ownership for the whole complex would require a vote of the entire membership to amend the association's legal documents. In my opinion, this would be unnecessary and unfair to the other owners.

BOARD PRESIDENT SAYS HE HASN'T READ THE CC&RS

Q *I recently attended my association's board meeting and questioned a board decision. When I quoted certain parts of the declaration of covenants, conditions and restrictions (CC&Rs), the president's response was, "I've never read them, so I take other people's word for what the documents say." Doesn't the president have an obligation to read these governing documents?*

A Of course, every owner should read the CC&Rs and all of the governing documents. Certainly, the board has an obligation to read, understand, comply with and enforce them. If they cannot understand them, then they should consult an attorney. I assume that the president thought the response was a clever one. I personally feel that if board members haven't read the CC&Rs, then they should not be serving on the board of directors.

WHAT DOES THE WORD "NOTWITHSTANDING" MEAN?

Q *This question is in reference to California Civil Code 1366. The law states: "Notwithstanding more restrictive limitations placed on the board by the governing documents, the board of directors may not impose a regular assessment that is more than 20 percent greater than the regular assessment for the association's preceding fiscal year . . . " The wording is very possibly not as explicit as many people believe. Perhaps the word "notwithstanding" awkwardly serves the purpose of acknowledging the right of the CC&Rs to be more restrictive.*

A Sorry, it does just the opposite. The word "notwithstanding" means "in spite of" as used in the following sentence. Notwithstanding the threatening clouds, Robert packed a picnic lunch and started off into the woods.

Many people are confused by this word but those who drafted the law understand its meaning and purpose. Though I am not an attorney, I am familiar with many who represent community associations as the primary focus of their law practice. I have spoken with several of them about the reasons that the legislature felt that the law was needed.

It is my understanding that during the early 1980s when the inflation rate was high, associations that had five percent or even ten percent assessment increase limitations in their documents were unable to keep up with the cost of living increases. At the same time, associations were faced with huge increases in their insurance costs.

There were many associations that were unable to adequately fund their reserves for future repair and replacement because of these limitations. Some associations were faced with financial instability or even bankruptcy because their budgets were so inadequate that there was no way to catch up and establish a realistic financial plan.

In my opinion, the law is a good one because it was adopted so that associations would be able to increase assessments as needed, with a cap of 20 percent per year. Exceptions can be made for emergencies such as special assessments and emergency assessments, which are defined in Civil Code Section 1366.

SHOULD ASSESSMENTS BE BASED ON SIZE OF THE UNIT?

Q *We own a one-bedroom unit in a 72-unit condominium complex. There are 23 one-bedroom units and the rest are two-bedroom units. All owners pay the same assessment amount. The owners of the one-bedroom units feel that their monthly assessments should be less than the assessments paid by the two-bedroom owners.*

Our board of directors is going to increase the monthly assessments soon. We would like to know if the assessments could be increased for two-bedroom units so that two-bedroom unit owners are paying more than the one-bedroom unit owners. What would be involved in making the change?

A Since you are writing about an association located in California, that tells me that your initial budget and the association's legal documents were reviewed for compliance with specific requirements of the Department of Real Estate. The Department of Real Estate usually requires that assessment amounts be set up in correlation with the units' square footage if the variance is more than ten to fifteen percent. Voting power would also be weighted according to the square footage of the units.

In my opinion, it would be nearly impossible to change to prorated assessment amounts. Trying to do so will not bring you any popularity awards from your neighbors since a majority of the owners have two-bedroom units.

You should read your legal documents, especially the declaration of covenants, conditions and restrictions (CC&Rs), in order to find out if equal assessments are mandated. Attorneys tell me that any change in the established assessment provisions and voting percentage would require an affirmative vote of the full membership to amend the CC&Rs. Your CC&Rs might require that mortgage lenders also vote on the matter.

PARKED MOTORHOME IS A VIOLATION OF CC&RS

Q *I live in a homeowners association that consists of 150 single-family homes on one- to two-acre lots. Last year, I purchased a motor home and I have been parking it on my property for the last few weeks.*

The association president called and told me that motor homes are not allowed in the neighborhood. I had no intention of moving the motor home, but before I could get any further information, I received a very official letter. The notice stated that I would be fined if I didn't remove the motor home or attend a hearing to answer the accusation that I am violating the declaration of covenants, conditions and restrictions (CC&Rs).

I don't have a copy of the CC&Rs but information that was enclosed with the letter says that motor homes, boats and trailers can't be parked or stored on the lots or in the driveways. Why wasn't I informed about this when I purchased my property? Does the association have the right to tell me what I can do? Do they have the right to fine an owner for violation of the CC&Rs?

A The declaration of covenants, conditions and restrictions (CC&Rs) should have been included in the disclosure information that you received prior to the closing of escrow when you purchased your home. The CC&Rs contain certain restrictions that owners are required to obey. By purchasing the property, you automatically agreed to abide by these restrictions. The association, through the board of directors, does have the right to enforce the legal documents. You need to read these to find out what obligations you have as an owner and what authority the association has regarding fines or other forms of enforcement.

Remember that the board of directors is an elected volunteer board. They should be glad to respond to your questions. If you need to obtain a copy of the CC&Rs, you should talk with the board president. If the association has a property management company, the manager should be able to provide a copy for you. You may be required to pay a photocopying charge.

I hope that after researching the association's authority you will resolve this problem by removing your motor home. The other owners have the right to expect that everyone will abide by the governing documents. The board has the authority and the obligation to carry out the enforcement process in a fair and business-like manner.

IS AN APPOINTED BOARD MEMBER "OFFICIAL?"

Q *The board of directors of my 54-unit association asked me to serve on the board. I was appointed to fill out the remaining term of a board member who resigned after just three months of his two-year term had elapsed.*

Our annual meeting and election of directors is coming up soon. Some people have suggested that I should resign and submit my name in nomination in order to be "duly elected."

What is your opinion?

A As long as the appointment was official and the board action was noted in the meeting minutes, I don't feel that being appointed is any less official than being elected by the membership. Unless the association's legal documents require that you run for election, don't allow others to discourage you from serving out the full term of your appointment. The association's bylaws usually state the procedure for filling board vacancies. The association should comply with the bylaws. If the bylaws say that you may do so, then continue to serve for the full term of the person that you were appointed to replace.

Since you mention that the board members are elected to two-year terms, I assume that your association has board member terms that are staggered so that not all board members' terms end at the same time. In that case, you should complete the entire term so that the provision for staggered terms is not altered.

PARALEGAL GIVES ASSOCIATION SOME BAD ADVICE

Q *Our homeowners association was recently contacted by a paralegal from a neighborhood legal and bookkeeping service. He told the board that the association's declaration of covenants, conditions and restrictions (CC&Rs) must be updated every year. He also stated that the association must have an audit done every year.*

The proposal for the cost of the legal work seems very reasonable, but we are wondering whether the advice regarding updating the CC&Rs is correct. What do you advise?

A You have been given incorrect and misleading information. I recommend that the association obtain the services of an attorney who specializes in community association law and stays informed about all of the laws and new legislation that govern common interest real estate developments and nonprofit mutual benefit associations.

Associations do not have to update their CC&Rs every year. Amendments to the CC&Rs should be done only when necessary. Amending the CC&Rs usually requires the approval of either two-thirds or three-fourths of the voting membership. Amendments must be recorded with the county recorder upon certification of the prescribed number of affirmative votes from the full membership.

All condominiums, homeowners associations, planned developments, cooperatives and "own your own" community apartment projects must distribute a financial report each year. Associations with annual income greater than $75,000 must have a financial review prepared by a state-licensed accountant. A full-scale audit is not required annually unless the association's legal documents specifically state that an audit is mandatory. Incorporated associations that have annual income between $10,000 and $75,000 must prepare an annual financial report according to Corporations Code Section 8321.

Please refer your questions to an attorney who can review your association's legal documents and advise you. As you can see, this particular neighborhood paralegal service is not your best resource.

HOW TO CHANGE THE RULES AND REGULATIONS

Q *I live in a condominium. Please provide some information on the legal way to change or add to the association's rules and regulations.*

A Changing or adding to the association's rules and regulations is usually the responsibility of the board of directors, but changes to the declaration or bylaws require a vote of the entire membership. Your association's declaration of covenants, conditions & restrictions (CC&Rs) will state whether your board has the authority to adopt rules and regulations.

Before your association considers making any changes to any of the governing documents, you should understand that a California association that has pet prohibitions cannot change any of its declaration of covenants, conditions and restrictions (CC&Rs), bylaws or rules and regulations without losing its ability to enforce pet prohibitions. Therefore, if you currently have a CC&R restriction that prohibits dogs, and your association decides it wants to change any portion of the governing documents and negate your "no dogs" provision, it might be prudent to also add to your rules some reasonable controls about dogs, their acceptable behavior and size, where they are allowed in the complex and the association's enforcement procedures. The board of directors should consult the association's attorney to discuss the need of allowing all owners to vote on a change that will do away with the pet restrictions in the CC&Rs.

When considering a rule change, the board should also think about the following issues:

1. Does the board have the authority to adopt new rules or make changes in the existing ones? Usually, the answer is "Yes." However, in rare instances I have seen CC&Rs that state that rule changes must be put to a vote of the full membership.
2. Is the proposed rule needed? If it isn't really needed, don't waste the association's time. Rules and regulations are necessary, but if your rules booklet is an inch thick, it's time to weed out a few rules and get back to the basics. Adopt rules that are for the good of the community and its owners.
3. Is the proposed rule legal? Is it in conformance with the other legal documents of the association? Does it contain anything that might be in conflict with state or federal law? You will need to obtain the advice of an attorney who is well-versed in community association law.
4. Is it reasonable and fair? Don't adopt a rule that is so restrictive that makes owners feel that they are living in a police state. What do your rules say about your community association? Remember that the word reasonable is often debated. A rule that is reasonable to one person is often unreasonable to another.
5. Is the proposed rule enforceable? If so, how will it be enforced? Will penalties be used to enforce the rule? Will a penalty result from the first offense, second, or third?

After considering all of the issues and deciding that a rule is needed, the next step is the actual wording of the rule. It should be as clear and concise as possible. The wording should be positive rather than negative in its tone. If your rules say "Don't...don't...don't" owners will feel that they are being treated like children.

Before going further, have the association's attorney review the proposed rule and the wording, primarily to see if it is legal and enforceable. He or she may also advise the board about procedures to follow in distributing the rule to the owners. I recommend that the proposed rule be sent to all of the owners prior to the actual adoption of the rule. Invite the owners to attend a board meeting to give feedback. Giving the owners this opportunity to be heard should build their trust and promote consensus.

It's best to find out at this stage if a majority of the owners are in favor of the rule. If a majority of the owners are against it, enforcement may be difficult.

After the rule is adopted, determine how it will be distributed to all the owners and tenants. Yes, tenants need to be included, too. It's the owner's responsibility to inform the tenant, but if the association does so, the little bit of extra effort is worth it. Decide whether the association should reprint the rules booklet. Usually replacing an entire page of the rulebook is preferable to just sending a written notice that the rule has been adopted. The revision date and the date that the rule becomes effective can be shown in the margin next to the new rule. If a monetary penalty will be levied against the violators, that should be stated and the schedule of monetary penalties must be distributed if it is changed from a previous distribution.

An attorney should review your association's rules and regulations when changes are made. It is wise to have the rules reviewed by an ad hoc committee or the board of directors at least every two years. If a rule seems unnecessary, unfair or unenforceable, take a board vote to repeal it.

HOMEOWNERS CAN VOTE TO CHANGE CC&RS

Q *Although homeowners can vote to change their declaration of covenants, conditions and restrictions (CC&Rs), some CC&Rs have amendment provisions that require lender approval. Obtaining a favorable vote from a majority of the mortgage lenders of all of the units seems like a formidable task. This, coupled with the requirement of a super majority vote of the homeowners, may make the amendment process impossible.*

An association could spend a great deal of money on legal expenses and still be unsuccessful in passing the CC&R amendment. Why should an association pay for costly revisions if there is a possibility the amendments will not be approved by the owners?

A As years pass, most associations need to amend their declarations. This is not easy to do but it is rarely impossible. Most associations have CC&Rs that require at least 66 percent approval of the owners. In many associations, the percentage of affirmative votes required is 75 percent.

If a CC&R amendment fails to get the approval of the owners, it is usually not because the attorney failed. It could be that the amendment is not a popular or prudent change, so it fails because it lacks merit. In some cases, an attorney might draft an amendment that the board requests even though the attorney advises against presenting the amendment to the owners. Another reason for amendment failure could be lack of communication with the owners or lack of an organized campaign to obtain the needed votes.

Attorneys who are experienced in the amendment process are knowledgeable about the methods of obtaining approval from a super-majority of the owners and the mortgage lenders. Drafting the language for the amendment is only a portion of the assistance that the attorney can provide. The attorney will guide you from the planning stage all the way to the recordation of the amendment after the owners have adopted it.

The successful adoption of a CC&R amendment depends upon teamwork and communication. The board should communicate with the owners so that they will understand the need for the amendment. Meetings for all of the owners should be scheduled prior to the vote so that the owners will have an opportunity to ask questions and become informed about the amendment process and the reasons that the amendment is good for the association.

California Civil Code Section 1356 explains the procedure to follow in order to reduce the percentage requirement. If the amendment is approved by more than 50 percent but less than the super-majority required in your CC&Rs, you can petition the superior court in your county to accept the lower percentage.

Contact an attorney who specializes in providing legal services to community associations.

WASHER AND DRYER IN UNIT BANNED BY DOCUMENTS

Q *I own a condominium unit that is listed for sale. The prospective buyer wants to install a washer and dryer; however, an amendment to the declaration prohibits washers and dryers within the units. The amendment was made because the association did not want owners putting in additional drain connections in the common area plumbing.*

I suggested that the washer and dryer could be installed next to the kitchen sink and the washer drain hose could drain into the sink. The dryer could be vented to the balcony. My unit is on the second floor and there is only one unit above mine.

Can the association prohibit owners from draining the wastewater from the washer into the kitchen sink and installing a dryer vent on the balcony?

A Yes, the association can prevent you from doing anything that is prohibited in the CC&Rs and its amendments. Legally, the governing documents are presumed to be reasonable and enforceable. Your ownership of the unit does not give you or your buyer the right to do whatever you please within the unit. When there are valid reasons for restrictions within the unit, the association has the right to exercise control. When you own property in a community association, you give up some self-determination that you would have in a single-family dwelling.

I can think of several reasons why you should be prevented from carrying out your plan. If the original plumbing was not designed to handle wastewater from washers, then washers should not be allowed.

Washers send a sudden high volume of water down the drain lines and the buildup of suds combined with the volume of water can cause backup in the lines. A washer installed in the manner that you suggest could result in damage to your unit and the one below you. Your kitchen drain line is probably not designed for the high volume of water.

Even if you could get the permits from the city building department to install the dryer vent, the association has the right to prohibit it because you would be venting the dryer through the exterior wall of the building. The exterior wall is common area and the association has the right to control or prevent any changes to common area.

If the association turns down your request, do not defy their decision. Besides the enforcement power of the association, any unit owner who disagrees with your washer and dryer installation could file legal action to uphold the CC&Rs. As the old saying goes, you could be in hot water . . . for a number of reasons.

ASSOCIATION IS CONTROLLED BY BUILDER

Q *The board of directors is controlled by the builder/developer of our association because only 40 percent of the homes have been sold. The board meetings are held during the day when most owners cannot attend. Letters to the board are not answered. They do not want to hear about any problems that might affect their sales activity.*

Some of the homeowners recently circulated a petition. The board president sent a letter demanding that the signature gathering must stop. He stated that the petition was a violation of the provision in the declaration of covenants, conditions and restrictions (CC&Rs) that prevents "interference with the quiet enjoyment of the occupants."

What are the rights of the homeowners?

A Even though the developer still owns a majority, the owners have a right to attend meetings and the board must give the owners an opportunity to speak at the meeting. You are entitled to receive copies of the minutes or a summary of the minutes or a draft copy within 30 days of a meeting.

In my opinion, circulating a petition is within your rights. Most associations have bylaws that provide for petitioning for the purpose of calling a special meeting of the membership, for instance.

If the board prevents you from going door-to-door, you can submit a written request for the name and address list of all the owners so that you can do a mailing to all of the owners. The board must comply with your request, offer an alternative method of communicating with the other owners, or state the reason that they are denying your request. According to California Corporations Code, the board must respond within 10 days.

Don't do anything radical like staging a demonstration outside the sales office. You should not attempt to interfere with the developer's ability to sell the homes. After all, as more homes are sold, the homeowners will soon have representation on the board of directors.

WHO IS RESPONSIBLE FOR ENFORCING RULES?

Q *I own a townhouse in a 24-unit complex. I am dissatisfied with the way the association is being operated. We have parking rules that no one is enforcing. The board member that I spoke with says that she doesn't want to make her neighbors mad. She doesn't think the violations are a problem. Who is responsible?*

A The board of directors is responsible for upholding the governing documents of the association, including the rules and regulations. Parking rules should be reasonable and enforceable and then the association board should enforce them fairly and consistently. If the illegal parkers are not causing a problem, then the board should eliminate or change the rules rather than just ignoring the violators.

You are not specific about the type of parking violations you are seeing. If certain owners are habitually parking in a guest parking space, this can be very frustrating to the other owners. The board's failure to enforce parking rules can quickly create anger and resentment. Obviously, fire lanes must be kept clear and towing of violators' cars is allowed if state laws regarding towing of cars, specifically Vehicle Code Section 22658.2, are followed.

OWNER COMPLAINS THAT BIKES NOT ALLOWED ON BALCONIES

Q *Our association's rules and regulations state that only patio furniture and plants are allowed on the balconies. I have been keeping my bicycle on the balcony and I have been cited for violations. I feel that since it is my balcony, I can put anything I want on it. Is this rule legal?*

A The way you have stated the rule, it seems that even people are prohibited from using the balcony, though I presume that is not the case.

The association can prohibit the storage of articles on balconies. I have seen a balcony where the owner had so many boxes and lumber stored on the balcony that rainwater could not drain out. Then the owner complained to the association that water came over the balcony doorframe and damaged his expensive carpet. He expected the association or its insurance carrier to pay for the damage. In this situation, the owner had created a water damage risk and a fire risk.

On another occasion, a roll of carpet was stored on a balcony. Rats had climbed up the vines on the exterior wall and were living in the rolled carpet. Some owners clutter their balconies with so much junk that the neighbors are embarrassed to look at it.

These examples are just some of the reasons that associations adopt rules that state what can and cannot be stored on the balconies. Rules are usually adopted for reasonable purposes that we fail to see if we disagree with the rule.

Perhaps your neighbors have complained about your bicycle being on your balcony or being brought through the common halls. Have your dirty wheels caused damage to the carpet?

Communicate with your association board to see if a better storage place is available. Boards can make exceptions to the rules if there is justification. If the balcony is the only safe place for your bicycle and if your neighbors who can see it are agreeable, the board may consider granting you the right to store your bicycle on your balcony.

CAN BOARD MEMBER BE HELD LIABLE FOR BICYCLE ACCIDENT?

Q *I live in a planned unit development in which several units share a common driveway. Some of the children ride their bikes in the driveways even though the association's rules prohibit it. As a member of the board of directors, could I be held personally liable for the injury or death of a child in this circumstance where the child was violating a rule?*

A Since I am not an attorney, I urge you to seek the advice of your association's legal counsel regarding California Civil Code, Section 1365.7, which specifically addresses this type of liability. The law states that "any person who suffers bodily injury, including, but not limited to, emotional distress, or wrongful death, shall not recover damages from a volunteer officer or volunteer director if all of the following criteria are met:

1. The act or omission was performed within the scope of the officer's or director's association duties.
2. The act or omission was performed in good faith.
3. The act or omission was not willful, wanton, or grossly negligent.
4. The association maintained and had in effect, at the time the act or omission occurred and at the time a claim is made, one or more policies of insurance, which shall include coverage (a) general liability of the association and (b) individual liability of officers and directors of the association for negligent acts or omissions in that capacity, provided that both types of coverage are in the following minimum amount: a) at least five hundred thousand dollars ($500,000) if the common interest development consists of 100 or fewer separate interests [units], or b) at least one million dollars ($1,000,000) if the common interest development consists of more than 100 separate interests."

There are further stipulations in the law that clarify who is and isn't protected under the law based upon their volunteer status and whether the officer or director lives in the complex or owns more than two units. You can research this at your local library's law reference section.

DOOR WREATHS ARE NOT ALLOWED

Q *I live in a townhome in a community association of 88 homes. We have rules prohibiting door wreaths but the board of directors is not enforcing the rules.*

Our new management company recently sent out violation notices to cite the door decorations. The board rescinded the notices and said that they would only enforce the rules if there were complaints.

Shouldn't the board take a proactive approach to enforcing rules that they know are being violated?

A Yes, the board has a duty to enforce the rules, but the board also has the authority to determine how the enforcement will be handled. Obviously, the management company representative was under the impression that the company had a duty to cite the violations. Some associations require that owners file a written complaint regarding rule infractions. If your association procedures require a complaint, then you can file a complaint.

If the board does not intend to enforce a particular rule, then the rule should be removed from the Rules and Regulations. Some boards are very lax about enforcement. They don't want to be the "police" because they fear that their neighbors will dislike them. Then, they offend the owners who prefer strict enforcement of the rules. As long as the rule exists, the owners have a right to expect that it will be enforced.

In my opinion, prohibiting door wreaths is overly restrictive.

BOARD MUST RESPOND TO REQUEST FOR CC&RS

Q *When I served as treasurer of our community association, I often completed questionnaires from Realtors and lenders who requested information about the association prior to the sale or refinancing of a unit.*

The new board of directors has decided that answering such forms is beyond the scope of its duties and refuses to perform this task. Does the board have the right to refuse to respond?

A The seller of a separate interest (unit or lot) in a community association has the obligation to provide certain documents and information to the buyer as stated in Civil Code Section 1368. However, if the association receives a written request for this information, the association must respond within 10 days or the association may be subject to liability for damages and a civil penalty of $500.

The information that must be supplied includes all governing documents: the Articles of Incorporation (if the association is incorporated), the Declaration of Covenants, Conditions and Restrictions (CC&Rs), Bylaws, and Rules and Regulations. If the seller has unresolved violations of the governing documents, a copy of the written notice is to be included with the disclosure documents.

If there are any age or occupancy restrictions in the governing documents, a statement must be attached that clarifies the enforceability of the age restrictions to the extent permitted by the Unruh Civil Rights Act, which can be found in Civil Code Sections 51 through 53. The Federal Fair Housing Amendments Act also nullifies age restrictions unless your association qualifies as senior housing.

The association must provide a copy of the annual budget and the most recent annual financial report if the annual income for your association is greater than $75,000. An incorporated association must provide a financial report if the annual income is greater than $10,000. The amount of the regular assessment, any special assessment or emergency assessment that is currently due on the unit, including late charges and other fees that could result in a lien must be disclosed. If this information is not provided correctly, the association may not be able to collect delinquent assessments and fees owed to the association.

In addition, any changes in the assessment amount or special assessment that has been approved by the association board or membership for future implementation must be disclosed.

If your association is aware of any construction defects, consult the attorney who is advising the association regarding the matter and include the information that is required by Civil Code 1375.

As you can see, there are many disclosure documents that the association is required to provide upon request. The association is allowed to charge a reasonable fee for providing the documents and also for transfer fees when ownership changes. If you have a management company, the management contract will usually specify its fee for this service.

In order to protect your association from liability, the board should consult an attorney who specializes in the representation of community associations and discuss all of the ramifications of providing disclosure information for lenders and buyers.

CAN BOARD DISREGARD OWNERS' DUTY AS STATED IN CC&RS?

Q *The board of directors of our homeowner association recently engaged the landscape contractor to plant and maintain the area behind several homes. These areas are designated as "restricted common area/homeowner maintained" in the declaration of covenants, conditions and restrictions (CC&Rs). The board felt that they were acting properly because weeds had become a fire hazard in the unmaintained areas.*

I notified the board in writing that they did not have the authority to change the maintenance responsibility that is stated in the CC&Rs. I feel that a more appropriate action would be fining the owners who have failed to maintain their restricted common area and calling the fire department to enforce weed abatement.

The manager told me that the board might advocate a CC&R amendment and conduct a homeowner vote. The board is displeased that I questioned their actions and it appears this may escalate to a legal battle.

What can you suggest?

A The CC&Rs may have a provision that allows the association to bill the owners for the cost of maintaining the areas that the owners failed to maintain. Perhaps that is the board's intent. Make sure that you are fully informed about the entire matter before you criticize the board's action.

The board has an obligation to uphold the CC&Rs. Perhaps they have notified the owners who were in violation of the maintenance requirements of the CC&Rs, conducted hearings to encourage the owners' cooperation, and levied monetary penalties against those owners who failed to correct the problem. If the CC&Rs allow the association to pay for correcting the problem and then billing the owners, that would be the ultimate course of action.

Relying on the fire department to enforce weed abatement is a good example of using outside sources and governmental services to assist the association. I agree with your suggestion.

It is not appropriate for the board to use association funds to pay for expenses that are beyond the scope of the association's responsibility as stated in the governing documents. If they treat you as the enemy because you disagree with their decision, they are just compounding their error. The board should understand that it is healthy to have "watchdogs" in their midst. Boards sometimes make improper decisions. They should be willing to revisit a decision and change it if they determine that their decision was wrong.

It is ridiculous if this disagreement is allowed to cause legal expense for you or the association. Perhaps the board needs legal advice to learn about the scope of their authority and alternative enforcement methods. That is appropriate use of funds.

If the board fails to correct their alleged bad decision, you can request mediation to resolve the matter.

CHAPTER 8 ARCHITECTURAL CONTROLS

ASSOCIATION WILL NOT ACT ON COMPLAINT

Q *My wife and I live in a homeowner association. Our neighbor has constructed a block wall between our properties. The footing of the wall is exposed on my side of the wall and there is no reasonable way for me to elevate my yard. The wall stands partially on my property and was built on top of my sprinklers. It has altered the ground drainage resulting in flooding of my property when his lawn sprinklers are turned on. Lighting that shines in my window has been installed on a pilaster at the end of the wall.*

We learned that our neighbor obtained construction approval from the association after the wall was already constructed. There are several CC&R violations involved but our association has not responded to our complaint other than to indicate that this is a "civil matter." How do we make the association enforce the CC&Rs?

A First, if you haven't already done so, file a written complaint with your association board of directors and request a written response. In their written response, the board of directors should tell you why they are declining action. For instance, there may be a time limit imposed on the board by the association's legal documents. It may be too late for the board to act.

Second, you should check with your city or county to see if building permits for this type of construction are required and whether permits were obtained. You may get some assistance from local government if the work was done without the proper permits. Alteration of original grading that affects drainage is a serious matter. This should be brought to the attention of the inspection department.

Finally, you must determine the answer to this question. Is the aggravation and expense of your corrective repairs to the lawn and sprinkler system worth the additional time and expense of pursuing this with an attorney? Remember that you may be living in this association next to this neighbor for some time to come. If you wish to file a lawsuit, your attorney can advise whether to sue the association, the offending neighbor, or both.

TWO OWNERS MADE CHANGES IN UNITS' EXTERIORS

Q *Two owners in my association have remodeled the exterior structure of their units so that they differ from the others in the complex. The board president was out of town when the work was done. The remodeling is completed now and I'd like to know what my rights are regarding rectifying this matter. Where do I begin?*

A Is the work that was done contrary to the declaration (CC&Rs)? Have you checked to see if the remodeling owners obtained approval from the association? Did they obtain permits from the city planning and/or building departments? If the work was done without proper authorization and building permits, you and the association may have recourse. Even though the president was out of town, you should have notified the other board members of your concern as soon as you noticed the construction in progress. If you haven't already done so, you should start by sending written notification to your board, stating that you object to the changes that were made. The board should then determine if they are going to take any action.

California law provides that, unless your association's CC&Rs state otherwise, the covenants can be enforced by legal action of any owner, the association, or both. Consult your attorney if you wish to pursue this further after you have obtained all the facts.

HISTORICAL STATUS OF BUILDING INHIBITS CHANGES IN UNIT

Q *I recently purchased a condominium unit in a delightfully quaint building that is designated as a historical site. Prior to my purchasing the unit, I was not informed that I would not be allowed to make some interior changes in the unit. I was unaware that there are complicated requirements established by the city's Historical Preservation Commission and federal guidelines for historic buildings.*

The condominium association's architectural committee requires a lengthy application process and they have already informed me that some of my proposed remodeling will not be allowed. Do I have any recourse?

A You may have recourse against the real estate agent and the seller if they failed to adhere to disclosure requirements.

It is usually very difficult for a property to attain historical status. This designation enhances the building's appeal, contributes to an increase in value and enhances the association's ability to obtain grants for restoration projects. Architectural guidelines that might seem unreasonable in any other building are quite appropriate in the type of building that you describe.

The architectural committee has a duty to protect the delightfully quaint building that attracted your interest. In addition to protection of authenticity, the architectural committee is probably overseeing particular problems with electricity and other "modern conveniences." Though it may be tedious, you must work within the restrictions of the governing documents and the guidelines of the architectural committee.

It is unfortunate that you did not review this information prior to your purchase.

OWNER SAYS ASSOCIATION NEEDS MORE STORAGE SPACE

Q *Our association has open carports that are assigned and deeded to the owners of the units. The units have balconies. The carports and balconies are "exclusive use common areas" and the association does not allow items to be stored in or on these exclusive use common areas.*

The complex is in a beach resort area, right across the street from a well-used bike path. Many residents use bicycles to commute. The only bike storage area provided by the association is a bike rack that is in plain view of passers-by. Owners have been fined for storing their bikes and other items in the carports or on their balconies. When the bikes have been moved to the bike racks, they have been stolen.

The units are less than 1,000 square feet so there is limited storage within the units and no storage space on the exterior. Residents do not have any safe place to store baby strollers, surfboards, bikes and other bulky items.

Is the association liable for the stolen items since the association has not provided a safe storage place? What methods have other associations used to handle storage?

A It seems that one can never have too much storage space. No matter how much space we have, we are able to accumulate more than enough stuff to fill it. If the association wasn't controlling the tendency to store items, the stealing would probably be worse and the whole complex would look awful.

You and the other owners must have known prior to your purchase that there is very little storage space in the units. I am not an attorney or an insurance expert so I won't guess about liability, but I can offer suggestions for dealing with the lack of storage. The board of directors should study the alternatives and consult an attorney before taking any action.

Some associations allow owners to build locked storage closets in their garage spaces. The carports are exclusive use common areas and visible, so the association probably has the right to determine the type of construction for the safety and appearance of the storage closets. Many associations allow a wall- and/or ceiling-mounted storage closet that projects into the space above the car's hood. Since you have open carports instead of garages, even padlocked storage may not provide enough protection.

Perhaps the association could build a small storage facility for bikes and other items. Controlling access could be a problem and it would probably be filled up quickly. The liability is still a concern.

Another suggestion: The board can find out how much it will cost to enclose the carports and then, if it seems feasible, get competitive bids from contractors and present the idea to the rest of the owners. If the association members vote to build this capital improvement, a special assessment could be levied to fund the project. This would provide a safe storage area for each owner and also increase the value of your units.

OWNER MAY APPEAL COMMITTEE'S RULING ON ROOM ADDITION

Q *My wife and I own a two-story townhouse. Because of an illness, my wife is unable to use the stairs. Since our unit is on the end of a row of townhouses, we would like to build a one-room addition on the ground floor. I submitted our idea to the architectural committee. Even though I explained our reason for the addition and assured them that it would conform to the existing structure's appearance, our request was denied.*

My wife and I are both disabled and we do not want to have to sell our unit and move. What can we do?

A Do you own the land where the room would be built? If you are asking to build your addition on common area that belongs to the association, then neither the architectural committee nor the board of directors would have the authority to grant your request.

Find out why your request was denied. If you feel that you want to overturn the decision, ask to appear at the next meeting of the board of directors to see if you can appeal the architectural committee's ruling.

The association has the authority and the responsibility to control architectural changes. In some associations, the legal documents set up the architectural committee to operate separately from the board of directors. In such a situation, the board may not have the authority to overrule an architectural committee's decision. If both the architectural committee and the board of directors turn you down, then you will have to decide whether you want to challenge their decision in court. An attorney can advise you as to the strength of your case.

NEIGHBOR INSTALLS OBJECTIONABLE WINDOW

Q *In our townhouse association, our board of directors has allowed reasonable exterior wall changes requested by the owners. Recently my neighbor installed a window in a portion of the wall that overlooks the roof of my unit. I had registered an objection based on the notion that a common wall should be left intact without any openings even though there is empty space above the roof on my side. The board approved the new window. Has our board exceeded their powers in this case?*

A It may have been improper to approve the window installation if the wall is a firewall. Common walls between units are often fire barriers. Check with the local fire marshal. You could also check with the city's building department to see if a permit was obtained. Since the window overlooks the roof of your townhouse, I assume that your privacy is not affected, so if the fire marshal and the city can find no fault with the installation, you will have to live with it. Of course, if the window is improperly installed, a leak could result which would be a concern for both you and your neighbor.

BOARD REFUSES TO TRIM TREES IN COMMON AREA

Q *We bought our condominium in 1983. It is located on the third floor overlooking flower gardens and tennis courts. The trees outside our unit are not pruned often enough. Every unit overlooks the gardens and all we can see is trees. My requests to the board to trim the trees have fallen on deaf ears and even my two-year stint as a board member did not change the board's attitude. What can we do to correct this situation?*

A As you have learned, it is sometimes impossible for an individual to have an impact on a board of directors. Is the board ignoring their responsibility to maintain the area properly or is this just your opinion?

The landscaping is a major asset that should be maintained properly. Perhaps the board is listening to another faction that likes the trees and the privacy that they provide. Trees are a major asset that must be protected and cared for properly. Most trees need to be trimmed regularly and checked for disease by a qualified arborist.

I would suggest that you try to enlist the help of some other owners who feel as you do. Then, as a group, you may be able to convince the board to hire an arborist or a landscape architect that would make recommendations as to the proper maintenance of the landscaping. You may feel so strongly about this that you are personally willing to pay for an expert's opinion.

This may be one of those situations that you will always be at odds with the board. Remember, when you live in a community association, you cannot expect that every decision the board makes will be agreeable to you. The board must also realize that it is impossible to please all of the owners. If you cannot live with that realization and abide by the majority rule, then you may not be suited to the condominium lifestyle. Sometimes people realize this only after living in a condo for a few years.

BELATED NOTICE FROM ASSOCIATION REGARDING PAINT JOB

Q *I live in an association in Palm Springs where owners are responsible for their own roofs. We put a new roof on our condo about a year and a half ago. Recently the association notified me that I must have the flashing painted. My husband passed away six months ago and he took care of things of this nature. I contacted the roofer but he said that he didn't do painting work. I finally had to hire a painter at a cost of $80. Why did they wait so long to notify me about this? What recourse do I have?*

A Shame on the association for waiting so long! You have obviously had some difficulty dealing with this situation and I can understand your frustration.

The association probably has the right to control improvements and ensure that work is properly completed even though you are paying for the work. Therefore, I think that you did the right thing when you responded to the association's letter and paid for the painting work. You can now rest assured that the work is completed and the flashing is protected from the wind and rain.

The association's board or architectural control committee should have acted promptly if the work did not meet with their approval. Perhaps they contacted your husband about this prior to his death. Remember, these people are volunteers and, since you live in a resort area, board meetings may be difficult to schedule. If I were you I wouldn't be too hard on the board. Their job is not an easy one.

Since you asked about recourse, though, you can check your association's CC&Rs, the architectural guidelines, and the rules and regulations. Some associations have documents that state that if an improvement has been completed for a specific period of time without notification of a violation from the association, then the improvement is acceptable and the association cannot take action at a later date.

OWNER DOESN'T LIKE PEACH-COLOR EXTERIOR

Q *I live in a 294-unit homeowners association. I have recently learned that a two-person committee has recommended that the exterior of our buildings be painted in varying shades of peach.*

The board is reviewing bids and will be going ahead with the work very soon. I am extremely upset by the way this decision was made. There has been no communication to the owners about the change in paint color. Our CC&Rs state that the board has the responsibility to paint and maintain exteriors of all the buildings. I don't believe they have the right to change the color of the complex. I would not have purchased here if the original paint color had been peach. What can I do?

A You indicate that you feel that most of the owners are not aware that this change is going to take place. Though the decision is one that the board has the authority to make, this is an issue that should be disclosed to the owners. If the board does not communicate, the board may be faced with a lot of irate owners when the job is in progress or upon completion. Then they may wish that they had communicated more effectively with the owners.

Your letter also indicates that you have done just about everything you can do to let the board know how you feel. Unfortunately, you cannot control every action that your board approves. You may have to accept this as being one of those situations. There is also the possibility that when the work is completed, you will like the new appearance. Color schemes come and go for aesthetic reasons and this update may appeal to most of the other owners.

UNIFORMITY SOUGHT WITH DRAPERY COLOR RULES

Q *My friend and I both own units in townhouse complexes that have rules specifying the "acceptable" colors for window coverings; however, no one can tell us the reason for such a rule. Both complexes have assorted buildings set at angles in heavily landscaped grounds. It takes a real effort to see even three windows at a time and there is no regulation as to the type of covering or whether they have to be open or closed. We understand that this rule is a common one in many associations.*

What is the purpose and how far can an association go in regulating what homeowners do inside their units?

A The purpose of the rule is uniformity. It may seem unnecessary in complexes like the two that you have cited, but try to imagine what it would look like if residents had purple, red and chartreuse drapes in their windows. Most associations require that at least the lining of the window treatments is white so that the appearance is consistent from the outside of the buildings.

Since the configuration of your buildings makes the rule seem unnecessary, consider this possibility. Attorneys who draft governing documents and management companies that provide sample sets of rules often have this rule as part of the standard "boiler plate" rules and regulations. This could be the reason that they are included in your rules.

The association usually does not control much within the unit except the outward appearance and factors that pertain to health and safety. As you stated, your rules do not require that the drapes be closed or open. That would be rather restrictive; however, I know of several condominiums with central heating/cooling systems that have passed rules during the 1970s that required that window coverings be closed for energy conservation. Closed drapes keep out the hot sun in summer and conserve heat in winter so there is a valid reason for conservation when everyone in the condominium shares the skyrocketing cost of heating and cooling. Consider yourself lucky that the rules aren't that restrictive in your complex.

OWNER OFFERS TO DESIGN AND COORDINATE REMODELING

Q *Our condominium lobby and corridors are beginning to look dated. The association has enough funds to redecorate. However, the board of directors is very concerned about how we should proceed.*

One of the owners is an interior designer. She has volunteered to design and supervise the redecorating work. She insists that she can get the work done at minimum expense for the labor and materials. She will not charge us for her work, but the materials will be ordered through her firm, so she will probably get some profit from the project.

The board's main concern is that the owners will not like the new decor. However, they feel since she is offering to do the work at minimum cost, they should accept her offer. Can you give us some guidance?

A The board of directors should take steps to ensure that they stay in control of this project. If they allow one person to make major decisions about the new decor and the cost without the input of the owners, it is very likely that it will result in controversy. The board should take steps to prevent the appearance of conflict of interest.

First, I would suggest that a letter and survey be sent to all the owners to inform them that this project is in the planning stages. The survey could ask for their ideas and for volunteers to serve on the redecorating committee.

Second, the board of directors and the redecorating committee should visit the interior designer's office and see some of her work. Visit other similar projects that she has completed and talk with former clients.

Some associations pay for two or three designers to put together a selection of plans within the association's budget and then the committee makes recommendations to the board of directors for the final decision. Some associations allow the owners to vote on the plans after the committee or the board has narrowed the choice to two or three decorating plans.

With this kind of project, it is impossible to please everyone, especially if you are changing from a distinctive decor to something completely different. Therefore, I recommend open meetings to get acquainted with the designer, discuss the plans and the cost. Later on, all the owners and residents need to be told how the work will be accomplished so that they know when and how the redecorating may inconvenience them.

Involving a lot of decision-makers is not really expedient; however, I believe that the owners will all be happier with the results if they are kept informed about the decisions, cost and redecorating schedule.

TREES ARE OBSTRUCTING OWNER'S OCEAN VIEW

Q *Four months ago I bought a condominium with a beautiful view of the beach. Some trees are growing and obstructing my view. I have sent three letters to the board president but nothing has been done. What can I do?*

A You do not state whether the trees are on a neighbor's property or on association property. If it is a neighbor's property, perhaps the board has no power to act or perhaps they have requested that the trees be trimmed and the neighbor has not taken any action.

Let's assume that the trees are on association property. Depending upon the size of the trees and the expense involved, the board may have decided to trim the trees annually. Also, the species of the tree may determine the best time of year to trim for the good of the trees. In other words, there may be a valid reason for the board's delay, but they do owe you a timely response. I suggest that you attend the next board meeting to inquire whether the board intends to take any action on your request, or write to the board again and request a written response by a specific date. Since the trees are not on your own property, you should not resort to trimming the trees yourself.

Bear in mind that unless your view is protected in the CC&Rs, with specifications as to the acceptable height of the trees, the association may not have a legal obligation to trim them. There may be other owners who value these trees and do not want them trimmed. In that case the board will have to try to work out a compromise.

CAN BOARD PROHIBIT ALL REAL ESTATE SIGNS?

Q *The board of directors at my condominium association has decided to prohibit all real estate signs advertising a unit for sale or lease. Our CC&Rs allow real estate signs that are reasonable and proper. Though a recent newsletter says that a vote of the membership was taken, the CC&Rs have not been amended to prohibit the signs.*

Can the board make this decision based on a vote taken at an annual meeting?

A No, the board cannot enforce this restriction against signs that are placed for advertising the sale or lease of the property. Even if the CC&Rs had been amended based upon the vote of the membership, the restriction is still not enforceable because a California law supersedes it. Civil Code 713 gives the property owner the right to display a sign of reasonable dimensions, as determined by the city or county where the property is located. The sign may be placed on the owner's property or on the property of another owner, with that owner's permission, in plain view of the public.

The sign may include the location or direction to the property and the owner's or the agent's name, address and telephone number. Since you own a percentage of the common area, your association may allow you to place a sign on the common area in public view, though some associations only allow a sign to be placed in the window of the unit.

OWNER REMOVED FIXTURE AND INSTALLED FLOODLIGHTS

Q *I live in a large condominium complex. All of the units have the same type of exterior light fixture next to the front door. One of our neighbors has violated the condominium association's declaration of covenants, conditions and restrictions (CC&Rs) by removing the exterior light fixture and installing an ugly dual-socket flood lamp. The hole still remains in the stucco where the original fixture used to be. Both the hole and the floodlights are visible from the common area walkway.*

I spoke to the board of directors about the violation. I did not find out whether my neighbor has been fined or even cited for the violation. The board seemed to think that if they charged a fine for the violation, the owner could just pay the fine each month and continue to ignore the problem. Isn't there a more effective way of requiring action from the offending owner?

How should the association's board be enforcing the governing documents?

A I believe that your board of directors is misunderstanding the effectiveness of monetary penalties when enforcing architectural restrictions and rules. Paying the monthly fine does not give the owner the right to continue with his unacceptable behavior. The board should notify the errant owner that he or she must attend a hearing regarding the alleged violation. The owner should be required to restore the wall by patching it, if possible. If it is a common area wall, the association can make repairs and bill the owner for the cost. If the board determines that a floodlight is needed for security reasons, they have the authority to allow it to remain. The board should enforce the association documents in a prudent manner.

If the board fails to take any action, you have the right to serve the association with a request for mediation.

ASSOCIATION SHOULD HIRE AND RELY ON EXPERTS

Q *There are numerous hairline cracks in the exterior stucco of the structures owned by our homeowners association. Since our reserves will not cover the $46,000 needed for painting, our board has determined that we should take out a long-term loan. The owners will have to pay $25 per month for the next ten years.*

I am not convinced that the repairs are needed immediately. I would prefer increasing the assessments to build up the reserve funds so that we will be able to afford this kind of expense when it becomes necessary.

Will the extra $25 added onto our monthly assessment make the units more difficult to sell? Will the rental population increase if owners are unable to sell their units?

A I doubt if the long-term loan will make the units sell any slower than a general increase in assessments. It appears that your association has to increase its reserve fund in addition to accumulating money for the cost of the painting work.

Perhaps the rental population will increase if owners cannot sell. That will be the case also if the association has an inadequate reserve fund. Buyers and mortgage lenders are becoming very wary of associations that do not have adequate money set aside for future repairs and replacement of the major components of the property.

From the tone of your letter, it appears that you are convinced that this costly project is not needed at the present time. Do you feel that the board failed to conduct proper research prior to making the decision?

I would recommend that the board rely on the advice of an independent consultant. By hiring a consultant that is not involved in bidding on the work, they should be able to obtain impartial advice. Perhaps the cracks are simply cosmetic. If the problem is more than cosmetic, then waterproofing and texture coating may be preferable to just painting. Since the association is not wealthy, it may be difficult to convince the board to pay a consultant, but wiping out the reserve fund or saddling the association with a ten-year loan is not the type of action that the board should approve without thorough study and planning.

LACK OF COMMUNICATION UPSETS OWNERS

Q *Our association's board of directors makes important decisions without notifying the owners. For instance, a portion of the complex was scheduled for painting. However, notification to the owners was not sent and there was no discussion of color or other considerations. Two people on the board approved the color and the homeowners were amazed that they were not notified prior to the work being done.*

Then, another phase of the project was scheduled for painting and again, the owners were not notified. Three board members approved an entirely different color from that used in the previous phase.

What recourse do we have?

A Most of the authority for making the association's business decisions is given to the board of directors. The association members should elect board members who will be responsive to the owners' desire to be informed about the board's decisions.

In my opinion, even though the board may have the authority to make a decision of this type, they should be communicating these decisions to the owners so that the owners' surprise and resentment does not create a problem.

Communication is extremely important. Boards need the support of the owners and good communication builds consensus for changes that the board is contemplating.

On the other hand, if the board allowed all of the owners to actively participate in every decision of this type, the association's work would be less than efficient.

Selection of paint color is always one of those decisions that generate complaints because owners' color preferences will vary greatly and it is impossible to please everyone. Perhaps the board decided not to notify the owners because they didn't want the owners' input.

Now that the work is completed, repainting would add unnecessary expense. I suggest that you, and other owners who feel strongly about the color, should volunteer to give your input to the board of directors prior to any additional painting work being done. Perhaps the board will appoint you to a committee that would make recommendations for future projects of this type.

COMMON AREAS ARE SHABBY AND OUTDATED

Q *I am looking for a condominium unit to purchase. I found a unit that I like very much but the common areas seem to be a bit shabby. The lobby furniture and paint colors are 1970s vintage and the carpet in the halls needs replacing. An acquaintance of mine lives in the complex so I asked a few questions about reserve funds and when the association will be redecorating the lobby and halls. I was told that there were no plans and a vote to increase the assessments was recently voted down.*

My real estate agent says that I should buy the unit if I like it and not worry about the rest of the building. He suggested that I could get elected to the board of directors if I felt strongly about upgrading the common areas.

What advice can you give me?

A Don't marry someone thinking that you can change your mate's faults after you are married. The same advice applies to associations. It is very hard to change the status quo. Even if you were elected to the board, if the majority has a different opinion, you will be powerless.

As for your real estate agent's advice, the common areas do affect the value of your property and, perhaps more important, your happiness. Imagine yourself living there and seeing the shabbiness every day. I think you would regret your purchase. Keep looking and keep asking questions of the owners in the buildings where you are interested in purchasing.

If you can see deferred maintenance, be wary of the *unseen* problems.

OWNER NEEDS APPROVAL FOR ARCHITECTURAL CHANGES

Q *One of the owners in our homeowner association wrote to all of the other owners telling them about proposed remodeling of his home that would include architectural modifications. These modifications require board approval, not the approval of the owners. Isn't the owner's action inappropriate?*

A In my opinion, any owner has the right to communicate with the other owners about association issues. The owner may have felt that his informing all of the owners might engender support for his proposed changes.

Though your letter indicates that the board may feel that the owner's course of action was inappropriate, the owner could be unaware of the proper procedure for obtaining approval of architectural changes. Now the board must communicate with the owner informing him that architectural changes require the approval of the board of directors and that remodeling work must not begin until proper authorization is given. Even if this information can be found in the association's governing documents, the board should not assume that the owner has read it or that he will comply with it.

Periodically, association boards and/or their management companies should send out information about the architectural restrictions contained in the governing documents and the procedures for applying for approval of architectural changes. Be proactive. Don't wait until after someone builds a purple gazebo to communicate with all of the owners.

DOES BOARD HAVE THE AUTHORITY TO CHANGE FENCE?

Q *Our condominium complex, built in 1973, consists of over 200 units. There is a six-foot wrought iron fence with brick columns around the perimeter with two electric gates for vehicles. The fence needs to be replaced. Since replacement would cost $15,000, the board wants to remove the perimeter fence and install smaller fences at the gaps between the buildings. This would leave the front units exposed to vandalism.*

Some of the owners feel that the board does not have the authority to change the architectural design of the complex. The declaration of covenants, conditions and restrictions (CC&Rs) states, "The Board shall have the duty and power to maintain and otherwise manage all of the common areas and all of its facilities..."

Does the board have the authority to change the fence?

A The association is responsible for the common areas and the CC&Rs state that the board has the duty to maintain the common areas. In my opinion, changing the fencing and eliminating some of the exterior fence would be a substantial change in appearance and it would eliminate access control.

Attorneys might differ in their opinions regarding the board's authority to alter the fence based upon the entire CC&Rs rather than one clause. However, I believe the board should not alter the location of the fence. They should consult the association's attorney and insurance agent regarding the board's authority and the association's potential exposure to risks and liabilities.

The board has the duty to maintain the fence. It is inappropriate for the board to neglect maintenance and then alter the architectural design and access control when replacement is needed. Perhaps the fence was well maintained but over a period of time, the fence has deteriorated to the point that replacement is necessary. The association should have gradually accumulated the money in the reserve funds to pay for the new fence. The board is responsible for long-term financial planning and budgeting based on a reserve study.

Now, instead of using reserve funds or perhaps because there are no reserve funds, the board wants to reduce the cost. Replacing the existing fence amounts to about $75 per unit. If the association does not have enough funds in the reserves, the board could vote for a special assessment from the owners to pay for the replacement of the existing fence. In my opinion, the money saved from changing the fence is not worth the additional exposure to vandalism and other risks.

NEW OWNER FINDS SCREEN DOOR IS NOT IN CONFORMANCE

Q *Soon after we took possession and moved into our condominium unit, we received a notice from the association's architectural committee that our front screen door was not in conformance with the architectural guidelines. The previous owner installed the screen door. It was gold anodized aluminum with a peacock grill. The association only approves bronze doors with no grillwork.*

This was a pre-existing violation known to the previous owners. We feel that the association should bear the $250 cost of replacing the screen door since no one notified us of the architectural violation.

What advice can you give us?

A Prior to your closing escrow, you should have received a form called the Real Estate Transfer Disclosure Statement. The seller has an obligation to disclose any alterations or repairs that are not in conformance and "any notices of abatement or citations against the property."

Effective January 1, 2001 the association's authorized representative (board member or manager) does have a duty to disclose such violations prior to the sale. If the association cited the violation and sent a notice of disciplinary action to the previous owner, a copy of the notice or a summary of the violation should have been included in the disclosure information.

If you had known about the architectural violation prior to the closing, would you have required that the seller pay for the new screen door? If so, small claims court is an option for you.

When I purchased a home in an association a few years ago, I asked for verification from the association that there were no architectural violations and that all improvements (pool, patio cover and brick hardscape) were approved by the association. Sometimes buyers just don't know the right questions to ask. I'm sure that is the purpose of the law that requires the disclosure of violations.

If the correction of the violation amounted to only $250, perhaps you should consider yourself lucky. My advice would be to pay for the door, forget about it and don't let this minor disappointment deter you from enjoying your new home and your new neighborhood.

OWNERS' PATIO COVERS MUST ALL BE WHITE

Q *Our association has given the owners permission to build wood patio covers at our own expense. The only paint color that the association will allow on the patio covers is white.*

I would prefer to have a natural wood finish but the association will not approve anything other than white paint for the exterior because the patio cover is visible from the street.

Since I am paying for this improvement myself, can the association dictate the color?

A Yes, many associations have very strict control over any exterior improvements even if the owner is paying for the architectural change. Architectural controls vary from one association to the next. The requirements usually promote uniformity, quality standards and aesthetic factors that might affect the overall appeal of the neighborhood.

You can learn about the specifics of your association's architectural control by reading the governing documents of the association. The declaration of covenants, conditions and restrictions (CC&Rs) will state the association's authority to adopt and enforce architectural guidelines.

CHAPTER 9 MEETINGS

PREPARATION IS KEY TO A SUCCESSFUL ANNUAL MEETING

Q *The annual meeting for our 200-unit homeowner association is often a time when the board of directors receives a lot of criticism from the owners. Last year, the board president was disorganized and became angry when the owners expressed their frustration. The atmosphere was ruined and the board president was not re-elected, primarily because the owners felt that he showed poor leadership.*

Since I am now the board president, I want to be prepared for the next annual meeting so that it runs smoothly and efficiently. What advice can you give to me so that we can get a quorum and have a pleasant business meeting?

A As you have witnessed, an annual meeting can be a frustrating experience for not only the person conducting the meeting, but also for those who are just the attendees.

An efficient annual meeting will encourage people to participate in the future. Some owners only see the association in operation at the annual election meeting. Preparation is the key to having an efficient business meeting and a worry-free election.

Advance planning is important but you must also review the requirements in the association's legal documents to be sure that you are complying with all aspects of the meeting procedures.

About three months prior to the date of the annual meeting, read both the association's declaration of covenants, conditions and restrictions (CC&Rs) and the bylaws to find out about board member term limits, proper notice, voting percentages, quorum requirements and nominating committee requirements.

At the board meeting three months prior to the annual meeting, discuss with your board members the agenda items, especially those that require advance planning such as proposed CC&R amendments or bylaw changes.

The most important agenda item is the election of the board of directors. The annual budget is a hot topic at many annual meetings when, in fact, it is not usually an action item for the members.

Consult the association's attorney to ensure that your election procedures comply with the California Corporations Code Sections 7510 through 7517 and 7520 through 7527, as well as the association's governing documents.

Discuss Internal Revenue Service requirements regarding excess income with the attorney or the association's certified public accountant. Since it is a nonprofit corporation, your community association membership must determine how to allocate any excess income that exists at the end of the fiscal year. This should be an agenda item for the annual meeting. Most associations vote to use any excess funds to lower the assessments for the ensuing year.

The board should discuss appointing a nominating committee and if they choose to do so, make sure that it is set up in accordance with the CC&Rs and bylaws.

If the association does not have sufficient space to have an on-site meeting, choose a location and appoint someone to make the arrangements for room rental and any special needs such as the rental of chairs, podium, microphone and other equipment.

Before confirming the meeting date, determine if the association's attorney is available to attend, if needed. Legal questions often arise during the election and the attorney should be well-versed in handling any unforeseen occurrence or controversy.

Two months prior to the meeting, the board should review the first draft of the contents of the mailing to the owners, including:

1. the official notice of meeting,
2. the agenda for the meeting,
3. the proxy form, which must give the owner the option of designating the proxy for quorum purposes only, voting for specific people or actions that the voter designates, or voting as the proxy holder wishes to vote,
4. cover letter with pertinent information about the location with directions and parking information, the importance of the owners' participation and how and where the proxy is to be returned.

The proxy should include the names of any individuals who have been nominated at the time that the notice is mailed.

If the association documents provide for suspension of voting rights of owners who are delinquent in paying their assessments, the board should send proper written notification to the delinquent owners giving them an opportunity to appear at a hearing prior to the meeting. One month prior to the meeting, or as directed in the bylaws, the meeting information should be mailed to all the owners. Some associations include a return envelope with prepaid postage to encourage the return of the proxy.

The board should organize a proxy gathering campaign if good attendance seems doubtful. Most association bylaws require 50 or 51 percent attendance for a quorum.

The secretary should see that copies of last year's annual meeting minutes are available to bring to the meeting so that the members can approve the minutes.

Two to three weeks prior to the meeting, the president should designate the officers and committee chairmen who will present reports at the meeting, decide on potential inspectors of election to oversee the voter registration, verify proxies and tally the votes. The board may decide to plan some type of recognition or awards for the volunteers who have served on the board or committees. The board should decide on refreshments, if desired, or appoint a committee to take care of refreshments.

One week prior to the meeting, confirm any special arrangements for the meeting room, remind board members about their proxy gathering duties, and put together the meeting materials, which may include:

1. oath of the inspector(s) of election stating that they will oversee the voting procedure with fairness and diligence,
2. a certificate or affidavit that the secretary will sign regarding the number of persons voting and the number of proxies held,
3. an official tally sheet for counting the ballots,
4. the ballots,
5. a copy of the governing documents to have at the meeting for reference,
6. sign-in sheets to register the voters and proxies, some extra pens, nametags,
7. copies of the agenda and last year's minutes,
8. other handouts pertaining to agenda items,
9. awards, if desired.

If your association uses voting percentages, you must prepare ballots with the proper voting percentage on each individual ballot. The owner's name and/or unit number can be stapled to the ballot and then removed by the voter before the ballot is turned in. This will provide a method for secret ballots.

Owners do not enjoy waiting in a registration line to pick up their ballots. Since your association has many members, the sign-in procedures must be well organized. A helpful crew of volunteers will keep the line moving. Refreshments can be served during the sign-in process so that those who arrive early will chat and mingle until all members are signed in and a quorum has been verified.

This advance planning and organization will help to make your annual meeting a better experience for everyone. Remember to check the requirements in the legal documents as you go through the planning stages since some of my advice may conflict with specifics in your documents.

Failure to adhere to the legal documents could result in a contested election. If you have questions about the interpretation of the documents, contact an attorney who specializes in community association law. A property management company that specializes in the management of community associations will be able to assist you if you need advice about the content of the meeting notice, the agenda or the effective methods of registering the proxies and voters.

ONLY INCUMBENTS WERE NOMINATED FOR ELECTION

Q *Our homeowner association recently held its annual meeting. Prior to the meeting the president sent out a notice encouraging members to submit their names to the nominating committee. Another member and I submitted our names but when the ballots were mailed out, our names were not listed. Only the two incumbents were named on the ballots. The president said we could be nominated at the meeting but we did not receive enough votes to be elected. The people named on the mailed ballots obviously had an advantage.*

The election was not an election, but rather an appointment of the incumbent directors, and although legal, it was not in the best interest of the homeowners.

A Read your association's bylaws to see how the nominating process is supposed to work. Some bylaws give the nominating committee a lot of power to determine the outcome of the election. There are good reasons for having a nominating committee. For instance, a nominating committee can weed out the potential nominees who are delinquent in paying their assessments or those who are running for self-interest. If there are troublemakers who want to run, their divisive strategies can be very detrimental to the association.

I usually advise boards and management companies to get as many names as possible on the list of nominees. However, there are times when it is better to use a nominating committee and limit the number of nominees.

After you realized that your name was not on the election proxy, you could have campaigned by sending a notice to all of the owners about your candidacy. The association is obligated to give you the list of addresses or send a mailing for you at your expense so that you and others in the association can participate in the democratic process.

I hope that you will give the elected board your full support. Next year, if you get elected, you will find that serving on the board is not an easy task. There are often other members who are quick to criticize, yet slow to take responsibility when there is work to be done or tough decisions to be made.

BALLOT RECOUNT SHAKES UP THE BOARD

Q *Our association's annual meeting took place last month. The manager announced that a sufficient number of proxies had been received to constitute a quorum. There were two board positions open. Three owners who were present at the meeting were nominated. Ballots were distributed with an incumbent director's name already printed on the ballot.*

The president appointed a committee of one to count the ballots. Two new directors were elected to the board.

A few weeks later, the defeated former director insisted on a recount of the proxies and ballots. It is alleged that there were sufficient proxies to establish a quorum but several proxies were only to be counted for that purpose and not to be used for voting. The votes were recounted and the defeated director was found to have enough votes to be elected.

Is this action by the board legal? If not, what is our recourse?

A I assume your question means that the board has reviewed the recount and has accepted the director who was previously defeated. Did the board seek legal advice before they reversed the decision of the inspector of election? They may have felt it was their duty to correct the vote count or their attorney may have advised them to do so.

Corporations Code specifies that one (1) or three (3) inspectors of election are to oversee the election process. The law states that inspectors must "perform their duties impartially, in good faith, to the best of their ability and as expeditiously as possible" and that "any report or certificate made by the inspectors of election is *prima facie* evidence of the facts stated therein."

An attorney can provide legal advice about your course of action. You have nine months to file an action to challenge an election, appointment or removal of a director.

DOES PROXY FORM COMPLY WITH THE LAW?

Q *There are more than 100 units in our condominium association. Prior to the annual meeting, the management company sends out a proxy form that includes an option for the owner to check the proxy "to be used for quorum purposes only."*

The corporate proxies that I have seen do not have this wording. I maintain that, absent the naming of an appointed proxy holder, the proxy is invalid. I believe that a quorum is only satisfied by the presence of the appropriate percentage of voters and proxy holders appointed by owners who are unable to attend.

At the annual meeting, the proxies marked "for quorum purposes only" are counted to establish the fifty percent needed to conduct the meeting.

Please share your opinion of this method of obtaining a quorum. Is this correct?

A Based on the information provided in your letter and review of California Corporations Code Section 7514, I believe that the association and the management company are providing the correct type of proxy and they are counting the proxies properly.

Since your association has more than 100 units, the owners should also be given the opportunity to indicate their vote on any issues, including the election of directors that will be voted on at the meeting. This proxy form is called a "directed proxy" and the proxy holder that the owner appoints must vote according to the directed proxy. For that reason, many associations use the directed proxy as the ballot to ensure that the owner's wishes are respected. The owners who use a directed proxy give up their right to a secret ballot, but they are able to vote as they would if they attended the meeting.

California Corporations Code Section 7514 specifically addresses proxies and written ballots. The law reads:

"Any form of proxy or written ballot distributed to 10 or more members of a corporation with 100 or more members shall afford an opportunity on the proxy or form of written ballot to specify a choice between approval and disapproval of each matter or group of related matters intended, at the time the written ballot or proxy is distributed, to be acted upon at the meeting for which the proxy is solicited or by such written ballot, and shall provide, subject to reasonable specified conditions, that where the person solicited specifies a choice with respect to any such matter, the vote shall be cast in accordance therewith.

"In any election of directors, any form of proxy or written ballot in which the directors to be voted upon are named therein as candidates and which is marked by a member "withhold" or otherwise marked in a manner indicating that the authority to vote for the election of directors is withheld shall not be voted either for or against the election of a director.

"Failure to comply with this section shall not invalidate any corporate action taken, but may be the basis for challenging any proxy at a meeting or written ballot and the superior court may compel compliance therewith at the suit of any member."

An attorney who is familiar with this law probably prepared the proxy form for the association and I see no reason to criticize it. Consult your own attorney if you feel that you need legal advice on this matter or other association procedures.

BOARD CANDIDATE LIST KEPT SECRET UNTIL MEETING

Q *Our association's annual election meeting took place recently. Prior to the election I telephoned the management company twice to ask for the names of the board candidates; however, the list of candidates was not available until the night of the meeting.*

At that time I asked why the list (six candidates for five positions) was not sent prior to the meeting so that those who were unable to attend could vote by absentee ballot. The answer that I received was that "for this type of election, absentee ballots are illegal in the State of California." The property manager stated that if members wanted to know for whom they were voting, they had to come to the meeting.

It's difficult for me to believe that each member is entitled to vote but is not entitled to know for whom he or she is voting. Please explain.

A You are probably describing a "directed proxy" rather than an absentee ballot. Most attorneys recommend using a proxy form that allows the member to show which candidate is to receive his or her vote, which is a "directed proxy." Therefore, the names of the candidates should appear on the meeting notice and the proxy form.

Most proxy forms give the voter three choices: 1) the proxy can be used only for quorum purposes, 2) the proxy can be used to vote in the manner that the proxy holder, either a board member or other person that the voter designates, sees fit, or 3) the proxy can be used to vote in the manner that the voter indicates on the proxy form (a directed proxy).

The manager should have provided the names of those who were on the list of nominees when you requested them. You and all the other owners have a right to this information. It would have been helpful to you, especially if you were considering nominating someone or running for the board yourself.

California Corporations Code Section 7511(a) requires that the "notice of any meeting at which directors are to be elected shall include the names of all those who are nominees at the time the notice is given to members." Therefore, when the Association sends out its annual meeting notice and proxy form, if anyone has announced his/her candidacy, then his/her name should be on both the notice and proxy that is sent to the members. Additional candidates may also be nominated from the floor at the annual meeting, which is the normal election process.

Some association boards cleverly skirt this law by sending out the notice and proxy before the members are given an opportunity to submit their names for nomination. It is important to review the association's bylaws to see if there are nominating procedures that the board of directors is ignoring.

If an owner decides to challenge an election because his or her name was not placed on the proxy form, the court might find that the election was valid in spite of the failure to include the name. However, the court could also determine that the name was omitted intentionally and a new election might be required.

PROPER PROCEDURE TO CHALLENGE VOTE COUNT

Q *What is the proper procedure to follow in challenging the results of votes cast in a board election or a board recall? Should a demand for a recount be stated immediately upon the announcement of the result of the vote? Who would have the duty to recount the votes? Could the challenger ask to participate in the recount? Would the same procedure apply when challenging the results of a 70 percent affirmative vote for document changes?*

A If you question the announced result of any vote, you should speak up immediately and state your request for a recount. The president or person conducting the meeting should avoid the appearance of a conflict of interest, especially if his or her name is on the ballot for the election. Additional people could be appointed to review the tally sheets that were prepared by the Inspectors of Election. It would probably be acceptable for the challenger to assist or observe.

Janet L. S. Powers is an attorney specializing in community association law, with the law firm of Fiore, Racobs and Powers located in Irvine, Coachella Valley and Riverside, California. Powers writes that the legal authority to challenge elections appears in Section 7614 of the California Corporations Code. That section states that in advance of an election meeting, the board may appoint inspectors of election to oversee the voting.

Powers states, "If inspectors of an election are not appointed or if any person who is appointed fails to appear, then the chairman of the meeting may, and on the request of a member shall, appoint inspectors of election at the meeting. The number of inspectors must be either one or three. If the inspectors are appointed at the meeting on the request of a member, then the majority of members present either in person or by proxy will determine whether one or three inspectors are to be appointed."

The inspectors of election are responsible for verifying the number of memberships, the voting power of each, the number represented at the meeting, the existence of a quorum, and the authenticity of the proxies. They are responsible for the fairness of the election, the balloting process and the accuracy of the vote tabulation.

The member who wishes to challenge the results of an election should so state to the inspector of the election and request a recount at that time. Powers writes, "If the inspectors are confident that the count has been properly tallied, they could deny the member's request. However, since the inspectors are charged with acting in a fiduciary capacity and must sign a certificate evidencing the results of the election, it is hard to imagine that a truly fair inspector of election would not agree to the demand of a member and order a recount."

If the member is still convinced that the election results are inaccurate, the member can file a court action within nine months of the election. In the absence of fraud, any election, appointment or removal of a director is presumed to be valid if no action is filed within the nine-month period.

Attorney Timothy G. Dallinger whose law firm is located in Sherman Oaks, California, cites Section 7616 of the California Corporations Code. "Section 7616 provides that any member or person who had the right to vote in an election may file an action in the Superior Court to determine the validity of any election or appointment of any director of any corporation. The court is obligated to hold a hearing within five days in order to determine the propriety of an election.... including voting rights and all relevant issues.

"In answer to the writer's question, though a public statement at the election may help to resolve a challenge without the need for litigation, no such statement is required in the Corporations Code as a prerequisite to the filing of a court action."

Attorney Dallinger cautions, "Be careful of any and all statements made at a meeting of members that are critical of another person or which expressly accuse another person of any dishonest, unprofessional, fraudulent or potentially criminal act. While challenging the results of an election, one may create personal liability for oneself by having defamed or caused emotional distress to another."

ASSOCIATION IS EMBROILED IN PROXY DISPUTE

Q *We have a five-member board that is sharply divided, three to two. There has been an ongoing dispute over the handling of the proxies since our annual meeting took place three months ago.*

The association uses a management company only for clerical needs, assessment billing and collection. The board members handle the other business affairs of the association. The board requested that all proxies be returned far in advance of the meeting. When I asked who had access to the submitted proxies, I did not receive a reply.

I submitted a proxy, but then attended the meeting. When I and other owners asked to have our proxies returned so that we could vote at the meeting, we were refused.

Must an owner use the proxy form submitted by the association, or can a self-prepared proxy be submitted? Should an owner's proxy be returned to that owner if he or she attends the meeting and asks to retract the proxy? How many people should be involved in the handling of proxies and when should they be registered for the meeting?

A In most associations, an owner can submit any form of proxy. I've heard attorneys say that a proxy written on a scrap of paper or a cocktail napkin is acceptable, but I've found that homeowners don't go along with that idea. Homeowners often believe that only the proxy form provided by the association is acceptable.

Arguments over proxies are so prevalent in some associations that they always have an attorney present to assist the Inspectors of Election. Because of election controversies, some associations have even taken a vote of the members to amend the bylaws so that only the "official proxy" sent out by the association can be used. Such a bylaw change is allowed according to Corporations Code if the proper member majority approves the bylaw amendment.

You and others who wanted your proxies returned at the meeting were acting within your rights. However, attorney Timothy G. Dallinger of Sherman Oaks, offers the following advice, "Condo associations and their members should be aware of the fact that California law does not require the return of the proxy form to a member as a condition to that member's right to vote in person at a meeting or as a condition to that member's right to revoke his or her proxy. California Corporations Code Section 7613 (b) provides that:

> "Every proxy continues in full force and effect until revoked by the person executing it prior to the vote pursuant thereto, except as otherwise provided in this section. Such revocation may be affected by a writing delivered to the corporation stating that the proxy is revoked or by a subsequent proxy executed by the person executing the prior proxy and presented to the meeting, or as to any meeting by attendance at such meeting and voting in person by the person executing the proxy. The dates contained on the forms of proxy presumptively determine the order of execution, regardless of the postmark dates on the envelopes in which they are mailed."

Dallinger continues, "As you can see, the mere attendance at the meeting by a member and voting in person has the effect of *permanently revoking* any prior proxy given by that member. Only a newly executed proxy received from that member will be enforceable once the prior proxy is revoked by virtue of the member's having attended a meeting and personally voting. *It is not necessary for the old proxy from to be returned to the member in order for that member to vote personally and thereby revoke the old proxy.* Indeed, it is arguable that, to be safe, the old revoked proxy form should be retained by the association in its corporate records along with a dated notation on the proxy form that it was duly revoked by means of personal attendance by the member who voted at the meeting."

If you feel that the outcome of the election was affected, you have a right to file an action to have the election examined by the court. Legal action must be commenced within nine months following the election. Over a period of time, the evidence sometimes disappears, so it is prudent to investigate sooner rather than later. Dallinger adds, "Once filed, an action by a member to determine the fairness of an election is by statute given the highest priority on the courts' calendars in California. Courts take these election disputes very seriously and hear them rapidly."

Regarding your right to a secret ballot, bylaws usually state that proxies are to be registered prior to the start of the meeting. When proxies are being gathered, privacy of the voters should be protected. If an association has a management company, the voters are often instructed to return their proxies to the manager. In many associations, the board secretary receives the proxies and registers them just prior to the meeting. Of course, voters who choose to use a directed proxy should assume that they are giving up their right to a secret ballot; however, they should not have to fear that everyone in the association is going to know how they voted.

Votes should be counted by the Inspector(s) of Election, either one or three impartial people, who are appointed to oversee the election process and the tallying of the votes. An inspector *should consider all voting information to be confidential.*

"The Condominium Bluebook" by Branden E. Bickel and D. Andrew Sirkin explains the outcome of the *Chantilles v. Lake Forest II Master Homeowners Association* litigation that took place in 1995.

Attorneys Bickel and Sirkin write, "There is no absolute right to inspect secret ballots after an annual election—even by an incumbent candidate-director—where less intrusive ways of verifying the vote count are available that preserve the privacy of member votes. Article I, Section I of the California Constitution guarantees association members the right to privacy in their voting decisions, even though some votes are cast by proxy, and that right must be balanced against the need to verify election results."

OWNERS CANNOT BE EXCLUDED FROM MOST BOARD MEETINGS

Q *My wife and I live in a property owners association. The architectural committee reviews and approves or disapproves home plans that are submitted by owners wishing to build a home on their property.*

The architectural committee and the board of directors hold secret meetings and owners are not allowed to attend unless the president invites them. Minutes are not available even after repeated requests.

I believe that this conduct is immoral and possibly illegal. What are my options?

A After reviewing the exchange of correspondence between you and the board president that you enclosed for me to read, it is clear that the board views you as a troublemaker. Perhaps you are a "pain in the neck" for the board, but that does not give them the right to exclude you and all the rest of the owners from their board meetings. The president is using Robert's Rules of Order in a way that stifles owner communication. Shame on board presidents who think that once they are elected they do not have to listen to the other owners!

According to California Civil Code Section 1363.05, community association board meetings must be open meetings. The association must publicize the meeting dates and location and the board must give owners an opportunity to address the board within reasonable time limits.

Minutes, other than executive session (closed meetings) minutes, must be provided to any owner who requests copies. The requesting owner must pay the copying costs unless the association has a policy of distributing them to each owner without charge.

As an owner, you have a right to attend the meetings unless the board is meeting in an executive session to discuss personnel issues, litigation issues, the formation of third-party contracts and disciplinary hearings that require discretion in order to protect the privacy of individuals. Owners who are accused of a violation may request that their hearing be conducted in executive session and the board must comply.

You should be allowed to *attend* the regular board meetings, though you do not have the right to participate in the board's discussion or disrupt the meeting in any way. Read your association bylaws to find out about the procedure for conducting board meetings.

I recommend that boards allow some time prior to the meeting to hear owners' comments or questions. Consistent time limits should be imposed so that owners do not unnecessarily delay the formal meeting. California law requires that owners have the opportunity to speak at a board meeting, within certain reasonable time limits that are adopted by the board.

Boards that hold secret meetings are often accused of having something to hide. Your board has compounded its problem by refusing to allow you to have access to the minutes. Now they are probably offended by your criticism and wishing that they could resolve the matter, but it has escalated to open animosity. If they do not provide access to the board meeting minutes or allow your attendance at meetings, you can take legal action. Contact an attorney to discuss your options.

Regarding architectural committee meetings, it is not unusual for committee members to meet on short notice to consider matters that must be resolved within a short period of time. Architectural committees are often pressured to act on a moment's notice and approve plans and improvements because the owner has already scheduled the contractors! That isn't the way the procedure is supposed to work, but if you ever serve on an architectural committee you will find out how difficult it is to hold scheduled public meetings.

ASSOCIATION HAS NOT HAD A MEETING IN THREE YEARS

Q *Our condominium has not had an annual meeting in three years. Most of the officers of the board have moved away so I don't know who is going to schedule the meeting and conduct the annual elections. The manager says that he will take care of everything but nothing happens. How can the annual meeting take place if the manager doesn't make the arrangements?*

A It sounds as though the board of directors is not supervising the manager. Scheduling the annual meeting is a board responsibility, but the manager is neglecting his duty to the association if he doesn't work with the board members to see that the legal documents of the association are obeyed.

If some of the board members are inactive, then the remaining board members should appoint or elect new members according to the procedures in the association's bylaws. Then an annual meeting should be scheduled at the proper time specified in the documents.

Since your annual meeting is long overdue, a special election could be scheduled to elect directors who will serve only until the next regularly scheduled annual meeting takes place.

ASSOCIATION HELD ANNUAL ELECTION WITHOUT A QUORUM

Q *Our community association held our annual election eight months ago. We did not have a quorum present; however, the manager conducted the meeting. She said that she would use proxies from previous meetings to have enough proxies to make the meeting legal.*

Our bylaws state that a proxy is valid for 11 months; however, the manager said that a proxy may be used for four years for any future meetings or elections.

If our meeting was not a legal meeting, is this current board of directors a duly elected board?

A It sounds like the meeting may not have been legal and the manager may have been too zealous in her efforts to see that the election took place.

Every owner should read the declaration and bylaws to find out how the association's meetings are to be conducted. Then read any meeting notices and election material carefully to see if the association's procedures are in compliance with the legal documents. Obviously, owners should read the proxy form very carefully before signing over their voting rights.

If you choose to contest the election, you must do so within a specific period of time. Before you decide to challenge the validity of the election, ask yourself this question.Would the outcome of the election have been different if the meeting had been postponed because of a lack of a quorum? Remember that another election should be occurring in roughly four months, so you can also prepare yourself for the next election by learning how state laws affect and, in some cases, supersede your association's procedures.

I have assisted many associations with their annual meetings. From the information that you provided to me in your letter, I can see why you are concerned about the election procedure that was used. State law differs from some of the information that your manager provided.

In my opinion, if the association had proxies on file from previous meetings, those proxies should have been registered at that meeting to show evidence of a quorum. The manager should have had them with her so that there was no question about the validity of the proxies. If the "old" proxies did not state on the proxy form that they were valid for three years, then they should not have been used for this election.

Corporations Code Section 7613 (b) states that: "No proxy shall be valid after the expiration of 11 months from the date thereof unless otherwise provided in the proxy, except that the maximum term of any proxy shall be three years from the date of execution." If your manager said it was four years, she is misinformed.

You need to quickly obtain legal advice. Provide copies of the proxy and any other meeting materials to an attorney if you want to contest the election. Corporations Code 7527 states, "An action challenging the validity of any election, appointment or removal of a director or directors must be commenced within nine months after the election, appointment or removal. If no such action is commenced, in the absence of fraud, any election, appointment or removal of a director is conclusively presumed valid nine months thereafter." Your attorney can explain Corporations Code 7616 and the legal procedure for challenging the election.

BOARD HAS DUTY TO CORRECT THE MINUTES

Q *The secretary of our association board was absent at a recent board meeting. The vice president acted as the secretary. When the board received copies of the meeting minutes, they found that most of the business that had been conducted at the meeting was not noted in the minutes at all. Many of the items in the minutes were incorrect. The secretary who was absent from the meeting signed the minutes.*

What is the liability of the board members who accepted these minutes at the subsequent board meeting? Is it proper for a secretary to prepare and sign minutes of a board meeting that he or she did not attend?

All board members have a duty to see that minutes are true and correct. The minutes that are approved at a subsequent meeting are the official record of the association.

Robert's Rules of Order, the manual of parliamentary procedure that most associations rely upon, says that the approved minutes may be corrected or amended regardless of the amount of time that has elapsed, so it is still possible for the board to correct the errors.

I always recommend that the name and signature of the person the took the meeting notes and wrote the minutes appear at the end, for example, "Submitted by John Doe, vice president, in the absence of the secretary."

After approval, the minutes should be dated and signed by two officers, usually the president and the secretary. The signatures of the secretary and president affirm that the minutes were approved by a board vote. Therefore, I do not feel that it is improper for the secretary's name to appear on these minutes that someone else prepared.

BOARD KEEPS ITS "CLOSED SESSION" ACTIONS SECRET

Our homeowners association has a seven-member board that meets two times per month in "open session." An agenda is set forth for discussion by the board with comments from the members present. Very few homeowners attend these meetings.

All issues that are of prime concern to the homeowners seem to wind up in "closed session" for board members only. The only way we hear of the results of these closed sessions is by rumor or word of mouth. No minutes of these meetings are ever published or distributed to the general membership. What can we do?

What's their big secret? Are they tearing their hair out, shouting at each other, planning dastardly acts? Secret meetings wrongfully stifle member participation. Owners lose respect for a board that takes action behind closed doors and then the deadly "us-against-them" syndrome will set in.

Board members should not conduct association business in closed sessions. The board should give the owners an opportunity to bring their concerns and questions to the board meeting. Depending upon the size of the association, a fifteen-minute open forum at the beginning of a meeting usually works well. After the board meeting begins, homeowners should not be allowed to interrupt the meeting to give further input on any issue that the board discusses. The president should run an efficient meeting without infringing on the rights of the owners who want to communicate with the board.

All owners have the right to request information about the topics of discussion and any action taken at board meetings. Minutes should be taken at all board meetings and those minutes should be available to any homeowner in the association. Some associations charge a small fee for copying minutes while others distribute the board meeting minutes to all owners with the monthly billing or in a newsletter.

There are exceptions when the board should meet in private. When a personnel matter or litigation is being discussed, then closed sessions are permissible. The board may also meet in closed session for formation or negotiation of third-party contracts or when an owner is invited for a disciplinary hearing. Minutes should be taken even during closed sessions, though these minutes may be kept confidential due to the nature of the discussions. Some states, such as Florida, have laws that permit closed meetings for discussion purposes only and any motions that result from the discussion must be made in an open meeting.

AGENDA SHOULD STATE ALL ISSUES OF MEETING

Q *Can a proxy be used at a homeowner association annual meeting for voting on any issue other than the items stated on the agenda? During our association's annual meeting, the subject of assessing owners for the cost of painting was introduced. The president stated that he could use the proxy votes to approve or disapprove a painting assessment. Is this legal?*

A The annual meeting agenda should state any items that will be voted upon at the meeting. In my opinion, it is improper to vote on any additional matters.

It is permissible for the painting assessment issue to be brought up during discussion, but the vote should have been postponed until all owners could be informed.

Remember that in California the association's board of directors has the authority to approve special assessments without a vote of the membership unless the special assessment exceeds five percent of the current annual assessment. If the painting assessment is less than five percent, the vote at the annual meeting was unnecessary.

MINUTES MUST BE TAKEN AT EVERY MEETING

Q *Our homeowners association holds an annual meeting each year to elect a board of directors. Until the last two years, meeting minutes were written that stated the names of the candidates and the number of votes each received. The current board chairman says that there is no need to have such minutes. The association bylaws state, "The secretary shall record the minutes of all meetings."*

During the past year, two special meetings were held which included recall elections. No minutes were written for these two meetings because the chairman states that they are unnecessary.

Is the board chairman correct?

A No, the chairman is incorrect. The annual meeting minutes are read or distributed at the subsequent annual meeting and approved or amended by the general membership. Minutes should be taken at all meetings. This is especially important at an election meeting where a quorum is necessary and election results should be a matter of permanent record.

California Corporations Code Section 8325 requires the association to provide the voting results to any member requesting this information within 60 days after an election. This does not mean that the requesting member has the right to review secret ballots; only election results have to be provided.

At most annual meetings that I have attended, the election winners have been announced without stating the exact number of votes that each candidate received, though that information should be available to any voting member who requests it. Recall election meetings have special significance since they often result from some type of controversy within the association. Minutes should be kept of these important meetings also. Since your association bylaws specifically state that minutes should be kept of *all* meetings, the board secretary should write up the meeting minutes whether the board chairman wants them or not.

All of the board members are obligated to uphold the bylaws, so the other board members should speak up when the board president is wrong.

ANNUAL MEETING REQUIREMENTS FOUND IN BYLAWS

Q *Our condo hasn't had an annual meeting for the general membership for more than eighteen months. How often should meetings occur? How and when should board members be elected?*

A You should be able to find the answer to these questions in the bylaws of your association. Usually, the general membership of the association meets annually. Your bylaws may not state a particular month of the year because this may depend on the original sale of a majority of the units. For instance, here is the wording of the section pertaining to annual meetings in the bylaws of an association: "The first meeting of the Association shall be held within forty-five (45) days after the closing of the sale of the first Lot in the project which represents the fifty-first percentile interest... and each subsequent meeting shall be held on the same day of the same month of each year thereafter..." In other words, as soon as over half of the homes (or lots) were sold, the association scheduled the first annual meeting to occur within 45 days. Each year's meeting for this association is to take place on that same date. Your association's bylaws may be quite different.

The bylaws will also tell you about the manner in which owners are to be notified of the meeting, the number of owners needed for a quorum, the procedure for election of officers, and other pertinent details.

After you have read your bylaws, you will have to consult your association minutes to find out when the last annual meeting occurred. Then you can determine whether your board is lagging in their responsibility to schedule annual meetings in a timely manner.

ASSOCIATION BOARD MUST HAVE BOARD MEETINGS

Q *My homeowner association never has any meetings. I think that one of the board members is making all of the decisions without communicating with any of the other board members or the owners.*

Is the board supposed to have regular meetings? How frequently are the board members elected?

A If your association is like most, the owners should be meeting for an annual membership meeting every year. The purpose of the meeting is to elect the board of directors of the association.

The board of directors has most of the decision-making authority for the association. Even in a small association with less than 30 units or lots, the board should meet at least on a quarterly basis to review financial reports and bank statements and follow up on any delinquent owners or rule violations. Written minutes of the annual meetings and the board meetings must be taken to provide a permanent record of any action taken by the membership or the board.

Check your association's legal documents for the frequency of meetings. Usually, the bylaws will specify when and how the membership meetings and board meetings are to be conducted. The bylaws will also indicate the terms or number of years that board members serve on the board and how vacancies on the board are to be filled.

SUGGESTIONS FOR EFFECTIVE BOARD MEETINGS

Q *Our association board has monthly board meetings. We try to conduct our meetings properly and yet there are some people who are disrespectful and interrupt the meetings with complaints and demands. Our meetings become long and non-productive because one former board member wants to give his opinion on every topic of discussion.*

It is hard to remain patient when the troublemakers take up so much time. How can we control the meetings so that we can take care of business without a four-hour meeting?

A The board is required to allow the owners to speak; however, they should not be allowed to disrupt the meeting. Time limits have to be imposed in a fair and consistent manner. It is my belief that any association board meeting that lasts longer than two hours to too long. Board members become bored and so do the owners. It is difficult to find board members when the meetings are inefficient or unnecessarily lengthy.

Advance communication is so important, but remember that communication is a two-way street. Owners have a right to know what is happening in their association. I think that some association boards do not communicate well enough with the owners and boards sometimes don't like to listen to their fellow owners. Boards have an obligation to listen and the law requires it, so find a way to make it work.

Conducting an effective board meeting requires advance planning and effort. Every association board meeting should have a written, detailed agenda showing that the board will be conducting a business meeting: approving prior meeting minutes, reviewing financial reports, reviewing committee and management reports and acting on the motions that will be addressed at the meeting.

If there is a central location near the mailboxes or an association bulletin board, post the agenda in advance of the meeting. Mention on the agenda that there will be an opportunity before the meeting starts for owners to express their opinions or share their concerns with the board. With twenty years of experience as a manager, I can tell you that having the open forum at the beginning of the meeting is usually the most effective.

After the board starts their meeting, the owners become observers, not participants. If disruptive owners cause problems, the president should politely ask them to leave so that the business affairs of the association can be handled. If this occurs, it is best for a calm board member to call or meet with the disruptive people a day or two after the meeting to try to mediate the problems and gain their cooperation.

Some associations adopt rules of conduct for their meetings. The president conducts the open forum much like a city council meeting. Each person who wishes to speak fills out an information card with his or her name and the subject that they want to discuss. Depending upon the number of people who wish to speak, the open forum time is divided fairly so that each person has equal time.

A detailed agenda distributed to the owners in advance is helpful. The owners will know what motions are being considered and they can give their opinions prior to the meeting.

I prefer using a timed agenda because that informs the owners that their time is limited and the board is conducting a business meeting. Having the time noted in the margin of the agenda will help the president keep the meeting on track. You will be surprised how much you can accomplish just by staying focused on the time factor.

By preparing a written agenda a week or so before the meeting and attaching any supporting information (for the board members only), the board will arrive ready to make decisions. If they have any questions or concerns, table the item until more research can be done or form an ad hoc committee to gather additional information for the board. The president should not allow extensive discussion by the board members if it appears that a decision will not be reached.

Boards should be cautious about making hasty decisions but they should also try to deal with matters as speedily as possible so that the same agenda items don't remain on the agenda for months and months. Seek the advice of professionals when the decisions are weighty and costly.

A professional manager assists the board with the planning of the agenda and preparation. He or she can greatly enhance the meeting experience with advice at every step of the process, including handling difficult people. If your association does not have a manager, you might want to seek the advice of a community association manager, a parliamentarian or your association's attorney.

As a last resort, if an owner is repeatedly abusive and disruptive, an attorney can assist you with legal steps, such as an injunction, to prevent the person from continuing to harm the association by undermining the effectiveness of the board.

BOARD NEEDS TO FIND WAYS TO SHORTEN MEETINGS

Q *You have often advised against lengthy board meetings. I serve on my homeowner association's board of directors. We have over 200 owners in our association and many of them attend meetings.*

Our declaration of covenants, conditions and restrictions requires open meetings. Our board feels that we are obligated to hear comments from the owners who want to participate in the decision-making process.

We would like to take your advice and shorten our meetings, but this seems impossible in our case. How can we comply with the open meeting requirement in our declaration and get all of the agenda items covered in a reasonable amount of time?

A The term "open meeting" means that the door is figuratively open. All owners and residents should be allowed to attend unless owner violations, legal issues, personnel issues or contract negotiations are being discussed.

Owners have a right to speak to the board. However, you are mistaken if you believe that each owner must be allowed to give his or her input on every agenda item. Remember, you are conducting a board meeting, not a full membership meeting for all the owners. The open meeting requirement means that owners must be allowed to attend as spectators, not as participants in the board discussions or decision-making process.

I recommend that some time be set aside prior to the meeting for an "open forum" for owners who would like to address the board. Their comments should be brief. The board can establish reasonable time limits. Then it is the president's responsibility to limit the speakers' time so that each person has the opportunity to participate. City council meetings usually have a two- or three-minute time limit. The board should not feel obligated to respond to owners' concerns immediately unless it is an actual emergency. It is acceptable to study the matter, refer an item to committee or to check on the proper course of action and get back to the owner at a later time.

After the president calls the meeting to order, the owners should not be allowed to interrupt or participate in the board's discussions.

If an owner wants to engage the board in lengthy discussion on a non-agenda issue, then the issue can be tabled until a future meeting when adequate agenda time can be scheduled.

Some very large associations require that owners submit their specific agenda topic in writing at least a week in advance. In my opinion, this is a reasonable way for the board meetings to be conducted in a large association.

Owners should be informed about the board's procedures. The board has a responsibility to listen to input from the owners but the decision-making power rests with the elected board members. Opinions voiced in an open forum may not be the opinions of the majority. The board must weigh the owners' input and then act in the best interests of all the owners.

PROXY DOES NOT COMPLY WITH SECRET BALLOT PROVISION

Q *The proxy form that is used for our homeowner association's annual election has three options. I can mark it for quorum purposes only, or my proxy holder can receive my ballot for voting, or I can show on my proxy how I would like the votes to be cast.*

Our bylaws state that the election of directors "shall be by written secret ballot." If I show on my proxy how I want my votes to be cast, this is not a secret ballot. I must return my proxy to the management company, and then it will be forwarded to the election committee. The election committee will give it to the inspectors of election for tallying at the annual meeting. Many individuals will know how I voted. How does this comply with the secret ballot requirement in our bylaws?

A If you use a proxy to indicate your vote, you give up your right to a secret ballot. Your proxy can be used to indicate the way that you want your vote cast. Strictly speaking, it is not a ballot and will obviously not be secret since other people will be inspecting the signed proxies and tallying them or distributing them to the designated proxy holders.

If you are unable to attend the meeting, you could enclose your proxy in an extra sealed envelope inside the mailing envelope for additional privacy. You could request that only an Inspector of Election open it.

Individuals who feel strongly about a secret ballot should plan to attend the meeting and vote in person. That is the only way that you can feel certain that no one else will know how you voted.

BOARD MEETINGS DRAG ON AND ON

Q *Our board of directors has a very nice president who is intimidated by the rest of the board members. He does not control lengthy discussions and consequently our board meetings often last well over three hours.*

I do not serve on the board but I like to go to the meetings just to find out what is happening in our association. After seeing how the board meetings are conducted, I don't think I would be interested in serving on the board because they never seem to accomplish anything.

What can be done to silence some of the board members or homeowners who appear to engage in long monologues just to hear themselves talk?

A Your president may be a nice guy, but that does not mean that he is an effective president. Obviously, the president is the one who must control aimless discussions and eliminate gossip or unnecessary conversations. An ineffective president and an inefficient board will turn off people like you who might be good prospects to serve the association.

Information packets containing bids for contracts, committee reports, correspondence and all pertinent information should be distributed a few days prior to the meeting. If all participants are prepared to make decisions, then the meetings shouldn't last longer than an hour and a half.

I find that a timed agenda helps to move the meeting along in a constructive way. By having a written agenda with approximate times for each item shown in the margin of the page, everyone can keep the president on track by gently reminding him that time is slipping away. Volunteers will be more likely to participate and less resentful of their obligations if meetings start on time, accomplish goals, and end on time.

OWNERS CANNOT BE FINED FOR NOT VOTING IN ELECTION

Q *My husband and I live in a 64-unit condominium association. We were unable to attend the association's annual meeting because we were out of town.*

Soon after the meeting, we received a notice from the association that we were being fined $25 for not voting in the election. Do we have to pay this fine?

A This is outrageous! According to Civil Code Section 1363, the board cannot levy a fine without giving you an opportunity to attend a hearing. If you don't want to pay the fine, you should write to the board requesting that you be given an opportunity to protest. If they fail to respond, then you should attend the next board meeting and calmly discuss it with your board of directors.

Everyone should participate in the election; however, voting is a right, not an obligation. This must be a new tactic that your association is using in an attempt to get the attention of the owners who ignore their opportunity to vote. Just think of the revenue that could be generated if our federal government used these tactics!

I would challenge the board's authority to impose a fine for this purpose, especially if you weren't notified prior to the meeting that fines would be levied against those who failed to participate. The law does not allow this type of enforcement.

I understand the reason that the association's board of directors wants to encourage attendance at the annual meeting. If the meeting has to be postponed because of the lack of a quorum, the association has to pay the cost of sending out another meeting notice. Sometimes there are other costs such as meeting room rental, management fees or attorney fees. It is a waste of everyone's time and money when meetings must be rescheduled.

The board probably feels that most owners will not argue over $25 and this is a way of encouraging participation of owners who are apathetic. They may feel that the results will justify their methods, but I disagree.

Now that the board of directors has "reminded" you of your responsibility to vote, I hope that you will attend your next annual meeting. If that is not possible, then be sure to sign and return a proxy form to be used for either quorum purposes or for voting.

ASSOCIATION HAS NOT HELD ELECTION FOR TWO YEARS

Q *My homeowner association has not held an election for almost two years. The board president keeps making excuses. On a number of occasions she has said that the meeting will be held "next month" but then nothing happens. She has also stated that if no one will run for the board there is no point in having an election. When should our annual meeting take place? Are the owners supposed to approve the annual budget? What can I do to cause the election to take place?*

A Read the association's governing documents. Usually the meeting requirements can be found in the bylaws. The annual meeting is often conducted on the approximate anniversary date of the association's first organizational meeting.

The election of directors is the primary purpose of the annual meeting. This is an important task because the board of directors has a lot of authority. One of the board's responsibilities is the setting of the annual budget. Unless the association's governing documents state otherwise, the owners do not vote on the annual budget. The budget would require a vote of the owners only when the board recommends a proposed increase of more than 20 percent over the previous year's budget or if the board failed to get the budget distributed within the legal time limit and an increase is needed.

I suggest that you write a letter to the board of directors asking when the annual meeting will be scheduled. Be sure to send a copy to each of the individual directors. If the board fails to act, five percent of the owners can petition the board to schedule a meeting. Read the bylaws and consult an attorney if you need further advice about compelling the board to hold the election.

DIRECTORS WILL NOT POST MINUTES OF MEETINGS

Q *My wife and I own a condominium unit in a community association of more than 100 units. The minutes of the board meetings were being posted in the common area. The board of directors and the management company have informed us that they will not post the minutes of the meetings. They say that they are not required to post them. Now the homeowner must request a copy of the minutes and they will make them available for a $3.00 fee for one set of minutes or $25.00 for the year. Isn't there a state law about this?*

A Yes, the state law regarding availability of minutes can be found in Civil Code Section 1363.05 (d):

"The minutes, minutes proposed for adoption that are marked to indicate draft status, or a summary of the minutes, of any meeting of the board of directors of an association, other than an executive session, shall be available to members within 30 days of the meeting. The minutes, proposed minutes or summary minutes shall be distributed to any member of the association upon request and upon reimbursement of the association's costs for making that distribution." The charges that are now being imposed by your association are probably in compliance with this law.

The law also states that the association must give written notice to the owners regarding how and where minutes can be obtained. This notice can be included with the annual budget information or any general mailing that is sent to all owners.

Since your association is a large one, your association may have an office where the minutes are available for your review. There should be no charge for just reading the minutes in the association's business office or management company's office. Call first to make sure that the minutes are ready and it is courteous to make an appointment at a time that is convenient for the manager or office staff.

Some associations have determined that the minutes should not be posted in a public location where people other than owners and residents can view them. There may have been a valid reason for the association board to discontinue the posting of the minutes.

HOW TO GET A QUORUM AT ANNUAL ASSOCIATION MEETINGS

Q *Our association's annual election is coming up in a few months. We never get a quorum at our annual meetings, so we have to postpone the meeting and schedule another date so that the quorum requirements are lower.*

How can we encourage owners to attend the meeting or send in their proxy so that the election can take place?

A What a waste of time and money when the turnout is insufficient. Some associations have to pay for a room for their annual meetings and so there is additional expense when the meeting has to be postponed.

Schedule a social event a couple of months prior to the annual meeting. Encourage all the owners to come and meet the current board and the slate of board candidates. Include the nominating committee in the planning. If your association needs to find people who are qualified and willing to serve, this is a good opportunity.

The social event can be very informal but it requires planning and organization. Decide how you will invite the owners. If your association consists of one building where everyone goes to a mailbox area, you may be able to reach everyone by simply posting a notice. Larger associations with several buildings or planned developments with single-family homes may have to deliver or mail flyers or organize a telephone tree to reach all of the owners. The notice should remind the owners that the annual meeting is coming up and that the purpose of the social event is to meet their neighbors and board candidates.

Be creative. Find ways to encourage people to attend so that they will want to participate in the election and become actively involved in their association. Offer refreshments, door prizes and coupons from local businesses.

At the social event, use nametags to encourage getting acquainted. Announce the annual meeting date, time and location and remind the owners of the importance of their attendance or sending their proxy. Explain the proxy procedure to new owners or those who do not understand. Discuss issues and pending decisions that the board will be facing during the next year.

Promote the election in a positive way. For two months prior to the annual meeting, remind the owners by sending notices or include announcements about the meeting in the association's newsletter. If you have had lengthy, disorganized or contentious meetings in the past, that may discourage people from attending. Make sure that the owners know that the election meeting will be brief, well organized and that good attendance is important to the future success of the association.

Refer to the association bylaws and consult the association's attorney to make sure that the official notice of the meeting, agenda and proxy form are in compliance with the law and the association's governing documents. Make it easy to return the proxy for those who are unable to attend. Enclose a stamped, addressed return envelope.

Finally, a group of owners can canvass their neighbors the final week or two before the meeting. The friendly, personal invitation is the most successful way of encouraging attendance. If the owner cannot attend, get their proxy. If no one is home, leave a reminder notice with the date, time and location of the meeting and a phone number to call if they have questions.

A successful annual meeting this year will encourage the participation in the future. From beginning to end, the meeting should be friendly and informative. Serve light refreshments during the sign-in process because there is usually a delay until everyone is registered. Use name tags if your association is larger than just a few units. You may want to identify board members and candidates with special nametags.

Rely on your management company and attorney to ensure that the voter sign-in process is streamlined and only one ballot is distributed for each unit or lot. The professionals will also advise the president and the inspectors of election so that the meeting is well-organized, appropriate minutes and records are kept and the voting process is efficient.

ANNUAL MEETINGS SHOULD NOT TURN INTO A BATTLE

Q *Our homeowners association will be having its annual meeting in January. As a member of the board, I am not looking forward to getting skewered by a few malcontents who seem to try to turn each annual meeting into a battle. Many of the complainers are owners who do not attend board meetings and would never run for the board themselves but they delight in asking vague and challenging questions like "Where are you spending all of our money?" Some bring up trivial complaints that could easily and more appropriately be addressed at a board meeting.*

One year we actually had an owner insist that we fill the whirlpool spa with soil and convert it to a flowerbed. She made a motion and demanded that we take a vote of the owners right then. When the board president tried to reason with her, she and her cronies complained loudly and accused the board of "Gestapo tactics."

I gladly volunteer my time to serve my association. As a board, we do our best to communicate with the owners and respond to their concerns. This takes more time and patience than most of the owners will ever know. Why should we have to endure verbal abuse from people who seem to thrive on conflict?

A Your frustration is showing. Ah, yes, it's the dreaded "Us Against Them Syndrome." Try to stamp it out before the whole association is infected. I wish I had a cure for this awful malady. It damages your board's self-esteem and reduces the prospects for getting new board members to serve.

You should not be subjected to verbal abuse at your annual meeting. However, some owners love to "grandstand" in front of a captive audience. They should be aware that they are not only hurting their image, but also the association's image. If you and the rest of the board can handle impertinence with grace, your association will be less damaged by the complainers.

California law provides that owners have the right to speak at all board meetings and general membership meetings within reasonable time limits set by the board. I encourage boards and management companies to ask members to communicate with the board in writing or at a board meeting rather than addressing all of the owners at the annual meetings.

The board president should maintain control of the meeting at all times. He or she should explain to the owners that the annual meeting is a business meeting. All attendees should conduct themselves in a respectful and business-like manner.

Some associations hire policemen or security guards if controversy is anticipated. Hot topics like special assessments often cause heated discussions, so be prepared to withstand the heat with dignity. A respected member of the community or a former board member serving as parliamentarian can often help the president to remain in control of the discussion.

The main purpose of the annual meeting is to elect directors. It should also be a celebration of the accomplishments of the past year (reports by the officers) and a time to thank the board and committee members for their service. Most annual meetings can be finished in one hour from the time that the meeting is officially called to order. I've attended many annual meetings where the registration of the voters took more time than the actual meeting.

The annual budget, maintenance complaints, landscape suggestions and requests for service are all board matters that should be addressed at a board meeting instead of the annual meeting. If an owner starts talking endlessly about these kinds of issues, it is appropriate for the board president to interrupt and ask the person to attend the next board meeting or write to the board.

If your association has a large number of owners, it is necessary that a timekeeper monitor the speakers' time allotted by the board so that everyone who wants to speak has an equal opportunity to do so.

Any agenda items requiring a vote of the owners must be announced to the membership ahead of time. Therefore, your board was correct when they did not allow a vote on converting the spa to a flowerbed. If it wasn't on the agenda, then the owners should not vote on the issue.

BOARD MEMBERS NEED TO CORRECT ERROR IN MINUTES

Q *I am the secretary of our homeowner association board. I just realized that there are a couple of problems with our association minutes. At a recent board meeting, we approved the annual budget for the coming year and we voted to file a lien on the property of an owner who is over 90 days delinquent in paying his monthly assessment.*

Here is the problem. In the meeting minutes, I neglected to include the approval of the budget and I made a typographical error on the address of the property to be liened. I have checked with the property manager to verify that the correct property was notified and liened. However, I believe that the minutes should be corrected.

The meeting minutes with the mistakes were approved at our subsequent meeting. Can I make a motion at the next meeting to change the minutes that have already been approved by the board of directors?

A Yes, you can make a motion to modify minutes that have already been approved. As you know, the minutes are the association's corporate record. The minutes should include all of the motions and reflect all of the board action that is approved at a meeting.

Robert's Rules of Order, the manual on parliamentary procedure, is a resource that many associations rely upon for advice on how to conduct their meetings. *Robert's Rules of Order* says that meeting minutes can be revised or amended regardless of the time that has elapsed.

You are correct that the approval of the budget should have been in the minutes and the typographical error should be corrected. The motion to revise the minutes, including the specific items that need to be corrected, will appear in the current meeting minutes. Then you, the board secretary, can create an addendum that includes the motion to approve the amount of the budget and the correction of the typographical error that was approved at a subsequent meeting. I recommend attaching a copy of the approved budget to the minutes so that it is in the permanent record.

It is preferable to get this taken care of before the end of the fiscal year. If it is not corrected, the certified public accountant, who does your year-end audit or review, will question why the approval of the budget does not appear in the minutes. The CPAs who do financial reviews and audits for community associations have specific guidelines from the American Institute of Certified Public Accountants, which include the review of the minutes.

The minutes should be a complete and accurate record of all of the board's actions. You or the board president could make a quick phone call to the association's attorney if the board has any questions about the procedure to amend the meeting minutes.

BOARD OF SMALL ASSOCIATION MEETS SPORADICALLY

Q *Our condominium association is very small and the board meets sporadically. Shouldn't the board be meeting on a monthly schedule? Can the rest of the owners attend the board meetings?*

A The association's bylaws will probably state how often the board should be conducting meetings. Some bylaws only require a quarterly meeting; however, the board can meet more frequently if needed.

All association members (owners) have a right to know the date, time and location of the meetings so that they can attend. All board meetings are open meetings unless the board is conducting a disciplinary hearing, discussing litigation or possible litigation, personnel issues or third-party contracts.

The boards that meet less frequently than monthly will often rely on the board president to make some emergency decisions that need to be made between meetings. For the board president's protection from liability, any actions taken between meetings should be noted in the minutes and ratified by the rest of the board.

Individual board members do not have the authority to take any action without a board vote unless the board has granted specific authority to the individual. The rest of the board members have a duty to oversee that individual board member's actions and curtail his or her decision-making if they do not agree with the way the association is being operated.

CAN ASSOCIATIONS PROHIBIT TAPE RECORDINGS?

Q *Our community association has adopted a board policy that forbids tape-recording the meetings. Are there civil penalties for secretly taping the meeting? Does an individual have privacy rights that are violated when secret taping occurs?*

A There seems to be a lot more audio and even videotaping going on these days. To complicate the enforcement of your association's policy, small voice recorders are easy to conceal in a pocket.

Some associations use their own tape for the purpose of writing the minutes. In that case, anyone addressing the board or participating in the meeting should be made aware that the meeting is being recorded. Many attorneys say that the tapes should be erased as soon as the minutes are approved, because the minutes are the official record of the meeting, not a tape recording. Tapes should never be transcribed word for word by the recording secretary.

In general, I am not in favor of tape recording meetings and I have advised several associations to adopt a policy prohibiting tape recordings. I believe your association's policy of not allowing taping is proper and the policy could include ejecting the person who refuses to comply, but I'm not sure how you can enforce it if someone is either blatantly or surreptitiously taping a meeting and they refuse to stop. I have heard of associations that had the offending owner removed by the police, which seems a bit drastic. Even attorneys disagree on the manner of enforcing the restrictions on tape recordings. Discuss privacy rights and civil penalties with your attorney.

CHAPTER 10 INSURANCE

JEWELRY DAMAGED IN SPRINKLER MISHAP

Q *A lawn sprinkler leak flooded the entire front of our condo. I made a frantic call to the manager who came over and turned the sprinkler system off. About one month later, I opened a floor safe and found that several thousand dollars worth of jewelry was sitting in four inches of water that had seeped through the exterior wall and into the safe. I called management and was told that the association is not responsible for damage inside the condominium.*

My pearls, previously appraised at $6,000, were destroyed. A watch had to have the inner works replaced and all of the jewelry had to be cleaned. My homeowners' insurance would only partially cover the damage and my insurance company feels that the association's liability policy should cover my loss. Please advise.

A Steve Segal, Steven G. Segal Insurance Agency, Burbank, states, "If the damage was a direct result of a faulty sprinkler on common area maintained by the association, then the association's liability policy may cover your loss. If you have already taken care of the damaged jewelry and do not have documentation or evidence, it may be difficult to collect at this point. Contact your board of directors or the management company and request the name of the association's insurance carrier for the purpose of filing a claim. The association does not have the right to bar you from filing a claim. Enlist the help of your own insurance agent if necessary."

WHO PAYS DEDUCTIBLE WHEN A CLAIM IS FILED?

Q *Our condominium's governing documents are unclear regarding the association's or the unit owner's responsibility to pay for the deductible amount in the event of a claim under our association insurance policy.*

What criteria should be used to determine the association's procedure when a loss occurs? What is the procedure in most condominium associations?

A I asked Timothy Cline, owner of Timothy Cline Insurance Agency in Santa Monica, California, to respond to your question. He is one of the most experienced community association insurance agents in the United States. Here is Cline's response:

"Unfortunately, nearly all CC&Rs and bylaws are silent on the handling of the deductible under the association's master insurance policy.

"The prevailing practice in most associations would be the following: The majority of association boards believe that the unit owner should be responsible for payment of the deductible if the loss occurred due to the negligence of the individual unit owner.

"Likewise, if the loss resulted from the failure of a structural element or equipment that is described in the governing documents as being the owner's maintenance responsibility, the owner should pay the deductible. For example, the payment of the deductible on a water damage loss due to the bursting of the flexible pipe leading to the dishwasher would be the owner's responsibility.

"On the contrary, if the loss occurred due to the association's negligence or due to a failure of a portion of the premises that is described in the governing documents as being within the association's 'care, custody and control', then the association should pay the deductible."

Cline recommends that the association's board of directors establish a policy for this matter, a "Deductible Handling Policy" that is consistently followed. Under any circumstances, the board should obtain legal counsel before establishing the association's procedures.

Then the association members should all receive written notification of the association's established "Deductible Handling Policy" that spells out the circumstances that may cause the owner to be held responsible for the deductible. This is important information for the owners because some individual owners' policies will pay the deductible amount that is required under the master association policy when the individual unit owner is responsible. This would reduce the owner's out-of-pocket expenses when a loss occurs.

Individual unit owners should check with their insurance agent or broker regarding coverage for the deductible amounts of the master policy.

LIABILITY COVERAGE FOR BOARD OF DIRECTORS

Q *Our association's governing documents are not specific about the type or amount of liability insurance that the association should have. I believe that we should have directors' and officers' liability insurance that is similar to a corporation's errors and omissions policy.*

I cannot convince our board to purchase this coverage because there is one very intimidating board member who feels that it is an unnecessary expense. She says that a general liability policy is sufficient.

Could you please give us your opinion?

A Associations should always obtain as much insurance as possible, within reasonable cost limitations. At the very least, the board should obtain insurance according to the stipulations in the legal documents. If the documents are outdated or non-specific, the board should be very conscientious about making sure that coverage is adequate.

Since your association's documents are not specific I can give you some general guidelines found in the California Civil Code.

In addition to having *at least* $2,000,000 general liability coverage if your association is fewer than 100 units, your association should purchase directors' and officers' liability coverage with at least $500,000 limits. If your association consists of more than 100 units, the coverage should be *at least* $3,000,000 of general liability and at least $1,000,000 of directors' and officers' liability coverage. The California Civil Code Sections 1365.7 and 1365.9 specify these minimum requirements for insurance coverage.

Directors' and officers' liability coverage protects the board members and the association if the board or one of the board members makes a decision that results in legal action. For instance, if your replacement reserves are not adequately funded, an owner might decide to sue the board for negligence or mismanagement. This kind of legal action is not a result of property loss or damage. It is the result of a decision or alleged lack of proper action on the part of the board of directors.

Boards that are very careful about making all the right decisions are still vulnerable to a lawsuit because of the complexity of the business affairs of the association. Even an unjustified suit requires legal expenses to get the action dropped or submit it to mediation or arbitration. Every owner shares in the cost of legal action so it is in the best interests of all the owners to have proper protection.

I recommend that your board discuss its liability with the association's attorney and insurance agent and then make an informed decision as soon as possible.

WHAT DOES EARTHQUAKE INSURANCE POLICY COVER?

Q *Our condominium association does not have earthquake insurance. Since the most recent earthquake, the board of directors has received many calls from our unit owners asking why we don't have coverage. Some people are demanding that the association obtain coverage. What does an earthquake insurance policy cover?*

A The earthquake insurance policy covers the structure of the building or buildings, common areas including equipment and contents owned by the association. In most situations, the association's policy would not cover the interior portion of the individual units or the furniture and personal belongings inside the units. However, following the disastrous Northridge quake that struck California in 1994, we found that many adjusters who handled claims for the associations were including at least some interior improvements in the individual units.

MUST THE BOARD OBTAIN EARTHQUAKE COVERAGE?

Q *Some owners feel that the board members have an obligation to obtain earthquake insurance for the association. Must the board do so? Is the board liable if they don't vote to obtain the coverage?*

A Some associations' legal documents require that the association have earthquake insurance. However, most declarations of covenants, conditions and restrictions (CC&Rs) leave this decision to the association's board of directors.

The board members should consider their personal liability for this important decision. I know of many associations that have had major controversies about whether or not earthquake insurance was advisable. Some boards of directors feel that the responsibility for this decision should be shared by all of the owners so they survey all of the owners or call a special meeting to let every owner vote on the matter.

Bob Little, Robert W. Little Insurance Agency, Inc., offers the following advice, "Most Directors and Officers 'errors and omissions' policies contain an exclusion for any 'act, error or omission' that a board member might make in procuring the right forms and kinds of insurance." In other words, if the board is sued for negligence because they didn't obtain the insurance, the directors and officers liability policy might not have to defend the suit or pay any court costs. The board might be personally liable.

Little advises the board of directors to consult legal counsel and attempt to limit their liability by conducting a vote of all of the owners. He states, "We encourage the board to prepare a mailing for each unit owner explaining the insurance coverage and the effect, if any, the addition of the earthquake coverage will have on the monthly assessment that each owner pays. The mailing should include a written ballot. If the majority of the owners do not want the coverage, place the written ballots in a safe place so that the board will have evidence to support their decision. The owners should be informed about the outcome of the vote."

EARTHQUAKE INSURANCE HAS HIGH DEDUCTIBLE

Q *Our condominium association has earthquake insurance but we do not have enough funds available for the deductible. How can we force all of our 30 unit owners to obtain loss assessment coverage on their individual homeowner insurance policies so that our units are eligible for Freddie Mac loans?*

A In my opinion, educating your owners about loss assessment coverage and encouraging them to obtain the coverage is a wise course of action, regardless of the Freddie Mac requirements.

Demanding that owners purchase insurance is a difficult thing to enforce. Some owners will not purchase insurance unless their mortgage lender requires it. If the unit is not mortgaged, an owner might refuse to obtain insurance. The association would not have the authority to require the individual owners to purchase insurance coverage unless the association's legal documents grant that authority.

There may be other reasons why the units in your complex would not be eligible for Freddie Mac funding anyway. In California, only 10 percent of Freddie Mac's loan purchases involve condominium units. Try to become informed before the association adopts extraordinary procedures to deal with the Freddie Mac requirements.

First, check with all of the other owners to see if you can find out which lenders are currently funding mortgage loans in your complex. Ask these lenders if they sell their loan packages to Freddie Mac or other secondary mortgage corporations. The lenders may be able to tell you whether the units within your complex are eligible for Freddie Mac funding.

Second, even if you are in a moderate or high-risk zone, a seller may be able to get an exemption from the earthquake insurance requirement. If a unit owner wants to sell his or her unit, try to obtain an exemption by contacting Freddie Mac's risk analysis adviser, Risk Management Solutions, Inc., at (800) 767-9131. Risk Management Solutions charges a fee to provide a document called a Site-Specific Earthquake Risk Analysis.

If your association cannot satisfy the Freddie Mac requirements and cannot obtain the exemption, it is not a hopeless situation. This simply means that a buyer will have to obtain mortgage funding from a lender who will not be selling the loan to Freddie Mac on the secondary mortgage market.

Read more about insurance in the chapter entitled "Before Disaster Strikes."

CHAPTER 11 MAINTENANCE AND REPAIRS

CEILING AND PAINT ARE DAMAGED FROM ROOF LEAK

Q *My condominium unit is on the top floor of the building. The roof is common area. For the past two years, the roof leaks every time it rains. The ceiling and paint in our unit have been damaged and discolored with mold. I have begged the board of directors to repair the problem before the next rainy season begins. I am afraid the next rain will cause the ceiling to collapse.*

The association's handyman has made four attempts to fix the leak, but the problem still exists. The board will not call a licensed roofer. Do I have the right to repair the roof myself?

A As an individual owner, you do not have the authority to engage a roofing contractor or repair the leak yourself. You should resort to self-help only if your written requests yield no response from the board.

You can file a claim with your insurance company or file a claim under the association's coverage. Since this is a two-year-old problem that the board has not resolved, the association's directors' and officers' liability insurance may protect you if all else fails.

Write to the board of directors giving them a 30-day response deadline. Your letter should state the number of times that the roof repairs have failed to correct the leak. Enclose interior photographs with your letter and keep copies of pictures and correspondence for your own records.

The board has a duty to hire someone who can determine the cause of the problem and complete the repair in a reasonable amount of time. The board's failure to take appropriate action has caused damage to your unit. Their cheap solution has created a costlier problem because they can probably be held responsible for the interior repair in your unit. Because of the probability of mold growth, which could be injurious to your health, a certified industrial hygiene expert or toxicologist should investigate the damaged area of the ceiling as soon as possible. When the roof repair has been completed and water-tested, the ceiling can be replaced.

If the board ignores your written demand, perhaps a letter from your attorney will spur them to action. Follow your attorney's advice regarding alternative methods of resolving the problem.

Civil Code Section 1354 states that your claim against the association, if less than $5,000, should be submitted to mediation or arbitration prior to filing legal action.

OWNER SAYS REPAIRS ARE UNSATISFACTORY

Q *Our condominium complex is relatively small but we have a huge problem. The contractor who performed the post-earthquake repairs did such poor quality work. We all had to pay a large special assessment and move out of our units for several months. We were limited as to the choices of carpet and other replacements and the board of directors handled everything.*

When we moved back into our units, the work was not completed and we immediately noticed poor workmanship. Many of the senior citizens are concerned but most of us are intimidated because the board president is an attorney and no one wants to have conflicts with the board.

A The board president is out of line if he or she uses intimidation to stifle the legitimate concerns and complaints of the other owners. The board president is not a supreme ruler.

Unfortunately, there are many associations that are still struggling with similar problems. Any large construction project can result in problems if the board doesn't seek adequate professional help to oversee the contracts, supervise the work, monitor payments and follow up on poor quality work. The board members are volunteers and they should not be expected to know everything. To protect the owners and reduce their own liability, the board should rely on professional help.

The board entered into the contracts on behalf of the owners. Now the board has a fiduciary duty to ensure that the contractor's mistakes are corrected. Even though the board president is an attorney, he or she may simply not know whom to contact. The board should seek the advice of several construction defect attorneys.

If the board fails to act, you and the other owners should get together and obtain legal advice immediately. If warranties have already expired, the owners may have to file legal action against the board and the contractors.

For most people, especially senior citizens, their home is their largest investment. Don't allow your investment to go down the drain simply because the board is ignoring you.

MANAGEMENT WILL NOT CLEAR DRAINS AND GUTTERS

Q *After months of letter-writing and phone calls to our association's property management company, my neighbors and I had to fix some common area problems. Our complaints about clogged gutters and lawn drains filled with rocks, weeds, dirt and other debris received no response from the manager.*

Yesterday, a huge storm hit. Again, we called the manager and received no response. The water was 10 inches deep near the clogged drains and both of my neighbor's units could have been flooded. My neighbors and I got our rain gear and boots and cleared the drains.

What are our rights? In addition to getting the manager's attention, I would like some compensation for doing the management company's work.

What advice can you give us?

A First, your sole compensation is that warm feeling in your heart because you helped your neighbors. I'm sure the other warm feeling that you experienced was your temperature rising because of the anger and resentment against the manager. Don't expect any monetary reward. However, if you had to purchase supplies or tools, you have the right to turn these items over to the association along with your receipts and request reimbursement from the association. You should have informed someone from the board or management company prior to purchasing supplies if you intended to get reimbursement.

Your board of directors is responsible for the supervision of the manager. Check with your board of directors to see if contracting for drain cleaning and gutter maintenance has been on the board meeting agenda. Does the management contract provide for these kinds of services? Does it include emergency response? Perhaps you were asking for something that is beyond the scope of the manager's duties, but that does not excuse the manager's failure to return phone calls. The board should be informed about the lack of response and then they can decide whether to complain to the manager's supervisor or the owner of the company.

Any property manager who would ignore numerous phone calls and letters about this problem must be over-worked or incompetent, but he or she might be held liable for gross negligence. Competent managers realize that they should return phone calls and letters as soon as possible. Even if the manager could not provide an immediate solution to the problem, he or she should have responded to you and your neighbors. For example, if the manager does not have authority to engage contractors, the only response needed would be that the matter has been placed on the board meeting agenda for board action. In case of emergency, the manager should contact the board president or other officer of the association who can authorize the emergency work that is required.

If the association does not have procedures for the type of problem that you experienced, it is time for the board of directors to address this issue and adopt procedures for the future.

REPAIR SCHEDULE FOR CONSTRUCTION DEFECTS

Q *I am purchasing a unit in a condominium association. The association sued the builder/developer for construction defects. The settlement agreement has been signed and work is progressing. I have a letter from the association's attorney stating that the reconstruction work will be completed within nine months.*

Is this letter legally binding? What recourse do I have if the work is not completed on schedule?

A I doubt if the letter carries much weight. Reconstruction projects often run into delays because of bad weather or problems coordinating the schedules of various subcontractors. When this happens, the association can simply issue another letter explaining the reasons for the delay. If you check the wording of the original letter, you will probably find some "wiggle room" or "weasel language" as one association attorney described recently in a discussion of this subject.

You did not state the extent of the repairs or the amount of inconvenience that you will endure until the work is completed. It seems that if you like the unit and the association that you may have to take your chances.

Consult an attorney regarding the wording that can be inserted in the escrow instructions that might provide for penalties to be paid by the seller if repairs are not completed in a timely manner. Bear in mind that your seller has no control over the repair schedule and therefore, the seller may not agree with any penalty that you propose.

DAMAGE TO LOBBY FLOOR OCCURRED DURING MOVE

Q *I have a conflict with the condominium association where I formerly lived. I was aware that residents are not allowed to move into or out of the building on Sundays, so my move was scheduled to take place on a Monday. Both my parents were hospitalized on Friday prior to my move. Because of the emergency, I decided to move out on Sunday. I hired some helpers and did not move any large furniture. We were done in two hours.*

One of the owners complained to me but she seemed to accept my explanation about my parents' hospitalization. However, four months later I received a bill for $475. When I questioned the bill, I was told that the charge was for polishing a two-foot by two-foot area of marble floor in front of the elevator.

No one told me that the floor was scratched. I had no advance warning that they were going to hold me responsible. None of the people that I have spoken to in the building noticed any damage or any work being done to correct any damage. I have written to the management company and the board president and have not had any response.

I am continuing to pay my monthly assessments but I haven't paid the $475 bill. Each billing statement has more threats about paying it. Can the association place a lien on my unit if I refuse to pay?

A I don't believe the association has the authority to place a lien on your unit for the cost of the damage. They will probably charge you for any collection costs or legal fees, so it is wise to resolve this as soon as possible.

Both you and the association have made mistakes. First, you admit that you knew that a Sunday move was against the rules. If you wanted the association to waive the rules for you, you should have asked for permission from a board member that weekend when the emergency arose.

The association's mistake was its failure to notify you immediately that there was damage. They should have given you an opportunity to see the damage. They also should have notified you in writing that there was damage and that they were going to be billing you for the cost. It is inexcusable for the association and the management company to ignore your letters. The association should allow you to state the reasons that you don't feel that you owe the association for the damage. That is due process, a legal term that means "an opportunity to be heard" by the board. Write to the board again and request a hearing at the next board meeting. The association board or management should respond to your request.

If the association continues to ignore you, this is a good example of a conflict that should be resolved through mediation but even mediation could cost you more than the $475. It's your call whether continuing to try to fight the bill is worth your time, energy and money.

WINDOWS ARE STAINED FROM LAWN SPRINKLERS

Q *I live in a large community association where the association is responsible for the landscape maintenance. The common area irrigation sprinklers spray water on my windows and I now have permanent stains on my windows. The landscapers have tried unsuccessfully on several occasions to correct the direction of the flow of water.*

What can I do?

A There has to be a way to change the sprinklers so that the water does not spray onto the structure. I assume that you not only want the sprinklers adjusted, but you also want the association to remove the stains from your windows. In most cases, this should only require a phone call to the manager to find out if the association is going to take responsibility.

If the manager is not responsive, then here is step two. Write to the association board of directors and the management company explaining your problem. Tell them that you expect to hear from them as soon as possible, but you will give them thirty days to respond regarding their solution to your problem. Be as specific as possible, giving dates that you have complained in the past and telling them what was done.

If your board meets monthly, you may want to request that the matter be placed on the next meeting agenda. You have a right to know if the matter is on the agenda and you have the right to attend the meeting to discuss it with the board. I feel that the board should consult an irrigation technician since the landscape crew cannot resolve it.

The association's failure to correct this problem can result in far more serious problems than stained windows, however. I believe your letter should notify the board that you will hold the association responsible for window frame damage, dampness, structural damage or any other result of their failure to correct the direction of the flow of irrigation water.

The stains on your windows are probably just mineral deposits from the hard water. In my opinion, it is the association's responsibility to have their workers clean the windows with a special cleaner such as Lime-Away or CLR. However, your association's declaration of covenants, conditions and restrictions (CC&Rs) may say that you, the homeowner, are responsible for maintaining, cleaning and replacing windows. If that is your situation, it is cheaper to hire a window washer than it is to hire an attorney to argue with your association about the CC&Rs.

ROOF LEAK CAUSED DAMAGE TO CEILING AND WALLS

Q *A roof leak has caused substantial damage to the ceiling and walls of my condo unit. The association is in the midst of negotiations with the developer because of structural defects. The association is unwilling to make any permanent repairs until the case is settled. Now the developer is finally repairing the roof, but is not repairing the interior damage. Isn't the developer responsible for my interior repairs also?*

A Yes, the developer should probably repair the interior damage, but you may have to take the right steps to protect yourself. If the association's negotiations with the developer become protracted, you may have a long wait.

Contact your own insurance company to inquire about filing a claim. The insurance adjuster will probably want to review the association's CC&Rs to ascertain the party who is responsible for the drywall and ceiling repairs. Your insurance may take care of your loss and subrogate against the developer's insurance or the association's insurance after they have paid your claim.

TERMITE DAMAGE IN BEAM OF OWNER'S UNIT

Q *I live in a planned development. My unit is an end unit attached to two other units. A 35-foot supporting beam in our living room is infested with termites. The association is not responsible for termite treatment.*

The other two unit owners in my building say that they do not have any termites so they are refusing to allow the building to be tented or to share the cost.

What can I do?

A Your neighbors would be wise to allow a thorough inspection of the entire structure. If they refuse to cooperate with you, you will have to treat the termites with some type of localized treatment. If localized treatment is not possible or is not successful, you can obtain three opinions from reputable, licensed companies and try to convince the others that they should protect their units by working with you to eradicate the termites.

If other owners in your association are having similar problems, the board of directors may want to survey the entire association to see if there is any interest in taking the legal steps to make the association responsible for termite treatment. Civil Code Section 1364 specifies the procedure for making the termite abatement an association responsibility. The association would then have the legal authority to require the owners to cooperate with the most effective treatment method on a case-by-case basis. The association would pay for the work and bill the owners for a special assessment to cover the cost of the treatment.

NEIGHBOR'S UNSIGHTLY REPAIR TO GARAGE DOOR

Q *An owner in our community association almost destroyed his garage door. He tried to repair it but it is still unsightly and detracts from the appearance of the complex. Can the board of directors demand that he fix it and give him a deadline for completion? If he doesn't take care of it, can the association fix the door and then bill the owner for the cost of the repair? Can the board file a lien on the property and start foreclosure if he fails to pay?*

A In some associations, the garage doors are maintained by the association. First, the board should decide who is really responsible for this repair. If it is the owner's responsibility, can the association ensure that the work is completed properly?

These are legal issues that depend upon your association's power and authority. The governing documents of the association explain the association's enforcement procedures that can be implemented when an owner fails to maintain his or her property. This information can usually be found in the declaration of covenants, conditions and restrictions (CC&Rs). The board should consult the association's attorney if this is an issue that they have not had to deal with previously.

Unless the association's documents clearly give the board the authority to repair or maintain on behalf of an owner, it is not advisable to do so. If the association does have the right to proceed, it is essential that the board communicate in writing with the owner to let him know that the repair is not acceptable. I recommend giving the owner an opportunity to meet with the board. The board should determine what the cost of the repair will be and include that information in the correspondence with the owner. Then the board should give the owner an opportunity to correct it himself or respond in writing if he is unable to complete the work within a specified amount of time.

Civil Code allows foreclosure only for nonpayment of monthly or special assessments. I have seen declarations that allow a damage reimbursement to be considered a "special assessment" against the owner who fails to pay. Since there are many specific situations that vary from one association to another, it is wise to proceed with caution and only with the advice of legal counsel.

More information about responsibility for repairs can be found in the chapter titled "Who Is Responsible?"

CHAPTER 12 MANAGEMENT

WHAT ARE ADVANTAGES OF PROFESSIONAL MANAGEMENT?

Q *What are the advantages to having a manager or management company for our association?*

A There are many laws that associations must obey. Most associations find that it is very difficult to comply with the legal requirements of record keeping, annual reports, disclosures and financial planning without the assistance of a professional manager.

Without professional management, the board is faced with doing the day-to-day tasks such as getting bids for maintenance projects, enforcing rules, paying bills and collecting assessments. A manager can handle many of these tasks more effectively.

Board members can become burnt out very quickly because most association documents require that board positions are voluntary. Unless the governing documents state otherwise, board members are not entitled to pay, perks or privileges. It is unfair for the rest of the owners to expect the board members to give endless hours of volunteer time to the association. However, paid board members do not have the same protection from liability that volunteers are granted.

The fairest way for associations to operate is to hire management to operate the association at the direction of the board. The board members can then serve as a policy-making body and delegate the day-to-day responsibilities to management. All of the owners share in the cost of management through payment of their monthly assessments.

A competent manager will educate the board about proper procedures, legal requirements and changing laws. When the board needs specialized services, a manager can refer other professionals and vendor experts.

CAN THE BOARD HIRE A MANAGEMENT FIRM?

Q *I own a townhouse in a 24-unit complex. Our association has been self-managed by the board members for several years. Now the board has hired a management firm that charges about $600 per month. Can the board spend our money in this manner?*

A The board of directors has the authority to delegate management responsibilities to a management company. This authority is usually stated in the association's declaration of covenants, conditions and restrictions (CC&Rs).

Boards often find that they do not have the time or knowledge to take care of all of the business affairs of the association. It is difficult to find board members who are willing to handle rule enforcement, assessment collection, property maintenance and all of the other responsibilities.

The cost of doing just the accounting for an association of 24 units (collecting the monthly assessments and paying the bills) would probably be at least $600. Depending upon the scope of the management contract, your association may be getting a real bargain. I have worked as a manager and consultant for many years. I find that very few people understand the number of hours and the level of skill that association management requires.

BOARD IS NOT SATISFIED WITH PROPERTY MANAGER

Q *A property management company manages our homeowners association. The board of directors is not satisfied with the performance of the manager. The manager does not return phone calls promptly and is often unprepared for board meetings. One of the board members feels that we need to pay the manager more to get better service. What should we expect from our manager? Should we look for another management company?*

A The level of service can vary greatly from one company to another. The board must read the management contract to find out exactly what services the manager is supposed to provide.

Before the board decides to change management companies, the board president should discuss your concerns with your current manager. Be specific about the reasons for your dissatisfaction. Review the management contract with the manager, noting the areas that need improvement. If the service that you want is beyond the scope of the contract, then perhaps the board will want to renegotiate.

If you feel that the manager's performance is unacceptable, be fair and honest as you verbalize your complaints. Open communication is very important but you don't want to destroy the relationship at this point.

Make notes during your conversation and follow it up with a letter to the manager outlining the topics discussed and the date that you wish to re-evaluate the manager's performance. A copy of your letter should be sent to the manager's supervisor or management company owner. Be sure to allow a reasonable amount of time for the manager to improve his or her performance.

If improvement isn't noted within a reasonable time, talk to the supervisor and the management company owner about getting another manager assigned to your association. Try a different manager before you write off the entire management company. Changing management companies should be the last resort.

MANAGEMENT IS RELUCTANT TO STOP LOUD MUSIC

Q *My condo complex is having a problem with a noisy neighbor who blasts music all day long. I have called our security officers and the police. I have asked our manager to enforce our CC&Rs, which specifically prohibit loud noises. The association has the authority to fine this neighbor but the management seems to be reluctant to do so. What is my next step?*

A Have you contacted your neighbor yourself? That may be more effective than going through the association. You could invite the neighbor to your unit to hear what you are hearing.

Then, if you haven't contacted your board of directors, that should be your next move. It is the board's responsibility to oversee enforcement of the CC&Rs. Usually, management carries out the association's enforcement procedures as directed by the board.

As you have learned, calling the security officers or police will only provide peace and quiet for a short time. As soon as the authorities are gone, the volume knob is probably turned up again and you have to go running for the earplugs.

The association needs to get the attention of the offending neighbor. One way to do this would be to send written notification of the violation, asking the owner to attend a hearing regarding the unacceptable noise levels. The notice of the hearing should also include the amount of the fine that will be levied if the board decides to levy a fine, what will happen if the owner does not attend the hearing and the procedure that will be followed if the owner continues to violate the rights of other owners.

If the offending neighbor is a tenant, then the association should be notifying and disciplining the owner of the unit, in addition to notifying the tenant.

If the association is unwilling to act or if the neighbor is totally uncooperative, you are entitled to bring suit to enforce the CC&Rs or to simply enforce your right to peace and quiet. Consult an attorney if you are interested in getting a court order to prohibit the resident from playing loud music. I have heard of owners who used a sound engineer to measure the decibels in order to prove that the noise coming into their unit was excessive.

MANAGER WANTS EXCLUSIVE LISTING AGREEMENT

Q *I serve on the board of a condominium complex. We have recently heard from a management company that is owned by a real estate broker. This management company states that the association should sign a management contract with their firm and amend the association's legal documents to include the following:*

1. Owners wishing to sell their condominium unit must list the unit with the management company.

2. The management company will place the property on the multiple listing service.

3. Owners offering their unit for rental must contract with the management company to handle the rental of the unit.

The management company offers huge discounts on the association's management fee based upon units sold.

What is your opinion? Would it be wise to revise our documents for this purpose?

A Wow! What a deal! Does the manager want the amendment to state that the association can only be managed by his company?

The owner of the management company knows that unless the restriction is placed in the declaration of the covenants, conditions and restriction (CC&Rs), it can't be enforced. In my opinion, the amendment that is suggested would unduly restrict an owner's rights. For instance, if one of the owners is a real estate agent, he or she would not like the idea of having to list his/her unit with the management company.

Owners should have the right to select any agent they choose for either rental or resale of their unit. A restriction like this could end up being challenged in court. Why go through the expense and work of changing your legal documents and then have the amendment challenged at some point in the future?

I urge you to select your management company based on the merits of their management ability and experience, not on the basis of a real estate license and the offer of projected discounts.

If your association is definitely considering hiring this management company, consult an attorney who specializes in community association law. Find out what your attorney advises regarding the management contract and this type of amendment to the CC&Rs before you sign on the dotted line.

ASSOCIATION WANTS TO CHARGE STEEP TRANSFER FEE

Q *Our association would like some advice regarding the extra fees that we can charge to new owners. Can our homeowners association assess a new buyer a transfer fee of twice the monthly assessment fee for the unit being sold?*

A That sounds like an unreasonable fee based on the laws governing ownership transfer fees. The seller is obligated to provide to the prospective buyer certain documents listed in California Civil Code Section 1368. The association may be asked to provide these documents through the escrow company. The law allows the association to charge only the amount of the association's reasonable cost to prepare and reproduce the requested documents.

Many management companies, operating as the agent for the association, charge $200 or more for this service. The cost is customarily passed on to the buyer at the closing of escrow. The transfer fee includes more than just supplying copies of the legal documents and changing the name on the account. The manager and the person who handles the escrow disclosures often spend a great deal of time on the phone with escrow and loan officers, real estate agents and others involved with the resale. The manager is often pressured to provide governing documents and fill out disclosure forms on very short notice.

The association must provide the requested documents to the seller within 10 days of the written request. This duty is usually delegated to the management company. Any person or entity that willfully violates this section of the law is liable to the purchaser for actual damages as well as a civil penalty not to exceed $500.

WHO OWNS THE ASSOCIATION'S RECORDS?

Q *Our homeowners association is just going into its second year. We have been frustrated with our management company's lack of follow up. This is the company that we inherited from our developer, and they have given us excuses instead of leadership in dealing with the developer. Our new board will probably vote to change management companies next month.*

What documents and records can we expect to have transferred to the new management company? Do the association's records and files belong to the management company or to the association?

A All of the association's documents, records, and files, including contracts, financial statements and correspondence files, belong to the association. Personnel records should be turned over to the association if employees work directly for the association rather than the management company. If the management company wants to retain any of the records they should make copies of the specific records that they need.

You will probably find that the current management company will request that someone from the association board of directors be present for the transfer of records. Most management companies will have a release form, which lists the documents and records that are being transferred. Reputable management companies will be very efficient and cooperative during the transition process.

Though you didn't ask for my advice about changing management companies, I would suggest that you have a face-to-face meeting with the owner of the current management company to discuss your concerns. During the development phase, the management company is often perceived as being on the side of the developer. However, the developer who serves on the initial board of directors and the manager must act in the best interests of the association, even if the management company is a division of the developer's company.

Terminating the current management company should be your last resort. Transition to a new company is not always smooth and there are bound to be some problems while the new company is becoming familiar with the association's procedures and its members, contractors, and vendors.

If you do change management companies, an audit should be performed by an independent certified public accountant. Ask for the accountant's advice regarding the management transition. I recommend closing any bank accounts that have the current management company's personnel as signators, leaving just enough funds to cover any outstanding checks that haven't cleared the bank.

SHOULD MANAGER ATTEND EXECUTIVE SESSIONS OF THE BOARD?

Q *Is it appropriate for the on-site manager of our condominium complex to attend board meetings and answer questions from the owners and residents that are directed to the board? It seems to me that she is not a member of the board and that she should not be seated at the board table.*

Is it appropriate for the manager to attend executive sessions of the board? We have a board secretary who is supposed to take minutes, but the association manager performs this task for both regular board meetings and executive sessions.

A In every on-site management position that I have held, I was expected to attend and participate in almost every board meeting including executive sessions. As an agent of the association, the manager is entitled to attend at the discretion of the board members. If the board wishes, the manager may be seated at the board table and that is where most managers sit. A professional, experienced manager often has a great deal of influence on the board's decisions. The board has the right to rely on the manager and other professionals' opinions when making business decisions.

The board may rely heavily on the manager's advice and information since the on-site manager often knows more about the day-to-day business affairs of the association than the individual board members know. The board usually hires an on-site manager in order to remove themselves from those day-to-day tasks. Meetings then become a time for management to exchange information with the board as well as the members.

Most governing documents give the board the authority to delegate duties to a manager or other agent. Many associations have the minutes prepared by a manager or recording secretary. The bylaws may state that the board secretary is responsible for the board meeting minutes but in many cases the secretary simply ensures that the work is done in a timely and accurate manner and signs the minutes after they have been approved. The board is still responsible for timely production and approval of the minutes. If they feel that the manager is slanting the wording of the minutes, the board can appoint someone else or pay for the services of a recording secretary.

SERVICES THAT MANAGEMENT COMPANIES PERFORM

Q *I serve on the board of an 80-unit association. We are currently self-managed. The board members take responsibility for overseeing the landscape contractor and the janitorial service. The treasurer keeps track of the assessment payments from the association members and pays the association's bills. He is retiring soon and has decided not to run for the board again at our next election.*

Our vice president has been handling the transfer information when a unit is sold but she has sold her unit and will soon be moving away. She has been providing copies of the association legal documents and financial reports and responding to the escrow and real estate agents' requests.

None of the rest of the board members can accept the responsibilities that these two people have been doing for the association. We have talked about hiring a management company. What does a management company do and how much would it cost?

A Management companies provide a wide array of services ranging from basic financial services (just collecting assessments, paying bills and preparing a monthly or quarterly financial statement) to full-service management which might include handling the details of rules enforcement, owner correspondence and preparation of board meeting agendas and minutes.

The cost will depend upon the scope of the services that you would like the management company to perform. Before you contact management companies to obtain their proposals, the board of directors needs to decide what functions can still be done by volunteers and what functions you would like the management company to provide.

Here is a list of some of the many services that property management companies will perform for your association:

1. collect assessments, pay association bills, keep financial records of receipts and expenses, prepare financial statements, carry out the associations procedures for collecting delinquent assessments,
2. prepare the annual budget showing estimated income and projected expenses,
3. oversee the operation and maintenance of the building and grounds by supervising the landscape and janitorial staff or contractors,

4. assist in finding insurance agents, attorneys, accountants and other professionals who will provide services to the association,
5. receive and respond to homeowner complaints and correspondence or refer homeowner concerns to the board of directors for further action,
6. attend board meetings and report on the status of current projects,
7. assist with the preparation of notices and voting procedure for the annual meeting,
8. keep the current owner roster list and respond to escrow demands for resales,
9. assist with communication to the owners, such as preparation and mailing of an association newsletter.

As a consultant, I have helped many association boards analyze their needs so that they fully understand what they want the management company to do for them. This is an important step. Written specifications should be submitted to the management company when you request a management proposal. Miscommunication at this stage can lead to dissatisfaction or disputes about services at a later date.

I urge you to contact companies that are knowledgeable about the legal requirements of community associations. Find out what professional affiliations or licenses the managing agent holds. The California Association of Community Managers (CACM) can verify the management company's affiliation and professional designations attained by the managers who work for the company. CACM's statewide headquarters are located in Irvine, California. The phone number is 949-263-CACM. Their website is *www.cacm.org*.

The local chapter of Community Associations Institute can provide a list of management company affiliates and the managers who have attained professional designations. Check your local phone directory or call directory assistance to find the CAI chapter in your area. CAI is a national organization located in Alexandria, Virginia. Their website is *www.caionline.org*.

UNRELIABLE MANAGEMENT PLAGUES ASSOCIATION

Q *Our homeowners association is faced with changing management companies for the second time in the past year. They all seem to be great during the initial interviews but after hiring a new company, we soon find that they are unreliable or slow to respond to our requests for service. The previous management company's financial statements were inaccurate or not available on time. Now we have a manager that seldom returns phone calls and makes excuses for his tardiness in getting bids and completing other assigned tasks. Can you give us some suggestions to help us in our selection of a new management company?*

A First, I suggest that you contact the owner of your current management company and discuss the manager's shortcomings. Before you cancel the contract, give them a chance to respond to your complaints. Perhaps another manager can be assigned to your association. Make sure that your expectations are reasonable. Does your contract with the management company include all of the tasks that you are expecting the manager to do? Read the contract thoroughly, especially the termination clause.

I have provided consulting services to a number of boards that did not fully understand the functions that a management company should perform. There are several different levels of service ranging from basic financial service to full service management including supervision of contractors and the association's staff or on-site employees. Don't look for the lowest bidder! Some companies overload and underpay their employees, which leads to manager burn-out or poor job performance.

Management companies are required to disclose their professional affiliations and certifications. Look for companies that have a professional community association manager (PCAM), certified property manager (CPM), or certified public accountant (CPA) among the owners or staff. A certified community association manager is especially knowledgeable about California laws pertaining to associations.

Examine the services that are included in the contract fee. Most management companies bill the association for postage, photocopying, stationery and supplies. These "extras" are the association's business costs and should be separate from the monthly management fee.

"Choosing a Management Company," a booklet written by Michael E. Packard, provides community associations with excellent guidance on the preparation of management specifications, the interview process, the screening and final selection of a management company. The booklet is available from Community Associations Institute. Remember, a good relationship with your management company requires frequent communication and adequate supervision from the board.

ASSOCIATION'S FUNDS NOT KEPT IN SEPARATE ACCOUNT

Q *Our board of directors recently asked to see the bank statements for our association. The manager would not show us the bank statements because the account also holds funds belonging to other associations that are deposited in the management company's account. It seems that this requires a great deal of complicated bookkeeping in order to ensure that our money is properly tracked. The manager does not want to set up a separate bank account for our association. Should we have our money in a separate account?*

A Yes, your association should have its own bank accounts. Community associations should have at least two accounts: a checking account for operating funds and another interest-bearing account for reserve funds. Assessment payments from the owners are deposited into the checking (operating) account and then that money is used to pay the association's common expenses. Reserve allocations should be transferred from the operating account into the reserve account on a regular basis according to the annual budget.

The board of directors, according to California Civil Code Section 1365.5, must review, at least every three months, the account statements prepared by the financial institution where the funds are deposited, and a reconciliation of the accounts. Has your board ever seen reconciled statements? If not, what do you know about the current financial condition of your association? Do you rely solely on the financial reports that are prepared by the managing agent? If that is the case, you are not fulfilling your legal duty according to the law. Your common interest development, planned development, condominium association, stock cooperative or community apartment project ("own-your-own") is governed by this law whether you are incorporated or unincorporated, large or small, rich or poor. The board must protect the assets of the association.

Civil Code Section 1363.2 (d) allows the managing agent to deposit your funds into a commingled account for only ten days, and only if very specific legal requirements are in place to protect the association. Here is the actual wording of the applicable code:

The managing agent shall not commingle the funds of the association with his or her own money or with the money of others that he or she receives or accepts, unless all of the following requirements are met:

1. The managing agent commingled the funds of various associations on or before February 26, 1990, and has retained a written agreement with the board of directors of each association that he or she will maintain a fidelity and surety bond in an amount that provides adequate protection to the associations as agreed upon by the managing agent and the board of directors of each association.

More information in this subject can be found in the "Financial Matters" chapter.

CAN MANAGEMENT COMPANY TAKE THE PLACE OF THE BOARD?

Q *We live in a 36-unit condominium association. If all of the officers want to resign from the board of directors, can they hire a management company to take over the management of the association? Do all of the owners have the right to vote on hiring a management company? How does the voting take place?*

A The board cannot stop functioning. The association must have directors who are responsible for making decisions and setting policies even if a management company is hired. The management company only has the authority that the board delegates.

You can find out if the board has the authority to hire a management company by reading your association's declaration of covenants, conditions and restrictions (CC&Rs) and bylaws. Usually, the board has the authority to make the decision without a vote of the owners.

If the cost of hiring management would increase the annual budget more than twenty percent, then approval of the owners would be required. The board can call a special meeting of the owners. At least 50 percent of the members must attend or be represented by proxies. The budget increase must be approved by a majority of the voters who are in attendance at the meeting.

MANAGER GETS ANGRY WHEN EXPENSES ARE QUESTIONED

Q *Our homeowner association has a contract with a management company that includes all of the janitorial and landscape work. We have had the same management company for several years. They perform most of the repairs without obtaining competitive bids.*

I believe that our association is being overcharged for supplies, parts and extra labor. In most cases, the board does not approve the extra work before it is done. The manager becomes very angry if any of these expenses are questioned. Several thousand dollars in reserve funds have been used, but the manager refuses to disclose where the money was spent.

How can we report this to the Department of Real Estate for investigation?

A The California Department of Real Estate is responsible for overseeing only the development stage of a project. After the project is sold out, the management of the association is the responsibility of the volunteer board of directors. After control is turned over to the homeowners, the Department of Real Estate does not handle any complaints about the operation or management of the association.

Supervision of the management company is the responsibility of the board of directors. The contract may give the management company the authority to perform extra services as you have described. However, the reserve funds should not be available to the manager.

California law requires that reserve funds be under the control of the board of directors. Reserve funds must be kept in a separate bank account that requires two board members' or officers' signatures for withdrawals. Expenditures that are paid out of the reserve funds should always be approved by a vote of the board of directors and noted in the minutes of the association's board meetings.

The board of directors can delegate management responsibilities to the management company but the board has a duty to see that the terms of the contract do not allow the management company to take advantage of the association.

MANAGER WILL NOT DISCLOSE THE COMPANY'S ADDRESS

Q *Our homeowner association is managed by a management company that closed its office and obtained a post office box so that most of its business is conducted by mail. Even the board members do not know the location of the manager's office or the whereabouts of our association records. A recorder takes our phone calls and many of the calls are not answered.*

It seems peculiar that the company does not want their business address known. The board of directors is sympathetic to our complaints but they haven't changed management companies.

Is the company obligated to provide the services that we need? What can we do?

A The company is obligated to fulfill the terms of the contract. Hopefully, someone on the board has a copy of the contract!

Reputable management companies have a business address and they answer phone calls promptly. If the contract does not specify that they must have a business office that is accessible to the members, then they may not be required to provide one. However, the association's board of directors should know the location of their records and they should be cautious about a company that is, in effect, going into hiding.

Managers have disappeared without notice and taken association funds with them. The board should be diligent about obtaining a business address. If the company is failing to operate in a professional manner, the board should probably look for a new company.

As owners, you can attend a board meeting or write to the board to let them know that you are concerned about the current management company's performance. If the board fails to respond, you can petition the board to hold a special meeting of the owners to discuss the matter. Consult your association's bylaws about the method of calling for a special meeting.

MANAGER REFUSES TO SIGN CHECKS FROM THE RESERVE ACCOUNT

Q *Our homeowner association was managed by the board of directors until we recently signed a contract with a management company. They separated our funds into an operating account and a reserve account. The management company writes the checks from the operating account to pay all of the regular bills.*

The reserve account is for roof repair and other major expenses. The manager set the account up for us but she refuses to sign checks on the account. We had $6,000 worth of painting work. The manager said that we should have the approval for the painting work written in the board meeting minutes. When the work was completed, she brought the check to the board president for two board members' signatures instead of following up herself.

We hired a manager to do the work for us. We were tired of doing it ourselves. The manager's refusal to take care of the reserve funds is very disappointing.

Though most of her work is satisfactory, I feel that we aren't getting our money's worth if we still have responsibility and liability for the reserve funds.

Who is right?

A I have good news for you. Your manager is doing it right, even though it probably means extra work for her. California law requires that a community association's board members must control the reserve funds and the reserve account must have two board members' or officers' signatures for withdrawals.

By having the reserve expenditure approved in the board meeting minutes, the manager is protecting the two check signers from liability if any questions arise in the future. The written documentation in the minutes will show that the board authorized the withdrawal.

Signing a reserve check is not something that is a frequent occurrence, so I don't think you should be concerned about having to do it this way. You should be glad that the manager is following the letter of the law.

Every board of directors for every association should make sure that there is a special insurance policy called a fidelity bond to cover the association's reserve funds and operating account. It is preferable to have the management company named in the fidelity bond coverage so that your operating account is fully protected.

MANAGEMENT COMPANY IS NOT SATISFACTORY

Q *Our 45 unit condominium association has a contract with a property management firm for collection of the monthly assessments, paying the bills and providing a monthly financial statement. The board of directors was satisfied with the management company but one of the homeowners came to us with a proposal from another company. Since the bid from the competition was $200 less per month, the board finally decided to change companies about six months ago.*

As treasurer, I deal with the management company almost as much as the president of the board. The new company has been less than adequate even though I have spoken to the owner many times. It was three months before we got the first financial statement. Yesterday, the gas company notified me that our service was going to be shut off because the bill had not been paid.

The owner of the management company has a glib excuse for every complaint. He took care of the immediate problem but I feel certain that this same thing could occur at any time.

Should we change management companies again?

A It sounds like you have communicated your concerns to the management company. If I were you, I would check the contract to see if you can cancel it without a penalty or claim from the management company.

The board of directors should write a letter to the company stating the reasons that they have failed to perform satisfactorily.

Associations should not jump from one management company to another without trying to resolve the problems. In this situation, communication with the owner of the company is not eliminating the problem, so you should recommend to the other board members that the association go back to the previous company that was providing satisfactory service.

The transition to a new company is not always smooth, but since you are going back to a company that is familiar with your association, the change should not cause a problem. In my opinion, you should cancel the contract as soon as possible before the new company completely messes up your records and your credit history.

The board of directors should see that timely bill payment procedure is a requirement in the management contract. If a utility company has to shut off service, it will often require a large deposit before service is restored.

Your problem shows that the low bid is not always the best way to go.

CHAPTER 13 OWNERS' RIGHTS AND BUYERS' RIGHTS

OWNER ENTITLED TO OBTAIN OR COPY MAILING LIST

Q *I would like to contact the other owners in my condominium association regarding the next annual meeting. I have requested the association mailing list from the board of directors but they will not release it to me. They say that they don't want to give the list out because it might be used to advertise my business. Actually, they know why I want the list and they do not want to cooperate or assist me in any way. What can I do?*

A You are entitled to inspect the names and addresses of your association members and make copies for your use or the association is obligated to offer another method of providing the information that you are seeking. There have been many lawsuits that have been decided in favor of the requesting owner. Several states now have laws that compel the board of directors to provide access to membership records. In California, the association board is supposed to act on the request within 10 days.

Send a letter to your board of directors requesting permission to inspect and copy the membership list and mailing addresses. Request that the board discuss and act upon this matter at the next board meeting and notify you in writing within ten days after the meeting. If your board does not meet on a monthly basis, then send your letter to the board president, requesting action within 30 days.

WITHHOLDING ASSESSMENTS IS A BAD IDEA

Q *I live in a 34-unit condominium. I am concerned that the association's money is not being handled responsibly. I have refused to pay the monthly assessment for the last four months because the board president will not show me the bank statements.*

Yesterday, I received a letter from an attorney that the association has hired. I am furious that they are spending the association's money to hire an attorney for this purpose. What are my rights?

A First, you must understand that they are not using the association's money to pay for the attorney. It's going to come right out of your pocket.

You have an obligation to pay your monthly assessments, even if you disagree with the way the association is being run. The association has the right to demand payment from you for reasonable expenses incurred for collection purposes.

The longer you delay paying the money that is owed, the more you are going to be paying in the long run. The association has the right to file a lien and even foreclose on your property if you refuse to pay. Each legal step along the way costs you more money.

You have a right to see the association's financial reports but you will have to find some other way of exercising your rights instead of withholding your assessment payment.

OWNERS ARE ENTITLED TO ATTEND MOST BOARD MEETINGS

Q *I live in a property owners association. The architectural committee reviews and approves or disapproves home plans that are submitted by owners wishing to build a home on their property.*

The architectural committee and the board of directors hold secret meetings and owners are not allowed to attend unless the president invites them. Minutes are not available even after repeated requests. We are being treated with open hostility.

I believe that this conduct is immoral and possibly illegal. What are my options?

A You have the right to attend board meetings unless the board has a legitimate reason to have an executive session (closed meeting). In my opinion, you have the right to attend the architectural meeting if they are considering plans that you have submitted for approval. You should conduct yourself in a business-like manner. Neither you nor the board members or committee members should be confrontational.

Your first approach might be to educate the board about California laws. According to California Civil Code, Section 1363.05, community association board meetings must be open meetings. The association must publicize the meeting dates and location and the board must give owners an opportunity to address the board within reasonable time limits. Board decision-making and official action should take place at a duly noticed meeting.

Minutes, other than executive session (closed meetings) minutes, must be provided to any owner who requests copies. The requesting owner must pay the copying costs unless the association has a policy of distributing them to each owner without charge. The association must provide the actual minutes, a draft or summary within 30 days of a meeting, even if the board has not approved the minutes.

As an owner, you have a right to attend the meetings unless the board is discussing personnel issues, litigation issues, the formation of third-party contracts and disciplinary hearings, which require discretion in order to protect the privacy of individuals. Anyone accused of a violation may request that their hearing be conducted in executive session and the board must comply.

You should be allowed to attend the open meetings and speak to the board briefly, though you do not have the right to participate in the board's discussion or disrupt the meeting in any way. Read your association bylaws to find out about the procedure for conducting board meetings.

I recommend that boards allow some time prior to the meeting to hear owners' comments or questions. Time limits should be imposed fairly so that owners do not unnecessarily delay the formal meeting.

Boards that hold secret meetings are often accused of having something to hide. Your board has compounded their problem by refusing to allow you to have access to the minutes. Now they are probably offended by your criticism and wishing that they could resolve the matter, but it has escalated to open animosity. If they do not provide access to the board meeting minutes or allow your attendance at meetings, you can take legal action. Contact an attorney to discuss your options.

CAN BOARD HIRE MANAGEMENT WITHOUT VOTE OF OWNERS?

Q *Our association board recently hired a management company without a vote of the owners. We have a small number of units and have never needed a management company previously.*

Now we cannot get any information about our finances. The board refers us to the management company and the management company will not allow us to look at any records.

What are our rights as homeowners? Can the board spend our money on a management company without getting a vote of the owners?

A If you will read your association's governing documents, you will see that the board has a great deal of authority. Normally, the board has the authority to delegate management tasks to a management company. Even in small associations like yours, the responsibility of doing the accounting work and following up with delinquent owners can be a daunting task.

The board has a responsibility to see that accurate records are being kept. If they are unable to find volunteers to fulfill these duties, the reasonable business decision is to hire a management company to perform the duties the board cannot do. Board members are volunteers who serve as decision-makers. They are not required to spend many hours every month performing tasks that make them the unpaid servants of the association members.

Owners do have rights. You have the right to be informed when meetings are taking place and you have the right to attend the meetings. The exceptions are listed in the prior answer. You have the right to attend an annual meeting and vote for board members who will make decisions in the best interests of the association.

Corporations Codes Sections 8310 through 8320 state that written minutes, records and accounting reports are to be kept. Members have the right to review the books and accounting records of the association. This right is usually stated in the association's governing documents. Monthly or quarterly accounting reports must be prepared for the association. Usually, this information is sufficient for an owner to understand the financial status of the association.

Normally, the owner must request an opportunity to review the records with reasonable advance notice and at a reasonable time if the accounting reports that are distributed do not contain the specific information that you are seeking. Attorneys disagree as to the right of owners to review every detail of the accounting records of the association. If you are being prevented from seeing certain records, you have a right to ask why this is the association's procedure.

If you feel that the association is not being operated properly, you have the right to petition the board for a special meeting of the owners. You will find specific instructions for petitioning in the bylaws of your association.

CAN NEW BOARD TIGHTEN UP RULE ENFORCEMENT?

Q *The board of directors of our association is fining owners all of the time for the slightest infraction of the rules. The former board members did not enforce the rules so this is a drastic change. Is the board allowed to just put an extra charge on the assessment account of an owner without giving us the opportunity to explain? We were cited for speeding but our car is similar to one that is owned by a teenager who lives in the neighborhood. We are being billed for something we didn't do. We will have late charges added if we don't pay the bill soon. What can we do?*

A The board has the obligation to enforce the rules, especially if safety is an issue. It is unfortunate that the former board did not understand or carry out this responsibility. Now it is difficult for the new board to enforce rules without looking like the bad guys.

Owners who feel that rules are too harsh may attend a board meeting to let the board know their opinion. Usually, boards have the authority to change the rules and regulations, but they cannot change the other governing documents without a vote of the owners.

You have the right to be heard if you disagree with the citation. Many associations have specific means of "due process" in the declaration of covenants, conditions and restrictions (CC&Rs) or the bylaws. Due process allows an owner to address the board to protest a violation notice. It is very important that the association's board follows the procedures for enforcement that appear in the governing documents.

The alleged rule violator is entitled to written notice of the rule that he or she is accused of violating. Then the association must give the owner the opportunity to a hearing with at least 10 days' notice. The hearing can be in executive session with only the board members and the alleged violator in attendance. The board must comply with an owner's request to have the hearing in executive session.

After the hearing, the board can decide how to proceed. They have the right to waive the fine or levy the fine based upon a majority decision. Notice of the board's decision should then be sent to the owner as soon as possible. California law says that a written notification of the board's decision must be sent out within 15 days. The law specifically states that the board's disciplinary action is not valid if the ten-day notice or the 15-day notification of their decision is not provided to the member.

If the owner fails to respond to the notice or fails to attend the hearing, the board can proceed with their decision without the member present.

In summary, the board has the obligation to enforce the rules but they must do so in accordance with the governing documents of the association. If the association levies monetary penalties, all of the owners are entitled to be informed about the amount of those penalties in advance. The penalties must be reasonable and enforcement must be fair and consistent. The association's attorney should be consulted to ensure that the board is following the association's procedures correctly.

BUYER SHOULD REVIEW ASSOCIATION DOCUMENTS

Q *I am considering purchasing a condominium. I found one that I really like but I don't know how to determine the financial strength of the association.*

What documents shall I ask for, in addition to the financial statements? After I obtain the documents, what should I look for when I review them?

A Be prepared to spend considerable time analyzing the association and the surrounding area before you make your decision. Prior to signing a purchase agreement, make sure that there is a clause in the agreement that allows for cancellation if the following documents are not provided or if they do not meet with your approval:

1. The declaration, often called the covenants, conditions and restrictions (CC&Rs), is the association's "constitution." It explains the powers and duties of the association and the board of directors, the restrictions that owners must obey, the authority of the association to collect assessments to pay for the maintenance costs of operating the association, and many other detailed legal requirements such as insurance protection and financial controls. Look for architectural controls and use restrictions in the declaration. Architectural controls govern what alterations or improvements are allowed in the interior and the exterior of your unit.
2. The bylaws explain how the association is to be operated. This document expands upon the declaration, giving the specific procedures for carrying out the responsibilities of the association, i.e., election procedures, frequency of meetings, responsibilities of the officers of the association and more detailed information about the powers and duties of the board of directors.
3. The rules include the "do"s and "don't"s for everyday living such as parking regulations and pool rules. The rules will often include the architectural guidelines for modifications. If you are a person who likes to "do your own thing" and the association's rules consist of a 50-page document, I can tell you that you aren't going to enjoy living in this particular association.
4. The latest annual financial report will tell you whether the association is operating without a loss and reserving funds for future repairs and replacement. An independent licensed accountant must do the annual financial review or audit if the association's annual income is greater than $75,000. Check to see if the association has a detailed reserve analysis or reserve study that

shows the amount of money needed for maintaining the association's common areas such as roofs, painting, mechanical equipment and other major components. Further explanation can be found in the chapter on Financial Matters.

5. The current budget will reveal the planned expenditures. You will find out whether the association employs personnel or contracts with a professional management company. You'll learn how much the association is supposed to be setting aside for reserves out of each month's assessment income.

Don't look for an association with low monthly assessments. The assessment amount depends upon the type of amenities and the level of services as well as the reserve funding. An association with low assessments may not be setting aside the reserves, which pay for future repair and replacement of the common area components.

The minutes of board meetings for the prior 12 months will reveal the current projects that the association is working on and whether there are problems that are not being resolved. Since minutes do not always reveal legal matters, you should ask for written disclosure of lawsuits or construction defects. In addition to reviewing these documents and records, you may want to ask some of the residents how long they have lived there and how they feel about the association. Sometimes this is the only way to find out about noise problems, average age of the owners, traffic or parking problems and other factors that may have an impact on your day-to-day living and your future happiness.

OWNER THINKS BOARD IS DISCRIMINATING AGAINST HIM

Q *I live in a large association of single-family homes. The association maintains the landscaping on the slopes behind of the homes as well as the "green belt" or walkways and parks. There are large weeds growing on the slope behind my house. One spot is almost bare and the soil is starting to erode.*

Other areas of the development look much better than the area where I live. I think the board is discriminating against me. I attended a board meeting and questioned the board about maintenance costs when our assessments were increased last year. Now, it appears that they have directed the landscape company to cut back on the maintenance of my area.

How can I combat these unfair tactics?

A Your use of the word "combat" makes it sound as though you are preparing for war. Don't think of your association board as your enemy without giving them the benefit of the doubt. I have seen boards that try to punish owners. It is unfortunate when that happens. Boards have a duty to treat each owner with respect and to see that the association is maintained in a fair and consistent manner. Owners should treat the board with respect also.

Put your past contact with the board out of mind and proceed as though you are just informing someone of a problem. Since you live in a large association, you probably have a manager. The normal way of reporting a maintenance problem is to contact the manager. Start with a phone call to report the condition of the slope. Be specific about the location and the problems so that the manager will have enough information to pass along to the landscape maintenance company.

If you do not see improvement within a couple of weeks, put your complaint in writing and send copies to the board. Be business-like and courteous. Invite the board to look at the slope so that they will see and understand the problems. Slope erosion is serious and the problem should be addressed without delay.

OWNER IS UNABLE TO PAY HER MONTHLY ASSESSMENT

Q *I recently lost my job and have had financial problems. I have been unable to pay the monthly assessment to the association for the past four months. I just received a notice that the association is going to file a lien on my property. I am working again but it will be impossible for me to pay all of this debt immediately since I have other financial obligations.*

I spoke to the treasurer and explained my financial situation. He said that the association has a delinquency policy and they must treat everyone consistently without regard for an individual's financial problems. Now I will have additional expenses added to my account because of the warnings and notices. How can I deal with this situation?

A The board is handling this situation correctly, in my opinion. It is not a kindness to you to allow your delinquency to get so high that you can never pay it back. It may seem harsh but it is unfair to the other owners if you are allowed to ignore your responsibility to pay.

I recommend that you request a special meeting with the board, which should be an executive session to protect your privacy. Let them know what you can afford to pay and offer a payment plan that will eventually pay off the delinquency, preferably within six months. If you offer a "good faith" plan, perhaps the association will cooperate with you so that your additional costs are kept at a minimum.

Do not ignore the notices from the association. Extra collection costs will continue to increase and the association has the right to foreclose on your property if you cannot pay your assessments.

BOARD MUST PROVIDE ANNUAL FINANCIAL REPORT

Q *I own a unit in a condominium association. My unit is rented out to a tenant. I do not feel that the board is spending money wisely. When sending in my monthly assessment payment to the management company, I requested a financial statement. There was no response. The board does not give a financial report at meetings and they are hostile when questioned. In two years I have received no explanation of expenditures. What are my legal rights?*

A You are entitled to receive an annual budget 45 to 60 days prior to the beginning of each fiscal year. Section 1365 of the California Civil Code says that, unless your association documents impose more stringent standards, the association should provide to each owner an estimate of the income and expenses on an accrual basis.

This annual budget should also show the total cash reserves that are set aside for future use and the estimate of the current replacement cost, remaining useful life, and the methods of funding the repair or replacement of the major components of the property that the association is required to maintain.

If your association's annual gross income exceeds $75,000, the association must provide a financial review that is prepared by a licensed accountant (CPA). A copy of the review of the financial statement must be distributed within 120 days after the close of the fiscal year. If the association is incorporated with revenues of at least $10,000, a financial report must be issued that is also in compliance with Corporations Code Sections 8321 and 8322. You can refer to the chapter on Financial Matters for more information.

The information should be provided to all owners whether you live in the unit or not. Perhaps it was distributed door-to-door and your tenant did not pass the information on to you.

In the future, do not enclose your request for information with your monthly assessment payment. Write to your board president or the association's manager or both.

MANAGEMENT CAN CHARGE AN OWNERSHIP TRANSFER FEE

Q *I recently bought a second unit in a condominium association where I have been an owner for several years. After the closing, the association manager informed me that I owed $175 for an ownership transfer fee.*

There is nothing in the association's governing documents or the management agreement that states that a fee is charged when owner-

ship changes. The manager's contract simply states that it is the manager's duty is to record changes in ownership and maintain ownership records.

Is a transfer fee normally imposed for this purpose and, if so, what amount would be normal?

A There is almost always a transfer fee that is charged to the buyer or the seller. The transfer fees vary from zero to $400 or more. In general, self-managed associations tend to charge less than professional management. If an unpaid board member is providing the service, a transfer fee might consist of only photocopying costs.

Civil Code Section 1368 includes a long list of documents and disclosure information that must be provided from the seller to the prospective buyer. It states that when the association receives a written request for these documents and disclosure information, the association must respond within ten (10) days. The association may charge a reasonable fee. Since it is the manager who usually performs this service, the fee is normally established in the manager's contract, even though the amount is collected from an individual seller or buyer.

In my opinion, the manager certainly has a right to collect a fee and $175 is reasonable for the complete ownership transfer packet and related services. Many managers provide an itemized list of charges.

Kathleen Windsor, a former real estate agent in Tustin and Irvine, California says, "I have seen transfer fees as high as $400 or more, especially in Orange County where the property might be in a sub-association under a larger master association. In such a situation, the documents and disclosures may be provided by two different management companies, one for the sub-association and one for the master association."

On the first page of the standard residential purchase agreement used by the California Association of Realtors, there is a place to check whether buyer or seller will be responsible for payment of the homeowner association transfer fees. The escrow company then charges the appropriate party at the time of closing. You may want to review your purchase agreement and escrow documents to see if an ownership transfer fee was included in the escrow fees that were paid at the time of the closing.

If you acquired the property without the assistance of a Realtor or escrow company, that would explain why the manager is now billing you for the fee. You have obviously done some research to determine whether there is any documentation to show that the manager is entitled to this fee. In my opinion, the services provided in conjunction with transfer of ownership are worthy of reasonable charges.

In general, buyers and sellers are unaware of the large amount of time that a manager spends on an ownership transfer. An itemization of charges would include a long list of services. It is not simply changing an owner's name on the computer. Buyers must be provided with complete and current copies of the governing documents, financial statements and disclosures, reserve study, insurance coverage, litigation disclosure and board meeting minutes. An accurate statement of the status of the seller's assessment account must be prepared. Usually, lengthy lender documents and disclosures must be filled out. Sometimes there is more than one loan application. The manager may have many phone calls from real estate agents, escrow company representatives, lenders and others. If the property has some form of controlled access, the directory at the entrance must be changed and common area keys must be provided.

Since you already owned a unit in the association, you may feel that some of the disclosure information was superfluous, but each transfer is a separate transaction and the seller is obligated by law to meet the legal disclosure requirements and lender requirements. Usually, the task falls on the manager's shoulders. It is a time-consuming responsibility with a great deal of liability.

NEIGHBOR'S CIGARETTE SMOKING BOTHERS UNIT OWNER

Q *I have lived comfortably in my condominium unit for the past six years. Recently, the owner of the unit located directly below me rented out the unit to a heavy smoker. Every time the tenant smokes on his patio, the smoke comes up into my deck. If we both have windows open on the same side of the building, wind will frequently carry the smoke into my unit.*

I have spoken to the tenant and the manager, but nothing has changed. What other options do I have?

A Since I have some sensitivity to cigarette smoke, I can certainly empathize with you. Smoke is bothersome to a great many people and is also a health risk, as scientific studies have shown.

Many associations have rules that prevent smoking in common areas. However, the patio is probably "exclusive use common area."

Living in proximity to others means that some of our privacy and our individual rights are reduced. For instance, some associations prohibit the use of barbeque grills on patios and balconies, not just because of the obvious fire hazard but also because of the nuisance of the smoke and food odors.

In my opinion, you should not have to endure your neighbor's cigarette smoke. However, it may be very difficult to convince your neighbor not to smoke on his patio. I doubt if you want to go to the extreme of trying to obtain a court order to prohibit his smoking.

You have two other reasonable alternatives. The first is contacting the owner of the unit to ask for his or her cooperation. The owner might convince the tenant that he should smoke only inside the unit with the windows closed. The owner has the authority to control the tenant's actions to a certain extent.

The second alternative would be to write to the association's board of directors to see if they would consider prohibiting smoking on the patios and balconies. The board may resist making this type of rule unless a large number of owners would support and comply with it. You may want to take an informal survey of some of your neighbors to see if others are bothered also.

If neither the owner nor the board is responsive to your problem, then you may have to resort to closing your windows and doors when your neighbor is at home. This may require that you run your air conditioning more, but you may decide that it is worth the additional expense so that you can have clean air and stay on friendly terms with your neighbor.

For your health and peace of mind, you may want to consider moving. It is a drastic and expensive solution but it may be the best solution.

OWNERS ARE IN CONFLICT OVER NOISE

Q *We live in a 20-unit condominium association. Two of our owners are in conflict over a noise issue. One lives above the other. The one residing on the lower floor has complained about the upstairs neighbors allowing skating and riding toy vehicles across hard surfaces, slamming cabinet doors and using the washing machine after midnight.*

The prior owner of the downstairs unit moved out because of the noise. The new owner has lived here for about a year. He has retaliated by turning his stereo volume up to a deafening level.

Communication between the two owners has now completely deteriorated. We don't want to have another owner moving out because of the upstairs owner's noise.

What can the condominium association do to help resolve this problem?

A Ideally, this type of problem should be resolved between the two owners. Too many owners expect the association to solve problems with their neighbors because they don't feel comfortable about confronting the offending neighbor and trying to resolve the problem. Perhaps they are afraid that they will make matters worse if they try to solve it neighbor-to-neighbor. It is also difficult to predict how the "friendly neighbor" approach is going to be received. This situation has probably escalated to the point of causing problems for the other neighbors if there is frequent noise and retaliation, so now it is the association's problem.

The board of directors should assist with some mediation techniques. Invite both owners to meet with the board to discuss the problem. The board member who is conducting the meeting should require that both of the neighbors remain calm and discuss with each other how the problem can be resolved. Perhaps that will be effective and no further action will be necessary.

Your letter doesn't state whether the association has any rules that are being broken. For instance, many associations have rules that state that no noisy appliances can be used after 10:00 or 11:00 p.m. If either one of the neighbors is violating a rule, then the association board should notify them of the violation and ask for their cooperation.

If the association's legal documents provide the board with the authority to adopt rules and levy penalties for failure to comply with rules, the board should consider adopting rules that would require owners to limit appliance use to daytime and early evening hours. Rules may help but inconsiderate neighbors often disobey rules, so the board needs to decide on reasonable penalties and then implement them as needed.

The board must be fair and reasonable when confronting those who don't comply with restrictions and rules. If the board has the authority to charge the violating owner with a monetary penalty or fine, this should only be implemented after giving the owner the opportunity to meet with the board to discuss the complaint. The hearing procedures appear in a prior answer in this chapter.

All of the owners should be fair and reasonable also. In most buildings, you will be able to hear your neighbors occasionally. You may not appreciate your neighbor's noise but retaliation is seldom wise or effective. When the conflict is out of control or noise is used to harass, then it may be necessary to seek legal advice about protecting all of the owners' rights to quiet enjoyment of their homes.

BOARD CHARGES HIGH FEE FOR COPIES OF MINUTES OF MEETINGS

Q *Our cooperative association board recently announced that there would be a $10 charge for requests for minutes of board meetings and a $100 charge for requests for the minutes of the general membership's annual meeting.*

In addition, a fine of $50 will be charged for any materials delivered under the door to the owners in the building. How are owners going to communicate if there is a common concern? If we place an announcement on the bulletin board, it is removed within the hour. Does this sound reasonable or legal to you?

A It sounds neither reasonable nor legal! As an owner or shareholder of a nonprofit mutual benefit corporation, you are entitled to see the minutes of board meetings and annual membership meetings without charge. If you request your own photocopy, it seems unreasonable that the board would charge anything beyond the photocopying cost. California Civil Code Section 1366.1 states, "An association shall not impose or collect an assessment or fee that exceeds the amount necessary to defray the costs for which it is levied." Your cooperative association must comply with this law.

The board's attempt to control communication may be evidence of a fear that people will find out what is going on and do something about it. That is the larger problem, in my opinion. You have a right to communicate with the rest of the cooperative's members; however, if you are doing so by shoving anonymous "poison pen letters" under everyone's door, I can't support your methods of communication. I do not understand why letters delivered to one's neighbors would justify a $50 fine. Is this a littering charge or is there a specific rule that bans any material being delivered under the door?

You should not allow your association board to trample on your rights as an owner. I recommend that you discuss this with the board and urge them to seek the advice of an attorney. In California and in many other states, the law establishes certain rights for owners. If you submit a written request for the mailing list of the members, for instance, the California Nonprofit Mutual Benefit Corporations Code, Section 8330, sets the association's response time as 10 days.

ASSOCIATIONS MUST COMPLY WITH STATE LAWS

Q *I live in a stock cooperative. Our fiscal year will end on December 31. Are the stockholders entitled to budget information if the monthly assessment is going to increase next year?*

A Yes, the California law that governs common interest developments or community associations, Civil Code Sections 1350 through 1376, pertains to stock cooperatives and community apartment projects ("own your own" apartment complexes) as well as condominiums, homeowner associations and planned unit developments (PUDs). These sections of the Civil Code govern all community associations, large or small and incorporated or unincorporated.

The annual budget, including the estimated expenses of both the operating fund and reserve funds, must be distributed to all owners between 45 and 60 days prior to the beginning of the fiscal year. The distribution of the annual budget is required even if the amount of the budget does not change.

Other disclosure requirements, which include the notice of the community association's delinquency procedures for unpaid assessments, the association's schedule of monetary penalties for violation of the governing documents, a summary of the association's insurance coverage and the summary of Civil Code Section 1354 (the statute regarding alternative dispute resolution) can be distributed in the same mailing.

If the association's board does not distribute the budget within the specified time frame, the budget cannot be increased unless a majority of the owners attend a membership meeting and a majority of the owners in attendance can then approve or disapprove the increase.

WHAT CAN OWNER DO IF BOARD DOESN'T COMPLY WITH LAWS?

Q *Your advice is a wealth of knowledge for boards of directors and community association owners. However, my association board seems to ignore regulations and the Davis-Stirling Act that you write about so frequently.*

Our last reserve study was done in 1994. The board boasts about the $49,000 currently in the reserve fund but the reserve study says that our fund should be $89,000 this year. Maintenance projects are not being done. Stucco has fallen off the front of the building and tree branches need to be trimmed so that further damage to the building is prevented.

What can an owner do to enforce the laws and rules that the board is ignoring?

A Are you ready to work to get your association on the right track? You will need to find other owners who are also concerned about deferred maintenance and low reserves. You and other concerned owners can volunteer to serve on a finance committee with the goal of updating the reserve study. If the board rebuffs your assistance, then you may want to enlist the help of other owners to vote for new directors in the next election.

Obviously the reserve study needs to be updated to comply with state law and the building must be maintained according to the governing documents of the association. These are basic responsibilities of the board.

Inadequate budgeting and failure to accumulate adequate reserve funds is a common problem in associations. However, there are always some owners who want to keep their monthly assessments low and they don't want the board to spend the reserve funds. Boards sometimes try to please the vocal penny pinchers instead of doing what is best for the whole association.

There is no question that the board must carry out the association's duty to maintain the building. To put it bluntly, the board is supposed to protect the owners' investment regardless of the owners' personal views on keeping assessments low. When the association's curb appeal is affected, owners lose respect for their property and vandals are more apt to damage it or paint it with graffiti.

There is no state or local agency to make the board comply with the law. If you are unable to convince the board to change their fiscal philosophy, perhaps a letter from your attorney reminding them of their fiduciary responsibilities will be the wake-up call that they need.

DO I HAVE TO GIVE THE BOARD THE KEY TO MY UNIT?

Q *I live in a three-story condominium complex consisting of 30 units. Our declaration of covenants, conditions and restrictions (CC&Rs) states that the association must have a key to each unit. This has not been enforced and I am one of the owners who has never complied. Now the board president is sending reminders that I must provide my key to the association.*

The thought of someone having access to my home is very unsettling to me. I do not want to give the board of directors my key. What are my rights and obligations?

A In general, you are obligated to comply with the CC&Rs, however you also have the right to protect your personal property and your privacy.

Keeping owners' keys is a huge liability for the association. It is both a legal issue and an insurance issue. If the board has not established procedures to ensure that the keys are handled responsibly, they should do so immediately with the advice of the association's attorney and insurance agent.

You have a right to know who keeps the keys and under what circumstances the key would be used to enter your unit. Since you live in a small building, it is unlikely that strict procedures are in place. Does the board president keep all of the keys? What happens when the board president is not at home?

Larger buildings usually have very strict procedures. For example, the on-site personnel of a large high-rise should have written key control procedures. The unit keys are usually kept in a locked cabinet or a safe that is only accessible to certain individuals. Some associations require that the owner seal the unit key in an envelope and if the seal is broken, the circumstances must be documented in a key control log. There are usually owners who refuse to provide a key to management despite the strict security procedures.

If there is a fire or police emergency in your unit, your locked door will probably be destroyed. That is a risk that you assume under any circumstances.

Emergencies can occur that are not life threatening. A water leak can be very destructive in a short period of time. If the water leak occurs in your unit and damages other units, you may be held liable for the damage. If the association's lack of a key increases the damage, will that increase your liability? You should discuss these matters with your insurance agent and your attorney.

OWNER BELIEVES BOARD MEMBER IS NOT PAYING ASSESSMENTS

Q *I am an owner in a homeowners association. I am wondering about my right to request a list of the owners in our association who are not paying their monthly assessment. Through an overheard conversation, I became aware that one of our board members is delinquent and, therefore, is voting against collecting assessments from other delinquent owners.*

I resent board members who establish a budget for the whole association and then fail to live up to their own financial obligation as an owner. If a director can't manage his or her personal finances, I don't feel that he or she should be in a position to manage corporate finances.

Our association's legal documents state that delinquent owners' voting rights are suspended but nothing is said about a delinquent board member's right to remain on the board. How can I follow up on the information that I heard? Do I have a right to see a list of delinquent owners?

A You have a right to review the financial records of the association because your homeowners association is a nonprofit mutual benefit organization. However, I know that there are association attorneys who defend the position of withholding this information in order to protect the privacy of the owners.

You and the other owners have a right to expect that your board of directors is upholding the governing documents and enforcing the delinquency procedures that are established for the association. The association members should challenge a board that ignores this basic fiduciary responsibility.

The association's written policy for handling delinquencies is supposed to be distributed annually to all of the owners. If the board fails to establish and uphold the policy, the entire board can be held liable, not just the delinquent board member.

Board members are entitled to human error now and then. Perhaps the late payment was a brief oversight. If it is a delinquency that lasts more than 30 days, I would question the board member's right to vote and participate in board meetings. According to your legal documents, voting rights for the delinquent member are suspended. Board members are not allowed any special favors or leniency.

OWNERS AND TENANTS ARE CHARGED PENALTIES FOR VIOLATIONS

Q *Our homeowner association has a graduated schedule of monetary penalties that are charged against owners or tenants who violate the declaration of covenants, conditions and restrictions (CC&Rs) or rules and regulations.*

We were told that California law limits the amount of penalties that can be charged per year to an individual owner. Are you familiar with this law and the limits for penalties?

A Your information is not completely correct. The law is California Civil Code, Section 1363(g): "If an association adopts or has adopted a policy imposing any monetary penalty, including any fee, on any association member for a violation of the governing documents or rules of the association, including any monetary penalty relating to the activities of a guest or invitee of the member, the board of directors shall adopt and distribute to each member, by personal delivery or first class mail, a schedule of the monetary penalties that may be assessed for those violations, which shall be in accordance with authorization for member discipline contained in the governing documents. The board of directors shall not be required to distribute any additional schedules of monetary penalties unless there are changes from the schedule that was adopted and distributed to the members pursuant to this subdivision. The board of directors of the association shall meet in executive session if requested by the member being disciplined and the member shall be entitled to attend the executive session."

The law does not limit the amount of penalties. However, the association's legal documents may include limits. As the law states, the association's penalty procedures must comply with the member discipline procedures that are specified in the CC&Rs or bylaws. Many associations have requirements in the legal documents for notification of the violator and other due process provisions that promote fairness and reasonableness in the discipline process.

Due process requirements in Civil Code Section 1363 include that the alleged violator receive notice of the specific restriction or rule that was violated, with at least ten days' notice of the date, time and place for the alleged violator to attend a hearing to answer the accusations and the opportunity to correct the violation. After the hearing takes place, the association must provide notification of the board's disciplinary action by personal delivery or first call mail within 15 days following the hearing.

OWNERS MUST RECEIVE MEETING NOTICES, ACCESS TO MINUTES

Q *Are owners entitled to receive adequate notice when membership meetings are scheduled? Are we entitled to know what issues are on the agenda for a membership vote?*

A Section 1363 of the California Civil Code has several other provisions regarding owners' rights, including:

1. The meeting notice that is distributed prior to a general membership meeting must specify the agenda items that will be presented for members' vote.
2. Membership meetings are to be conducted under some form of parliamentary procedure.

3. Members of the association are entitled to access to association records as described in California Corporations Code, Sections 8330 through 8338.
4. Any member of the association may attend any board meeting except when the board adjourns to executive session to discuss litigation, matters that relate to contract formation or negotiation, personnel matters or disciplinary hearings. Members may attend the board meetings and address the board within reasonable time limitations. They may observe the board meetings but the members do not vote or participate in the decision-making process during a board meeting.
5. If two or more associations are performing or managing the functions of the membership, such as a master association and sub-association, members may attend meetings of the joint or master association.
6. The minutes of any meeting of the board of directors or a draft copy of the minutes, or a summary of the minutes, must be available to the members within 30 days after the meeting. The minutes, draft copy or summary must be distributed to any requesting owner upon receipt of reimbursement of the association's costs for copying and distributing them.
7. The board of directors is required to notify all members that meeting minutes will be distributed upon request. The notice should specify how and where copies of the minutes can be obtained.

You will find more information in the "Meetings" chapter.

BUYER SHOULD GET CC&RS LONG BEFORE CLOSE OF ESCROW

Q *I have learned that a buyer should read the declaration of covenants, conditions and restrictions (CC&Rs) before purchasing property in an association.*

I am interested in buying a unit in an 18-unit complex but the real estate agent says that I will get the CC&Rs at the closing when the final closing documents are signed. Is this proper?

A No, you are entitled to see the association's governing documents long before you get to the closing.

A prospective buyer is entitled to see the CC&Rs, the bylaws, the rules and regulations, the budget and financial statements. Before I would consider signing a purchase agreement I would want to read all of these documents and possibly review the board meeting minutes of the prior twelve months. The real estate agent that represented me in my most recent purchase (a single-family home located in an association) efficiently gathered all the documents that I requested and we closed within thirty days.

You need to find an agent who will protect your interests. If you sign a purchase agreement without seeing all of the disclosure information, be sure that the agreement has a contingency clause that allows you a reasonable number of days to review the documents with the right to withdraw from the agreement if there is anything that doesn't meet with your approval.

I would be curious about the reason that the seller or real estate agent is not disclosing the CC&Rs. Are there pet restrictions that exclude your Great Dane? Do you have five cars and the outside parking is reserved for guests only? These are restrictions that you need to learn about *before* you decide to buy.

NEW OWNER SURPRISED ABOUT ASSESSMENT INCREASE

Q *I recently purchased a townhouse. Fifteen days after the close of escrow, I received notice of a homeowner meeting. The notice of meeting was dated one day prior to my closing date and it referred to an imminent assessment increase. The board approved a 20 percent increase in the monthly assessment. Then I learned of water intrusion problems and costly testing that is being conducted. Neither of these matters was disclosed to me prior to my purchase. I informed the management company that I was very disturbed about the lack of disclosure.*

What recourse do I have?

A Any sales transaction is accompanied by several disclosure documents. Of course, there are more documents connected with the transfer of property situated in an association than the number of disclosure forms required in the sale of a home that is not in an association.

If the assessment increase and water intrusion matters were known to the seller, the seller had the duty to disclose them and the real estate agent had the duty to inform the seller about full disclosure of any anticipated increase in assessments, construction problems and many other matters.

Your agent should have protected you by ensuring that you received from the seller, or seller's agent, a form called the Real Estate Transfer Disclosure Statement that includes information completed by the seller and the seller's agent. Additional disclosure information required in Civil Code 1368 is supposed to be provided by the seller "as soon as practicable before transfer of title" so that the buyer has an opportunity to reject the offer if any of the disclosure information is unacceptable. The lender usually reviews this specific disclosure information prior to deciding whether to fund the mortgage. If the disclosure was sent to your lender and not provided to you, that is another mistake on the part of the agent or the escrow company.

Information required in Civil Code Section 1358 includes, along with many other disclosures, "Any change in the association's current regular and special assessments and fees which have been approved by the association's board of directors, but have not become due and payable as of the date disclosure is provided." This information should not be held back and presented to the buyer at the escrow closing when there isn't adequate time to review all of the documents and forms.

From your information about the specific dates of the transfer of ownership and the notice of meeting about the impending assessment increase, it appears that you should have been informed about it.

Seek the advice of a real estate attorney who can review all of the documents and advise you of any recourse and applicable deadlines. Until you obtain legal advice, continue to pay your assessments in full or the association could file a lien on your unit and complicate your legal issues even more.

CHAPTER 14 NON-RESIDENT OWNERS AND RENTALS

HOW SHOULD BOARD DEAL WITH TENANT VIOLATIONS?

Q *One of the owners in our association has rented his unit to tenants who have noisy arguments that disturb the neighbors. We have asked the association's board of directors and management company to enforce our rules that prohibit excessive noise. The association has fined the owner for the behavior of her tenants in the past. The police have been called numerous times. What else can we do?*

Can the association evict the renter? Can the association continue to penalize the owner?

A Your rules should include the association's procedure for levying monetary penalties. These procedures are supposed to be distributed to all owners. In my opinion, it is information that all tenants should receive. The association must collect penalties from the owner. The governing documents usually say that the owner is legally responsible for the actions of family members, guests and tenants. The owner can't say, "It's not my problem."

Each time the tenants disturb the other residents, the neighbors should write a written complaint to the board and management noting the date and time of the disturbance. If you have on-site security personnel, they can document the complaints if they are instructed to do so in the service contract.

In most associations, management will send out citations as directed by the board. The association has no contractual relationship with the tenants, so the association should be dealing with the owner of the unit. The board could consult with the association's attorney regarding the proper procedure to follow; however, I can suggest a procedure that may be effective.

A letter should be sent to the owner and a copy of the letter should be sent to the tenants. The letter should state the date and time that the alleged violation took place and cite the section, paragraph or page number of the governing documents that pertain to the violation. Request that the owner attend a board hearing and state that the violation may result in a specific amount of monetary penalty if the owner does not respond.

If your governing documents establish the procedure and schedule for notice of the hearing and the specific penalty involved, the board and management company should carefully follow those procedures. The owner is entitled to have reasonable advance notice of ten days or more prior to the hearing. If the owner is unable to attend, he should respond in writing to ask for a postponement of the hearing. The board should honor the owner's request and work with the owner to find a solution to the problem.

The board should not view the hearing process as a means of discipline but rather as a means of learning how the owner is going to deal with the problem. A monetary penalty can be levied at the hearing if the owner fails to appear and fails to respond to the hearing notice. The association must provide a written decision within 15 days after the hearing. The owner is obligated to pay the penalty unless the amount is unreasonable. Unpaid penalties can be added to the owner's assessment billing and small claims court is an option if the owner fails to pay.

Each time the tenants cause a disturbance, a written complaint should be initiated and the board should follow up with an enforcement hearing for the owner. It is time-consuming and frustrating, but it is usually effective in getting the owner's attention.

The owner, not the association, has the power to evict the tenant depending upon the wording regarding eviction that appears in the lease. So the association must prove to the owner that the tenants' behavior is a serious problem. If citations and penalties are ignored, a letter from the association's attorney is usually effective and the attorney's fees can be passed on to the owner.

Some associations have provisions in the declaration of covenants, conditions and restrictions (CC&Rs) that require a standard lease agreement between the owner and the tenant that spells out the tenant's obligation to abide by the governing documents, which includes the declaration, bylaws and rules and regulations. Even with that provision in the lease, it is still the owner's responsibility to evict the tenant if problems arise.

ASSOCIATION CAN'T CHARGE HIGHER FEE FOR RENTED UNITS

Q *Our condominium association is considering charging an additional fee or a higher monthly assessment for absentee owners who lease their units to tenants. There is additional work and expense when communicating with absentee owners. Our volunteer board performs our maintenance, accounting and other association duties and absentee owners do not participate in these responsibilities. We also feel that the increased fee may discourage absentee ownership.*

In our relatively small complex of 35 units, it is getting more difficult to find enough resident owners who are able and willing to serve on the board of directors. How do we resolve this problem?

A First, I don't think you will find more owners willing to serve on the board as a result of charging these additional fees. If owners are getting tired of serving, then it's time to consider a management company to handle the maintenance and accounting functions.

Second, you must read your association's legal documents to determine whether the association has the authority to charge a higher fee from absentee owners. Many declarations state that all owner assessments "shall be equal." Remember that the word "shall" means "must" in a legal document. If the assessments are not equal then the assessment amount is usually based upon the square footage of the unit.

Third, if the authority to charge a higher fee is stated in your documents, then you must decide what a fair and reasonable fee would be. Can the extra fee be justified by extra services provided, such as additional postage and extra copies of correspondence for both the owner and the tenant? Does the association provide common area keys or copies of the legal documents and rules that would be chargeable to the owner? What other charges do you feel are justifiable? After you have considered all these factors, then seek the advice of your association's attorney prior to approving the new fee. Proper notice should be given to all the owners so that they can respond with any questions or concerns before the new fee is initiated.

If one of your goals is to reduce the number of rental units, I doubt if the extra fee would effectively discourage owners from renting out their units. After further study and discussion, you may decide that the justification and extra bookkeeping involved with having the extra fee just simply isn't worth it.

CAN FEE BE CHARGED FOR TENANTS' MOVE-IN OR MOVE-OUT?

Q *Several units in our condominium association are rented out by the owners. The association must change the resident directory at the front entrance, change office records and provide rules and regulations to each new tenant.*

The move-in and move-out often results in damage to the common areas of the building. Though the owner is supposed to pay for any damage, sometimes it is difficult to determine the guilty party or to prove it.

When a unit is rented, can the association charge a $100 move-in fee each time there is a new tenant?

A Charging a flat move-in fee is a common practice in many condominiums but you should discuss this with your association's attorney before instigating any new fee.

If an owner challenges the fee, the association may have difficulty collecting the fee unless the board is able to show justification for the charges. If the charge is fair and reasonable based upon actual association cost such as those you mentioned, then the fee probably would not be contested.

Most association documents are written so that owners, both resident owners and non-resident owners, are all treated equally. The association has no contractual agreement with the renter that would require the renter to pay a fee to the association. If you are going to have a move-in or move-out fee, it is more equitable to charge the owner of the unit any time there is a change in occupancy.

If owners move in, they would be charged a fee. If tenants move in, the owner of the unit would pay the association and then get reimbursed by the tenant.

Charging for actual damages that occur during the move-in or move-out is always justifiable if you can determine who actually caused the damage. Sometimes charging a move-in fee does not ensure good behavior. Some individuals are not careful and then if damage occurs, they feel that they have already paid for the damage with the move-in or move-out fee.

The association members should realize that there will occasionally be damage that is not billed to anyone because of lack of evidence. In my opinion, this does not give the association the authority to punish all the owners who are leasing their units to tenants by charging an exorbitant fee that will eventually pay for the complete redecoration of the building. Owners who reside in the building also cause wear and tear and maintenance problems.

OWNER COMPLAINS ABOUT EXTRA ASSESSMENT

Q *I know that many of the rules and regulations of our condominium association are discriminatory and, therefore, probably unenforceable. I am being charged 50 percent more than other owners for my monthly assessment because I rent out my unit to a tenant.*

The association refuses to obtain legal advice. I have refused to pay the extra 50 percent and I have asked them to take me to court so that we could resolve the matter. The association board says that they will just wait until I try to sell the unit and then they will hold up the sale until I pay the association the unpaid balance.

What is my legal recourse?

A The association cannot adopt rules and regulations that conflict with the provisions of the declaration of covenants, conditions and restrictions (CC&Rs) or the bylaws. Rules that conflict with these other legal documents are not enforceable. Associations should seek legal advice in order to ensure that their rules and regulations are in compliance with federal and state laws and the association's legal documents. The board should rescind this rule as soon as possible before you or other non-resident owners challenge it.

If you want to take legal action, contact an attorney who specializes in community association law. You definitely have a reason to sue, but that should be the last resort.

The attorney could write a letter to the board of directors citing the provisions in the legal documents, which explain the method for calculating assessments. Usually assessments are either an equal amount for all owners or the amount is based upon the percentage of ownership (square footage of the units). Any additional charges levied against your unit, other than a monetary penalty for violation of the CC&Rs or rules, should be based upon actual services provided. For example, if your tenant needs an extra common area key or garage door opener, the association could charge you a reasonable amount for providing those items. You should not be charged any more than any other owner would be charged for the same service.

It is unfortunate that your association's board of directors has decided not to consult an attorney. Paying for an attorney's preventive legal advice is always less expensive than defending against legal action when an owner decides to challenge the association.

NON-RESIDENT OWNER CANNOT USE AMENITIES

Q *I am the owner of a unit in a condominium complex. The board has determined that the non-resident owners are not entitled to have access to the common areas of the association. The board says that I have forfeited my rights to the common areas by renting my unit to a tenant. Furthermore, the board has issued only one key per unit to the common areas so I am locked out of the complex. What are my rights?*

A I believe that since you are an owner, you have the right to have access to the common areas. However, having access to the property does not mean that you have the right to swim in the pool, play tennis or use any of the other amenities. When you leased your unit to a tenant, you transferred those rights to your tenant.

If you review the association's legal documents, you will probably find a restriction about this. It is not fair to the other owners if both you and your tenants are using the amenities.

NEIGHBOR COMPLAINS ABOUT LARGE NUMBER OF OCCUPANTS

Q *We reside in a homeowner association in Orange County. The association's declaration states that the homes are "single fam-*

ily residences." One of our neighbors has six or eight male boarders. Some of these men share one room, sleeping in the bed in shifts.

We are worried about the welfare of our children because of the large number of renters who are strangers. We also have a parking problem because of limited parking spaces.

Is there any way that the association can enforce the single-family concept and get rid of the large number of renters?

A If you live in an incorporated area of Orange County, you may get some help from your city officials. Find out if the city allows bedroom rentals. Your neighbor may be in violation of local zoning codes or health and safety codes. If you can report this to a higher authority to get the matter resolved, that is certainly beneficial for the association.

If the wording in the association's declaration of covenants, conditions and restrictions (CC&Rs) is clear and specific, you may be able to prohibit or limit the number of your neighbor's tenants. For example, if the association's legal documents clearly limit occupancy to two people per bedroom, then enforcement of that restriction is more likely. The association board should seek the advice of an attorney who specializes in community association law to find out if the wording in the governing documents is enforceable. If so, then the association should vigorously pursue enforcement before rentals and overcrowding becomes more prevalent.

RENTER IS CITED FOR LEAVING GARAGE DOOR OPEN

Q *I own a condominium unit that is rented to a very reliable tenant. The tenant was recently cited for violating the condominium rules because the garage door had been open "for a long period of time." The tenant said that the citation must be a mistake because he has valuable items in the garage and has not left the garage door open.*

What method is required to file a complaint about a violation, verbal or written? Who receives the complaint? Am I entitled to know who originated the complaint? What can the violator do to deny the allegation? What role does the management company play in the process?

A All of your questions should be addressed to your association's board of directors. You have the right to know the facts about your association's rule enforcement procedures.

Some association boards accept verbal reports of violations from owners while others require written notice of a violation. Written complaints reduce the chance of error.

Some associations keep the complaining person's name confidential while others will reveal the name of the person who filed the complaint. Confidentiality prevents resentment and retaliation.

The owner who is cited for a violation should always have the opportunity to respond to the violation notice either in writing or by appearing at a board meeting or both. Many associations have established methods for processing complaints and dealing with violators. If you are being charged a monetary penalty for the violation, the association must give you or your tenant the opportunity to state your innocence. You have the right to ask the board to consider your tenant's contention that he was cited in error. The board should then decide whether to withdraw the citation.

California Civil Code requires that the association provide written notice of the specific violation and schedule a hearing to consider the matter. The owner is entitled to 10 days' notice prior to the hearing and the association must send the written notice of the outcome of the hearing within 15 days after the hearing occurs.

OWNER'S TENANT IS BOTHERED BY NOISE IN ADJOINING UNIT

Q *I own a condominium that is rented out. The very noisy occupants in the adjoining unit bother my tenant. Our association rules say that only four people may reside in the units, however there are at least 6 or 7 people there all the time.*

I have asked the board and the management company to enforce the rules limiting the number of occupants but they say that the rule cannot be enforced.

I feel that I was misled when I purchased my unit if the CC&Rs and rules are not enforceable. I am ready to sell out and sue the board of directors for any loss. What else can I do?

A Many association boards and management companies are afraid to try to enforce limits on occupancy since the Federal Fair Housing Amendments Act went into affect. However, some restrictions are enforceable.

First, check to see if a governmental authority might provide assistance. Call the building and safety department of your city administration office or county health department to inquire about their codes and ordinances. Check to see if there are occupancy limits based upon the number of people per square foot of floor space or per bathroom. You may be able to get some of the occupants evicted with the city's help.

By referring you to the city or county, I do not mean to imply that the board has the right to ignore their obligation to enforce the governing documents. Unless the association's legal counsel has advised them that the rule is unenforceable, they have an obligation to enforce the rule. You may find that you need the support of other owners to convince the board to enforce rules.

If the vast majority of the owners are disobeying a rule or if the membership decides that a rule is no longer necessary, then it should be deleted. The board should appoint an ad hoc rules committee to evaluate the association's rules at least every three years. The rules are easier to change than the CC&Rs or bylaws. If the association is not going to enforce the rule than they should get rid of it so that it doesn't mislead the owners.

I urge you to pursue other alternatives before filing a lawsuit. Taking legal action should always be a last resort.

ASSOCIATION CHANGED THE RULES ON RENTAL DURATION

Q *In 1972 my wife and I purchased a condominium in a community association in Southern California. There were no restrictions on the amount of time that owners could rent out their units. We have rented out our condo unit for periods of one or more weeks during the ensuing years.*

Now the association membership, by a weighted majority, has approved amending the CC&Rs to prohibit rentals of less than one-month duration.

Is such a restriction now binding when the restriction did not exist at the time that we purchased our unit?

A Owners need to understand that even though the CC&Rs are the "Constitution" of the association, the CC&Rs can be changed by a super majority vote of the membership. Most CC&Rs require approval of 66% or 75% of the owners to amend the document. Assuming that the amendment procedure was done according to the CC&Rs, the new amendment is probably binding.

Though you may not be in favor of the change, I'm sure that you can understand the reason for the amendment. Short-term rentals can be a nuisance for the association, especially if the owners do not ensure that their tenants abide by the association's CC&Rs and rules and regulations. A large majority of the owners must have decided that the change was in the best interests of the association.

WHAT TYPES OF RENTAL RESTRICTIONS ARE LEGAL?

Q *I understand that a potential condominium buyer should be concerned if an excessive number of units are occupied by renters and should ask if the complex has rental restrictions.*

What types of rental restrictions can a condominium complex impose under California Law?

A Mortgage lenders want to know the percentage of non-owner occupied units. When the percentage of renters becomes too high, the lenders are more careful about approving a loan. One can assume that lenders believe that a high percentage of renters in a community association means that owning a unit in that complex is not a good investment.

Renters can be very responsible occupants; however, they can also be irresponsible about care of the property and obeying rules. Tenants bring another level of complexity to the rule enforcement process. The association must deal with the owner when a tenant is uncooperative. Only the owner can evict a tenant who is damaging the common area or creating a nuisance.

Some associations require that owners use the association-approved lease format, even though the association is not a party to the lease. The lease will state that the tenant must comply with the governing documents: the declaration of covenants, conditions and restrictions (CC&Rs), the bylaws and the rules and regulations of the association. If the tenant fails to comply, the owner has the right to evict the tenant.

Some associations restrict rentals to at least a one-month, or six-month or one-year term. Tenants who rent on a short-term basis may be less conscientious about abiding by rules. A steady stream of new occupants can cause wear and tear on the common area.

I know of some associations that have amended their CC&Rs to place a limit on the percentage of units that can be rented or leased. For instance, 20 percent rentals would put the association in the acceptable range for most lenders. When the 20 percent threshold is reached, no other owners can rent or lease their units. If the amendment passed with the proper supermajority required for CC&R amendments, it would probably be considered reasonable and enforceable.

A few years ago, there was a very interesting court case in Southern California involving the owners' right to rent. The court decided that the owners of a condominium unit were prevented from renting out their condominium unit. The owners did not have the right to rent out their unit because the construction and mortgage loans for the complex had been subsidized specifically for low-income buyers by the municipality. Buyers who could qualify for ownership and residency were required by the CC&Rs to keep their resident status and were not allowed to rent to someone else. Therefore, the court upheld the enforceability of the prohibition of rentals.

CHAPTER 15 RESOLVING DISPUTES

ALTERNATIVE DISPUTE RESOLUTION FOR ASSOCIATIONS

Q *My friend owns a home in a planned development. She told me that state law requires that associations inform their owners that alternative dispute resolution is required prior to filing a lawsuit. I have not received any notification from my association yet. Is my association in violation of the law?*

A This law, California Civil Code Section 1354, has been in effect since 1994. It explains that an association's declaration of covenants, conditions and restriction (CC&Rs) may be enforced by any owner, or the association, or both.

The law states that all community associations are required to send a summary of the law to all of its owners annually. The summary can be included in a newsletter or other written communication or it can be mailed along with the annual budget information that is sent out prior to the beginning of the association's fiscal year. The entire law is included at the end of this chapter.

Alternative dispute resolution (ADR) is the term for conflict settlement processes that can be used prior to or instead of going to court. The law requires that a plaintiff must attempt to settle a conflict through mediation or arbitration prior to filing a lawsuit, though ADR is not necessary when an association is attempting to collect delinquent assessments from an owner.

In addition, there are other situations that may not require ADR prior to obtaining an injunction or taking other forms of legal action. For instance, if an owner is in the process of violating an architectural restriction by constructing a pool without permission, the association or another owner could take immediate legal action to halt the construction since delay would only complicate the situation.

The alternative dispute process begins when one of the parties sends to the other party a "Request for Resolution" form. By signing the form, the two parties agree to try to settle the dispute through mediation, arbitration or binding arbitration. The "Request for Resolution" must include a brief description of the dispute, a request for either mediation or arbitration and a notice that the party receiving the Request has thirty days to sign and return a "Response to Request for Resolution" to the initiating party. If the respondent does not return the form within the 30-day deadline, then the offer of ADR is deemed to be rejected.

On the other hand, if both parties agree to submit the dispute to arbitration or mediation, the ADR must be completed within 90 days unless both parties agree to an extension. Both parties share in the cost of the ADR unless otherwise determined during the resolution process.

If one of the parties in the dispute refuses to use ADR and the case goes to court, the judge can take into consideration the failure of the party to agree to ADR when the awarding of legal fees is determined. For instance, one of the parties might be required to pay more of the attorney fees if he or she refused to use ADR.

Mediation and arbitration are two distinctly different forms of ADR. The two parties involved in the dispute may be more inclined to choose arbitration rather than mediation depending upon the nature of the dispute.

WHAT IS ARBITRATION?

When arbitration is used, the two parties present their testimony and evidence to an arbitrator, a third party who hears both sides of the argument and then renders a judgment. Arbitration can be either binding or non-binding. Binding arbitration means that both parties agree, prior to commencing the hearing, that the decision of the arbitrator will be final. Non-binding means that either party can proceed to court if they do not agree with the arbitrator's decision. In California, retired judges often preside at arbitrations. Arbitrations are often more formal that mediations.

WHAT IS MEDIATION?

Mediation is another method of resolving conflicts. The mediator is a third party who listens to both sides and encourages open discussion, which explores possible solutions to a dispute. A resolution is reached through the active participation of both parties with the mediator facilitating the communication. In California, the mediator does not have to be an attorney.

WHY DO COMMUNITY ASSOCIATIONS USE MEDIATION?

With community associations, the two parties involved in the conflict are often neighbors who will continue to live as neighbors after the problem is resolved. Therefore, all parties should be interested in preserving the well being and friendly atmosphere in their association. Resolving conflicts before they get to the litigation stage will save the association and the disputing parties from spending lots of time, energy and funds. Conflict is counter-productive and can have a negative impact on the association's reputation. Conflict can erode the cooperative attitude of the owners and discourages owners from becoming active in their association. Repetitive conflict will make volunteers less likely to serve on the board or participate on committees.

WHY IS MEDIATION A FAVORABLE METHOD OF RESOLVING CONFLICT?

Mediation is a less threatening way of resolving disputes. Both parties participate in finding a solution instead of having an arbitrary decision handed down by a judge. The outcome of arbitration or litigation is almost always uncertain, regardless of the facts of the case. Mediation removes that uncertainty because the parties participate in the outcome. Mediation considers the viewpoints of both parties, brings out the underlying causes for the dispute (often issues that are inadmissible in court) and works toward resolution in a non-adversarial atmosphere. On the other hand, litigation often accelerates negative feelings on both sides.

WHY IS MEDIATION ADVANTAGEOUS FOR THE ASSOCIATION?

Mediation can resolve problems quickly and efficiently in an informal setting. Whereas litigation can be detrimental to the owners' sense of community, mediation promotes a friendly, cooperative approach to problems. Effective conflict resolution will revitalize the association. Members tend to respect the association for its constructive approach to conflict and, after experiencing the ADR process, the association will be better equipped to handle future problems.

CALIFORNIA CIVIL CODE SECTION 1354

Here is the wording in the law:

"The covenants and restrictions in the declaration shall be enforceable equitable servitudes, unless unreasonable, and shall inure to the benefit of and bind all owners of separate interests [units or lots] in the development. Unless the declaration states otherwise, these servitudes may be enforced by any owner of a separate interest or by the association, or both.

"Unless the applicable time limitation for commencing the action would run within 120 days, prior to the filling of a civil action by either an association or an owner or a member of a common interest development solely for declaratory relief or injunctive relief, or for declaratory or injunctive relief in conjunction with a claim for monetary damages, other than association assessments, not in excess of five thousand dollars ($5,000), related to the enforcement of the governing documents, the parties shall endeavor, as provided in this subdivision, to submit their dispute to a form of alternative dispute resolution such as mediation or arbitration. The form of alternative dispute resolution chosen may be binding or non-binding at the option of the parties. Any party to such a dispute may initiate this process by serving on another party to the dispute a Request for Resolution. The Request for Resolution shall include (1) a brief description of the dispute between the parties, (2) a request for alternative dispute resolution, and (3) a notice that the party receiving the Request for Resolution is required to respond within 30 days of receipt or it will be deemed rejected. Service of the Request for Resolution shall be in the same manner as prescribed for service in a small claims action as provided in Section 116.340 of the Code of Civil Procedure. Parties receiving a Request for Resolution shall have 30 days following service of the Request for Resolution to accept or reject alternative dispute resolution and, if not accepted within the 30-day period by a party, shall be deemed rejected by that party. If the alternative dispute resolution is accepted by the party upon whom the Request for Resolution is served, the alternative dispute resolution shall be completed within 90 days of receipt of the acceptance by the party initiating the Request for Resolution, unless extended by written stipulation signed by both parties. The costs of the alternative dispute resolution shall be borne by the parties.

"At the time of filing a civil action by either an association or an owner or a member of a common interest development solely for declaratory or injunctive relief in conjunction with a claim for monetary damages not in excess of $5,000, related to the enforcement of the governing documents, the party filing the action shall file with the complaint a certificate stating that alternative dispute resolution has been completed in compliance with subdivision (b). The failure to file a certificate as required by subdivision (b) shall be grounds for a demurrer pursuant to Section 430.10 of the Code of Civil Procedure or a motion to strike pursuant to Section 435 of the Code of Civil Procedure unless the filing party certifies in writing that one of the other parties to the dispute refused alternative dispute resolution prior to the filing of the complaint, that preliminary or temporary injunctive relief is necessary, or that alternative dispute resolution is not required by subdivision (b), because the limitation period for bringing the action would have run within the 120-day period following the filing of the action, or the court finds that dismissal of the action for failure to comply with subdivision (b) would result in substantial prejudice to one of the parties.

"Once a civil action specified in subdivision (a) to enforce the governing documents has been filed by either an association or an owner or member of a common interest development, upon written stipulation of the parties the matter may be referred to alternative dispute resolution and stayed. During this referral, the action shall not be subject to the rules implementing subdivision (c) of Section 68603 of the Government Code.

"The requirements of subdivisions (b) and (c) shall not apply to the filing of a cross-complaint.

"In any action specified in subdivision (a) to enforce the governing documents, the prevailing party shall be awarded reasonable attorney's fees and costs. Upon motion by either party for attorney's fees and costs to be awarded to the prevailing party in these actions, the court, in determining the amount of the award, may consider a party's refusal to participate in alternative dispute resolution prior to the filing of the action.

"Unless consented to by both parties to alternative dispute resolution that is initiated by a Request for Resolution under subdivision (b), evidence of anything said or of admissions made in the course of the alternative dispute resolution process shall not be admissible in evidence, and testimony or disclosure of such a statement or admission may not be compelled, in any civil action in which, pursuant to law, testimony can be compelled to be given.

"Unless consented to by both parties to alternative dispute resolution that is initiated by a Request for Resolution under subdivision (b), documents prepared for the purpose of or in the course of, or pursuant to, the alternative dispute resolution shall not be admissible in evidence, and disclosure of these documents may not be compelled, in any civil action in which, pursuant to law, testimony can be compelled to be given.

"Members of the association shall annually be provided a summary of the provisions of this section, which specifically references this section. The summary shall include the following language: "Failure of any member of the association to comply with the prefiling requirements of Section 1354 of the Civil Code may result in the loss of your rights to sue the association or another member of the association regarding enforcement of the governing documents." The summary shall be provided either at the time the *pro forma* budget required by Section 1365 is distributed or in the manner specified in Section 5016 of the Corporations Code.

"Any Request for Resolution sent to the owner of a separate interest pursuant to subdivision (b) shall include a copy of this section."

RESOLUTION OF ASSESSMENT DISPUTES FOUND IN CIVIL CODE 1366.3

According to the wording in California Civil Code 1366.3:

"The exception for disputes related to association assessments in subdivision (b) of Section 1354 shall not apply if, in a dispute between the owner of a separate interest and the association regarding the assessments imposed by the association, the owner of the separate interest chooses to pay in full to the association all of the charges listed in paragraphs (1) to (4), inclusive [see below] and state by written notice that the amount is paid under protest, and the written notice is sent by certified mail not more than 30 days from the recording of a notice of delinquent assessment in accordance with Section 1367; and in those instances, the association shall inform the owner that the owner may resolve the dispute through alternative dispute resolution as set forth in Section 1354, civil action, and any other procedures to resolve the dispute that may be available to the association.

1) The amount of the assessment in dispute.

2) Late charges.

3) Interest

4) All fees and costs associated with the preparation and filing of a notice of delinquent assessment, including all mailing costs, and including attorney's fees not to exceed $425.

(b) The right of any owner of a separate interest to utilize alternative dispute resolution under this section may not be exercised more than two times in any single calendar year, and not more than three times within any five calendar years. Nothing within this section shall preclude any owner of a separate interest and the association, upon mutual agreement, from entering into alternative dispute resolution for a number of times in excess of the limits set forth in this section. The owner of a separate interest may request and be awarded through alternative dispute resolution reasonable interest to be paid by the association on the total amount paid under paragraphs (i) through (iv), inclusive, of subdivision (a), if it is determined through alternative dispute resolution that the assessment levied by the association was not correctly levied."

Author's comment: These two laws were intended to resolve disputes and lighten the burden in the court system. However, in my opinion, since it is so difficult for the average reader to understand the laws, very few individuals should pursue this method without obtaining the advice of an attorney. Obviously, if you need to use ADR, it is best to consult legal counsel to ensure that you are following the letter of the law and adhering to time limitations and other restrictions.

CHAPTER 16 PARKING, POOLS & PETS

OWNER PARKS IN SPACE RESERVED FOR GUESTS

Q *Our association has a problem with an owner who parks his vehicle in the guest parking spaces. He uses his garage space for storage. We have only seven guest parking stalls for 31 units.*

One place in our declaration of covenants, conditions and restrictions (CC&Rs) states that owners, lessees or guests may park in the guest parking stalls; in two other places in the same document it states that guest parking is for guests only and owners must park their vehicles in their garages.

Should we amend our CC&Rs so that this inconsistency is resolved?

A I believe that the intent of your CC&Rs is to reserve the seven guest parking spaces for guests only. Obviously, the person who wrote the document was inept if there are such glaring inconsistencies.

Most city codes stipulate a certain ratio of guest parking spaces be set aside based upon the number of units with owned parking spaces or garages. I advise you to check with the city planning or code enforcement division to see what they have to say about this.

Then check with an attorney who specializes in community association law to see if the attorney advises amending your legal documents. Some attorneys will say that the association should consider the needs of its owners rather than the needs of guests.

After you have checked with the city and the association's attorney, then you will know whether to go after the offending owner.

This is a common problem in many associations. You can be sure that unless the board takes steps to enforce the guest parking areas, other owners will soon be using the guest spaces.

In my opinion, if the owner who is parking in the guest spaces is doing so because his garage is stuffed to the rafters with stored items, he should be told to comply with the CC&Rs and park his vehicle in his garage. He is trampling on the rights of other owners who deserve a place for their guests to park. Contact the local fire marshal to see if the fire safety codes restrict the use of garage spaces for storage.

"TYRANNICAL" BOARD CRITICIZED FOR PARKING FINES

Q *We have a tyrannical board of directors that levies fines for parking violations and other infractions.*

It's my understanding that only the rulings of the U.S. Supreme Court are not subject to judicial review by a higher court. Yet our board levies unfair fines giving no consideration to our owners or their circumstances. It seems that the board's main goal is to make life miserable for the rest of the owners. There are about 1000 units in our complex and many of the owners are tired of putting up with this board's nonsense. How can we appeal their unfair actions?

A In a complex as large as yours, rules are a necessity. Otherwise, chaos reigns! Some board members feel that once they are elected to the board they don't have to listen to the homeowners who elected them. They loose sight of the democratic process. I've heard a board president say to a homeowner, "You elected us to run this association, now shut up and let us run it!" At the next annual meeting, this man was not re-elected. What a surprise!

Boards have a responsibility to govern the association. Most boards try to do so in the best interests of the association as a whole.

Homeowners have a responsibility to obey the governing documents, which includes the rules and regulations. However, all homeowners have rights! You have a right to a hearing with the board to explain your feelings and ask for their consideration if there are reasons for your infractions. The board should not levy a fine until after they have given you the opportunity to appear at a hearing (due process). If you wish to appeal the board's action, consult your association's governing documents to see what procedure to follow. Try to work this out amicably with your board. In too many situations like this, resentments lead to litigation, which should always be the last resort. If a majority of owners are dissatisfied with the board, you should have no difficulty getting a petition signed by other homeowners requesting a change in enforcement procedures. If the board does not respond to your petition, your easiest recourse is to vote them out of office at the next election.

PARKING CHAIRMAN IS BERSERK WITH POWER

Q *Our homeowner association has had difficulty in enforcing parking regulations. The board president appointed a new parking enforcement chairman. This new chairman, an owner volunteer, is now berserk with power. He continually walks around the complex confronting other owners. He uses a threatening manner with the teenage residents that I fear will result in some form of retaliation. I believe that he is being lenient with some people but is especially tough on those he calls "habitual violators."*

We board members are at odds. Some board members like the new "get tough" approach. Others don't want to offend a willing volunteer even though we don't like his tactics.

What can we do to restore peace without backing off from enforcing the rules?

A The parking enforcement chairman reports to and takes direction from the board of directors. Committee chairmen do not have any power beyond the authority granted by the board.

The board of directors should determine what the enforcement methods will be. Rules must be enforced but owners should not be treated in a manner that will create hostility against the association or its leaders. The parking enforcement chairman must be told that violators will be treated fairly, reasonably and consistently. The board of directors has a duty to see that the procedures are just. If parking penalties are being levied against owners, the owners have a right to a hearing with the board before the penalty is imposed. Do not ignore the owners' rights.

After the board has talked with the enforcer about his methods and responsibilities, determine whether he is suitable for this position. Perhaps you will want to consider contracting with a security firm to enforce the parking rules. Of course, the cost of contract security versus volunteer labor may be a factor, but the association's liability and reputation should be considered also. Remember that the board should make its decision based on the good of the whole association.

DOES ASSOCIATION HAVE THE RIGHT TO TOW PARKED CARS?

Q *Our association towed the cars of two of our adult children. Our children live in the complex and had valid parking stickers on their cars. We were not given any warning before the towing took place. We do not know why the cars were towed. I have asked the association to reimburse us for the cost of towing. If the board refuses, I may take this to small claims court.*

Does the board or the manager have the right to tow cars without warning?

A Unfortunately, some associations and some managers are unaware that there are specific California vehicle codes that apply to homeowner associations. The association's rules are void if they are in conflict with the state laws.

Daniel C. Shapiro, an attorney with the law firm of Wolf, Rifkin and Shapiro, Los Angeles, warns that associations must comply with Vehicle Code Sections 22658, 22658.2 and 22853. These laws are quite specific about the procedures that must be followed and they dictate even the size of the signs that must be displayed on the premises.

Vehicle Code 22658.2, regarding removal of vehicles from a common interest development, states that, "The association may cause the removal without notice of any vehicle parked in a marked fire lane, within 15 feet of a fire hydrant, in a parking space designated for handicapped without proper authority, or in a manner which interferes with any entrance to, or exit from, the common interest development or the separate interest [individual unit or lot] contained therein."

Associations should have their attorney review the parking and towing rules prior to attempting to enforce rules that may be superseded by state law.

OWNER USES WHEELCHAIR; ACCESS TO CAR IS HAZARDOUS

Q *I use a wheelchair. My condominium complex has an underground garage. I must get to my car using the driveways; some are on an incline where I cannot see the oncoming cars and they cannot see me. The board of directors will not take any action and they have not answered my correspondence. What can I do?*

A Have you requested a different parking space that might lessen your risk? Have you requested that the board inform the other residents that a wheelchair-bound resident is using the garage and that unsafe speeds will not be tolerated? Do you have documentation of your communication and correspondence to the board?

Perhaps the board of directors is not aware of the Americans with Disabilities Act, which is a federal statute that requires making accommodations for disabled owners or residents. If you feel that your rights are being ignored, you can contact the local offices of the Department of Housing and Urban Development. For telephone numbers, check the federal government listings in the front of the white pages of your local telephone directory.

CAN ASSOCIATION PROVIDE A HANDICAPPED PARKING SPACE?

Q *Ten years ago, when our 44-unit condominium complex was new, the board of directors designated a handicapped parking space for a handicapped owner. Recently, the manager advised the association that the handicapped space did not comply with city code. Then the association's attorney stated that the board did not have the authority to grant the space to the handicapped owner. Each owner has a two-car garage and the attorney said that all other spaces should be open to everyone's use.*

The attorney cited an Ohio case that states that the board would be breaking the law if they designated a handicapped parking space for one owner. The attorney says that we need to have 100 percent agreement of all the owners to allow the owner to use the handicapped space. We don't believe we would ever achieve the approval of every owner.

The board wants to abide by the law but because this handicapped space has been there for ten years, the board is reluctant to take it away. The disabled person uses a wheelchair and the space in the garage is not sufficient to allow easy access of the wheelchair.

How should we settle this matter?

A I am aware of the Ohio case, *U.S. versus Fairway Villas Condominium Association.* In that case, the association refused to grant a handicapped space to a woman who had chronic fatigue syndrome and several herniated discs in her back. The court sided with the association, basing the decision on specific clauses in the Ohio Condominium Act.

"These clauses provided that the common areas were owned by all unit owners as tenants in common. Because of that, each unit owner was entitled to use the common areas without interference from another owner. The court reasoned that only the owners, by unanimous vote, could convert a common area to a limited common area (a common area available for the use of less than all owners)," wrote attorney Seth Emmer in an article in *Common Ground* magazine.

It is difficult to predict what a California court would do in your case, but you should inform your attorney that this specific owner has been using the handicapped space for ten years. It seems that a precedent may have been established. The association's attorney should also consider the Americans with Disabilities Act and Fair Housing statutes.

The federal Fair Housing Amendments Act of 1988 provides that associations must allow handicapped residents to modify common areas at their own expense when changes are needed for the resident's use and access to the property. Emmer's article states, "Discrimination against a handicapped person includes a refusal to make reasonable accommodations in rules, policies, practices or services, when such accommodations may be necessary to use and enjoy a dwelling."

I believe that a wheelchair-bound person deserves some concession. The association should be very cautious about changing a ten-year-old decision. Perhaps the board members should use a wheelchair and navigate the owner's route from his or her garage into the building. Sometimes, decisions become very easy when we simply put ourselves in the other person's shoes (or wheelchair).

POOLS

RESTRICTIONS AGAINST CHILDREN MAY VIOLATE THE LAW

Q *I am serving on the rules and regulations committee of a newly developed homeowners association. Our association has a spa and a swimming lake that are fenced.*

Our committee is now trying to formulate rules that state the ages of the children that will be allowed to swim unsupervised. We are concerned about small children using the spa even when they are supervised. We would like to have your advice as to the age restrictions that other associations use.

A The rules that you are formulating affect the safety of your residents and should have been adopted before the swimming facilities were even opened for use. My advice is to eliminate any age restrictions other than those relating to health and safety.

You must check with your city or county code enforcement officials about age restrictions, spa temperatures, and the rules that should be enforced by the association. You should have the required health and safety ordinances or codes posted at the lake and spa or else you are probably in violation of your local codes.

Most community associations require that children under the age of fourteen be accompanied by an adult while using pool and spa facilities. Consult with the association's insurance agent to see what affect your regulations will have on your insurance costs.

Spas are unsafe for young children. The temperature in the spa should not exceed 104 degrees. It is typical that local health departments require that signs be posted discouraging spa usage by persons who have heart, circulatory or respiratory problems, pregnant women and children under the age of ten. Even healthy persons should limit the amount of time that they spend in a spa. Certain prescription drugs or alcohol consumption may influence an individual's tolerance.

You may be accused of age discrimination unless you carefully research this matter. The board should be able to show that the association's restrictions are for health and safety reasons. Most associations that have very restrictive rules controlling the hours of pool usage by children are finding those rules challenged by owners who want to swim with their families.

FEDERAL AND STATE LAWS PROHIBIT AGE DISCRIMINATION

Q *My husband and I reside in a high-rise condominium in Long Beach. After repeated requests the board of directors approved new pool rules that allow only children 48" or taller who have passed Red Cross certification or similar designation to use the pool with an adult homeowner accompanying them.*

I feel that these rules discriminate against all other children. Why can't other children enjoy the use of the pool if an adult homeowner accompanies them?

A The federal Fair Housing Amendments Act made sweeping changes to eliminate restrictions against children and provide for their full use and enjoyment of their residences. One of the few exceptions would be senior housing that provides special services and amenities for persons over 55 years of age. The law contains very specific requirements that associations must meet in order to qualify as senior housing.

The Unruh Civil Rights Act is California's law that provides protection from arbitrary discrimination in "accommodations, advantages, facilities, privileges or services in all business establishments of every kind whatsoever." In the case of *O'Conner versus Village Green Owners Association* in 1983, the California Supreme Court ruled that a condominium association is a "business establishment" and therefore the association could not discriminate against children by denying them as residents.

I recommend that associations restrict unwanted behavior rather than restricting children. For example, if you don't want noise or toys in and around the pool area, then restrict the noise and toys but don't have rules that are age-specific. A rule that states, "Running in the pool area is prohibited" is better than "Children are not allowed to run in the pool area." Obviously, to prevent injury, no one should run in the pool area regardless of his or her age, so eliminate the reference to children.

Because of California Civil Code 1352.5, all community associations, especially those that were formed prior to 1983, must evaluate all of their governing documents to remove any discriminatory provisions. Rely on the advice of an attorney who is familiar with both the federal and state laws prohibiting discrimination.

PETS

PET EXCLUSION O.K. ONLY IF CHANGE WAS MADE PRIOR TO 2001

Q *Our condominium board of directors has banned pets even though the declaration of covenants, conditions and restrictions (CC&Rs) allows pets. When I inquired, I was told that the declaration had been amended prior to my purchasing my unit and only pets that were here prior to the amendment are allowed to remain. I was given a copy of the amendment, recorded by the County Recorder, in 1998. Since the original documents bear the official seal of the State of California, has the board followed the proper procedure?*

Did this amendment require two-thirds vote signed by the members?

A California Civil Code, Section 1360.5 states that associations must allow pets only if the association's governing documents are written or amended after January 1, 2001. Since the amendment was recorded in 1998, the amendment would be a binding legal document if all of the following criteria were met. The declaration may be amended according to the procedures stated in the governing documents of your association. After the amendment has been approved by the percentage of owners required by the governing documents, then the amendment must be recorded by the county. Only the articles of incorporation are filed with the Secretary of State.

If the amendment procedure is followed properly and an officer of the association certifies the voting, then the county clerk would accept it for recordation.

All owners must be informed and given an opportunity to vote on an amendment to the articles of incorporation, declaration or bylaws. After an amendment has been approved and recorded, the amendment should be distributed to all owners because it is a part of the governing documents. There should be no reason for an owner being unaware of an amendment.

If you are a new owner and you weren't informed about the amendment or given a copy of it during the escrow process, you may have recourse against the previous owner or the escrow company.

OWNER CAN'T SLEEP BECAUSE OF DOGS UPSTAIRS

Q *I purchased my condominium unit about a year ago. A few months after I moved in, the unit above me was sold. The new owners installed hardwood floors in every room and brought two full-grown sheepdogs with them when they moved in. My unit is small and I cannot escape the sound of dog paws and footsteps above my head. I work very late hours and am awakened every morning by this noise above me.*

When I bought my unit the developer only offered carpet and tile as floor coverings. Therefore, I did not anticipate this kind of problem. I have written letters, spoken to the board at board meetings, and made numerous phone calls but nothing has happened. The man upstairs is now serving on the board. He was elected by other dog owners and insists that my complaints are vindictive.

Isn't there some way that I can get some peace and quiet?

A This is more than just a pet problem or non-dog-owners against dog-owners. I can imagine that this situation is certainly interfering with your enjoyment of your home. Hardwood floors are prohibited in many condominiums. Associations that permit hard-surface flooring often have specific requirements for soundproofing. It's a sensible restriction since many buildings were not constructed with adequate soundproofing for hard-surface floors.

First, check with the city building department to see if your city's building codes require sound insulation under hardwood floors. It's possible that the floor was not installed according to the building codes. Research the building codes for acceptable sound decibels and you might want to engage a sound testing firm to see if the noise is excessive.

Unless the association's CC&Rs prohibit hardwood floors, there is very little that the association board can do for you. Perhaps you can convince your neighbor to meet with you and a mediator to see what solution might be acceptable to both of you. The neighbor might be willing to carpet the bedroom areas or might even pay for modifying your ceiling to prevent the transfer of sound.

OWNER HAS ALLERGIES TO PETS

Q *I live in a condominium association that has common area elevators and corridors. Twenty years ago, I moved into this particular association that does not allow pets because I have pet allergies and breathing problems. My neighbor says that a new law was passed and our association cannot ban pets. I have to come in contact with other owners when I take the elevator or walk in the hallways to get to my unit. If our association must allow pets, I will have to sell my home and move. Do I have any recourse?*

A Your neighbor is not correct. Hopefully, you will not have to move. The law only applies to new associations whose documents are written after January 1, 2001 or to existing associations that amend or modify their governing documents after that date. Please refer to the following questions and answers for more details.

In my opinion, the new law ignores the rights of people with allergies, asthma and other breathing problems who choose to live in a pet-free environment.

ARE WEIGHT LIMITS FOR PETS ENFORCEABLE?

Q *Our high-rise condominium building has two elevators. Our association allows dogs but they must weigh less than 20 pounds and owners who are accompanied by dogs must use the freight elevator. Is this restriction enforceable?*

A Yes, your association is allowed to restrict the weight of dogs. The association can also restrict the areas where pets are allowed access. Civil Code 1360.5 states that pets are "subject to reasonable rules and regulations of the association." However, if a large dog was in residence prior to a weight limitation being imposed, the dog could remain until the owner moves or the dog dies.

The association members, especially the board of directors, should be aware that exceptions must be made for the disabled. If a disabled owner or resident owns a large service or assistance dog, the special needs of the disabled person must be accommodated.

SOME DOG OWNERS LET THEIR PETS ROAM

Q *A few owners in our homeowners association allow their dogs to run loose occasionally. I don't dislike dogs but I dislike owners who allow their dogs to roam. We have an association rule about controlling pets but the board seems unable to enforce it.*

A This is probably an instance where the association's rule is duplicated by city or county code. Contact your local authorities to seek help if the dogs are a nuisance or a safety hazard.

Then work with your board to "put some teeth" into your rule enforcement. Most associations impose fines upon rule violators; however, the owner must be given an opportunity to appear at a hearing. That may be an effective enforcement tool.

You can find out how to adopt new rules in the "Governing Documents" chapter.

BOARD DECIDES TO TRAP ROAMING CATS

Q *Some of the residents of our condominium have complained about cats roaming freely around the complex. The board has decided to place cat traps in various locations. Because there isn't a leash law for cats, it seems to me that trapping cats is illegal. The monthly newsletter has not disclosed what they will do with the trapped cats. Can you offer any suggestions or a remedy to this unpleasant situation?*

A Are you serious? Trapping cats is a pretty extreme measure. It sounds like the board is threatening this as a way to get the cat owners' attention. The owners have a right to know what will be done with the cats that are trapped.

If you are a cat lover who feels that cats are meant to roam, you may not like my response. First, let me say that I've never met a cat I didn't like. When we moved into a townhouse with our six-year-old cat, she became an indoor pet because the CC&Rs stated that no pets were allowed to roam. One *can* teach an old cat new tricks!

Your veterinarian will tell you that you are not being kind to your cat when you allow it to roam. What about traffic, other cats, dogs, mean neighbors? And now, cat traps?

Cat lovers seem to forget that cats can be a nuisance, especially in flower gardens, and a health hazard in children's sandboxes, etc. When living in proximity to others, even cats must give up some of their freedoms, just like humans.

Now, let's examine the board's action. Did they pass a new rule against roaming cats? Or is the board simply trying to enforce an existing rule? Even if the board didn't follow proper procedure for establishing this rule, I urge you to comply with it for your cat's sake.

RULES ARE MORE RESTRICTIVE THAN CITY CODES

Q *We own a townhome in an association that allows pets; however, all pets must be on a leash when they are in the common area. Our cat is outside during the day and stays in our garage at night. We cannot bring the cat into our unit because it will fight with our other cat.*

The board of directors sent us a complaint letter because our cat is in the common area without a leash. They are threatening to fine us.

We checked with the Los Angeles Police Department and were told that, under Section 53.06 of the Municipal Code, cats are not required to be on a leash. A representative from Animal Regulation also stated that cats are roaming animals and that there is no leash law for cats.

We informed the board of directors about the Municipal Code and they indicated that they would check further with local agencies. However, they still intend to fine us. We do not want to file a lawsuit but the board is leaving us no choice. Do association rules supersede municipal code regarding the control of pets?

A Community associations often have rules and regulations that go beyond the restrictions in the local codes. For example, architectural controls and paint color restrictions are often far more stringent than city regulations.

Your association does have the authority to enforce this pet restriction, especially if it appears in the declaration of covenants, conditions and restrictions (CC&Rs). If you allow your cat to roam the neighborhood, other cat owners will be resentful. Cats can be a nuisance and a health hazard, especially when Morris leaves his "calling card" in a child's sandbox or digs up flowers in the common area. Perhaps the board has received complaints from other owners about your cat.

Any veterinarian will tell you that a roaming animal is not a safe animal. Freedom to roam is not a kindness. I urge you to keep your cat inside if you really care about its health and happiness. If your two cats fight when they are confined together, then put them in separate rooms. You are not allowed to disobey the rules just because your cats are incompatible.

This may seem like an important issue to you, but it is not an issue that should be litigated. Filing a lawsuit over this would be a waste of your time, money and energy.

Contrary to your statement, you do have a choice. You have chosen to live in a community association that has CC&Rs, bylaws and rules. If you cannot comply with the legal documents of the association, then you should move somewhere else. I can tell you with certainty that if you decide to sue, you will want to move anyway by the time the lawsuit is resolved.

PUPPY WILL VIOLATE WEIGHT RESTRICTIONS SOON

Q *I recently bought a puppy that will be about 80 pounds when full-grown. Someone in my condominium complex has complained that my dog will be in violation of a restriction that prohibits pets that weigh over 40 pounds. Other owners have or have had pets that were above the weight limit. Can the board of directors enforce this restriction against me and not others?*

A Yes, the association can enforce this restriction. Perhaps the other dogs that are present in the building are service dogs. Handicapped owners with service dogs are exempt from pet restrictions. If the rule prohibiting dogs over forty pounds was passed after those other dogs were in residence, the association would have to "grandfather" those dogs. In other words, the existing dogs have a right to stay until the owner/resident moves or the dog dies.

If you want to have an 80-pound dog, you moved into the wrong condominium complex. And if you want reassurance from me that you can keep your pet, you've asked the wrong person. I am not an attorney but I am aware of a number of legal cases on this subject. Though I am a pet lover, I take a very strong stance against anyone who willfully violates pet restrictions. However, you will definitely find attorneys who disagree with me on this matter.

You are risking a legal hassle when you disobey the legal documents of your association. The board of directors has an obligation to uphold the documents even if they like you and your puppy. The CC&Rs cannot be ignored. By purchasing your unit, you agreed to abide by the restrictions in the legal documents.

Though you say that you may not be the only one violating this restriction, you have not given me any specific details. At the present time, the association's board may be attempting to correct the problem and your impending violation may intensify their efforts.

It is true that the board should not discriminate against you if there is another violator; however, one must look at all of the facts and you may not be aware of all of the facts. Perhaps the board is not pursuing the other violation because the pet is only slightly over the limit.

The board may have determined that a few pounds is not worthy of the expense of a legal battle and therefore, they granted a variance.

It is impossible to accurately predict how this case would be decided in a court of law, if it goes that far. There are always many factors that a judge or jury must consider. On the way to the courtroom, you will make many enemies among your neighbors.

Why would you want to anger your neighbors and cause the association to spend resources on legal advice when you know that the CC&Rs prohibit your 80-pounder? Even if the board doesn't take action against you, any owner has the right to take legal action to require compliance with the legal documents of the association.

In my opinion, you are making a big mistake if you decide to keep your dog knowing that any of your neighbors may take legal action against you. In California and many other states, when a lawsuit is instigated in order to enforce the CC&Rs, the prevailing party is entitled to reimbursement of reasonable legal expenses.

DOGS IN CONDO AT THE TIME OF AMENDMENT CAN STAY

Q *I am a dog owner who has just moved into a condominium association that does not allow dogs. I saw a woman with a dog when I was touring the complex prior to purchasing my condominium unit. The real estate agent told me that if other dogs were present in the building, the association could not make me get rid of mine.*

I have been notified that the association will not allow me to keep my dog. The association's attorney sent me a copy of an amendment to the declaration, which states that after a certain date in 1998, owners are not allowed to have dogs. He stated that the dog that I saw in the lobby was "grandfathered" and that no other dogs can be brought into the building.

What can I do?

Assuming that the association has not made any changes to their governing documents since January 1, 2001, you have two choices. You should either keep your dog and move to another location or, if moving is out of the question, you must get rid of your dog. You are the only one who can decide which solution is less painful. You may or may not have recourse against the real estate agent. If you received and signed for a set of the association's legal documents, then the real estate agent has the right to assume that you read them and were aware of the amendment to the declaration.

A lawsuit against the real estate agent for verbal comments is not very practical, but you have a right to bring your problem to the attention of the agent, the broker and possibly the local Board of Realtors.

If you try to keep your dog, the association has grounds for a lawsuit against you. Any of the individual owners could also file a lawsuit to enforce the association's legal documents. At the very least, you will become a very unpopular resident if you do not comply with the restriction. The other owners may like you and your dog, but they aren't going to like paying the attorney's bill to educate you about your responsibility as an owner.

NEW ASSOCIATION DOCUMENTS CANNOT PROHIBIT PETS

Q *Our condominium association is a twenty-story high-rise complex. The declaration prohibits dogs and we have never allowed dogs during our association's 15-year existence.*

Now a new owner has moved in with his large dog. The real estate agent informed the owner that pet restrictions are illegal because of a law that became effective on January 1, 2001.

Is this information correct? If our dog restrictions are legal, what can we do about this new owner if he refuses to get rid of his dog?

A The law, Civil Code Section 1360.5, only applies to new association documents or to those associations that amend their governing documents after January 1, 2001. Since your documents were in place long before the law was passed, you can enforce your pet prohibition as long as you don't amend your declaration, bylaws or rules and regulations. The real estate agent needs to read the law, especially subparagraph (e).

Here is the wording of Civil Code Section 1360.5:

"No governing documents shall prohibit the owner of a separate interest within a common interest development from keeping at least one pet within the common interest development, subject to reasonable rules and regulations of the association. This section may not be construed to affect any other rights provided by law to an owner of a separate interest [unit or lot] to keep a pet within the development.

"For purposes of this section, "pet" means any domesticated bird, cat, dog, aquatic animal kept within an aquarium, or other animal as agreed to between the association and the homeowner.

"If the association implements a rule or regulation restricting the number of pets an owner may keep, the new rule or regulation shall not apply to prohibit an owner from continuing to keep any pet that the owner currently keeps in his or her separate interest if the pet otherwise conforms with the previous rules or regulations relating to pets.

"For the purpose of this section, "governing documents" shall include, but are not limited to, the covenants, conditions and restrictions of the common interest development, and the bylaws, rules and regulations of the association.

"This section shall become operative on January 1, 2001, and shall apply only to governing documents entered into, amended, or otherwise modified on or after that date."

What can your association do about the new owner in your association? Perhaps by showing this information to him, you will be able to persuade him to comply with the pet restriction. Since your association has always enforced the restriction, you should not have a problem enforcing it now. The board should consult the association's attorney regarding your alternatives.

If the owner refuses to comply with the pet restriction, your association attorney could write a letter to him informing him that his lack of compliance is a serious matter. He should also be informed that he will be charged for the legal expenses. In California and many other states, the violating owner can be held responsible for the payment of reasonable legal expenses incurred by the association to enforce the CC&Rs.

PET RESTRICTIONS ARE ENFORCEABLE

Q *A new resident who owns a dog has moved into our 24-unit condominium complex. When we board members spoke with her to inform her of our condominium's pet restrictions, we met with strong opposition.*

Our declaration of covenants, conditions and restrictions (CC&Rs) clearly state that cats and dogs are not allowed in our building. Through the years, we have enforced the restriction diligently.

The new owner says that her real estate agent told her that the Nahrstedt case makes enforcement of pet restrictions illegal. The real estate agent is not able to give us any specific information about this legal case and, therefore, we do not believe her argument.

Are pet restrictions enforceable? If so, what is our association's next step? What is the buyer's next step if she wants to file a complaint against the real estate agent?

A Yes, your pet restrictions are enforceable unless the animal is a seeing-eye dog or is used for some other type of assistance for a disabled person. As stated in the previous question, the restrictions must have been in affect prior to January 1, 2001 and the declaration, bylaws and rules and regulations must be the same as they were prior to January 1, 2001.

It is unfortunate that the real estate agent provided incorrect information to the buyer. The buyer may be upset with the condominium association's board members; however, her real adversary is the agent who gave her the incorrect information.

The agent may be confused about a well-publicized lawsuit, *Nahrstedt v. Lakeside Village Condominium Association*. If the agent was relying upon the appellate court decision in this case, she needs to be aware of the final decision in the California Supreme Court.

The owner of three cats, Ms. Nahrstedt, moved into a condominium unit at Lakeside Village in Culver City. When the association's board of directors attempted to enforce the association's prohibition of cats, Ms. Nahrstedt filed a lawsuit. She felt that she should be allowed to keep her cats since they stayed inside her condo unit and did not create any noise or other nuisance. At the Superior Court level, the case was dismissed. The court felt that the association's pet restriction was enforceable and refused to hear the case.

Then, Ms. Nahrstedt filed an appeal. The Court of Appeal determined that each challenge to the association's CC&Rs should be analyzed on a case-by-case basis by looking at the impact of the governing document's restrictions on the individual owner. The appellate court ruled that Ms. Nahrstedt could keep her cats.

However, the appellate court's decision contained an ominous threat to the enforcement of many of the provisions in every association's documents throughout the state. Lakeside Village appealed the case to the Supreme Court, and the outcome was anxiously awaited.

On September 2, 1994 the Supreme Court handed down its ruling. The court upheld the association's pet restrictions. Ms. Nahrstedt was told that her cats were not entitled to reside at Lakeside Village. This is an important, precedent-setting decision. In my opinion, it was a great victory regarding the enforceability of the legal documents.

The Nahrstedt case reinforces the legal validity and the strength of the declaration (CC&Rs) in California community associations. New owners sometimes purchase their condominium units without understanding that the declaration is a binding document. When they are informed of the declaration's provisions, they sometimes decide to ignore them, rather than live harmoniously with their fellow association members. We now have the Nahrstedt case to educate the general public about the importance of every community association's legal documents.

The law firm of Wilner, Klein and Siegel represented Lakeside Village Condominium Association in the lawsuit. Laura J. Snoke, one of the attorneys who was instrumental in the association's victory, said, "The Supreme Court set forth a clear and sensible standard for CC&R enforcement: CC&Rs are enforceable if they are rationally related to a legitimate purpose of the association. In determining whether a restriction is enforceable in the future, the court will analyze the restriction as it affects the community as a whole. No longer will boards of directors have to evaluate, on a case-by-case basis, whether a restriction is unreasonable as it applies to a specific homeowner. Instead, unless the restriction is unreasonable on its face, i.e., it is arbitrary or violates public policy, the restriction will be enforceable."

Pet problems are often the topic of discussion at association board meetings. A pet that is unconditionally loved by its owner is sometimes a serious aggravation for the rest of the association's residents. Pets often create undesirable noise, odors and clean-up problems. If the owner is negligent, the result can be unsanitary conditions in and around the property.

On the other side of any debate about pet restrictions are those who are so firmly convinced that pets are therapeutic that they are appalled that anyone would try to restrict them. The heated debates will probably continue in spite of the final court decision.

Those of us who recommend enforcement of pet restrictions are not necessarily pet haters. We are simply aware of the importance of protecting the integrity of the association's legal documents and protecting the rights of the owners and residents who may have moved into the association because of its pet restrictions.

The new buyer who was misled by the real estate agent should talk with the broker of the real estate agency and also consult a real estate attorney. In order to sell the unit, the agent has committed an offense that could lead to suspension of her license or a lawsuit.

The association and the pet owner can file a complaint about the agent's misrepresentation with the local Board of Realtors, a voluntary self-policing trade organization, and the Department of Real Estate, which is the state's agency that oversees the licensing of real estate brokers and agents.

VISITING PETS NOT ALLOWED IN "NO PETS" CONDO

Q *The governing documents of my condominium association state that pets are not allowed. My parents will be visiting for about one month this summer. They have a dog that travels with them.*

Does the association have the authority to keep all pets out of the building, even those that are temporary?

A Yes, depending upon the wording of the legal documents, the association can probably bar even the temporary stay of a pet. In my opinion, it is important for the association to be careful about allowing "guest dogs."

I have heard of several situations where a "guest" turned into a permanent resident. "I'm just taking care of Aunt Susie's poodle while she's gone on vacation," said the offending owner. Obviously, that is not an adequate or truthful response when the dog has been on the premises for six months.

If either one of your parents has a handicap and the dog is a service animal, one that is specially trained to assist a handicapped person, then the association should make an exception upon your written request. In my opinion, the association has the right to ask for a physician to provide verification that the animal's assistance is needed.

ASSOCIATION WANTS TO PROHIBIT PETS

Q *I live in a 56-unit community association. The units are townhouses built on a seven-acre parcel of land. Since pets are a continuing source of problems for our association, the board sought the advice of our attorney.*

The attorney states that it is possible to amend the CC&Rs to prohibit pets, using a "grandfather clause" to allow the existing pets to remain.

What can you tell us about other associations that have dealt with this problem? What knowledge can you share that would be helpful?

A It's too late to amend your documents to prohibit pets since Civil Code Section 1360.5 took effect on January 1, 2001. Please refer to the question with the heading "New Association Documents Cannot Prohibit Pets."

If pets are a problem for your association, I would suggest calling a meeting of the pet owners. After all, the pet owners are the real problem, aren't they? The board should communicate with them and ask for the owners' help in resolving the problems. Encourage the pet owners to abide by the rules. Levying monetary penalties may be effective.

Find ways of reducing the nuisance factor. Perhaps somewhere in your seven-acre complex, you have an area that can be set aside for walking and exercising the dogs. By improving communication and involving the pet owners in the solutions, you may find that the situation improves.

CHAPTER 17 BEFORE DISASTER STRIKES

Author's note: The following information was provided in my *Los Angeles Times* column, "CONDO Q & A," after the Northridge earthquake in 1994. The advice originated a long time ago, but the information is helpful for boards and members whose associations might be susceptible to catastrophic fire, flood, hurricane or other disasters.

BOARD MUST ACT CAREFULLY AFTER DISASTER OCCURS

Q *The recent earthquake damaged our condominium extensively. Though we have earthquake insurance coverage, the insurance deductible is a major expense that some of our owners will probably be unable to pay. Some unit owners have told the board of directors that they plan to abandon their units. It appears that the association may be unable to rebuild even with the insurance proceeds.*

There are so many complex issues that my fellow board members and I need some advice so that we can set some priorities. Where do we start?

A For many association board members, aftershocks aren't the only cause of sleepless nights. As board members, in addition to your own personal losses and concerns, you must deal with the association matters, too. You are undoubtedly getting numerous phone calls from anxious owners wanting to know what is being done. You should not be embarrassed to tell the other unit owners that you just don't have all of the answers yet. I recommend that the board schedule a special meeting of owners to let them know what is happening and what the board is doing. If possible, invite the association's attorney, insurance agent, manager and any other professional who can assist the board in answering the owners' questions.

Attorney Leonard Siegel, with the law firm of Wilner, Klein and Siegel in Beverly Hills, recommends that the board's first priority is to review the association's declaration (CC&Rs) concerning destruction and condemnation of the project. Several attorneys with Wilner, Klein and Siegel have prepared an excellent checklist to assist community association boards of directors that are dealing with post-earthquake issues.

The checklist states, "Most likely, the CC&Rs of your association will contain provisions that will require that the Board take certain actions as a result of the earthquake. Because the CC&Rs of your association are unique, your Board should review your CC&Rs for pertinent provisions with the assistance of the association's attorney.

"For example, CC&Rs of a community association may contain provisions which require that the structures be rebuilt where damage is extensive, provided that insurance proceeds are sufficient to finance some percentage (often 85 percent) of the costs of rebuilding the Project. Likewise, your CC&Rs may require that the Board initiate the reconstruction pursuant to existing plans. However, if the Board wishes to modify these plans, your CC&Rs may provide that reconstruction in accordance with modified plans requires approval of some percentage of the association's members and some percentage of the holders of the first trust deeds ('Senior Lenders').

"If the insurance funds are not sufficient to finance the stipulated percentage of the rebuilding costs, your CC&Rs may provide that rebuilding may only be initiated with the approval of members and Senior Lenders." Your CC&Rs also probably address how insurance proceeds must be distributed, to whom and on what basis. "In the event your Project will not be rebuilt, your CC&Rs probably authorize the partitioning of units, and require that certain notices be made.

"Finally, if the buildings of your Project have been condemned, your CC&Rs should address how these condemnation proceeds are to be distributed, to whom and on what basis. You must review *your* CC&Rs to determine the rights and obligations of your Board and your members."

I have added some of my comments and summarized Wilner, Klein and Siegel's checklist of steps that the board of directors should take:

1. Notify the homeowners about damage, liability and other issues as soon as reliable information can be obtained. Try to limit the information to statements of fact that can be substantiated. Be sure to disclose the statements or conditions that need further research or clarification and put a date on the material that is distributed. As the information is updated or revised, owners will be able to see from the date which information is most reliable. If the board has consulted with independent sources or professionals, inform the owners. For example, your notice could state, "The Board of Directors has been advised by the association's insurance agent that...."
2. Apply for Federal Emergency Management Agency (FEMA) assistance. Call your local directory assistance to obtain the local FEMA phone numbers. They will mail to you the Small Business Administration (SBA) loan application. All loans are processed through the SBA.
3. Obtain a list of all senior lenders (first mortgagees) for all of the condominium units. Your insurance agent may be able to help with this list. The association CC&Rs probably state that the senior lenders have the right to vote on any decision not to reconstruct and the senior lenders are entitled to their pro rata share of any insurance proceeds or condemnation awards.
4. Notify the lenders and the unit owners of any actions that may require their approval. Some lenders may have already filed an

official request for notification of any occurrence that may affect their interests.

5. If any units are uninhabitable, advise the owners to check their individual insurance policies to see if relocation expenses are covered. The owner should check with their insurance agent regarding the specific coverage and then keep records of reasonable expenses resulting from the relocation. I assume that most insurance companies will challenge a claim that includes five-star accommodations with caviar on the room service bills. Many hotels are offering discount rates to those who are displaced by the earthquake.

   The owners may have earthquake coverage under their individual condominium owners' insurance policies. One of the options available is "earthquake loss assessment coverage" which protects the unit owner when a special assessment is approved by the board or the association members.

6. The board should retain a structural engineer as soon as possible to identify the extent of the damage and estimate the cost of repairs and the estimated time that repairs will require. The board should consult the association's attorney for referrals to engineers, architects and other professionals. Relying on the advise of these professionals will tend to reduce the board's liability.

7. Adopt a plan for funding the reconstruction. The board must decide how the insurance deductible will be paid and how to finance any repairs that are not covered by insurance. Consult the association's attorney regarding the procedures for special assessments and emergency assessments.

8. If the association is already a party to a loan agreement, consult the lender regarding deferred loan payments, an increase in the line of credit or any other special benefits that the lender might offer to the association. Advise owners to check with their mort-

gage lenders about deferred loan payments or other special arrangements that will temporarily ease their financial burden.

9. Review vendor contracts and equipment leases if revision or termination seems advisable. Consult your attorney regarding any changes that are needed.
10. Advise homeowners to contact the county assessor's office about a reassessment of the property taxes on their unit.
11. Inform homeowners about their responsibility for repairs to the interior of their units. Wilner, Klein and Siegel's advice is, "Under the CC&Rs of your association, homeowners may be responsible for the repair of damage to the interior of their units (including the interior surfaces of walls, ceilings and floors), as well as fixtures and personal property in the units, to the extent that these damages are not covered under the association's master insurance policy. Typically, this will be true if there is not major exterior damage to your project." After consulting an attorney, the board's written notice to the owners should cite the attorney's advice regarding the owners' responsibilities.
12. Consider hiring a construction engineer and/or architect before hiring a contractor. Most of the law firms that I have talked with, including Wilner, Klein and Siegel, advise associations to hire professionals who can work as a team to complete the repair work that the structural engineer has recommended. Damage must be inspected, reconstruction plans need to be designed and specifications need to be prepared so that contractors can submit competitive bids. A construction engineer or architect may be able to assist the board in reviewing the bids, inspecting the work of the contractor as it progresses and interfacing with the insurance carriers. The additional cost can be submitted as part of the insurance claim.

Wilner, Klein and Siegel's firm advises, "Even if there is no coverage, it is our opinion that the benefits such a professional [construction engineer or architect] brings far outweigh the cost."

They advise the association board to "exercise the same care with this reconstruction as you would with any construction project your association undertakes. Many of our clients advise us that they are under great pressure to reconstruct their project as quickly as possible, even if this means neglecting to take the kind of precautions they would take under ordinary circumstances. These precautions include soliciting competitive bids, checking references, having your construction agreement reviewed by the association's attorney, and monitoring the work performed to insure that no payments are made unless the work to date has been satisfactory and all lien releases have been obtained.

"Although exercising this level of care may delay the date your project is reconstructed by several weeks or more, these precautions are essential. A year from now, if your project has been reconstructed properly, no homeowner will care that the board proceeded methodically. However, if in the upcoming year the workmanship is so poor that the board has to hire a substitute contractor to complete the job, and at great additional time and expense, no homeowner will forget and many may not forgive the board."

CAN OWNER BUY INSURANCE FOR STRUCTURAL DAMAGE?

Q *If the condominium association does not have earthquake coverage, can an individual owner purchase an earthquake insurance policy that would cover structural damage?*

A I don't believe that an insurance company will allow you to purchase coverage for something that you do not own. Since the condominium association owns the structure of the building, each individual owns just a percentage of the structure and an individual would probably not be able to purchase a policy.

WHAT DOES EARTHQUAKE INSURANCE DEDUCTIBLE MEAN?

Q *The association received bids for earthquake insurance coverage from various insurance companies and they all had deductibles of ten percent. Does that mean that the association would have to pay $5,000 of a $50,000 loss?*

A No, the deductible amount of an earthquake insurance policy does not apply to the amount of the loss. The deductible would be ten percent of the total replacement cost of the structure or the total policy limits. If the building were a $10,000,000 structure, the loss would have to be greater than $1,000,000 in order to file a claim. For example, if the association filed a claim for $1,200,000 worth of damages, the association would have to pay the $1,000,000 deductible amount and the insurance company would pay $200,000.

WHAT IF RESERVE FUNDS DO NOT COVER THE DEDUCTIBLE?

Q *How would the association be able to pay the deductible?*

A If reserve funds were inadequate, the owners would have to pay a special assessment. Let's say the condominium association has 100 units. Each owner would have to pay a special assessment of $10,000.

There is protection that an individual owner can obtain that will help to pay a special assessment in these circumstances. The individual owner can obtain earthquake coverage for their personal property and the unit's contents. In addition, some insurance carriers offer "earthquake loss assessment coverage" which will protect the unit owner when the association must levy a special assessment to cover the cost of the repairs.

The individual owner may be able to obtain "earthquake loss of use coverage" to cover the cost of temporary relocation if the unit is uninhabitable. Some policies will cover hotel costs and other expenses if the owner has to leave the unit until repairs can be completed.

OWNERS SHARE THE COST OF REPAIRS

Q *Will I have to help pay for repairs even if my unit is not damaged in the earthquake?*

A Yes, you own a share or a percentage of the entire property and you must share in the cost of the repairs so that everyone's investment is protected. If the association levies a special assessment, the cost of the special assessment is shared in the same way that all expenses are shared. If the CC&Rs specify that all units pay the same amount for regular assessments, then that is the way special assessments are collected.

WHAT IF I CAN'T PAY THE LARGE EMERGENCY ASSESSMENT?

Q *What if an owner is unable to pay a large special assessment?*

A When an owner is delinquent in paying a regular monthly assessment, a special assessment or an emergency assessment, the association can file a lien on the unit and take the property through foreclosure, if necessary.

Owners who are unable to pay should contact their bank or lending institutions immediately to see if loans are being made available in response to the disaster. Some banks offer low-interest loans to assist their customers.

INSURANCE COMPANIES' ABILITY TO PAY CLAIMS

Q *Will the insurance companies be able to pay all of the claims that will result from another disaster? What can we do to verify an insurance company's financial stability?*

A Each disaster that occurs, such as hurricanes in Hawaii and Florida and major fires or floods, has a devastating affect on the insurance industry. Several companies have gone out of business. Be sure to check the A. M. Best Key Rating Guide to Property-Casualty Carriers to find the bidding companies' ratings and their financial integrity.

You can call the California Department of Insurance to see if the companies have a good record for claims processing. I have heard complaints from some people who had losses during a previous quake. They were very disappointed that claims took several months to be processed. Contact the Department of Insurance if you want to file a complaint about the manner in which your claim is handled.

UNIT'S VALUE HAS DEPRECIATED BELOW AMOUNT OF LOAN

Q *My condominium association has levied a special assessment of $4,000 to cover the cost of repairing earthquake damage to the common areas. I also must pay for damage inside my condominium unit. My unit has depreciated in value so that I now owe more on my mortgage than the unit is worth. It seems unwise to put more money into repairs.*

I love my unit and the location is near my work. I don't really want to move. However, because of the financial situation, I have been advised by some friends to simply walk away from the unit and default on my loan and the association assessment payments. What can I do?

A Walking away will have dire, long-term effects on your credit rating and it won't win you any friends in your association. If the bank forecloses on your unit, the bank generally is not required to pay the unpaid special assessment. The burden of your regular assessments (that remain unpaid until the bank foreclosure) and the special assessment will have to be shared by the other owners in the long run. There may be a way for you to get some financial assistance so that you can stay in the unit.

Contact the SBA to see if refinancing is a possibility. You may be able to refinance your mortgage loan at the unit's current appraised value and obtain the assistance that you need for the special assessment and the damage to your unit.

After disaster strikes, applications to the SBA must be filed within a specified time limit. Local telephone numbers or toll-free (800) numbers are established so that owners have a means of getting the information that they need.

OWNER'S RIGHT TO INSPECT REPAIRS TO UNIT

Q *My townhouse was damaged during the earthquake and is currently being repaired. The association has banned the owners from entering the grounds to inspect their units while the construction is going on. However, we have been asked to sign waivers to release the association from liability.*

Many homeowners are paying for upgrades to their units. Don't we have the right to see what we are getting and inspect the quality of the construction?

A The association, through its board of directors, acts on behalf of all of the owners. This is especially true when disaster strikes. If you read your governing documents, you may find that the association or its board has power of attorney which grants to the association the authority to file and settle the insurance claim, manage the reconstruction and pay out insurance proceeds to the individual owners. The board has the duty to protect everyone's investment and ensure that the association is made whole again.

The board should communicate with the owners about every aspect of the reconstruction process. If there is a possibility that owners could be injured, they should be kept out of the complex. If the contractor is dealing strictly with the association, then you are not a party to the transaction and you must rely on the association's board to see that your unit is reconstructed properly.

If you are paying for upgrades out of your own pocket and want to inspect the work while it is in progress, make your request to the board in writing. It seems that you should have the opportunity to see that the work that you are paying for is being completed to your satisfaction.

SBA ASSISTANCE FOR CONDOMINIUM UNIT OWNERS

Q *Our condominium association needs more information about the Small Business Administration (SBA) loans that are available for the association or for our individual unit owners. Must the association determine whether to 1) apply for an association loan or 2) levy an emergency assessment and allow the owners to apply for their own individual loans if they need assistance?*

A That is correct. The SBA will not approve an association loan and then fund the individual owners' applications also.

Your association must move quickly to comply with the filing deadline for SBA loan applications for physical damage to homes, personal property and businesses. The SBA's "Unit Owner's Fact Sheet" about disaster loans for condominiums and other common interest developments begins with the following definitions of the terms used in the information:

1. DEVELOPMENT - A condominium complex, or a planned unit development (PUD), or any other common ownership entity,

which has individual unit owners and common elements managed by an association.

2. UNIT - A physical portion of the condominium or planned unit development designated for separate, individual ownership, and for which the owner is responsible for paying the cost to repair or rebuild.
3. UNIT OWNER - The person who owns the unit.
4. ASSOCIATION - The unit owner's association, organized to manage and maintain the common elements of the development. Associations generally have the responsibility to repair or rebuild the common elements, and they decide how the project will be completed and financed.
5. COMMON ELEMENTS - Those portions of the development which are owned by the association, or which are owned in common by the unit owners and maintained by the association.
6. GOVERNING DOCUMENTS - The documents that define the development and establish the rights and duties of the unit owners and the association. The actual names of the documents vary depending upon location and state law. They are often referred to as "The Declaration of Covenants, Conditions and Restrictions" (CC&Rs), "The Declaration," "The Master Deed," or "The Master Lease" and the association's Bylaws.

Special Eligibility Rules for Developments: Eligibility rules for developments are different from the rules for other forms of real estate, because the association generally has the responsibility to maintain and repair the common elements, and it determines how the repairs will be financed. To fund the repairs, an association may use its own maintenance fund, or borrow funds from SBA. An association may also choose to pass a "one-time" assessment (due in one payment) against all unit owners for their proportional shares of the common element damage. Unit owners can apply to SBA for home loan funds up to $200,000 to cover individual unit repairs and "one-time" assessments which are for disaster repairs only and which do not duplicate SBA loans to the association. If the common element damage exceeds SBA's maximum business loan amount of $1,500,000, the association may apply to borrow $1,500,000 from SBA and pass a one-time assessment against the owners for the rest of the funds needed to repair the damage.

Unit Owner Loan Eligibility: Unit owners may apply to SBA for funds up to $240,000 to cover:

1. Uncompensated damage to personal property ($40,000 maximum);
2. Uncompensated damage to the unit, excluding common elements that are the responsibility of the association ($200,000 maximum);
3. "One-time" assessments passed by the association for damage to the common elements (also included in the $200,000 maximum).

All loans are subject to SBA's lending limits. Insurance and other compensation for your loss will be deducted from the loan after the compensation is received. SBA will require a mortgage or deed of trust on your unit, if your loan exceeds $10,000.

To Obtain Funds To Restore The Common Elements: If SBA loan funds are needed to pay for the restoration of your development's common elements, there are two different ways to obtain the funds:

1. *Association Loans* - Your association may apply for a loan to restore the common elements, even if it doesn't own them, because the governing documents give it the responsibility to restore the common elements damaged by the disaster. In order to repay SBA, your association will generally be required to levy a *special monthly assessment* against all the units in your development (SBA prefers that disaster related assessments be kept

separate from general improvement or other assessments). SBA generally requires an assignment of the proceeds of the special assessment as collateral for SBA's loan. If your association actually owns the common area, SBA may require a deed of trust or mortgage against the common area as additional collateral.

In addition, your local financial institution may be able to supply a "bridge loan" until the SBA funds are received. The California Trade and Commerce Agency is providing state loan guarantees to financial institutions that provide loans to businesses so that they can continue to operate until the SBA loan is funded. For further information about the California Trade and Commerce Agency's guaranteed loan program, contact your local financial institution.

2. *Unit Owner Loans* - Your association may decide not to apply for an SBA loan. Instead, the association may decide to levy a one-time special assessment against each unit. As a unit owner, you may be eligible to borrow the funds to pay for the one- time assessment, subject to SBA's loan limits. Special conditions may be required prior to commencement of repairs, to ensure that all the funds necessary to complete the project are available, and to facilitate orderly disbursement of construction funds.

Details Needed About Your Project: SBA can quickly process your loan application for funds to repair or replace your uncompensated *personal property losses.* However, before SBA can determine your loan amount for unit repairs and common element assessments, if any, SBA must know the course of action you and your association will take. SBA must know if the structure will be rebuilt or of the owners will relocate. SBA also needs to know the expected total project cost, so that they can determine the viability of the project and confirm that there are enough funds available, from all sources, to complete the project.

Information Needed To Begin Processing Your Loan:

1. An SBA Disaster Home Loan Application (Form is provided by SBA).
2. A listing of your damaged/destroyed personal property (Form provided by SBA).
3. Complete copies of your prior two years' Federal Income Tax Returns. If they are unavailable, SBA will assist in obtaining them from the IRS.
4. Details of any insurance coverage or claims.

A copy of a deed to your property, or a copy of the Title Policy you obtained when you purchased your property, is not required to file your application, but SBA may request this later.

Information Needed From Your Association: Your association should submit a list of the names and phone numbers of the members of the Board of Directors and the elected officers, a list of unit owners who are members of the association, a copy of the special assessment resolution (if it has already been passed), and a copy of the face sheet of the association's insurance policy.

SBA's Loan May Not Be Used To Upgrade Your Property: SBA's loans are for disaster related repairs only. SBA's loans *may not* be used to upgrade your property, or make additions to it. However, SBA's loan *can include* assessed costs to comply with building and safety code requirements. Furthermore, your loan can be increased by as much as 20 percent for mitigation to protect your property from a future disaster of a similar nature.

If Your Development Will Not Be Rebuilt: You, the unit owner, will be viewed by SBA as being forced to relocate. You are eligible for the replacement value of your personal property, your unit, and your share of the common area, minus any insurance recovery your have received, subject to SBA loan limitations and your ability to repay SBA. You should submit a *relocation proposal* for SBA review when you know where you would like to relocate. All relocation proposals *must be approved by SBA*. If you are purchasing another property or signing a lease, you should make any purchase contract or lease agreement "subject to SBA approval" to protect yourself if your proposed relocation plan is unacceptable to SBA.

If You Do Not Want To Participate In The Restoration Of Your Development: You will be viewed by SBA as choosing to *voluntarily* relocate. When you voluntarily relocate, you are only eligible for an amount equal to the uncompensated loss of your personal property plus the cost to repair your unit. You are not eligible to use your proportional share of the cost to repair the common elements for relocation if the association has voted to restore your development.

Current Interest Rates For SBA Loans: Interest rates are determined by formulas set by law. The applicable interest rates on SBA home loans for individuals and for condominium associations and other common interest developments are far less than regular loans.

CONTRACTOR'S WORK IS UNSATISFACTORY

Q *Our condominium complex is relatively small but we have a huge problem. The contractor who performed the post-earthquake repairs did such poor quality work. We all had to pay a large special assessment and move out of our units for several months. We were limited as to the choices of carpet and other replacements and the board of directors handled everything.*

When we moved back into our units, the work was not completed and we immediately noticed poor workmanship. Many of the senior citizens are concerned but most of us are intimidated because the board president is an attorney and no one wants to have conflicts with the board.

A Any large construction project can result in problems if the board doesn't seek adequate professional help to oversee the contracts, supervise the work, monitor payments and follow up on poor quality work. The board members are volunteers and they should not be expected to know everything. To protect the owners and reduce their own liability, the board should rely on professional help.

The board entered into the contracts on behalf of the owners. Now the board has a fiduciary duty to ensure that the contractor's mistakes are corrected. Even though the board president is an attorney, he or she may simply not know whom to contact. The board should seek the advice of several construction defect attorneys.

If the board fails to act, you and the other owners should get together and obtain legal advice immediately. If warranties have already expired, the owners may have to file legal action against the board and the contractors.

For most people, especially senior citizens, your home is your largest investment. If the board is not protecting you, you must take care of yourselves by seeking legal advice. Don't allow your investment to go down the drain simply because the board is ignoring you.

DEFINITIONS FROM CALIFORNIA CIVIL CODE SECTION 1351

[The comments in italics and brackets are the author's explanation or clarification in non-legal terms.]

Association – a nonprofit corporation or unincorporated association created for the purpose of managing a common interest development.

Common Area – the entire common interest development except the separate interests therein. *[A "separate interest" is an individual unit or lot that is owned by a member of the association.]*

Common Interest Development – a community apartment project, a condominium project, a planned development or a stock cooperative. *[Community apartment projects, sometimes called "own-your-own" projects, are similar to real estate cooperatives, though somewhat different in the legal structure of the organization. In a townhouse-type planned development, depending upon the governing documents and the property deeds, the unit owners share in the ownership of the common areas and the owners individually might own the land under their unit. Planned developments can also be associations with single-family, detached homes and the owners own the lot where the home is constructed as well as an undivided ownership of the common areas.]*

Community Apartment Project – a development in which an undivided interest in land is coupled with the right of exclusive occupancy of an apartment located thereon.

Condominium Plan – a plan consisting of (1) a description or survey map of a condominium project, which shall refer to or show monumentation on the ground, (2) a three-dimensional description of a condominium project, one or more dimensions of which may extend for an indefinite distance upwards or downwards, in sufficient detail to identify the common areas and each separate interest, and (3) a certificate consenting to the recordation of the condominium plan pursuant to this title signed and acknowledged by the record owner of fee title to the property included in the condominium project. *[The Condominium Plan is a separate document, not a part of the Declaration of Covenants, Conditions and Restrictions. The three-dimensional description and explanations in the Condominium Plan are often helpful in determining exactly what is and is not common area or separate interest.]*

Condominium Project – a development consisting of condominiums. A condominium consists of an undivided interest in common in a portion of real property coupled with a separate interest in space called a unit, the boundaries of which are described on a recorded final map, parcel map or condominium plan in sufficient detail to locate all boundaries thereof. *[In general, the condominium association, consisting of the homeowner members, owns the land and structure(s) and the individual owners own "airspace" within the bounds of the unit that he or she purchases. For instance, if there are ten units in the complex, each owner owns 10 percent of "undivided interest" in the common property. The individual owner is assessed real estate taxes on the unit and the percentage of undivided interest in the common area. The association does not pay real estate taxes.]*

Declarant – the person or group of persons designated in the declaration as declarant, or if no declarant is designated, the person or group of persons who sign the original declaration or who succeed to special rights, preferences or privileges designated in the declaration as belonging to the signator of the original declaration.

Declaration – the document which contains the information required by Civil Code Section 1363: a) A declaration, recorded on or after January 1, 1986, shall contain a legal description of the common interest development, and a statement that the common interest development is a community apartment project, condominium project, planned development, stock cooperative, or combination thereof. The declaration shall additionally set forth the name of the association and the restrictions on the use or enjoyment of any portion of the common interest development that are intended to be enforceable equitable servitudes *[fair and equal requirements or restrictions that each owner agrees to when purchasing a unit or lot in the development.]* b) The declaration may contain any other matters the original signator of the declaration or the owners consider appropriate.

Exclusive Use Common Area – a portion of the common areas **designated by the declaration** *[author's emphasis]* for the exclusive use of one or more, but fewer than all, of the owners of the separate interests [units or lots] and which is or will be appurtenant to the separate interest or interests. *[Appurtenant means an "accessory having a legal connection" to the unit, for example, deeded garage or garage space, patio or balcony areas.]*

Unless the declaration states otherwise, any shutters, awnings, window boxes, doorsteps, stoops, porches, balconies, patios, exterior doors, door frames and door hardware, screens and windows or other fixtures designed to serve a single separate interest *[unit or lot]* but located outside the boundaries of the separate interest, are exclusive use common areas allocated exclusively to that separate interest.

Notwithstanding *[regardless of]* the provisions of the declaration, internal and external telephone wiring designed to serve a single separate interest, but located outside the boundaries of the separate interest, are exclusive use common areas allocated to that separate interest.

Governing Documents – the declaration and any other documents, such as bylaws, operating rules of the association, articles of incorporation, or articles of association, which govern the operation of the common interest development or association.

Planned Development – a development (other than a community apartment project, a condominium project or a stock cooperative) having either or both of the following features: a) the common area is owned either by an association or in common by the owners of the separate interests who possess appurtenant rights to the beneficial use and enjoyment of the common area; b) a power exists in the association to enforce an obligation of an owner of a separate interest [unit or lot] with respect to the beneficial use and enjoyment of the common area by means of an assessment which may become a lien upon the separate interests . . .."

Stock Cooperative – a development in which a corporation is formed primarily for the purpose of holding title to improved real property, and all or substantially all of the shareholders of the corporation receive a right of exclusive occupancy in a portion of the real property, title to which is held by the corporation.

RESOURCES

ORGANIZATIONS

California Association of Community Managers
2171 Campus Drive, Suite 260
Irvine, CA 92612-1430
(949) 263-CACM or 2226
www.cacm.org

California Legislative Action Committee (community association issues)
1401 P Street, #412
Sacramento, CA 95814
(916) 658-0257
www.clac.org

Community Associations Institute – National Office
225 Reinekers Lane, Suite 300
Alexandria, VA 22314
(703) 548-8600
www.caionline.org

Executive Council of Homeowners
1602 The Alameda, Suite 101
San Jose, CA 95126
(408) 297-3246
www.echo-ca.org

BOOKS

The Condominium Bluebook
By Branden E. Bickel, Esq. and D. Andrew Sirkin, Esq.

This paperback book, updated annually, contains the exact wording of the Davis-Stirling Common Interest Development Act and other portions of the California Civil Code, Corporations Code, Labor Code and Vehicle Code that pertain to community associatons, as well as helpful forms and checklists for associations.

For information about the cost of the book, contact Piedmont Press, 1375 Grand Avenue, Suite 200, Piedmont, CA 94610. The email address is piedmontpress@condolawfirm.com.

The Davis-Stirling Act in Plain English
By Beth Grimm, Esq.

Attorney Beth Grimm self-publishes this book each year. The contact information for Beth Grimm is Private Mailbox 1000, 3478 Buskirk Avenue, Suite 1000, Pleasant Hill, CA 94523, phone (925) 746-7177, or visit her website at www.bgcondolaw.com.

Finding the Key to Your Castle
By Beth A. Grimm, Esq. and Jim R. Lane

This is a cleverly-written and entertaining book that is full of practical advice. The Condoguru is witty and wise. The book was written in 1995 and self-published by the authors. Though some laws have changed since the book was published, it is still an informative resource that addresses the problems and personalities of owners and board members.

For information about purchasing the book, see the listing above for *The Davis-Stirling Act in Plain English*.

Home and Condo Defects: A Consumer Guide to Faulty Construction

By Thomas E. Miller, Esq. and Rachel M. Miller, Esq.

This book explains what homeowners and associations should look for in order to determine if defects exist and contains a step-by-step explanation of attorney selection, expert investigation, alternative dispute resolution and litigation.

The book may be purchased from The Miller Law Firm, phone (800) 403-3332, or from the website at www.constructiondefects.com.

INDEX

Q

R

V

W

ABOUT THE AUTHOR

Jan Hickenbottom is the owner of Condo Consulting Services, Irvine, CA, a company she formed in 1987 to provide professional guidance to community associations, management companies and developers. She lives in Orange County, California.

A professional in the community association industry since 1979, Jan's management and supervision experience runs the gamut . . . from high-rise condominiums, planned developments and townhouse complexes to large estate-type associations and retirement communities. She has clients throughout the state of California and provides consulting services ranging from crisis management, manager recruitment and board training to mediation of association disputes and annual meeting supervision. Qualified to serve as an expert witness, she has fifteen years of experience providing court testimony in legal cases involving community associations.

In 1990, she achieved the Professional Community Association Manager (PCAM®) designation from Community Associations Institute in recognition of her education, professional experience and service to the community association industry.

In 1994, she was given the Community Associations Institute's prestigious national award, the Byron Hanke Award, in recognition of the outstanding advice provided in her newspaper column during the aftermath of the Northridge earthquake. The column appeared in the *Los Angeles Times* Real Estate Section from 1989 until 2001.

An active volunteer for the betterment of the community association industry, she was instrumental in forming the California Association of Community Managers, a self-regulatory trade organization that was formed to educate and elevate the professional standards of care and ethics of community association managers. She is also a recipient of the Certified Community Association Manager® designation.